THE ITALIAN SOLO CONCERTO, 1700–1760

Rhetorical Strategies and Style History

The Italian solo concerto, a vast and important repertoire of the early to mid eighteenth century, is known generally only through a dozen concertos by Vivaldi and a handful of works by Albinoni and Marcello. The authors aim to bring this repertoire to greater prominence and have, since 1995, been involved in a research programme of scoring and analysing over eight hundred concertos, representing nearly the entire repertoire available in early prints and manuscripts. Drawing on this research, they present a detailed study and analysis of first-movement ritornello form, the central concept that enabled composers to develop musical thinking on a large scale. Their approach is firstly to present ritornello form as a rhetorical argument, a musical process that dynamically unfolds in time; and secondly to challenge notions of a linear stylistic development from Baroque to Classical, instead discovering composers trying out myriad different options, which might themselves become norms against which new experiments could be made.

SIMON MCVEIGH is Professor of Music, Goldsmiths College, University of London; JEHOASH HIRSHBERG is Professor in the Musicology Department, Hebrew University of Jerusalem.

THE ITALIAN SOLO CONCERTO, 1700–1760

Rhetorical Strategies
and Style History

Simon McVeigh and Jehoash Hirshberg

THE BOYDELL PRESS

First published 2004
The Boydell Press, Woodbridge

ISBN 1 84383 092 2

The Boydell Press is an imprint of Boydell & Brewer Ltd
PO Box 9, Woodbridge, Suffolk IP12 3DF, UK
and of Boydell & Brewer Inc.
668 Mt Hope Avenue, Rochester, NY 14620, USA
website: www.boydellandbrewer.com

A catalogue record for this book is available
from the British Library

Library of Congress Cataloging-in-Publication Data
McVeigh, Simon.
    The Italian solo concerto, 1700–1760 : rhetorical strategies and style history /
    Simon McVeigh and Jehoash Hirshberg.
        p. cm.
    Includes bibliographical references (p.) and index.
    ISBN 1–84383–092–2 (hardback : alk. paper)
    1. Concerto – Italy – 18th century.   2. Ritornello.   3 Music – Italy –
    18th century – History and criticism.   I. Hirshberg, Jehoash.   II. Title.
    ML1263.M28 2005
    784.18'6–dc22   2004004670

This publication is printed on acid-free paper

Typeset by Pru Harrison, Hacheston, Suffolk
Printed in Great Britain by
Cromwell Press, Trowbridge, Wiltshire

Contents

To Alice and Israela

Acknowledgments

We are deeply indebted to Michael Talbot for his generous advice and support throughout our work on this project. Much of the background scoring and analysis has been carried out with the help of a team of researchers at the Hebrew University, Jerusalem and Goldsmiths College, University of London. We would like to acknowledge in particular the contribution of Na'ama Ramot, who played an active part in the project throughout, as well as Bella Brover-Lubovsky, Michal Ben-Tzur and Miri Gerstel at the Hebrew University, and Ann van Allen-Russell at Goldsmiths College. It was in animated and often passionate debate within the team that many of the ideas developed in this book took shape.

A special word of thanks to Jane Terepin for her meticulous work on the musical examples, and her patience as ever-changing versions flew around the globe. The bibliography was compiled with the assistance of Meredith McFarlane, and Alice McVeigh brought her customary alert editorial eye to the final text.

We are especially grateful to Ada Beate Gehann and Richard Maunder for sharing some of their scorings with us; and to Bathia Churgin, Albert Dunning, Paul Everett, John Walter Hill, Rosamond McGuinness, Rudolf Rasch and the late Eugene K. Wolf for their helpful advice and assistance. Librarians too numerous to mention have responded to our queries, and we are particularly indebted to Antonio Fanna for permission to reproduce musical examples from *Le opere di Antonio Vivaldi*. Chapter 12 draws, with kind permission, on our article 'The "Virtuosi Instromenti" and the Milanese Concerto in the Early Eighteenth Century', in *Giovanni Battista Sammartini and his Musical Environment*, ed. Anna Cattoretti (Turnhout: Brepols, 2004).

A great and close friend, Cyril Ehrlich, passed away just as we were putting the final touches to the manuscript. Having sensed our common interests, he had prompted our collaboration, and throughout the research and the writing was a constant source of support and advice. We regret he did not live to see the book.

The research has been aided by grants from the Israel Science Foundation; the Leverhulme Trust; the Irwin Trust, University of London; the Schonbrun Research Endowment Fund of the Hebrew University, Jerusalem; and Goldsmiths College, University of London.

Simon McVeigh, London
Jehoash Hirshberg, Jerusalem
April 2004

Editorial Conventions

For the sake of brevity, every reference is to the first movement of a concerto, unless otherwise stated; likewise it can assumed that the soloist is a single violin unless indicated otherwise. Major keys are identified by upper case Roman numerals (I, II etc.), minor by lower case (i, ii etc.). In harmonic analyses, // is used to indicate hiatus.

Wherever possible, musical examples have been taken from original sources listed in the Catalogue, and only very lightly edited in the interests of consistency; figuring has been omitted from the bass. Since most ritornello movements are marked Allegro, tempo markings have only been given in other cases. All Vivaldi examples have been taken from the collected edition *Le opere di Antonio Vivaldi* (1947–72); this edition has been entirely adequate to our purposes, but it should be recognised that it is now somewhat dated, and the editorial methods do not always measure up to modern musicological standards. The thematic catalogues at the end of the book also serve as music examples whenever references to the motto and the opening of the first solo are made.

INTRODUCTION

'To Think Musically'

This book stemmed from an independent yet shared everyday teaching experience – a search for a typical ritornello form to demonstrate the essential principles of late Baroque music. We both not only failed completely to find any concerto that encapsulated the supposed 'model', but also learnt far more from the experience: that it was a limited and meaningless attempt in the first place. Indeed anyone who has performed or studied the concertos of Vivaldi will already have recognized the endlessly rich inventiveness and variety of this repertoire. But we became increasingly rankled by the memory of Stravinsky's glib quip that Vivaldi 'composed the same form so many times over'.[1] Certainly our further intensive research has revealed that no two concertos can be described as identical even at larger levels of formal analysis. To appreciate the subtlety and sophistication that Vivaldi brought to the concerto requires a listening experience that goes well beyond the daily sampling of Vivaldi concertos as acoustical backdrop in airports, lifts and department stores. And then what about the hundreds of other concertos by the many other Italian violinists whose music was heard and admired all over Europe? As our project developed, we turned in two different directions: uncovering the deeper musical secrets of this pioneering instrumental genre, and unravelling the history of style change in an enormous and neglected repertoire.

The early eighteenth-century concerto deserves and requires the listener's closest attention in order to follow the development of a rhetorical musical argument in real time. We will deal with the events in the concerto movement not as static objects bounded by preconceived formal constructs but as contributors to an unfolding process of musical invention.[2] Early eighteenth-century music used to have a reputation for static or architectural qualities, with entire movements supposedly representing no more than a single musical idea. This interpretation conveniently exaggerates the contrast with the more dynamic emotional transformations of the classical sonata. Yet such a view severely downgrades the potential within the older concerto for musical exploration and argument, especially through the ritornello form that Vivaldi developed to early fruition. It was, after all, Vivaldi's 'Harmonic Inspiration' that proved the most significant guide to Bach in his search for musical 'order, connection, and proportion':[3] Johann

---

[1] Igor Stravinsky and Robert Craft, *Conversations with Igor Stravinsky* (London: Faber & Faber, 1959), p. 76.
[2] Cf. Dreyfus, *Bach and the Patterns of Invention*, p. 10.
[3] *L'estro armonico*, Vivaldi's first set of published concertos (1711).

Forkel even went so far as to claim that it was the study and transcription of Vivaldi's concertos that taught Bach how 'to think musically'.[4]

Listening to a concerto movement in ritornello form should therefore be an active process for the listener, who reacts to musical events on two levels simultaneously as the movement unfolds:

(1) relating each new musical idea to its immediate past and anticipating elaborations later in the movement;
(2) drawing on familiarity with a large repertoire of music of the period, and not just of concertos.

The listener of Vivaldi's time, whose daily repertoire consisted largely of new music, locally composed, would surely have been alive to subtle variants and novel formal strategies in each new concerto and would have appreciated and comprehended the selection of choices the composer was trying out. Yet the listener of today can, through extensive and attentive experience, build up a similar sensitivity to compositional strategies.[5] Such alert listening is much assisted by the shortness of ritornello movements, already highlighted in 1752 by Johann Joachim Quantz, who implied that five minutes was a 'suitable length' for the first movement; he explicitly referred to the vantage point of the listener who would prefer a piece 'too short rather than too long'.[6]

This direct listening experience forms a starting point for a more conceptualized analysis. Our approach builds on Sarah Fuller's concept of performative analysis, developed for an earlier repertoire: 'a process-based approach . . . [which] regards tonal structure not as an external property to be assessed rapidly from written notation or a score, but as a perceptual category'.[7] The exegesis of the concerto presented here is not designed to be prescriptive in any way, but rather one interpretation – not a definitive route map for the listener, but an indication of a possible way of listening. Above all, it represents a passionately held conviction that this music does indeed reward close attention, and that each concerto carries out musical arguments both intrinsically and by reference to the surrounding repertoire.

The Italian solo concerto has been selected for study as embodying the most innovative and dramatic expression of this musical rhetoric in the early decades of the eighteenth century. Though this repertoire might appear to be relatively well known, the general understanding is still based on the published works of a few major figures – Vivaldi and Albinoni predominantly – and on an even smaller sample of recordings (although, happily, a few pioneer editions and recordings of concertos by other composers, such as Andrea Zani and Carlo Tessarini, have

---

4   Johann Nikolaus Forkel, 'Johann Sebastian Bach, his Life, Art, and Work' (1802), in *The New Bach Reader*, rev. edn Christoph Wolff (New York: Norton, 1998), pp. 441–2. This passage has served as a point of departure for Wolff, 'Vivaldi's Compositional Art', pp. 3–5. Wolff suggested pairs of translations for Forkel's terms 'Ordnung, Zusammenhang, und Verhältnis': order/organisation, connection/continuity, and relation/proportion.
5   A point explored fully in Dreyfus, *Bach and the Patterns of Invention*, p. 30.
6   Quantz, *On Playing the Flute*, p. 315.
7   Sarah Fuller, 'Exploring Tonal Structure in French Polyphonic Song of the Fourteenth Century', in *Tonal Structures in Early Music*, ed. Cristle Collins Judd (New York: Garland, 1998), pp. 61–86.

recently appeared). Our central premise has been that any attempt to decipher the complex process of style change requires a comprehensive study of the entire available repertoire, applying the methodology of 'thick history'. Most previous stylistic surveys have departed from an unsound premise, either expecting the published editions to represent the process of change within the much larger repertoire, or else selecting small random samples from numerous composers as a basis for stylistic studies.[8] Consequently, there has been no satisfactory analysis of the process of stylistic dissemination and change over time. Composers who enjoyed an international reputation in their lifetime, such as Platti, Tessarini and Zani, have been relegated to the pejorative status of 'minor' composers without proper reassessment. Furthermore, despite repeated attempts to unseat it, the traditional paradigm of a stylistic dichotomy between Baroque and Classical has continued to pose an artificial division somewhere around 1750, interrupting the study of the continuous history of the solo concerto and imposing old-fashioned evolutionary concepts of historical progress.

The development of large-scale musical organization through ritornello form resulted immediately in more expansive and more complex musical structures; and indeed the concerto was the earliest autonomous instrumental genre on such a scale.[9] But still more importantly it enabled experimentation within some kind of common framework for the first time. Such a process of assimilation and comparison has long been recognized in connection with the symphony, yet its relevance for the concerto has so far been underestimated.

We therefore aimed in principle to study the entire surviving repertoire of Italian solo concertos from the period 1700–60, extending from the pioneering early publications of Albinoni, Torelli and Vivaldi, through the central, highly prolific phase from the late 1710s to the 1730s, towards the later concertos of Tartini. In practice, pragmatic considerations – as well as the chronological and geographical structure of the book – forced us to relegate a few interesting composers to a future project;[10] and we also omitted composers represented by only a handful of surviving concertos in disparate sources. Furthermore, we should make clear at the very outset that we have studied only the opening fast movements in ritornello form (or second movements in the case of concertos in the four-movement *da chiesa* pattern). This was again a pragmatic decision, resulting from the sheer size of the repertoire. Finales in ritornello form would make a fascinating point of comparison, building on the methodology developed here, and there is room for a specialized study of slow movements across the repertoire.[11]

---

[8]   Standard histories of the eighteenth-century concerto include Engel, *Das Instrumentalkonzert* ; Hutchings, *The Baroque Concerto*; Schering, *Geschichte des Instrumentalkonzerts*; White, *From Vivaldi to Viotti*. A new perspective on concerto scoring is offered by Maunder, *The Scoring of Baroque Concertos*; and Fertonani, *La musica strumentale di Antonio Vivaldi*, provides an invaluable guide to Vivaldi's instrumental repertoire.

[9]   Further on ritornello form in this repertoire, see Eller, 'Das Formprinzip des Vivaldischen Konzerts'; Eller, 'Geschichtliche Stellung und Wandlung'; Eller, 'Die Entstehung der Themenzweiheit'; Kolneder, *Die Solokonzertform bei Vivaldi*.

[10] Including Alberghi, Cattaneo, Dall' Oglio, Fiorenza, Leo, Morigi, Salurini and Visconti.

[11] On Vivaldi's use of ritornello form in slow movements see Kan, 'The Concerto Adagios of Antonio Vivaldi'.

Our analysis is nevertheless based on a very wide and significant sample – some 800 movements for one or two solo instruments, studied in modern editions, contemporary scores, and our own scorings from printed and manuscript parts. This has enabled not only a much more comprehensive overview than has ever been attempted before, but also the possibility of detailed and well-founded comparisons between composers' personal styles or idiolects, as well as broader conclusions about the processes of style change in the early eighteenth century.

Some methodological issues arise from the very scale of the sample. In the first place, it would be impossible to chart a purely chronological development across the entire repertoire – not only because of problems of dating the material, but also because such a linear view of style change is at variance with the diversity of individual creative impulses. We have therefore preferred to take each composer's repertoire as a single corpus for statistical study, grouping composers into regional centres. It is true that any attempt to map styles and strategies by centres is complicated by the diverse career patterns of travelling soloists and by the widespread dissemination of their concertos, in marked contrast with the situation of the newly developing symphony, which can be linked with reasonably permanent court orchestras. But still we have found certain preferences that can be tied to particular regions, so that a grouping of composers in this way retains some validity.

The point of departure has been the distinction between the Roman and north Italian models highlighted by Michael Talbot:

> Since the layout of string orchestras in Rome and in northern Italy (Venice, Milan, Bologna etc.) differed, correspondingly different approaches to the scoring and structure of the concerto developed in the two localities. Despite considerable cross-fertilization and hybridization of the two types, they remained distinct up to the end of the Baroque period.[12]

The first part of the book concentrates on the emergence of the solo concerto and its culmination with Vivaldi in Venice, as a way of exploring the diversity of strategies available in ritornello form. The reaction of composers in Rome, who in part continued the Corelli concerto grosso tradition, provides an immediate point of comparison and contrast. From here we proceed first to those composers whom we have regarded as part of the wider Venetian orbit, including Italians active across the Alps; and we then turn to five north Italian centres – Parma, Bologna, Milan, Turin and Padua – where the Vivaldian concerto was variously adapted and transformed.

The virtuosic solo concerto embodied a new spirit of individualism that departed from the sense of cooperation typical of the Corellian concerto grosso. At its furthest extreme, the two modes – solo and tutti, individual and community – could be sharply differentiated, not communicating.[13] But usually there was an engagement between the two parties, in which some interaction or dialogue permeates and shapes the developing musical argument. Inbuilt into the concerto,

---

[12] 'Concerto', NG2.

[13] For a contentious view of the social ideologies embedded in the early eighteenth-century concerto see McClary, 'The Blasphemy of Talking Politics'.

therefore, is a dichotomy between alternative meanings of the term itself, reflecting two sides to the Latin verb *concertare*: 'to work together' on the one hand, 'to contend, dispute, debate' on the other.[14] If the first was the primary meaning in Italian, there was nevertheless some awareness of the latter, and it was ultimately this dichotomy that inspired so much of the vitality of invention within the early solo concerto.

The sheer number of surviving concertos bears witness to the creative energy that the form released; their dissemination around Europe in manuscript copies or in printed editions attests to the enthusiasm it engendered outside Italy. While compiling the repertoire, we discovered many rewarding and worthwhile works that deserve the attention of performers and audiences, including many forgotten gems in Vivaldi's magnificent oeuvre. Our study will, in the first place, reveal the high degree of individuality and inventiveness that Italian composers brought to the solo concerto; and in proposing a new model to describe the evolution of the ritornello movement, it will go a further stage towards the core issue: the very process of style change itself.

---

[14] 'Concerto', *NG2*.

CHAPTER 1

Order, Connection and Proportion

Our exploration stems from actual experience of listening to numerous movements from the immense concerto repertoire, so our initial step will be to share that same experience in order to illustrate the principal issues and components of the ritornello movement. This chapter will present six detailed performative analyses, each focussing on particular aspects, and illustrating the multi-layered strategies developed by concerto composers in the early eighteenth century.

Ritornello form was 'the quasi-automatic choice for the first movement' in concertos by Vivaldi and his followers;[1] it was also frequently used in finales and even slow movements. Michael Talbot has outlined the concerto movement as an unfolding of a tonal scheme away from and then returning to the tonic, with musical periods of diverse duration delineating the process.[2] Central to the ritornello form was the establishment of a hierarchy of tonal centres visited in the course of the movement. Traditional modal theory and practice treated degrees other than the *finalis* as temporary stations, marked by rhythmic articulations and brief cadences. The emerging tonal practice around 1700 expanded the stations into full key areas, each supported by its own array of functions – allowing the emergence of the concept of tonal hierarchy. The tutti-solo contrast inherent in the Corellian concerto grosso was recruited as a powerful aid in articulating stable and modulatory areas by means of specialized tutti and solo sections. These sections may be linked (or, alternatively, differentiated) through the use of similar, transposed, altered or contrasting motivic material.

In this way, all musical parameters – melodic, rhythmic, textural and tonal – participate and interact in the development of the musical argument. They may be coordinated in varying degrees, resulting in a constant tension between articulation and continuity. But above all the ritornello movement unfolds as a succession of discrete events that delineate a process of departure from the tonic and arrival at several intermediate tonal centres, before the inescapable re-establishment of the home key.

The Ritornello Transformed

Our first shared experience will be the opening movement of Vivaldi's violin concerto in A major, RV 345, published in 1727 as Op. 9/2 and readily available

---

1   Talbot, *Vivaldi*, p. 111.
2   Talbot, 'The Concerto Allegro'.

in modern recordings. The analysis will be arrayed in narrative form, in order to reveal the unfolding process of musical invention. It will also serve to introduce the analytical symbols to be explained later in this chapter.

The movement opens with a short ritornello in the tonic (R1), based on a festive unison sonority with octave leaps (Ex. 1.1). Some historical awareness is needed to appreciate that such 'pounding octaves were novel, exciting and worthy of imitation', as Talbot has observed in connection with Vivaldi's Gloria of 1713 (RV 589).[3] The motto and its two ornamented repeats together span the octave and a half within which the entire ritornello is contained; and minorization and the Neapolitan B♭ add a chromatic tint to the otherwise diatonic harmonies. Such an arresting ritornello, encapsulating the very essence of the movement, 'impresses itself so strongly that the listener not only anticipates its recurrence but actually desires it', in the words of Paul Everett.[4] In this way, the ritornello functions as part of a developing compositional process that may depend as much on defeating expectations as on fulfilling them.

Ex. 1.1. Vivaldi, Violin Concerto in A major, RV 345 (Op. 9/2)

The first solo (S1) immediately differentiates the role of the soloist through figuration and high melodies in regular two-bar phrases, each time repeated in the upper or lower octave with corresponding accompaniment. Modulation to the dominant is effected imperceptibly, the new key established by a repeat of the solo phrase which only enhances expectation for the next ritornello (Ex. 1.2). This second ritornello (R2) is a transposition of the first, yet with two significant variants. By avoiding the expected leap to b″ in bar 32, the ritornello retains exactly the same register as R1; and it is compressed, forcing the syncopated phrase (bars 3–6) into two bars (31–32) and omitting bar 9 altogether (Ex. 1.3).

At the beginning of the second solo (S2) the dominant naturally pulls back towards the tonic, yet such a resolution would have been far too premature at such an early stage of the movement. Vivaldi's rhetoric at this point is based on the acknowledgment of this centripetal force through a brief touch of the tonic chord (ST), and its immediate rejection through a chromatic progression (Ex. 1.4). This intensification begins a modulation that leads directly to a mode change into minor for the third ritornello (R3a), beginning in iii (Ex. 1.5). This time there is yet further compression, as the syncopated phrase from bars 3–6 collapses into a

---

[3] *Vivaldi*, p. 74.
[4] *Vivaldi: 'The Four Seasons'*, p. 27.

Ex. 1.2. Vivaldi, Violin Concerto in A major, RV 345 (Op. 9/2)

Ex. 1.3. Vivaldi, Violin Concerto in A major, RV 345 (Op. 9/2)

Ex. 1.4. Vivaldi, Violin Concerto in A major, RV 345 (Op. 9/2)

single, non-syncopated bar at bar 56. Yet now, for the first and only time in the movement, an imitative texture is introduced, elaborating the semiquaver motive from bar 2 in a sequential pattern modulating to ii. The new key is confirmed by the closing ritornello phrase, this time devoid not only of the inapplicable minorization but also of the Neapolitan degree (bars 60–61).

The overall process corresponds to the model suggested by Leonard Ratner: from the dominant, the movement heads away still more remotely to the 'point of furthest remove', which then initiates a reversal of direction.[5] The point of furthest remove here is conveniently placed on ii to initiate (at least potentially) a direct return to the tonic, by the simple step of majorization (B major = ^{V}/V). Yet the expectation is thwarted by an alien E minor chord (bar 65), triggering a circuitous retransition. A straightforward circle-of-fifths progression (starting with C♯ at bar 66) does indeed arrive on the tonic five bars later, but the sequential

5   *Classic Music*, pp. 225–7.

Ex. 1.5. Vivaldi, Violin Concerto in A major, RV 345 (Op. 9/2)

momentum overshoots through D, G♮, and then (in striking disjunction) C♯ again, in order to lead to vi. The unexpected ritornello in F♯ minor acts as a false reprise: a recapitulation of R1 material in an unexpected key replacing the tonic missed at bar 72 (Ex. 1.6). The surprise move is immediately rectified in bar 79, with an abrupt jump to the tonic, a harmonic 'hiatus'.[6]

Ex. 1.6. Vivaldi, Violin Concerto in A major, RV 345 (Op. 9/2)

The first ritornello in the tonic (R4a) reintroduces the motto only. The ensuing solo (S4) is entirely in the tonic, apart from a brief recall of the two principal keys of the movement (E major and C♯ minor). This solo refers back to S1 in a number of ways: the entire phrase structure and texture are recapitulated, as well as the closing material, now transposed from the dominant to the tonic (compare bars 24–5 with bars 99–100). Finally the movement concludes with a second ritornello

---

6 The term introduced in Talbot, 'The Concerto Allegro', p. 12.

in the tonic (R4b), which compresses R1 from 12 to 8 bars by avoiding all internal repetitions and again omitting bar 9.

The movement illustrates Vivaldi's intention of creating a hierarchy of successive keys: highlighting the attraction of the tonic, placing the dominant as a powerful secondary key, and relegating the remaining keys to a peripheral status. The hierarchy of key areas is dependent not only on variants in rhythmic and melodic parameters. It is also reflected in the proportion of durations allotted to each stable key area in relation to the entire movement (Table 1.1). Tonic and dominant prevail, though the secondary nature of the dominant is reflected in the relative ease with which it is reached, only to slip back to the tonic. The subsequent ritornellos are modulatory, and thus unstable, in sharp contrast to the final tonic spanning R4a-S4-R4b, the longest stable key area in the movement. Having traced the unfolding of the movement in detail, we summarize the process in Table 1.2.

Table 1.1. Proportions of stable key areas in Vivaldi, RV 345 (Op. 9/2)

I	V	iii	ii	vi	I	TOTAL
20%	18%	4%	2%	4%	28%	76%

Table 1.2. Timeline of Vivaldi, Violin Concerto in A major, RV 345 (Op. 9/2)

Function	R1	S1		R2	S2a	(ST)	S2b
Bars	1–12	13–23	24–29	29–38	38–42	43–44	44–53
Key	I	I	V	V	V	(I)	→

R3a			S3	R3b	R4a	S4	R4b
53–56	57–59	60–61	62–76	76–79	80–82	82–102	102–9
iii	→	ii	→	vi //	I	I	I

This analysis supports Everett's contention that one of the fundamental principles of the Vivaldian ritornello form is 'that a movement's second and subsequent ritornellos are rarely identical to the first'.[7] Talbot goes further in observing that 'when Vivaldi recapitulates material, he likes to prune it drastically, eliminating the repetition of phrases or simply excising whole groups of bars ... He seems to regard a melody less as an organic whole than as a provisional arrangement of small units capable of recombination.'[8] The interaction of musical parameters – changing textures and registers; repeated, altered and new motives; shortened ritornellos; and different proportionate durations of sections – all collaborate in guiding the listener through the musical process. This is not to say that all parameters move in a synchronized fashion: indeed, it is one of the purposes of our analysis to

[7] *Vivaldi: 'The Four Seasons'*, p. 33.
[8] *Vivaldi*, p. 77.

demonstrate the imaginative potential of varying degrees of coordination of parameters. As Everett himself has persuasively argued, 'the predictability inherent in the alternation of solo and *tutti* periods . . . can be harnessed as a positive force for musical development provided that listeners' expectations are manipulated'.[9]

Functions and Symbols

Our analysis required a redefinition of the components of ritornello form, expanding the concepts of ritornello and solo beyond their conventional textural implications so that they designate structural functions. The symbols R and S with attached figures are used to refer to distinct structural stages within the tonal unfolding of the movement (Table 1.3). While it is the parameter of texture that most immediately distinguishes ritornello from solo, this is just one component among several in the multi-level articulation of the form. The numbering of ritornellos and solos therefore signifies not merely the order of events but also the tonal function of each section, with lower-case letters representing further subdivisions.

Table 1.3. Symbols and definitions

Column 1		Column 2	
Siglum	**Definition**	**Siglum**	Definition
R1 **M**	Ritornello in I Motto	**RT, ST**	Central ritornello or solo in I, followed by further tonal elaboration
S1	Solo modulating to secondary key	**R3**	Ritornello in a peripheral key (key other than secondary)
R1a-S1a-R1b-S1b	Ritornello; solo leading to another ritornello in I; solo modulating to secondary key	**S3**	Solo effecting retransition to I, or between two peripheral keys
R2	Ritornello in secondary key (V in major; III, v or iv in minor)	**R3a-S3a-R3b-S3b**	Analogous to R1a complex above (R3a and R3b may be in different peripheral keys)
S2	Solo in secondary key modulating to peripheral key	**S4**	Solo in I
R2a-S2a-R2b-S2b	Analogous to R1a complex above	**R4**	Ritornello in I
		R4a-S4-R4b	Ritornello in I with solo interpolation

---

[9] *Vivaldi: 'The Four Seasons'*, p. 33.

The numbering system is designed to reflect the incipient hierarchy of secondary and peripheral key areas, but by no means presumes or prejudges norms of tonal organization. Hence, most functions listed in the table are optional: so if there is no ritornello in a peripheral key, the ritornellos are numbered R1, R2 and R4 (omitting R3). Likewise, if the retransition from a peripheral key to the tonic is accomplished within a ritornello, there is no S3, but we have instead R3-R4.

We have preferred the term 'motto' to 'head motive'. Defined in the *Oxford English Dictionary* as 'a short quotation (or sometimes an original passage simulating a quotation) prefixed to a literary work or to one of its parts, and expressing some idea appropriate to the contents', the term brings out the particular properties and central role of the first musical idea. The motto is a short, distinct and easily memorable motive, which the listener would expect to hear later in the movement. The various ways in which the motto may be repeated, transformed or alternated with other important motives will be shown to be one of the most powerful and sophisticated devices available in ritornello form. The interaction of the recurrent motto with new material creates a dichotomy of unity-versus-diversity that is crucial to the individual trajectory of each ritornello movement. It is thus essential to view reprises of the motto not as static architectural signposts but as stages of a continuous argument.

The term 'period', which is also essential to our discussion, has never been universally defined: indeed, as Leonard Ratner has pointed out, there was already confusion surrounding the use of the term among German theorists in the second half of the eighteenth century. Three grades of definition may be suggested, from the broadest through a middle way to one that is highly specific. Ratner himself settles on a very general definition: 'accepting the traditional rhetorical definition of a period – the completion of a line of discourse at a final point of punctuation – then the most decisive element in musical periodic structure is its *final cadence*'.[10] At the most specific end, 'period' has connotations of matching antecedent-consequent, in which the antecedent typically moves to a half-close, and the two halves open with similar material. Such essentially symmetrical periodicity is most closely associated with the later classical style.[11]

For our purposes it will be convenient to retain an idea of a period having both closure and division into antecedent and consequent, following the terminology initiated by Talbot.[12] Yet, beyond stressing the interdependence of two phrases in creating a whole, this usage has no connotations of regularity, symmetry or thematic parallelism. Frequently the consequent will be much longer, itself subdivided into a spinning-out phrase and a closing phrase. The antecedent and the consequent may therefore encompass the familiar tripartite Fortspinnungstypus identified by Wilhelm Fischer: Vordersatz, Fortspinnung, Nachsatz (Schlusssatz

---

[10] *Classic Music*, p. 34.
[11] Rothstein (*Phrase Rhythm*, p. 18) distinguishes between two types of period. The one with parallel material has antecedent-consequent, whereas the other with no parallel material is composed of fore-phrase and after-phrase (Vordersatz and Nachsatz).
[12] 'The Concerto Allegro', pp. 9–11.

or Epilog).[13] The ritornello may be coincident with a single period; yet the more complex ritornellos may comprise two periods or more.

A crucial aspect of the composition of a ritornello movement is the decision about its tonal scheme. As Everett has indicated, Vivaldi 'typically writes a movement from beginning to end, fluently and quickly, without the aid of sketches'.[14] Yet we would not conclude from this compositional method that new, 'seemingly strategic' keys are arrived at 'almost by chance', nor necessarily that Vivaldi lacked a sense of tonal and structural planning – quite the reverse. For over the short timescale of a concerto movement Vivaldi would certainly have been quite capable of maintaining an acute sense of direction and proportion, especially while writing a movement in a continuous manner. Allowing the form of a movement to develop out of the material is by no means incompatible with this larger consciousness of structural memory and anticipation. To return to our example, the central B minor cadence must clearly have appeared to Vivaldi as a convenient point to start moving back to tonic. But the ensuing compositional process can be viewed in two quite different lights:

(1) In the course of writing, Vivaldi conceives a sequence that approaches the tonic, but he senses that this would be premature after the intensification in the C♯ minor ritornello. With a 'fine instinct for what seemed right'[15] he keeps the sequential pattern going. Drawing on his past experience he decides to stop on F♯, which under the circumstances would form a false reprise leading back to the tonic.

(2) Vivaldi had already planned a false reprise at a much earlier stage. Identifying F♯ minor as a strong possibility based on theoretical and practical norms of the time, he avoids it entirely until S3, which (in some tonal ambiguity) proceeds to the false reprise. This is further highlighted by the strongly dramatized hiatus to the tonic within the ritornello; and the final tonic is then prolonged by a lengthy solo. This process confirms the overall conception of the movement: a 'frame' of similar material – diatonic, tonally stable, in textural dialogue – surrounds a powerful and unstable core, in which all three minor-mode options are explored. The final F♯ minor forms a resolution of C♯ minor, in the same way as the recapitulation goes on to resolve the dominant.

Albinoni's Pendulum

The vast array of tonal schemes explored in the concerto repertoire may be grouped into two conceptual categories, characterized by Talbot as 'pendulum' (with at least one intermediate tonic in the course of the movement) and 'circuit' (traversing a series of different keys before the inevitable return to the tonic).[16] The pendulum model was advocated by the German theorist Joseph Riepel, who argued that tonal unity should be maintained through restatements of the tonic in

---

[13] Wilhelm Fischer, 'Zur Entwicklungsgeschichte', pp. 29–33. See also Dreyfus, *Bach and the Patterns of Invention*, pp. 60–1.

[14] *Vivaldi: 'The Four Seasons'*, p. 39.

[15] Ibid., pp. 39–40.

[16] *The Sacred Vocal Music*, pp. 128–9.

the course of the movement, since the tonic 'must never be lost to the eye or the ear'.[17] This is the case in Albinoni's concerto for two oboes in G major, published as Op. 9/6 in 1722 (Table 1.4).

Table 1.4. Timeline of Albinoni, Concerto for Two Oboes in G major, Op. 9/6

Function	R1a	S1a	R1b	S1b	R2	S2a	ST
Bars	1–15	15–18	18–22	22–36	36–43	44–45	46–47
Key	I	I	I	I → V	V	V	I

S2b	R3a	RT/ST	S3	R3b	R4	Coda
48–53	54–59	59–62	62–71	71–75	76–89	90–101
→ vi	vi →	I	→ iii	iii →	I	I

Here is an example of the full use of the pendulum process: indeed the tonic is reiterated twice (marked ST and RT), with each occasion providing a new point of departure for tonal excursion. Thus after R2 the two oboes state the motto first in the dominant, yet immediately repeat it in the tonic (Ex. 1.7), an emphatic and unmistakable assertion that initiates a move to the peripheral E minor. R3a leads swiftly back to a tonic restatement, yet this turns out to be a false tonic reprise, for the oboes instead divert towards another peripheral key (B minor). This time R3b prepares the dominant for a genuine reprise, consisting of a full Da Capo of R1. The tonic is prolonged by a lengthy coda that ties together some of the earlier material, closing with a compressed version of the ritornello in a kaleidoscopic interplay of soloists and orchestra.

The soloists in this movement are treated in a quite different way from the violin in the Vivaldi example. The sonorous potential of the oboes, their ability to enrich and stand out from a full string orchestra, is immediately exploited in R1, where the oboes move variously from imitation through solo interludes to full contrapuntal interplay. The palette is thus multicoloured, and the musical structure expanded, despite a reliance on only two chords. After the end of R1, the roles of tutti and soloists are at first separated. Talbot has noted that the oboe 'almost invariably enters, at the start of the second period, with a briefly stated solo motto (Riemann's *Devise*)'.[18] Here the oboes assert their individuality with their version of the orchestral motto (this is the Devise): after the usual orchestral interruption, the Devise is resumed and extended into the new key. Gradually the orchestral texture thickens and intensifies, subsuming the oboes, until R2 emerges in full daylight scored for strings alone. Similar shifts of focus, ranging from sharp highlighting of soloists or strings to unified contrapuntal textures, shape the textural argument through the rest of the movement, in parallel with

---

[17] *Grundregeln zur Tonordnung insgemein* (1755), cited in Ratner, *Classic Music*, p. 50. Ratner uses the terms 'solar' and 'polar', the latter better suited to the high classical style, with its essential predominance of tonic-dominant polarity.

[18] *Tomaso Albinoni*, p. 165: see p. 136 for a discussion of the Devise in Albinoni's vocal works.

Ex. 1.7. Albinoni, Concerto for Two Oboes in G major, Op. 9/6

tonal and motivic development. Paradoxically, following the orchestral R3b, it is the return of the oboes in R4 that clearly articulates the tonic return. The Da Capo thus fully reintegrates soloists and orchestra, and the coda continues this process of textural resolution.

Closing with a Da Capo of R1 is a strategy that occurs across the repertoire in many different contexts. In the simplest version, which has become enshrined as a textbook norm, the final solo (S3) modulates back from the peripheral area; the tonic is then articulated by the arrival of a ritornello (R4) presenting a complete Da Capo of R1. Yet, as will become apparent throughout the book, this procedure is not at all common. Instead, composers experiment with all sorts of relation-ships between tonic return, textural articulation and motivic recurrence; as well as varying the proportions of time spent in the tonic. Even where there is a full Da Capo, it may well be preceded by a tonic ritornello and solo, pushing the reprise further back into the movement and raising the proportion of final tonic.

Vivaldi's Circuit

By contrast to the pendulum process, the circuit requires a continuous progression through secondary and peripheral key areas, thereby increasing the anticipation for the final tonic. Early eighteenth-century composers realized how the strong directional pull of the dominant back towards the tonic could be used as a powerful device to extend the tonal process: for by postponing the implied resolu-tion at the centre of the movement, the overall trajectory of the movement could be sustained on a much more ambitious scale. Furthermore, the stronger the establishment of the dominant area, the more powerful the sense of avoidance of the immediate resolution.

An extreme example is Vivaldi's violin concerto in D major, RV 232, in which any suggestion of the tonic triad is conspicuously avoided across the centre of the movement. This is a virtuoso piece on a grand scale (Table 1.5). The first ritornello (R1) corresponds to Talbot's description of a 'well-rounded musical entity, almost a piece within a piece';[19] it is designed as a multi-sectional period, each component creating implications that Vivaldi will realize as the movement unfolds (Ex. 1.8). The antecedent recalls RV 345 in its powerful unison octaves, but they soon give way to more contrapuntal treatment; and at bar 11 there is a sudden textural change. A five-bar interruption in concertino texture (*piano* in the minor mode) acts as a rhetorical aside: as the example shows, bar 10 could have led directly to the motto in bar 16. This breakdown of continuity is rectified by a resumption of the motto in brilliant style and a frenzied drive towards closure, which serves to dramatize the solo entrance.

Table 1.5. Timeline of Vivaldi, Violin Concerto in D major, RV 232

Function	R1			S1		R2	S2	
Bars	1–10	11–15	16–23	24–36	37–52	53–59	59–76	76–83
Key	I	i	I	I	V	V	V	→ vi
Thematic	M			M var.		= 17–23		

R3	S4	R4
84–88	89–115	116–123
vi	I	I
= 11–12, 18–20	M var.	= 17–23

S1 begins with a flamboyant variant of the motto in a high register, staying in the tonic until a brilliant scale passage lands on the dominant (bar 36). This is accepted as a new key with no modulatory progression – that is, using the device of 'under-preparation'. The ensuing virtuoso solo over an A pedal argues persuasively for a reversion to the tonic, but this is strikingly avoided at bar 49 (Ex. 1.9). R2 is then based on the exciting culminating phrase of R1.

The second solo replicates the S1 procedure a fifth higher, thus leading to a V/V pedal on E. Yet in this case E does not become a new key area, but is instead diverted into a sudden modulation to vi (bars 76–77). Now the implication of the surprising minor interpolation in R1 is realized, when its opening two bars are quoted in B minor to introduce R3, this time in tutti scoring (bars 84–85). Thus the hierarchy is confirmed thematically: only R1 has the motto, R2 transposes the closing phrase, while R3 is based on the subsidiary concertino passage (Table 1.5).

---

[19] *Vivaldi*, p. 110.

Ex. 1.8. Vivaldi, Violin Concerto in D major, RV 232

Ex. 1.9. Vivaldi, Violin Concerto in D major, RV 232

Vivaldi overtly avoids any reappearance of the tonic prior to the recapitulation, where it is dramatized by a hiatus – the solo breaking in immediately after R3 with a literal reprise of bars 24–26. The superior function of the tonic is thus established by all parameters. The motto appears only in the tonic, whether in tutti or in solo, while the other ritornellos refer to the subsidiary sections of R1. The movement is direct and bold in its tonal design, with 99% consisting of stable areas and long pedals, and only one brief modulatory passage. Tonal hierarchy and specialization of motivic material collaborate in a highly sophisticated and well-planned structure.

A comparison between this movement and those analysed previously reveals quite different roles for the ritornello. In the earlier Vivaldi and Albinoni examples the motto articulated every ritornello, clearly marking salient reference points. The D major concerto, on the other hand, unfolds as a continuous process, distributing specialized roles to elements of R1 as required and emphasizing the circuit model by avoiding the motto until the re-establishment of the tonic. R2 and R3 provide closure of the preceding solos more than reassertion through the motto. This strategy further serves to highlight the soloist, who is entrusted with the important role of bringing back the tonic as well as the only return of the motto, a role dramatically emphasized by hiatus.

The comparison leads to more general observations. The mottos of both RV 345 and RV 232 are powerful assertive gestures, ideally suited both to articulate the form and to orientate the listener. Yet they are used in markedly different ways. The invention of the motto and the ensuing motivic material of the first ritornello in no way limits or determines the course of events. On the contrary, it opens up a wide range of potential moves.

The Minor Route

The dominant as secondary key is common to all three concertos discussed so far: this was already the preferred choice for the major mode. The minor mode was treated very differently, with III, v and even iv regarded as potential secondary keys; and the choice of key was often elevated to a matter of rhetorical argument. This will be illustrated in the following three examples. Although they share the same beautiful motto, each explores a different strategy in the unfolding of the ritornello movement.

Albinoni's oboe concerto in G minor, Op. 9/8, provides a further example of an argument carried out through the pendulum process (Table 1.6). The first

Table 1.6. Timeline of Albinoni, Oboe Concerto in G minor, Op. 9/8

Function	R1a	S1a	R1b	S1b	R2	S2a
Bars	1–10	11–13	14–20	21–31	31–37	38–39
Key	i	i		i →	III	III →
Thematic	M	M (Devise)	= 4–10	M	M	M

ST	S2b	R3a	S3	R3b	R4	S4	Coda
40–41	42–47	47–52	52–66	66–68	68–77	77–87	87–97
i →	→ v	v →	VII →	iv →	i	i	i
M		M		M	= R1a	= S1a, R1b varied	

ritornello corresponds to Fischer's tripartite pattern of opening Vordersatz (bars 1–3), Fortspinnung extending around a circle of fifths (bars 4–7) and closing Nachsatz (or Epilog, bars 7–10). The closing phrase is a melodic expansion of the motto, further stressing the self-contained nature of the ritornello (Ex. 1.10). The soloist adapts the Fortspinnung to reach the first tonal target, the relative major (III). Yet S2 reverts to the tonic and a new modulatory process is initiated, revisiting the sequential harmony of the Fortspinnung. This time the dominant is reached. Thus III and v are presented as part of a rhetorical argument, suggesting both secondary keys as possible targets: they are accorded equal weight in being marked by the motto, yet v is downgraded by the instability of the modulatory third ritornello. After the peripheral F major, a reversal and return to the tonic would be expected: indeed G is reached (bar 59) but only as a major chord which

Ex. 1.10. Albinoni, Oboe Concerto in G minor, Op. 9/8

Ex. 1.11. Albinoni, Oboe Concerto in G minor, Op. 9/8

resolves to the subdominant, marked by a strong statement of the motto by the tutti. Yet this proves to be a false reprise, instantly recognized and amended, diverting immediately to the tonic in mid-phrase and continuing without further ado to the end of R1 (Ex. 1.11). The solo S4 then reconfirms the tonic by presenting R1 in its entirety, again drawing soloist and tutti together in a characteristic gesture of summative recapitulation before the final coda.

Albinoni uses the pendulum process to build his rhetorical argument, presenting two options for departure from the tonic, the relative major (III) and the dominant. Eventually the subdominant is asserted, but it is immediately abandoned as a false reprise. While all are equally highlighted by the motto and by a ritornello, only III is privileged by a ritornello that is both stable and closed.

Table 1.7. Timeline of Vivaldi, Violin Concerto in G minor, RV 317 (Op. 12/1)

Function	R1	S1	R2	R3a	S3a
Bars	1–26	27–47	48–52	53–65	65–96
Key	i	i →	III →	iv	iv →
Thematic	M	M¹	M²	M³	

R3b	S3b	R3c	R4a	S4	R4b
96 – 108–114	114–138	139–142	143–148	149–182	183–197
VI → v	v [→ i?]	v //	i	i	i
M⁴		M	M	M⁵	

Vivaldi's violin concerto in G minor, RV 317, published in 1729 as Op. 12/1, provides another example of the continuous circuit process (Table 1.7). The rhetorical basis for the movement is again the search for a secondary key, resulting in a constant state of flux: indeed the two central ritornellos are equally modulatory and unstable. By contrast with the Albinoni example, each arrival is marked by a variant of the motto, gradually departing further from the original (Ex. 1.12). The dominant key is privileged over III by its long duration, culminating in a statement of the original motto in v at bar 139, which apparently confirms the priority of this key. Yet it turns out to be a false reprise, corrected immediately by a statement of the motto in the tonic, injecting a further note of ambiguity about the role of v (Ex. 1.13). Finally, the preferred status of the tonic is strongly supported by S4, which closely paraphrases the material of the opening

Ex. 1.12. Vivaldi, Violin Concerto in G minor, RV 317 (Op. 12/1)

Ex. 1.13. Vivaldi, Violin Concerto in G minor, RV 317 (Op. 12/1)

ritornello. The overall tonal argument is reinforced by the proportions of the stable areas, as shown in Table 1.8.

A third concerto based on the same motto is by Andrea Zani (1696–1757), a composer active in Lombardy and Vienna whose large concerto output will be discussed in Chapter 12. The violin concerto in E minor (Zan15) was published as Op. 2/12 in 1729, and also copied for the large Dresden court orchestra under Johann Georg Pisendel.[20] Zani's strategy differs markedly from those of Vivaldi and Albinoni, and requires separate discussion of ritornellos and solos.

The hierarchization of the ritornellos is based on a subtle manipulation of the phrase structure outlined in R1 (Table 1.9). The opening ritornello acts as the point of departure for the entire musical argument, relying on memorization of the

[20] Eds Hirshberg and McVeigh (2002).

Table 1.8. Proportions of stable areas in Vivaldi, Violin Concerto in G minor, RV 317 (Op. 12/1)

i	III	iv	VI	v	i
15%	7%	10%	3%	18%	28%

Table 1.9. Timeline of Zani, Violin Concerto in E minor, Zan15 (Op. 2/12)

Function	R1	S1	R2	S2	R3	S3	S4	R4
Bars	1–14	14–35	36–46	46–60	60–62	62–78	78–92	93–106
Key	I	i → III → v	v	v → iv	iv	→ ♭vii → VI →	i	i
Thematic	M a b c	M¹	M a b		c			= R1 D.C.

succession of brief phrases to set up long-range expectations. R1 is a full period with the tripartite division of the Fortspinnungstypus (Ex. 1.14). Yet the Nachsatz here, rather than resolving tension, instead triggers a new intensification with its rising suspensions: an additional cadential descent is required, which is further intensified through chromaticism. R2 confirms the preferred status of the

Ex. 1.14. Zani, Violin Concerto in E minor, Zan15 (Op. 2/12)

Ex. 1.15. Zani, Violin Concerto in E minor, Zan15 (Op. 2/12)

dominant by a near-complete transposition of R1 that only omits the final cadential phrase. R3 in the subdominant, potentially a secondary key area, is placed on a lower hierarchical level in that it is not marked by the motto, but instead transposes the final cadential phrase of R1 – the very phrase that had been omitted from R2. Its status as a peripheral ritornello is thus neatly encapsulated.

The solo sections proceed in a manner largely independent of the ritornellos. S1 introduces a new melody in *bassetto* texture (solo accompanied by upper strings), the onset of modulation being marked by a further change to solo plus continuo (Ex. 1.15). First the relative major is proposed with a contrasting motive, but it is eventually rejected in favour of the dominant. At this point the soloist surprisingly refers to the motto over a chord of E minor, the home key: this serves to recall its original form, yet at the same time anticipates the return of the motto in R2. S3 takes advantage of the peripheral associations of A minor, the key of R3, in leading to the remote D minor, which acts as the point of furthest remove. In returning towards the tonic via C major, the solo makes oblique reference to both the motto and to S1, thus predicting the return to the tonic through motivic retrospection (Ex. 1.16).

In this movement the tonal argument is entrusted to the soloist, whose thematic material is only tangentially connected to that of the ritornellos. The movement shares a number of features with those of Vivaldi and Albinoni – notably the tonal rhetoric and the hierarchization of key areas – but they are enacted by different means.

Ex. 1.16. Zani, Violin Concerto in E minor, Zan15 (Op. 2/12)

Rules and Strategies

The foregoing analyses converge on Leonard Meyer's theory of musical style, and, specifically, on his distinction between rules and strategies. Rules constitute 'the highest, most encompassing level of stylistic constraints . . . Rules specify the permissible material means of a musical style.'[21] On the other hand, strategies 'are compositional choices made within the possibilities established by the rules of the style. For any specific style there is a finite number of rules, but there is an indefinite number of possible strategies for realizing or instantiating such rules.'[22]

Any Vivaldian concerto movement will always follow the rule of departure from the tonic key to temporary key areas, followed by return to the tonic. In itself this embodies a further rule: an inherently hierarchical approach to musical thinking. Yet, as already suggested in the sample discussed above, there are many different itineraries that the composer may choose to take: these constitute

[21] Meyer, *Style and Music*, p. 17.
[22] Ibid., p. 20.

strategies. As Meyer has clarified, 'syntactic rules establish sets of *possible* functional relationships within parameters. In addition, because of the rules, some simultaneities and some successions tend to be more *probable* than others, [but such probabilities] are not in themselves rules. Rather they are aspects of strategy.'[23] As an example of this distinction, the development in the seventeenth century of syntactic rules for harmonic succession resulted in 'a repertory of possible progressions capable of denying as well as fulfilling implications, defining – instead of being subservient to – contexts, and forming hierarchic tonal structures'.[24]

At a larger level, the treatment of tonal schemes in our repertoire provides a potent illustration of Meyer's theoretical perspective. As will be discussed in detail subsequently, the number of tonal schemes essayed in the sample is well in excess of 200, of which 98 appear in Vivaldi's output alone. Some of the tonal schemes were prevalent, whereas others were very rarely used; some were common to many composers, others limited to a single one; some were common to the major and minor modes, others were mode-dependent. But alongside the exploration of new patterns, another process led in the opposite direction towards selection of certain schemes and elimination of others. Options used rarely by Vivaldi became more prevalent in concertos by other composers, whereas some of his preferred strategies were relegated to a marginal position or even eliminated altogether. At the same time, permutations that Vivaldi had never used were attempted by others, and, if found convincing, were maintained into the next generation. Similar processes were at the same time replicated across all the other parameters. In this way, an array of procedures within the general concept of ritornello form unfolded and transmuted.[25]

The analyses offered above have demonstrated how in any individual concerto movement a hierarchy of keys results from the varying degrees of coordination of the musical parameters – textural with regard to the tutti-solo alternation, thematic in terms of the repetition, variation and avoidance of the motto. These factors have a further impact on the listener. At one extreme, common material in all of the ritornellos and solos stresses unity; at the other, distinct and contrasting material for every solo emphasizes specialization as the movement progresses. The solos may proceed with a thematic argument of their own, or they may be related in various ways to the ritornellos. Numerous permutations are possible within this complex set of relationships, and usually only some of the ritornellos and solos are privileged with the recall of the motto. Since these thematic permutations may be enacted entirely independently of the permutations of the tonal schemes, the result is a staggering variety across the repertoire.

Italian concerto composers never settled for any single exclusive strategy, but rather experimented with a wide range of options in every parameter. This is a central premise in coming to grips with Vivaldi's compositional decision-making, as well as in understanding his relationship with contemporaries and

---

[23] Ibid., p. 19.

[24] Ibid., p. 19.

[25] An example of experimentation with the parameters of ritornello form is discussed in Hirshberg and McVeigh, 'The Making of a Ritornello Movement'.

followers. Statistical methods will take on a special importance in our study of Vivaldi's style, particularly in view of the limited information about chronology. Statistical data derived from his repertoire will then guide us in establishing the stylistic profiles of other composers: many options will turn out to be shared, yet each composer exhibits his own, idiosyncratic preferences. For this reason, statistics should not be used merely to establish the generally preferred options. Indeed, minority options may demand special attention, whether they represent (i) options that turn out to be limited and uninteresting, and are consequently discarded; or (ii) options that result from exceptional invention, highly individual to a particular concerto and hard to replicate.

The Ritornello Movement as a Rhetorical Argument?

Our detailed recreation of the experience of listening to these six movements has been unequivocally related to aspects of a rhetorical argument, leading us to address once more this controversial issue in the historiography of eighteenth-century music. We make a clear distinction between what we have considered the inherently rhetorical basis of the solo concerto and the contrived efforts by German theorists – interestingly, never by Italians – to apply terminology derived from classical Greek and Latin rhetorical texts to contemporary music. Particularly relevant to our study are the three basic relationships between motives in the small dimension, and between periods and sections in the middle dimension: recurrence, variation (including all degrees of change and elaboration that still bear an audible relationship to the original) and contrast. The German theorists characteristically fitted traditional rhetorical terms to these three devices, such as *anaphora* for repetition and recurrence (Mattheson), *variatio* (Bernhard) and *antithesis* for contrast (Scheibe).[26] The application of such terms to modern instrumental music must in part reflect the deep admiration of German composers, performers and theorists for Italian music and for concertos in particular. As well as performing Italian concertos and using them as templates for their own compositions, they also sought the best manner to express their admiration in writing, which was by relating Italian instrumental music to the venerable classical tradition.

Whether Italian composers themselves were aware of such ways of articulating the compositional process is a different matter, and it is here that the controversy lies. Drawing upon a penetrating critique by Brian Vickers, Talbot has sounded a note of caution for musicologists seeking to exploit 'rhetorical processes and effects as metaphors for musical ones', especially the application of German terminology to contemporary Italian music.[27] Yet it is our contention that we need not use traditional terms in the way that German theorists proposed in order to benefit from their perception of Italian musical processes and thereby enhance our own understanding of the ritornello movement as a rhetorical

---

26 These and other terms are discussed with extensive quotations in Bartel, *Musica Poetica*; see also George J. Buelow, 'Rhetoric and Music', *NG2*.

27 *The Finale in Western Instrumental Music*, pp. 84–5, referring to Vickers, 'Figures of Rhetoric'.

argument. Talbot himself has conceded that 'the models provided by the oration (which for the first time identifies the beginning and the end of a musical composition as discrete sections with distinctive functions) and also by its *figurae* (which have left an indelible mark on the conventions of word-painting and onomatopoeic reference within music) have proved, in their time, a highly potent fiction that the historian cannot ignore if he wishes to get inside the minds of those who composed, performed, and heard the music of past centuries'.[28]

The most extensive and systematic attempt to match the traditional rhetoric of oratory with an entire musical argument is to be found in Johann Mattheson's *Der vollkommene Capellmeister* (Hamburg, 1739). Describing the 'manifold and various' affects possible within the concerto, Mattheson suggests a general rhetorical interpretation, introducing the central term of *Elaboratio*: 'Much depends upon the full elaboration, indeed, one even overdoes it, so that it resembles a rich table which is set not for hunger but for a show. One can easily guess that in such a contest, from which all concertos got their name, there is no lack of jealousy and vengeance, or envy and hate, as well as other such passions.'[29]

Elsewhere Mattheson provides a much more detailed discussion of rhetoric, as it might be applied to the process of musical composition and to the understanding of specific musical examples. First he establishes his own five-part categorization of musical creativity: *Inventio, Dispositio, Elaboratio, Decoratio, Executio*.[30] The last two – ornamentation and performance – will scarcely concern us here. We shall be most concerned with the first three components of the compositional process: invention, reliant on 'fire and spirit'; disposition, displaying 'order and measure'; and elaboration, the routine working-out of musical ideas in 'cold blood and circumspection'.[31] Although disposition and elaboration might be thought to be inherently connected, the fact that Mattheson chose to distinguish them is significant in itself. *Dispositio* will be central to our discussion. Mattheson defines it as 'the neat ordering of all the parts and details in the melody, or in an entire melodic composition, about in the manner in which one contrives or delineates a building and makes a plan or design in order to show where a room, a parlor, a chamber, etc., should be placed'.[32] It is this concept of a larger design for the entire musical composition that we hope to trace.

Mattheson goes further in advocating a division of *Dispositio* into six stages: *Exordium, Narratio, Propositio, Confirmatio, Confutatio* and *Peroratio*.[33] He himself admitted the difficulties encountered in applying this sequence to every composition, yet such reservations do not diminish his strongly held adherence to the principle: 'For, though the cited parts should not always occur or follow one another in the same sequence, they will almost all be encountered in good melodies.'[34] In practice Mattheson's attempts to apply the Latin terms to the sections

---

[28] Ibid., p. 85.

[29] *Der vollkommene Capellmeister*, p. 467.

[30] See Dreyfus, *Bach and the Patterns of Invention*, pp. 5–8 for a full discussion.

[31] *Der vollkommene Capellmeister*, p. 480.

[32] Ibid., pp. 469–70.

[33] Ibid., pp. 470–6. Further on the genesis of these terms, see Hartmut Krones, 'Musik und Rhetorik', *MGG2*.

[34] *Der vollkommene Capellmeister*, p. 472.

of an actual musical example are undeniably awkward, leading modern commentators such as George J. Buelow and Laurence Dreyfus (as well as Talbot) to reject this detailed application of rhetorical thinking as 'empty scholasticism': Dreyfus has instead proposed that 'music and rhetoric are analogous, but not synonymous'.[35] However, if one does accept that German rhetorical thinking provides at least some contemporary insight into the listener's perception of instrumental composition, a more flexible use of Mattheson's concepts can still be usefully adopted – one that certainly does not require any rigid succession of required components.

For example, the notion of *Confutatio* may be fruitfully used in directing the listener towards a frequently encountered procedure: the deliberately misleading arrival and consequent refutation. Mattheson defined this notion as 'a dissolution of the exceptions . . . expressed in melody either through combining, or even through quotation and refutation of foreign-appearing ideas: For through just such antitheses, if they are well stressed, the hearing is strengthened in its joy.' Mattheson comments that although *Confutatio* is not always used, it is 'truly one of the most beautiful' aspects of musical disposition.[36] A less happy example is his assertion that a repeat of the opening material at the end of a piece implies that 'our peroration is replaced by our *Exordium*'. The logical weakness in this argument has been rightly identified by Dreyfus, since an *Exordium* (in the rhetorical sense) can only occur at the beginning.[37] A principal contention of our book will be to argue that no repeat of material can ever be completely identical in function with its initial presentation, not even an unaltered reprise. Thus a Da Capo of the opening ritornello is not a repeat of the *Exordium* – a built-in contradiction – but still a *Peroratio,* in this case the simplest kind of reinterpretation of the previous argument, such as will be discussed later in the context of recapitulation.

Rather than indulging therefore in futile attempts to force musical analysis into a rigid rhetorical framework, we will instead work the other way around, resorting to rhetorical concepts whenever they seem to contribute to our understanding of the unfolding of the ritornello movement. Our approach will thus concur with Dreyfus' view of analysis as 'the inverse of synthesis or composition'.[38] First, however, we turn to the vibrant social and musical context within which the Italian concerto originated and flourished during the early eighteenth century.

---

[35] Buelow, 'Rhetoric and Music', *NG2*; Dreyfus, *Bach and the Patterns of Invention*, pp. 5–6.
[36] *Der vollkommene Capellmeister*, p. 471.
[37] Ibid., p. 472; *Bach and the Patterns of Invention*, p. 7.
[38] *Bach and the Patterns of Invention*, p. 10.

CHAPTER 2

The Concerto in Context

The concerto as a rhetorical argument directed at a responsive group of listeners proved an extraordinarily versatile genre – as likely to be heard in public theatre or church as in court concert, on grand ceremonial occasions as in intimate chamber gatherings, performed by international virtuosi as by amateurs who bought manuscripts or printed copies. This chapter will explore the context for the concerto, from the viewpoint of the composer and soloist, and of the audiences and players for whom it was intended.

The Violinist and the Image of the Solo Concerto

While there had been violin virtuosi before, only in the eighteenth century was the concept openly expressed in terms that rivalled the great singers: compare Veracini's boast that 'there was but *one God*, and *one Veracini*'.[1] Indeed the great violinists were already attributed with supernatural powers a century before Paganini, something encouraged by Tartini's famous anecdote of the dream he tried to recapture in his 'Devil's Sonata'.[2] Locatelli ('il diavolo del violino') set out his claims in a collection entitled nothing less than *L'arte del violino*, a set of concertos with solo capriccios of staggering difficulty, the last headed with the challenging motto 'Il Labirinto armonico: Facilis aditus, difficilis exitus'.

The new virtuosity was variously regarded as wonderful, frightening, despicable and demeaning. For some it inspired more amazement than pleasure. The German traveller Johann Friedrich Armand von Uffenbach captured these ambiguous reactions in his description of Vivaldi's playing in 1715:

> He added a cadenza that really frightened me, for such playing has not been heard before and can never be equalled: he brought his fingers no more than a straw's breadth from the bridge, leaving no room for the bow – and that on all four strings with imitations and incredible speed. With this he astonished everyone, but I cannot say that it delighted me, for it was more skilfully executed than it was pleasant to hear.[3]

---

[1] Charles Burney, *A General History*, vol. 2, p. 450.
[2] Now normally the 'Devil's Trill' sonata.
[3] Diary entry of 4 February 1715, translated from Preussner, *Die musikalischen Reisen*, p. 67.

The association of the virtuoso violin with wildness and caprice, with abandon or loss of control, recalls attitudes to the Carnival, which was seen as playful but dangerous in its subversion of normal modes of life. Vivaldi encouraged such associations through the whimsical titles of some of his concerto collections: *L'estro armonico* (harmonic inspiration or caprice), *La stravaganza* (extravagance or eccentricity), *Il cimento dell'armonia e dell'inventione* (the trial of harmony and invention).[4]

In England there was suspicion amounting to hostility towards virtuosity and the associated imitation of natural sounds: Roger North was dismissive of the descriptive *'bizzarie* the masters of musick will undertake to represent. And many persons that doe not well distinguish between real good and evill, but are hurryed away by caprice, as in a whirlewind, think such musick the best . . . And as to these, in naming Vivaldi, (tho' he hath his fellows) I have instanced enough.'[5] Charles Avison was less reticent in naming the culprits, all central figures in this book: 'OF the first and lowest Class, are VIVALDI, TESSARINI, ALBERTI, and LOCCATELLI, whose Compositions being equally defective in various Harmony and true Invention, are only a fit Amusement for Children.'[6] For Avison these were composers 'who have erred in the Extreme of an unnatural Modulation', his particular scorn being reserved for Vivaldi's imitations of nature.

Detractors of the modern concerto decried its frivolous virtuosity and fantasy, its superficiality, its volatile and irregular eccentricities, upholding instead the chaste sobriety and well-worked contrapuntal style of Corelli, which was regarded as the touchstone of Arcadian good taste. By implication there was a further moral dimension: even Veracini came to view the modern idiom as a symbol of depraved taste, which he allied directly to moral corruption.[7] Like Geminiani, he reworked the music of Corelli in his later years, while Locatelli also returned to the concerto grosso.

Yet there was more than mere mechanical virtuosity in the violinist's appeal. As seductive siren, luring listeners out of themselves, he strove to match the enchanting effect of the finest opera singers. Already in the late seventeenth century the Neapolitan violinist Nicola Matteis, arriving in London on foot from Germany, captivated the diarist John Evelyn:

> I heard that stupendious Violin Signor Nicholao (with other rare Musitians) whom certainly never mortal man Exceeded on that Instrument: he had a strock so sweete, & made it speake like the Voice of a man; & when he pleased, like a Consort of severall Instruments: he did wonders upon a Note: was an excellent Composer also: here was also that rare Lutinist Dr Wallgrave: but nothing approch'd the Violin in Nicholas hand: he seem'd to be spiritato'd & plaied such ravishing things on a ground as astonish'd us all.[8]

This imaginative fantasy, the beauty and intensity of the vocal line – above all the magical aura that enraptured the audience – continued to inspire Italian violin

4   On these titles, see Everett, *Vivaldi: 'The Four Seasons'*, pp. 17–18.
5   *Roger North on Music*, p. 293.
6   *An Essay on Musical Expression*, p. 42.
7   Hill, 'The Anti-Galant Attitude'.
8   John Evelyn's vivid account of a private concert on 17 November 1674.

playing throughout the eighteenth century. In his *Trattato di musica*, published in 1754, Tartini repeatedly emphasized the natural expressive qualities of the voice ('la maggior perfezione del buon gusto sta nella voce, e nella espressione').[9] As the violin aspired to the highest form of musical expression – the reflection and intensification of literary text – so too did Tartini's concertos explicitly take on a new sensitivity and expressive meaning through the literary mottos he attached to them. Many slow movements, and some Allegros, are headed by emotional phrases from poetry or opera librettos, such as 'Lascia ch'io dica addio' or 'Torna, ritorna o dolce mia speranza'. Locatelli's concerto grosso, Op. 7 No. 6 ('Il pianto d'Arianna'), has an implicit programme with both musical and poetic models, and it even includes a violin recitative written in poignant operatic manner.[10] Such works form a close link between a reflection of classical ideals and a sensitive vocal expression that looks towards the new musical sensibility. Even Vivaldi's own concerto titles sometimes reflect more than purely pictorial representation, as with 'Il riposo' (rest) or 'L'inquietudine' (anxiety). Certainly Vivaldi's later concerto Allegros often require a slower tempo to provide space for a meditative violin cantabile, while Tartini also went on to develop his aesthetic of natural vocal expression in concertos of the utmost melodic simplicity and directness.

Whether through fantastical virtuosity or alluring vocal expression, the solo concerto embodied a new spirit, a modern individualism that threatened the cooperation, balance and moderation typical of the Corellian concerto. The increasing differentiation of the soloist resulted in a complex interrelationship between shared musical experience and the strong individual profile that became the hallmark of the concerto. Ritornello form provided a rational counterbalance that both contained and highlighted the soloist's virtuosic and seductive attractions. Those critics who were so distracted by eccentricity and caprice that they could not hear this dialogue were surely missing its very essence.

The Lives of Instrumentalists

The careers of celebrated instrumentalists reflect a similar dichotomy between individualism and conformity. The emerging concept of the international violin virtuoso (the idea did not as yet extend to other instruments) conflicted with traditional realities of making a secure living. While some violinists maintained fixed posts in Italy, or elsewhere in Europe, others – conscious of their new status and of the demands of a growing market – adopted a restless lifestyle that took them around the continent, mixing short-lived appointments with commercial exploitation of North European concert life and publishing. Many, too, were

[9] 'The highest perfection of good taste lies in the voice, and in expression' (quoted in Petrobelli, 'Tartini, le sue idee', p. 672).
[10] Giacomo Fornari posits an interesting connection with Locatelli's Roman friend Giovanni Valentini, the violinist and sonnet-writer (Introduction to Opera omnia, 7, pp. xxxviii–xxxix). See also Fertonani, 'Espressione strumentale', pp. 338–41, where the comparison with Tartini is drawn; and Bizzarini, 'I "buoni fondamenti degli Antichi" ', pp. 134–40, for a possible link with Benedetto Marcello's serenata *Arianna*.

intermittently involved with opera composition and promotion. These manifold and varied opportunities introduced not only the prospect of fame and fortune, but also new tensions into violinists' lives.

Vivaldi combined the traditional Venetian lifestyle – pieced together from employments or engagements with the *ospedali*, opera houses, churches and private patrons – with a much more diverse international career negotiating with Amsterdam publishers and cultivating patrons around Europe. These aristocratic connections had a direct effect on his concerto output. In the late 1720s Vivaldi assiduously cultivated the Austrian Emperor, dedicating to him the concertos Op. 9 in 1727 under the title *La cetra* (symbol of Habsburg musicality) and presenting him with a fine presentation copy of manuscript concertos with the same title in 1728. A year or so later Vivaldi went to Vienna as a private musician in the Emperor's circle, and at least one further concerto (RV 171) was probably intended for him.

These European ambitions certainly put a strain on his lifelong relationship with the Pietà, the *ospedale* where he was variously employed as violin-teacher and *maestro de' concerti*.[11] In 1723, after a lengthy interruption, he was re-engaged on a quite different basis, with a lucrative contract to compose two concertos a month (sending them by post if necessary), and to direct rehearsals when in Venice. Up until 1729 he contributed some 140 concertos for performance by the *figlie* of the orchestra. As late as 1740 the Pietà asked Vivaldi to compose three unusually scored concertos in honour of the young *Kurprinz* of Saxony; and in May they (somewhat reluctantly) bought twenty concertos before his final departure for Vienna.

Venice was the starting point for many of the violinists who form the subject of this book. The career of Carlo Tessarini reflects a pattern of European connections similar to that of Vivaldi, but taken to a further extreme.[12] He was appointed a violinist at S Marco in 1720, and three years later was engaged as a violin teacher at the Ospedale dei Poveri Derelitti (the Ospedaletto), rising to *maestro de' concerti* by 1729. His first set of concertos was published in Amsterdam (apparently without his knowledge) in 1724. In 1731 he obtained a post in the *cappella* of Urbino Cathedral, where he was based for the next twenty years, albeit with frequent absences that caused the cathedral authorities endless grief – and Tessarini numerous recriminations, fines and absolutions. The relationship provides a telling example of the inherent tension between the restless lifestyle of the concert virtuoso and the needs of the church authorities. In the mid-1730s, for example, Tessarini was working in the retinue of Cardinal Wolfgang Schrattenbach in Brno, while during the 1740s he was giving concerts and

11 He was engaged as a violin-teacher 1703–09 and 1711–16 (and composed sacred music from 1713). In 1716, having first lost his post, he was appointed to an apparently more important position, *maestro de' concerti*, confirming his responsibility for the instrumental music of the Pietà; this engagement lasted just one year, and only in 1735–38 was he again employed in this formal capacity (Rostirolla, 'L'organizzazione musicale', pp. 183–5; Vio, 'Precisazioni sui documenti', pp. 104–8).

12 Dunning, 'Some Notes on the Biography of Carlo Tessarini'; Hirshberg and McVeigh, Introduction to Carlo Tessarini, *Twelve Violin Concertos Opus 1*, where full sources are identified.

publishing in Paris, London and the Netherlands, where (after a further stint in Urbino) he spent his final years.

Even more variegated was the career of Francesco Maria Veracini, who left his native Florence in 1711 for Venice, appearing as soloist at S Marco. The following year he contributed a richly orchestrated *concerto a otto stromenti* to a celebratory Mass at the Frari church marking the accession of Emperor Charles VI.[13] In 1714 he was in London, appearing at public concerts and at the Opera House, before a brief spell at the Düsseldorf court. In Venice the *Kurprinz* of Saxony enticed him to Dresden, where he stayed for five years (1717–22), his special status inevitably causing friction with local (and lower paid) German instrumentalists. After a decade back in Florence devoted to oratorio composition, he returned to London in 1733, achieving a high profile as concert soloist and opera composer. He lived out his last years in Florence, again concentrating on church music – but still playing the violin, as on 6 October 1765, where at a private *accademia* at the grand ducal court 'the Old Veracini, *gran Professore di Violino*, played several concertos'.[14] Such a varied, apparently irrational lifestyle seems to reflect a strong vein of independence in Veracini's make-up. This is mirrored in his attitude towards the concerto: though one of the most famous violinists of his day, he nevertheless left only a small number of concertos, no doubt reflecting his increasing revulsion towards what he saw as the idle immorality of empty virtuosity and modern frivolity.

While it would be a mistake to speak of such violinists undergoing concert tours in the manner of Paganini, nevertheless it was this peripatetic lifestyle that secured the image of the soloist as an individual artist. Across all these diverse activities in Italy and beyond, the concerto was the musical enactment of this image, not only as a vehicle for virtuosity and an individual style of performance, but also as a mark of personal creativity attached to the composer. Indeed performance and composition were so closely intertwined that to specify the composer of a violin concerto was an irrelevance: for why would Vivaldi or Locatelli dilute their individual presence by performing a concerto by someone else?

The Italian Concerto in Italy: Composition and Performance

Court, church and ospedale

Within Italy, the solo concerto was cultivated in many different settings and for many diverse purposes. One such arena was the court, which still provided a stable environment for many instrumentalists. The violinist Giovanni Battista Somis, for example, spent almost his entire life in Turin in the service of the duchy of Savoy (later kingdom of Sardinia). The ducal court retained a large musical establishment for chapel, court concerts and opera, especially at the vast new Teatro Regio, begun in 1738. While Cathedral services were not among their duties, court musicians also played a major role at the annual exposition of the

---

[13] Hill, *The Life and Works of Francesco Maria Veracini*.

[14] Ibid., p. 57. Whether the pieces in question were really concertos, rather than sonatas, must be open to doubt.

Turin Shroud, which was housed in a special chapel between the ducal palace and the Cathedral.[15]

In Milan too, the court maintained an unusually large orchestra for similar purposes. The orchestra was revitalized with the building of the opera house (the Regio Ducal Teatro) in 1717, and three years later it consisted of thirty 'Virtuosi Instromenti', in addition to a *maestro di cappella* and his deputy: perhaps seven first and seven second violins, four violas, two cellos, three double basses, two oboes, three trumpets (two doubling horn), and two bassoons.[16] The stability of this prestigious ensemble is attested by the fact that nine of the thirty were still members in 1748, among them the prolific concerto composer Angelo Maria Scaccia. Milan may have had more significance as the centre of the emerging symphony around G. B. Sammartini, but the sizeable surviving concerto repertoire must, at least in part, reflect performances at court by members of the *cappella*.

Another stable environment was provided by the church. In 1721 Tartini was employed at the Basilica of S Antonio in Padua ('Il Santo') as *primo violino e capo di concerto*, a position he retained – with only one significant interruption – for the rest of his life. His most important duty was to perform concertos at major festivals in the church calendar. The more elaborate functions during Advent, Lent and Easter were graced with 'Organi con Instrumenti, e Concerti': the latter term simply implies concerted music that could be vocal as much as instrumental, but a resolution of 1726 is more specific, allowing after the Credo (i.e. at the Offertory) a 'sinfonia, which must be done as arranged by the first *maestro di cappella*'.[17] Concertos also contributed to the festivities surrounding the celebration of S Antonio on 13 June.[18] A large part of Tartini's concerto output was therefore destined for practical use at S Antonio. Exactly where concertos would have figured in the course of Mass is not documented: Pierluigi Petrobelli has hypothesized that as instrumental music was essentially decorative rather than functional, the first movement might have been played at the Offertory, the slow movement during the Elevation, and the third at the end of Mass.[19] Leonardo Frasson places the first two movements similarly, but the third at Communion, adding that a full concerto could also have been performed before or after Mass; with, on exceptionally grand occasions, several concertos by different instrumentalists.[20]

In Bologna, musical life was focussed around two institutions with a venerable musical history: the basilica of S Petronio, already the focus of an important school of instrumental composition in the late seventeenth century; and the

15   Burdette, 'The Violin Sonatas of Giovanni Battista Somis', p. 29.
16   As suggested by Barblan, 'La musica strumentale', p. 624. Barblan has traced records from 1720 and from 1748; no documents from the interim period exist.
17   Translated from Degrassi, 'Destinazione e aspetti esecutivi', pp. 155–6.
18   According to Leonardo Frasson, Tartini's concertos were reserved for the succeeding Sunday: only from 1745 were 'concerti' heard after the civic procession on the day itself (cited in ibid., p. 156).
19   Petrobelli, 'Giuseppe Tartini' (*Storia della musica al Santo*), p. 187.
20   Cited in Degrassi, 'Destinazione e aspetti esecutivi', pp. 156–9. See also Bonta, 'The Uses of the *Sonata da Chiesa*'.

Accademia Filarmonica, an association of professional musicians which acted as a guardian of contrapuntal standards, discussed at the weekly *esercizi* for composer members and *conferenze* for performers.[21] A central figure in both these institutions from the 1680s onwards was Giuseppe Torelli, whose early violin concertos and trumpet sonatas (written for the celebrated Giovanni Pellegrino Brandi) are of the highest significance. Three later concerto composers held posts at S Petronio, and all were also members of the Accademia Filarmonica: Giuseppe Matteo Alberti, Girolamo Nicolò Laurenti and Lorenzo Gaetano Zavateri. While trumpet sonatas were apparently designed to open Mass, the role of the violin concerto in Bologna is less clear: certainly Alberti's concertos Op. 1 were first performed under his direction at the home of Count Orazio Bargellini, rather than in either of the two main institutions. The focus of composition at the Accademia was on sacred vocal music (its declared mission 'to glorify God'), so it was clearly an exceptional honour when Laurenti was elevated from instrumentalist to composer member in 1710, 'having presented to such effect a *concerto a quattro* to the Accademia'. At the academy's annual festival in honour of S Petronio a 'sinfonia' was always performed as a *Sonata dopo l'epistola*: the predominant composer after Torelli's death was Laurenti, whose works were heard most years from 1710 to 1748.[22]

The principal locus for instrumental music in Venice – a republic lacking a permanent court, music at S Marco a mere shadow of its illustrious past – lay in a different direction. There the most vital instrumental music-making was to be found in the four *ospedali grandi*, Venice's main charitable institutions.[23] Each of these rather different institutions maintained a musical establishment, a choir and orchestra drawn exclusively from the female wards (*figlie di coro*). At the Pietà, with near 1000 foundlings, the musical establishment was an elite group, consisting of a choir of over 20 and almost as many instrumentalists: in 1739 Charles de Brosses counted 40 girls and women dressed in white, expressing his amazement at the precision of the orchestral playing.[24] The predominant purpose was not so much the education of the *figlie* (the phrase 'conservatoire' is clearly inappropriate, as departing *figlie* had to undertake never to perform in public), but a celebration of the religious and social mission of each *ospedale*, one which moreover attracted a great deal of money in the form of bequests and endowments. Many foreign dignitaries were attracted by the European renown of the performances, which took place at services in neighbouring churches on Sundays, feast days and during Lent. The *figlie* performed in elevated choir lofts concealed behind iron grills – serving both to heighten the effect of angelic asceticism and (at least in Rousseau's case) to nurture other fantasies.[25]

The most musically ambitious and secure of the four *ospedali* was the Pietà,

[21] Gambassi, *La cappella musicale di S Petronio*; Gambassi, *L'Accademia filarmonica di Bologna*.
[22] Ibid., pp. 108, 287–92.
[23] Further on the *ospedali*, see Baldauf-Berdes, *Women Musicians of Venice*; Ellero et al., *Arte e musica all'Ospedaletto*; Rostirolla, 'L'organizzazione musicale'; Vio, 'Precisazioni sui documenti'; and especially Talbot, *Benedetto Vinaccesi*, Chapter 3, which provides the clearest recent overview.
[24] Letter of 29 August 1739, translated from *Lettres familières*, vol. 1, p. 238.
[25] Baldauf-Berdes, 'Anna Maria della Pietà', pp. 135–6.

especially during the earlier decades of Vivaldi's association. The diversity of instruments played by the *figlie* – and thus of the instrumentation of his concertos – reflects this ambition, not least the desire to impress visitors with novelty. As de Brosses wrote in some amazement, '[They] play the violin, the recorder, the organ, the oboe, the cello, the bassoon; in short, there is no instrument large enough to frighten them',[26] not to speak of such curiosities as the viola all'inglese, the psaltery or the chalumeau. Although it was possible for a girl to leave if she married, became a nun, or found low-grade employment, many stayed well into adulthood. The most famous violinist was Anna Maria (1696–1782), who enjoyed an international reputation as one of the finest virtuosi of the day. First listed in 1704, by 1712 she was already a proficient performer trusted to participate in outside engagements, going on to become the principal violinist and teacher until she was elevated to the rank of *maestra di coro* in 1737.[27] Vivaldi was thus able to work with an outstandingly disciplined orchestra and soloists of mature musicianship.

Patrons and academies

While these large-scale establishments provided a relatively stable environment for the cultivation of the concerto, instrumental composition also flourished independently. Milan supported a vigorous musical life away from the court, with private concerts at aristocratic homes during Lent (when opera was prohibited), as well as outdoor concerts at the Castello. Many an aristocratic patron put on concerts and literary/musical evenings, known as academies, and a few of the most wealthy even maintained a small musical establishment. The term *accademia* was also used for more formal societies fostering intellectual debate – scientific, literary, philosophical or artistic – within which music might play a part. The most celebrated of these was the Arcadian Academy in Rome, which combined fanciful recreation of a supposed Grecian pastoral Arcadia with elevated discussion of classical aesthetic ideals.

In Rome musical life was focussed on independent musical enthusiasms, with which the roles of patronage and the church were closely intertwined. The concerto flourished under the aegis of Roman prelates and nobles such as Cardinals Benedetto Pamphilj and Pietro Ottoboni (Corelli's patron) and Princes Francesco Maria Ruspoli and Marco Antonio Borghese.[28] Ottoboni and Ruspoli were rivals in the splendour of their patronage within a lively intellectual environment, and each maintained a small musical establishment; their regular academies or *conversazioni* took place by arrangement on different days. For more elaborate occasions they drew in musicians from further afield: at the major

---

26 See note 24.
27 Baldauf-Berdes, 'Anna Maria della Pietà'; Talbot, 'Anna Maria', *NG2*; Talbot, 'Anna Maria's Partbook'; White, 'Biographical Notes'.
28 Further on Roman musical life and its patrons, see Della Seta, 'La musica in Arcadia'; Della Seta, 'I Borghese'; Hansell, 'Orchestral Practice at the Court of Cardinal Pietro Ottoboni'; Marx, 'Die Musik am Hofe Pietro Kardinal Ottobonis'; Kirkendale, *Antonio Caldara*; Kirkendale, 'The Ruspoli Documents'; La Via, 'Il Cardinale Ottoboni'; Marx, 'Die "Giustificazioni della Casa Pamphilj" '; Piperno, ' "Su le sponde del Tebro" '; Piperno, 'Musica e musicisti per l'Accademia del Disegno'; Rostirolla, 'Maestri di Cappella'.

festivals at Ottoboni's church (S Lorenzo in Damaso), lists of instrumentalists distinguish between leading players (such as Montanari, Ghilarducci and Mossi) and 'Instrumentisti per il Concerto Grosso'.[29] It is highly likely that instrumental concertos were played on these occasions, and at the annual festivals of religious institutions or the artists' Accademia del disegno di San Luca. Partly through the influence of Corelli as player and mentor, Rome retained an attachment to the traditional concerto grosso, at least into the 1730s; and such works are well represented in Ottoboni's own library. But increasingly they were joined or supplanted by solo, double and multiple concertos, sometimes featuring those wind instruments that were so characteristic of Roman musical life.

In Venice, too, a major role was played by aristocratic patronage, whether from the Venetian nobility or foreign ambassadors (many of whom were dedicatees of concertos).[30] The numerous private concerts and more formal *accademie* would certainly have cultivated the new Venetian concerto, and a post at one of the *ospedali* (even that of *maestro de' concerti*) allowed ample time for such extramural activities. Even the most intellectual *accademie* promoted musical events upon occasion: in 1735, for example, the Accademia Albriziana, which was devoted to science and letters, celebrated the Doge with a cantata accompanied by an orchestra of thirty strings and winds. Other *accademie* were dedicated primarily to music. The Accademia Filarmonica, an aristocratic organization founded around 1711, soon numbered 192 nobles, who formed an orchestra to play music twice a week throughout the year, except in Lent when spoken tragedies were substituted. Though no record of the repertoire survives, the latest concertos of Vivaldi and Albinoni were surely performed here: Giovanni Donato Correggio, the dedicatee of Albinoni's *Concerti a cinque*, Op. 7 (1715), was a member.

Foreign ambassadors to Venice played a particular role. Separated from indigenous social life, since Venetian nobles were strictly forbidden social interaction with them, they marked special occasions such as their potentate's name-day with elaborate festivities, including concerts, cantatas and allegorical serenatas. Distinguished visitors were greeted in style, as ambassadors vied with each other in munificence. When the two Princes of Bavaria were entertained in 1725 by the French ambassador, 'the banquet was followed by a concert of music given by the finest instrumentalists, and the famous Faustina [Bordoni] sang'.[31] The public entrance of Count Colloredo-Waldsee as imperial ambassador was an excuse for even more magnificent celebrations at his *palazzo*: two days of celebration with illuminations, banquets and concerts (replacing operatic performances during Lent). There is little indication of what instrumental music was performed on such occasions, but the music performed at the celebratory Mass in 1712 in honour of Charles VI survives. The fine presentation manuscript includes three particularly elaborate concertos, one by the Florentine violinist Veracini, one by

[29] La Via, 'Il Cardinale Ottoboni', p. 399.

[30] On Venetian patronage, see Bernardi, 'Il mecenatismo musicale' and Talbot, 'Musical Academies', from which the following paragraphs are largely derived; also Talbot, 'Vivaldi and a French Ambassador'.

[31] Translated from the quotation in Bernardi, 'Il mecenatismo musicale', p. 71.

the Novara cellist Giovanni Perroni and another by padre Ferdinando Antonio Lazari.[32]

Vivaldi's concertos were undoubtedly heard in widely varying contexts outside the Pietà. Three are designated to the festival of S Lorenzo, one possibly intended for Ottoboni's titular church in Rome, and the other two for Venice.[33] Concertos were also heard in Venetian opera houses as entr'actes. This is where the German traveller Uffenbach heard Vivaldi's 'frightening' display of virtuosity in 1715 and where (according to anecdote) the Dresden violinist Johann Georg Pisendel played Vivaldi's RV 571 at the request of the *Kurprinz* of Saxony – when his accompanists attempted to catch him out by deliberately rushing through a taxing high solo.[34]

Amateur composers

A small but significant group of concerto composers may be described as musical amateurs. Tomaso Albinoni, son of a Venetian playing-card manufacturer, was pursuing a successful musical career as a 'Dilettante veneto' long before his father died in 1709; following his exclusion from the family business, he pursued an independent devotion to music as a prolific composer with a European reputation, without reliance on any permanent position.[35]

From a different social stratum were the Venetian noblemen Alessandro and Benedetto Marcello, who both combined high office in the republic with the cultivated artistic and intellectual world of the Venetian academy.[36] By 1719 Alessandro was *principe* of the Accademia degli Animosi, a group devoted to the spirit of Classical antiquity in a classicizing and decorous resistance to ostentatious display. Benedetto made an important early contribution to the concerto, but it was Alessandro who continued to nurture the genre, his concertos no doubt being regularly performed at the weekly academy in his own home. One set of concertos was published in Augsburg under his Arcadian pseudonym, Eterio Stinfalico.

Another amateur composer of major significance was Franceso Antonio Bonporti, 'gentiluomo di Trento', although the main objective of his publications was apparently to impress dignitaries who might further his ecclesiastical career. His one major set of concertos, Op. 11, was inscribed to the Duke of Lorraine, an attempt at ingratiation no more successful than any of his previous dedications.

Italian Musicians across Europe

If the solo concerto was invented and nurtured within Italy, rare indeed was the prominent Italian musician who did not at some point exploit the growing demand for Italian music throughout Europe, whether through court

---

32 Hill, *The Life and Works*, pp. 11, 73–4.

33 Talbot, 'Vivaldi and Rome', pp. 34–7.

34 Manfred Fechner has, however, cast doubt on the identification of the concerto on source grounds ('Bemerkungen', pp. 778–9).

35 Talbot, *Tomaso Albinoni*.

36 Madricardo and Rossi, eds., *Benedetto Marcello*; Selfridge-Field, *The Music of Benedetto and Alessandro Marcello*.

appointments in central Europe or through commercial opportunities further north.[37] Even those with Italian bases made occasional forays across the Alps; many others were more permanently attracted, sometimes engaged in Italy, sometimes travelling more speculatively with letters of introduction.

Mobility was encouraged not only by physical proximity but also by political affiliations. The duchy of Savoy maintained strong historical links with France; indeed, the Turin court was modelled on Versailles and its orchestra on Louis XIV's *Vingt-quatre Violons du Roi*. The connection became even stronger when the Duke's relative, the Prince of Carignano, moved to Paris in 1718. Giovanni Battista Somis (who had been in the Prince's employ since 1709) visited the French capital in 1733, performing concertos twice at the Concert Spirituel; and his concertos figure prominently in the sumptuous manuscript collection made for Pierre Philibert de Blancheton, described below. Another Piedmontese violinist, Giovanni Pietro Ghignone, settled in Paris permanently. At first he was set up to represent the alien Italian style, taking part in a national 'duel' with Jean-Baptiste Anet at the Concert Spirituel in 1725. Five years later he became musician to the Prince of Carignan, but he was rapidly accepted into Parisian musical life, entering the service of the King in 1733 and becoming a French citizen in 1741 under the name Jean-Pierre Guignon. The Italian influence was also carried back to France by the Lyons-born Jean-Marie Leclair, who visited Turin as a dancer but, after tuition from Somis, became one of the leading French violinists of the age.

Even stronger were the musical interactions between Milan and Vienna after 1706, when Lombardy came under Austrian rule. The violinist Andrea Zani, for example, was born in Casalmaggiore near Cremona, but he spent much of the 1720s in Vienna, where a single set of concertos was published, before returning to his birthplace for the rest of his life. Others settled in Austria permanently: Giovanni Perroni was working in Milan in the late 1710s (his name appears in the 1720 orchestra list), but in 1721 he was appointed cellist to the imperial court in Vienna, where he built up a distinguished career.

Other concerto composers who settled outside Italy, some of whom will be considered in more detail in the course of this book, include three Bolognese violinists: Giuseppe Antonio Brescianello, first enticed from Venice to Munich, then from 1717 serving as Kapellmeister at the Württemberg court in Stuttgart; Francesco Maria Cattaneo, violinist at the Dresden court from 1726 and eventually Pisendel's successor as Konzertmeister; and Gaetano Maria Schiassi, who by 1734 was employed in the royal chapel at Lisbon. Tartini's students spread across Europe throughout the century; as early as 1735 the Paduan violinist Domenico dall'Oglio left his post at S Antonio for service at the Russian court. The career of the oboist Giovanni Benedetto Platti led in a different direction: in 1722 he was engaged among a group of musicians for the musical establishment of Johann Philipp Franz von Schönborn, Prince-Archbishop of Bamberg and Würzburg.[38] He was employed not only as an oboist but also as a singer and a performer on violin, cello, flute and harpsichord; yet his surviving solo concerto output is

[37] Strohm, ed., *The Eighteenth-Century Diaspora*.
[38] Lindgren, 'Count Rudolf Franz Erwein von Schönborn'.

almost entirely for the cello, reflecting the predilections of the Bishop's brother, the diplomat Count Rudolf Franz Erwein von Schönborn, at nearby Wiesentheid.

The commercially orientated cities of Northern Europe present a somewhat ambiguous picture with regard to the concerto. London, with its ample financial opportunities and wealthy Italophile patrons, proved a particular magnet for Italian musicians.[39] The Castrucci brothers, for example, were first employed in Rome by the Earl of Burlington on the Grand Tour. Travelling to London in 1715 as part of his retinue, they remained in his household for several years before adopting a leading role in the musical life of the metropolis. So, too, did the Milanese oboist Giuseppe Sammartini, a member of the Milan court orchestra in 1720, who moved permanently to London in 1729. But while solo concertos figured prominently in public concert programmes (Burney wrote that Vivaldi's *La stravaganza* was especially favoured 'among flashy players, whose chief merit was rapid execution')[40] the English predilection for the concerto grosso meant that the genre dominated publishers' catalogues, as well as the published output of both Castrucci and Sammartini. Two of the outstanding violinists of their generation, Geminiani and Veracini, both of whom spent extended periods in London, will figure little in this book. Geminiani (the most distinguished student of Corelli) largely eschewed public exposure, favouring the old-fashioned verities of the concerto grosso. In 1714 Veracini played concertos as entr'actes at the Italian Opera House, but on his later visits he clearly preferred the more earnest potential of the sonata, for reasons that have already been suggested.

The Bergamo violinist Pietro Antonio Locatelli also settled in the North, after sampling almost all the musical environments so far described: early musical experiences in Rome, private concerts in Venice, and appearances at German courts. Despite his Roman training he developed a persona as an itinerant virtuoso of supreme technical prowess. Yet when he arrived in Amsterdam in 1729 the attraction lay not so much in the lucrative potential for concerts as in publishing (*L'arte del violino* was brought out by Le Cène in 1733). Indeed Locatelli deliberately avoided public appearances, preferring concerts in the company of wealthy amateurs: 'he is so afraid of People's Learning from him, that He won't admit a Professed Musician into his Concert; and he never will Play any where but with Gentlemen'.[41]

Two English visitors in 1741 recorded their reactions to Locatelli's playing. Thomas Dampier, though lapsing into conventional French accolades, still captures something of the intensity of the performance:

> Locatelli must surely be allowed by all to be a Terre moto: Tate adds the three other Elements, Heavens & all; But in my opinion, That is rather saying too much. Mais pourtant, Mess[rs], quels Coups d'archet! Quel Feu! Quelle Vitesse! He plays his Laberinthe [Op. 3/12] & another piece, w[ch] he has lately composed 50 times more difficult, with more ease than I can humm y[e] Black Joke; and what is still more extraordinary, he never pulls off his Coat to play it, as I have

---

39 McVeigh, 'Italian Violinists'.
40 *A General History*, vol. 2, p. 445.
41 Letter of Benjamin Tate, 11 April 1741, in Dunning, *Pietro Antonio Locatelli*, vol. 1, p. 204. Further on Locatelli's patrons in Amsterdam, see Giskes, 'I dedicatari olandesi'.

observed most other great Musiciens do . . . He plays with so much Fury upon his Fiddle, that in my humble opinion, he must wear out some Dozens of them in a year.[42]

Benjamin Tate noticed two old-fashioned aspects of his playing – the short bow and the violin-hold 'upon his Breast' – which appear to suggest a certain insouciance to his supernatural powers:

[He] has the most affected Look just before he Begins to Play, that I ever saw in my Life. I have heard him Play that Concerto, which is so prodigiously difficult. He told me himself that the Laberinth was quite easy in comparison of this Spavento; which he calls his 'Queüe de Vache'. There is a Caprice in it of seven Sides of very Large Paper wrote very close; there is not a Rest in the whole Caprice, where he could possibly Turn over a Leaf. . . . I beg you'll let Fritz know, that Locatelli never sits by to Rest; but Plays on for three Hours together, without being in the least fatigued. I never in my Life saw a Man Play with so much ease: He Played that difficult Caprice with as much ease as old Fritz accompanys his Son.[43]

The virtuoso who conquers astonishing difficulties with careless facility, who yet destroys violins with the intensity of his playing, who captures an audience for hours on end with endless stamina – all these are images that Locatelli bequeathed to later generations. It is nonetheless striking that Locatelli deliberately avoided exploiting his gifts for commercial gain through public concerts, as he could so easily have done both in Amsterdam and in London.

Violin Schools, Regional Schools

Surveying this disparate range of environments for the concerto, a conflict appears between international universality and the idea of the local school around an individual master, a concept derived from art history. It may sometimes be possible to speak of centres of concerto composition, such as the Milan and Turin courts where musicians worked together on a daily basis. Other connections stem from training and musical background, but any such classification is fraught with pitfalls: witness the many violinists who may (or may not) have been pupils of Corelli. In any case, the lasting implications of musical training are by no means clear-cut. For all those who remained in the shadow of Corelli – the Roman group and London emigrés – there were others who broke away decisively from his influence, and in disparate directions.

Similarly diffuse was the influence of Vivaldi. Numerous German musicians (including opera composers and theorists such as Johann David Heinichen) gathered around Vivaldi as teacher or mentor in the 1710s. Pisendel, who in 1716–17 visited Italy with the *Kammermusik* of the Dresden court, joining the *Kurprinz* of Saxony in Venice in 1716 and again in 1717, was to become a prime figure in disseminating the Italian idiom north of the Alps. Yet while numerous Italian

---

[42] Letter of 4 April 1741, in Dunning, *Pietro Antonio Locatelli*, vol. 1, pp. 203–4.
[43] Letter of 11 April 1741, in ibid., vol. 1, pp. 204–5. The reference is to the violinist Gaspard Fritz.

violinists evidently came under Vivaldi's influence in Venice (and of course his violin music was ubiquitous), he does not appear to have taught directly any of the concerto composers under discussion here.

Among the teaching 'schools' that can truly be identified are those of Somis in Turin and Tartini in Padua. Tartini formalized his position as a teacher in 1727, and the subsequent fame of his 'Scuola di Nazioni' was acknowledged across Europe. He accepted only a small number of students (nine in 1737, though just four or five made him feel 'like the most worried man on earth'): all received a thorough training in violin-playing, some also in composition.[44] These devoted students took with them Tartini's ideals of violin-playing – clarity of execution and intonation, beauty of sound, subtlety of expressive nuance – and, to some extent, his compositional idiom as they dispersed across the continent.[45]

In general, however, the diversity of experience cultivated by most successful musicians had the effect of emphasizing the individual. The violinist who constantly travelled around Europe would have been influenced by a vast range of musical styles and genres. The balance between regional centres and the individual, within an overall European context, will be an important issue in our discussion of the concerto.

Italian Music across Europe

Concertos were, therefore, written for many different purposes: for the composer himself to play, for students, for patrons, and for sale either in manuscript or printed form. It is not surprising that the surviving sources reflect this diversity. Typically it appears that violinists would retain some repertoire for their own individual use, or the use of their immediate circle. Vivaldi's personal musical archive survives in the Turin Biblioteca Nazionale Universitaria (split between the Foà and Giordano collections); many of Vivaldi's autographs here are unique, and they were perhaps played only by himself or by *figlie* at the Pietà. A few of the Pietà's original performing materials survive, including isolated concerto parts dating from the years around Vivaldi's death; so too does Anna Maria's own part-book, dating from *c*1723–6 and containing the solo part for thirty-one concertos by Vivaldi, Tartini, d'Alai and others.[46]

The major Tartini collection preserved in the library of S Antonio, Padua – autographs and manuscript copies made by the scriptorium of the Cappella Antoniana – likewise includes some works not otherwise known. Others are duplicated in the enormous collection of manuscripts of the Tartini school now in Berkeley: this was apparently copied during the years around Tartini's death by musicians and copyists associated with S Antonio.[47] Taken together, these collections surely represent the core repertoire that Tartini and his followers played and studied.

[44] Petrobelli, 'Giuseppe Tartini', pp. 189–90.
[45] Petrobelli, 'La scuola di Tartini'.
[46] Talbot, 'A Vivaldi Discovery'; Talbot, 'Anna Maria's Partbook'; Tanenbaum, 'The Pietà Partbooks'.
[47] Duckles and Elmer, *Thematic Catalog of a Manuscript Collection*.

But just as violinists disseminated the Italian concerto across Europe through their own performances, so too was the repertoire spread in more tangible form. Not only were some printed editions extremely well known, but individual concertos frequently appear in several manuscript concordances, even among the (presumably limited) corpus that still survives today. The best known examples of the diaspora of the Italian concerto are Bach's keyboard transcriptions of Vivaldi's concertos, made in Weimar c1713–14: Bach's sources were apparently brought from the Dutch Republic by his employer's son, Johann Ernst of Saxe-Weimar, who studied at the University of Utrecht from 1711 to 1713. But while Vivaldi's Op. 3 had been published at this time, Opp. 4 and 7 had not, and some of Bach's arrangements match manuscripts that differ significantly from the versions eventually printed.[48]

Manuscripts
With Italian music publishing in serious decline since the heady days of Petrucci and his successors in the sixteenth and seventeenth centuries, Italian concertos were still disseminated primarily in manuscript, whether as scores or (more commonly) in individual parts.

The music library of Cardinal Ottoboni (now in the Henry Watson Music Library, Manchester) vividly illustrates the way in which such a collection might be built up. The paper-types of its main sub-groups have been painstakingly analyzed by Paul Everett, who has drawn up a convincing schedule of possible provenances.[49] The largest group consists of Roman manuscripts deriving partly from musicians connected with Ottoboni, including Mossi and Valentini; as well as a group of six Vivaldi concertos, probably copied from manuscripts brought to Rome by the composer in the early 1720s. A Bolognese group, including many concertos by Alberti, presumably reflects Ottoboni's period as protector of the Accademia Filarmonica; while a further group was perhaps accumulated from a Milanese connection. Finally, a group of sixteen Vivaldi concertos on Venetian paper, including an important early version of *The Four Seasons*, was perhaps sent subsequently: the high proportion of titled works is striking and may possibly reflect Ottoboni's French connections.[50]

Another Italian collection was put together by the Obizzi family in Padua in the decades around 1700: the 'Estensischen Musikalien' eventually passed via the Estense family to the Nationalbibliothek in Vienna.[51] This collection is of particular importance here for the substantial number of *unica* by Alberti.

Foreign courts also built up their Italian repertoires by collecting manuscripts. In the case of Dresden this was initiated directly by Pisendel's visit to Italy in 1716–17, when Vivaldi presented him with six concertos.[52] Scores of twenty-two

---

[48] Rasch, 'La famosa mano', drawing on an extensive literature. Heller, *Antonio Vivaldi*, p. 245, provides a summary list of Bach's sources.

[49] Everett, *The Manchester Concerto Partbooks*; Everett, 'A Roman Concerto Repertory'; Talbot, 'Some Overlooked MSS'; Talbot, 'Vivaldi's "Manchester" Sonatas'.

[50] As tentatively suggested in Talbot, 'Vivaldi and Rome', p. 31.

[51] Haas, *Die Estensischen Musikalien*.

[52] '. . . although the dedication seems in nearly all cases to have been an afterthought' (Talbot, *Vivaldi*, p. 46). Further on the Dresden collection see Heller, *Die deutsche Überlieferung*;

concertos by Vivaldi and sets of parts for another fifteen survive in Pisendel's hand; he also copied concertos by Albinoni, Benedetto Marcello, Tartini and Tessarini, and (presumably in Rome) concertos by Montanari and Mossi. These formed the basis of the Italian instrumental repertoire at the Dresden court, contributing to a gradual shift away from French taste: 1717 was also the year in which Veracini moved to Dresden with a troupe of Italian opera musicians, through the influence of the *Kurprinz*.

The Dresden court music library (now in the Sächsische Landesbibliothek) was evidently accumulated from many sources. Probably some of the manuscripts on Italian paper were taken back by Pisendel in 1717, but others may have been posted subsequently. Certainly Pisendel was an avid collector, requesting music from such composers as Alessandro Toeschi, who regarded it as an honour to comply. Still other concertos are on German paper, including two by Locatelli, perhaps copied on a visit as yet undocumented. Some of the Pisendel scores are accompanied by parts copied in Dresden, probably dating after 1728 when (as Konzertmeister) he became responsible for selecting the repertoire. Frequently the Dresden versions transmit a text differing significantly from those found elsewhere, either because they represent a different stage in the compositional process,[53] or because Pisendel shamelessly rewrote them: many concertos were recast to accommodate Pisendel's own violinistic demands and the wind section of the large Dresden orchestra.

During the first two decades of the century, Vivaldi supplied music to many other German and Austrian visitors. Thus during 1708–14 the Schönborn family received instrumental music via their protégé Franz Horneck (the three cello concertos he copied in 1708–09 are Vivaldi's earliest surviving concertos); and via Matthias Ferdinand von Regatschnig, the Mainz Resident in Venice, who in 1711 undertook to seek out 'some more select compositions by Vivaldi'.[54] Another customer was Johann Friedrich Armand von Uffenbach from Frankfurt, despite his grudging approbation of Vivaldi's violinistic showmanship.

In the following decade Vivaldi continued to deal directly with patrons besides Ottoboni and the Austrian Emperor. He supplied manuscripts – including at least seven concertos – to Count Wenzel von Morzin, who was also the dedicatee of Op. 8, published in 1725. The letter of dedication makes it clear that Vivaldi had already sent earlier versions of *The Four Seasons*, for performance by the count's 'virtuosissima orchestra' either in Prague or at his country seat. Finally, in his impoverished last year in Vienna, Vivaldi sold music cheaply to Count Vinciguerra Tommaso Collalto, a Venetian patrician who owned the nearby castle of Brtnice (Pirnitz): probably the fifteen concertos and a sinfonia listed in a contemporary catalogue.

Landmann, 'Katalog der Dresdener Vivaldi-Handschriften'; Pozzi, 'Il concerto strumentale italiano'. Manfred Fechner ('Bemerkungen zu einigen Dresdner Vivaldi-Manuskripten') has cast doubt on the generally held assumption that all the Pisendel Vivaldi manuscripts date from 1716–17. See also Landmann, 'The Dresden Hofkapelle'.

[53] Hirshberg and McVeigh, 'The Making of a Ritornello Movement'.

[54] Heller, *Die deutsche Überlieferung*, pp. 178–9. On the date see Talbot, 'Vivaldi and the Empire', p. 47 (from which article the following paragraph is drawn).

A quite different kind of collection is the lavish manuscript of instrumental music compiled for the French parliamentarian Pierre Philibert de Blancheton.[55] The Fonds Blancheton (probably copied in the 1730s, or at least by 1742) was presumably intended as a performing repertoire, although the part-books them-selves show no signs of use. The fifty concertos include many by Italian composers with some French connection, including seven attributed to G.B. Somis: he may well have been involved in the compilation of the collection during his 1733 visit or shortly thereafter. The works of Italian emigrés naturally gravitated towards a foreign employer's library. Much of Giuseppe Sammartini's surviving concerto repertoire, overlapping with some printed works but differing in detail, was presented to his patron Frederick, Prince of Wales: the collection is now preserved in the Royal Music Library at the British Library.

But sometimes concertos were destined for aristocrats to perform themselves. The cello-playing Count Rudolf Franz Erwein von Schönborn (1677–1754), whose family connections have already been mentioned, amassed an extensive collection of cello music via all the routes discussed so far. His musical interests were encouraged during student years in Rome, where he made the acquaintance of Corelli and started collecting Italian instrumental music – showing a distinct preference for music in older idioms.[56] As Count of Schönborn-Wiesentheid (from 1704), he served the Emperor as a diplomat, living variously in Wiesentheid, Mainz, Vienna and elsewhere. On his travels he continued to indulge his passion for cello music, playing concertos in a chamber manner with family, friends and musician-servants. Visitors to Italy were commissioned to send back music, including concertos by Geminiani, Locatelli and Mossi, as well as Vivaldi. The Count's music library at Schloss Wiesentheid contained numerous cello concertos, including twenty-eight by his brother's musician Giovanni Platti and a set of twelve by Andrea Zani – perhaps commissioned when he visited Vienna in 1732 to receive the prestigious Order of the Golden Fleece.

Only rarely, it seems, did violinists write concertos for other musicians, who must have been perceived as potential rivals. Vivaldi's gift to Pisendel was essen-tially a gesture of friendship towards a fellow musician from a far-distant German court, one who moreover would spread Vivaldi's reputation abroad. Of course his concertos for the extraordinary range of instruments played by the *figlie* at the Pietà are a quite different matter; as also are the concertos inscribed to Anna Maria (the way the titles to two viola d'amore concertos are spelt – 'AMore' – suggests a further interest). At least one bassoon concerto (RV 502) was written for a professional musician, the Venetian bassoonist Giuseppe Biancardi.

Venetian composers also sold their works commercially in manuscript copies made in the many *copisterie*, firms of scribes working together in the manner of the medieval scriptorium.[57] British and German visitors to Italy, enriching their

---

55 Now in the Paris Conservatoire library at the Bibliothèque Nationale. See Hirshberg, 'The Formation and Destination of the *Fonds Blancheton*'; Hirshberg, Introduction to *Ten Violin Concertos from Fonds Blancheton*; La Laurencie, *Inventaire critique du fonds Blancheton*.

56 Lindgren, 'Count Rudolf Franz Erwein von Schönborn'; Zobeley, *Die Musikalien der Grafen von Schönborn-Wiesentheid*.

57 Everett, 'Vivaldi's Italian Copyists', p. 32.

cultural experience on the Grand Tour, certainly sought out music in this way, whether for themselves or on behalf of musical friends at home. Edward Holdsworth, who acquired the Ottoboni library in 1742 for Charles Jennens (Handel's librettist), travelled to Italy five times as a private tutor to gentlemen tourists; his correspondence reveals an active role in obtaining music on Jennens' behalf. In 1733 he described how Vivaldi had abandoned publication for the more lucrative manuscript trade:

> I had this day some discourse with your friend Vivaldi who told me y^t He had resolv'd not to publish any more Concerto's, because He says it prevents his selling his Compositions in Mss wch He thinks will turn more to account; as certainly it wou'd if He finds a good market for he expects a Guinea for ev'ry piece. Perhaps you might deal with him if you were here to choose what you like, but I am sure I shall not venture to choose for you at that price. I had before been inform'd by others that this was Vivaldi's resolution.[58]

One guinea (about 48 lire) was indeed a substantial premium on what the Pietà paid for a concerto (22 lire).[59]

Vivaldi was clearly no mean salesman. Although by 1739 his star was well in decline, eclipsed by the arrival of younger and more modern composers, he was successful with de Brosses:

> Vivaldi has made himself one of my intimate friends in order to sell me some concertos at a very high price. In this he partly succeeded, as did I in my intention, which was to hear him play and get plenty of good musical recreation. He is an old man with a mania for composing. I have heard him boast of composing a concerto in all its parts more quickly than a copyist could write them down.[60]

Probably compiled in this way was a collection of concertos and sinfonias by Tessarini, Visconti and Zuccari now in the Rowe Library, King's College, Cambridge.[61] Written on Italian paper, its numbering and uniformity suggest a coherent collection designed for actual performance, although its provenance remains unidentified.

Other substantial collections of manuscripts of Italian concertos are now in the principal libraries of Paris (including the Conservatoire collection), in Berlin (from the Prussian royal library), in Schwerin (a collection largely copied by members of the Fick family),[62] in Karlsruhe (from the Baden-Durlach court) and in Lund (the collection of the organist Hinrich Engelhart).

Printed editions
The most public and widespread diffusion of the Italian concerto repertoire was, of course, through printed editions of individual parts. Though it may not always

---

58 Letter of 13 February 1733, quoted in Talbot, 'Charles Jennens', p. 71.
59 In 1741 Vivaldi received only 12 lire per work from Count Collalto (Talbot, 'Vivaldi and the Empire', p. 45).
60 Letter of 29 August 1739, translated from *Lettres familières*, vol. 1, p. 237.
61 Mss. 231–7, 240–2.
62 Heller, *Die deutsche Überlieferung*, pp. 165–8.

have been the most lucrative source of income, publication was still regarded as an important status symbol, and as a ready means of spreading a reputation throughout Europe. The name of a famous dedicatee on the title page gave authority to the publication, as well as increasing the likelihood of financial reward. While it was easiest to publish sonatas (the set of sonatas Op. 1 became a familiar rite of passage), many composers published at least one major set of concertos.

In some cases concertos are mixed in with ripieno works, a juxtaposition already found in Torelli's Op. 6 (1698) and Albinoni's Op. 2 (1700). Some later collections perpetuated this tradition: thus Tessarini's *La stravaganza*, Op. 4 (*c*1736/7), alternates concertos for one or two violins with symphonies and the like. Most collections consisted of one or two sets of six concertos, whose short duration and contrasting affects suggest that they were intended to be played in succession at a musical soirée.

The most influential publisher before 1740 was Estienne Roger in Amsterdam, together with his daughter Jeanne and his successor Michel-Charles Le Cène. Rudolf Rasch has proposed a useful three-phase model for the relationship between Italian instrumental composers and northern publishers.[63] In the early years up to 1710, Roger built up his list by actively seeking out saleable Italian instrumental music, and by pirating Italian editions if necessary. Italian composers were no doubt flattered by his approaches, and presumably sold their works inexpensively. But Roger's phenomenally successful first editions of Vivaldi's Op. 3 (1711) and Corelli's Op. 6 (1714) initiated a new phase. As Italian composers began to recognise their market value, they started putting their works forward and negotiating more astutely, resulting in a central phase of equilibrium during the late 1710s. This was the period of liveliest activity, both in terms of individual collections and of anthologies of works by Vivaldi and his contemporaries. The growth of demand is reflected in yet another indicator of buoyancy: the publication of concerto collections without the composer's permission, such as Le Cène's 1724 edition of Tessarini's Op. 1. Eventually equilibrium gave way to glut, as publishers were inundated with Italian compositions. In the 1720s Le Cène was even reluctant to maintain the firm's earlier level of output, with a remarkable delay in bringing out Vivaldi's Op. 8 (which may have been lying around for five years before it eventually appeared in 1725). On Le Cène's death in 1743 a large number of Italian concertos remained on the shelf, to judge from the manuscripts put up for sale. While the high price of volumes 3 and 4 of Tessarini's Op. 4 suggests imminent publication, concertos by Alberti, Albinoni, Montanari and Valentini had probably been gathering dust for years, victims of changing public taste.[64]

Although Britain continued an allegiance to the concerto grosso longer than anywhere else in Europe, Italian solo concertos were also highly marketable there, to judge from the London publications of John Walsh and his son. Many were in fact pirated directly from Roger: while Walsh occasionally sold off Roger prints legitimately, the theory that he acted as an agent for Roger has been

---

63 See 'Il cielo batavo', also his 'Corelli's Contract' and 'La famosa mano'.
64 Rasch, 'I manoscritti musicali'. Even more modern works by Laurenti and Schiassi lay ignored.

disputed.[65] Parisian publishers also began to play a role of some importance towards the end of the period, reflecting the gradual French acceptance of the virtuosic Italian instrumental style.

Although it is impossible to estimate the scale of dissemination through printed editions, we can be certain that the most popular sets were widely known throughout Europe. Collections appeared under such alluring international titles as *Harmonia Mundi*, 'Collected out of the Choicest Works of the most Eminent Authors viz Vivaldi Tessarini Albinoni Alberti never before Printed' – although the authenticity of works in such collections is sometimes dubious, as with the Albinoni concerto included here.[66] Some sets were published in several countries: Vivaldi's Op. 3, for example, was not only reissued by Roger and by his successor Le Cène throughout Vivaldi's lifetime, but was also speedily published by Walsh and others in London, as well as by French publishers during the 1740s. Amsterdam publications quickly spread to North Germany, to judge from the première of Telemann's comic intermezzi *Pimpinone* in Hamburg in 1725. Of the seven concertos proposed to open and close each intermezzo, four were taken from Tessarini's Op. 1 (Nos. 2, 8, 11 and 12; 1724), and the others from Vivaldi's Op. 7 (No. 2; 1720) and Albinoni's Op. 9 (Nos. 8 and 10; 1722).[67]

The most successful concertos by these and other composers were available for many decades. In London, Walsh was still advertising long lists of concertos into the early 1750s, including works by Alberti, Corelli, Geminiani, Locatelli, Tessarini and Vivaldi. Similarly Johannes Smit advertised in a Hague newspaper on 18 February 1750 a 'large selection of musical works by Corelli, Geminiani, Handel, Locatelli, Tartini, Tessarini, Valentini, Veracini, Vivaldi, and many more'.[68] Commercial demands, however, tended to mean that the most technically demanding and experimental concertos never achieved publication. This can certainly be observed in Vivaldi's output; and although it is true that some brilliantly virtuosic concertos were published (Locatelli's Op. 3 being the outstanding example), other printed sets deliberately avoided the high positions so dreaded by amateur players.

The surviving repertoire
An inevitable consequence of the haphazard way in which concertos were selected and distributed is that the surviving repertoire can be regarded neither as a complete record, nor necessarily an entirely representative one. Printed editions present particular problems, and some are undoubtedly suspect, whether in terms of authenticity (such as Vivaldi's Op. 7, published by Jeanne Roger) or of text (Le Cène's 'Spring', for example, lacks the additional lightning flashes given in the Manchester manuscript version).[69] But even without such defective transmission,

65 Rasch, 'Estienne Roger and John Walsh', pp. 403–4.
66 Talbot, *Tomaso Albinoni*, p. 254.
67 *Pimpinone,* ed. T. W. Werner, Das Erbe deutscher Musik, 1st series, Bd. 6 (Mainz: Schott, 1936), p. 102.
68 See Hirshberg and McVeigh, Introduction to Carlo Tessarini, *Twelve Violin Concertos Opus 1*, p. x.
69 See the edition of *Le quattro stagioni* by Paul Everett and Michael Talbot (Milan: Ricordi, 1996).

individual works were often circulated in different versions, as they developed compositionally or were adapted to different instruments. Vivaldi is known to have rethought details of solo passages every time he wrote out a new set of parts, introducing new figurations or decorative melodic variants: indeed, the fact that he sometimes chose to personally copy only the solo part, leaving the other parts to minions, suggests that this was his intention.[70] As a work was copied and recopied on different dates, a complicated relationship could emerge between different versions of the same work.

Sometimes such changes extended to new movements altogether. Op. 4/1 shares different movements with two manuscript versions, both of which may have been compiled after Vivaldi had already sent his score to Amsterdam for publication.[71] Vivaldi also recast whole concertos for different instruments in answer to some practical or publishing demand. Transformations illuminate not only his idiomatic solo writing (agile arpeggiation and leaps for the bassoon, smooth cantabile for the oboe), but also shed light on his compositional priorities. In some cases he preserved the ritornellos and accompaniments intact, merely writing out a new solo part.[72] But other examples show more sweeping changes, ranging from significant structural compressions to the radical change of tonal scheme between RV 406 and RV 481, which will be considered in more detail in Chapter 5.[73]

Tartini also constantly reworked individual concertos throughout his lifetime, resulting in equally complex textual relationships.[74] In many cases, therefore, it is misleading to contemplate the notion of a definitive text. Instrumental works were, like operas, in a constant state of flux: only when they appear in a presentational autograph or an authorized print can a certain final form be attributed.

It is also difficult to be sure whether the surviving repertoire accurately reflects the solo instruments preferred at the time, since it may well be skewed by circumstances (such as the preponderance of cello music in Wiesentheid and flute music in Karlsruhe). Of course, concertos for one or two violins dominate, but there is also a sizeable oboe repertoire, the first Italian oboe concertos published being those in Albinoni's Op. 7 (1715). Although the transverse flute was well known earlier in Rome, it was not popular in Venice until the mid 1720s: Vivaldi's flute concertos Op. 10 (1729) were the first set devoted exclusively to this instrument, contributing to its rapid rise in popularity with gentlemen amateurs. Lower instruments did not have the same currency among amateurs, so no concertos for cello

---

[70] Everett, *The Manchester Concerto Partbooks*, p. 187.

[71] RV 381 (on which Bach based his keyboard arrangement) shares only the first movement with RV 383a (Op. 4/1), while RV 383 (copied by Pisendel, presumably in 1716–17) shares only the last two movements with the printed version (Rasch, 'La famosa mano', pp. 99–100).

[72] As with RV 448 and 463 (Everett, 'Vivaldi's Paraphrased Oboe Concertos'). Everett has described in detail Vivaldi's practice of working above an existing bass line (*The Manchester Concerto Partbooks*, pp. 159–72).

[73] Regarding the flute concerto RV 438, apparently a compressed version of the cello concerto RV 414, see Kotsoni-Brown, 'The Solo Cello Concertos of Antonio Vivaldi', pp. 228–31. Cuts in Vivaldi ritornellos in the late Pietà manuscripts, not necessarily authorized by the composer, are described in Tanenbaum, 'The Pietà Partbooks – Continued', pp. 10–11.

[74] One example is D21, the compositional history of which is analyzed in Petrobelli, 'Per l'edizione critica'.

or bassoon were published in the period (except for an early collection by Jacchini); but a substantial number of manuscripts survive, as well as concertos for unusual combinations such as one by Brescianello for violin and bassoon. Vivaldi experimented with all kinds of extravagant combinations, mostly beyond the scope of this book: among the smaller-scale oddities are a concerto for violin and oboe in unison ('tutto pianissimo') and another entitled 'Il Proteo, o sia Il mondo al rovescio' in which the solo cello plays higher than the violin.

The large corpus of Vivaldi concertos forms the centrepiece of the present study, not only because of its individuality and its musical stature, but also for a further reason. Since all composers of the period must surely have known at least a few Vivaldi concertos intimately, they wrote their own concertos against the background of a universally shared idiom. It is therefore essential to our methodology that the Vivaldi repertoire takes a central position as a springboard for discussion. Yet at the same time it cannot be regarded as a monolithic body of work, to be analyzed as an entirety; for Vivaldi's own idiom and strategic preferences changed significantly across a professional career lasting more than thirty years.

At any given time, therefore, every composer would have experienced a certain amount of music by others, including Vivaldi, but we can seldom be sure about his knowledge of any specific work. Furthermore, with most works disseminated only in parts, aspiring composers did not have the luxury of studying large numbers of scores. Notions of influence, once ubiquitous in musicological enquiries of this kind, can therefore be advanced only with the utmost caution. Our method is rather predicated on large-scale comparisons of individual composers' repertoires. We begin with the period that has conventionally been regarded as the prehistory of the solo concerto: the first decade of the century and the development of what may be termed the 'proto-ritornello' stage.

CHAPTER 3

Assembling the Elements:
Towards the Vivaldian Revolution

This dramatic title draws on Michael Talbot's identification of a crucial moment in our history of the concerto.[1] Vivaldi's *L'estro armonico*, Op. 3 (published in Amsterdam in 1711) has universally been regarded as the start of the 'true' solo concerto, in which ritornello form is for the first time consistently and coherently used for most of the Allegro movements. And it is no exaggeration to write that this collection changed and shaped the course of instrumental music, through its incisive definition of the concerto idiom and strongly individual characterisation of each concerto, highlighting the potential of the violin soloist in the most vivid way – not to speak of the sheer quality and variety of its musical invention. It was, after all, the first collection of large-scale instrumental music ever to achieve a Europe-wide sensation.

Yet for all this 'epoch-making' quality,[2] *L'estro armonico* needs to be considered in a broader context, for it should not be thought that the Vivaldi concerto appeared here, Athene-like, in fully formed perfection. For even in these works the form is not entirely settled, reflecting many of the features that will be identified in earlier repertoire and that were largely abandoned in the later concertos of Vivaldi and his successors. This immediately raises the question of the role of the preceding decade.[3]

The present chapter is designed to look back from our study of later concertos – including of course the whole corpus of mature Vivaldi concertos – in what might appear to be an anachronistic perspective. Yet only apparently, because it is our contention that all the required elements were available during the 1700s: Vivaldi then synthesises them into 'order, connection, and proportion', resulting in a new compositional direction that is both dramatic and rhetorical.

The Vivaldian ritornello form then becomes the paradigmatic choice for the concerto Allegro. But does this musical concept represent some kind of ideal; or could the concerto have gone some other way with equally satisfying musical results? Put another way, are the concertos of the 1700s to be regarded as

---

[1]   'Concerto', *NG2*.

[2]   Talbot, ibid.

[3]   Among more detailed studies of the early development of ritornello form, see Dubowy, *Arie und Konzert*; Dubowy, 'Anmerkungen zur Form'; Kolneder, *Die Solokonzertform bei Vivaldi*; Talbot, 'The Concerto Allegro'. A complete survey of ritornello forms before 1711 is beyond the scope of this book, and is the subject of an ongoing study by Michael Talbot.

inadequate precursors, always failing in some respect to measure up to the Vivaldian achievement? And where later concertos differ from Vivaldi's approach, could they be following another tradition, with roots in some other musical background? We will first address some background issues, before going on to look selectively at the works of four composers working in the 1700s – Torelli, Albinoni, Benedetto Marcello and Valentini – and finally at Vivaldi's early concertos, including *L'estro armonico* itself.

The Concerto as a Genre

Terminology is itself a minefield: indeed many works that could be regarded as concertos go under different titles (such as sinfonia or sonata), while conversely, around 1700, the term 'concerto' did not at all indicate the presence of distinct solo passages in the modern understanding.[4] Where collections make a distinction between genres – as in Torelli's *Sinfonie à tre e concerti à quattro*, Op. 5 (1692) or Albinoni's *Sinfonie e concerti a cinque*, Op. 2 (1700) – this is not between symphony and solo concerto, but rather between differences of idiom and instrumentation. In this context, sinfonia refers to more contrapuntal sonatas, concerto to a more homophonic idiom dominated by the first violin (Torelli actually specifies multiple instruments to a part). 'Concerto' soon became a generic term for a large-scale multi-movement composition for strings, irrespective of its precise scoring. This apparent confusion of terminology may partly reflect our own preconceptions about what such words should mean, but it also reflects the contemporary fluidity and interaction between musical genres and usages. While this book will concentrate on works that are entitled concerto and incorporate soloistic ritornello form, we are conscious that boundaries, especially in the early period, are by no means so neatly drawn.

One controversial issue with which we shall not be concerned, since it is the subject of Richard Maunder's recent book, is the number of players per part.[5] In general, musical analysis is not affected by whether the accompanying string parts are designed for single players or for 'orchestral' doubling – especially in the solo concerto, where solo and tutti are contrasted by musical material and idiomatic virtuosity as much as by changes of texture. But the number of written parts is certainly a matter of importance in discussing the early ritornello form. The most important of the various possibilities are as follows:[6]

---

4   Maunder, *The Scoring of Baroque Concertos*, pp. 2–5. In particular Maunder stresses that the title 'concerti grossi', from Gregori's Op. 2 (1698) onwards, does not imply a particular genre allied to the Corellian concept of concertino and ripieno, but rather 'grand concertos'. Thus Torelli's Op. 8 (1709), considered below, uses the title for works that are unambiguously solo and double concertos. Further on the question of genre and terminology see the useful debate in Talbot, 'The Concerto Allegro', pp. 14–16.

5   Maunder, *The Scoring of Baroque Concertos*; see also Holman and Maunder, 'The Accompaniment of Concertos'. We are most grateful to Richard Maunder for sharing some of his findings with us.

6   This analysis is not concerned with the number of physical parts produced: separate parts for cello and continuo may be identical apart from figuring in the latter.

(1) *the Venetian type (five parts)*: soloist and accompanying four-part strings, the essential 'concerto a cinque' (in tuttis, soloist and first violin play the same line; if an additional violin soloist is required to partner the *violino principale*, the part is normally entrusted to the first violin, not the second; any independent cello solos may be found in a separate cello part);

(2) *the early type (four parts)*: four-part strings, with any solo passages simply resulting from the nature of the figuration or from reduced texture (for example, first violin and continuo only);

(3) *the Roman type (seven parts)*: for three-part concertino (two violins and cello) and four-part ripieno or 'concerto grosso', the normal layout for works that have come to be known as concerti grossi (in tuttis, the second solo doubles the ripieno second violin; viola may be added to the concertino; this can be adapted to make a solo concerto layout).[7]

In any of these types the viola part may be omitted or the texture may be enriched by the addition of a second viola.

The Ritornello Concept

In the first decade of the eighteenth century, there was therefore an abundance of different types of instrumental concerto, ranging from the concerto grosso and *ripieno* concerto without solos to the trumpet sonata and early solo concerto – as well as hybrids that cross such boundaries. Allegro movements in any of these may adumbrate some elements that contribute to ritornello form:

(1) differentiated periods, clearly articulated in at least one parameter, for example by a strong perfect cadence;

(2) alternating sections of contrasting textures (including tutti-solo);

(3) recurrent thematic material (such as a motto) articulating structural divisions;

(4) tonal departure and return;

(5) final recapitulation of some kind.

All of these elements impart for the listener a sense of function to the different sections, each taking its place within the dynamic and purposeful unfolding of the movement, rather than mere static decoration. A number of recurrent issues may be isolated by way of introduction, issues to which we shall return as we discuss each composer.

(a) Relationship with other genres and procedures

The solo concerto emerged from a combination of diverse procedures and genres. It drew directly on such genres as the Bolognese trumpet sonata and the trio sonata, and is clearly related to the operatic aria as well as to the opera overture or sinfonia; at the same time it easily assimilated fugal procedures and binary dance forms.

Yet it should not be assumed that the solo concerto simply took over a pre-existing three-movement model from the opera sinfonia, for the two genres

---

[7] See Talbot, ' "Lingua romana" ', pp. 313–14 for further clarification of this distinction.

undoubtedly developed in parallel.[8] Similarly it is by no means clear that the concerto simply adopted the form of the operatic aria, an area of debate which is beyond the scope of this book. While there is naturally a great deal in common between the ritornello-solo relationship in the aria and the concerto, the concerto did not merely adapt the ritornello pattern of the early Da Capo aria of the 1690s. As John Solie has pointed out, Albinoni's typical tonal schemes – in concertos I-V-I-vi-I, in Da Capo arias I-V-I ‖ vi-iii ‖ D.C. – are similar.[9] But there is a crucial difference in that the whole A-section I-V-I is automatically reprised in the Da Capo form, without alteration, a concept entirely alien to the ritornello concerto form. If alternatively one restricts comparison to the A-section only, then comparison is weakened by the absence in contemporary arias of a third ritornello in the peripheral key: suggesting that the eventual expansion of the aria's first section may have been influenced by the concerto rather than the reverse. In other words, aria and concerto developed in tandem, resulting in two different kinds of ritornello structure as each matured.

More closely connected in terms of tonal structure is the binary dance, the two halves of which frequently (although not always) describe a similar trajectory: I→V:‖:V→vi/iii→I. Still, the central caesura and the repeat structure naturally create an entirely different concept, and it is misguided to regard the ritornello form as intrinsically binary, for it rigorously avoids such a central break. But there is an important factor in the relationship of tonality and motive. If the two halves of a binary movement match motivically, then the opening naturally recurs in the dominant, while dominant material is reprised at the end in the tonic. This certainly has connotations for ritornello form.

Another related genre is fugue, which in any case has prior claim on the second movement in the *da chiesa* scheme. A similarly through-composed genre with no pre-ordained structural requirements, fugue inherently shares one important characteristic with ritornello form: the recurrence of the opening in different keys, resulting in an overarching tonal trajectory. When the episodes are taken by contrasting solo figuration, the two genres more or less coincide. A major distinction, though, is the propensity of the fugal exposition to alternate between I and V, meaning that there is less imperative on the soloist to confirm the dominant, but rather a tendency to move towards peripheral areas; the final section may also move freely between tonic and dominant, resulting in an overall sense of ternary design.

(b) Textures

The defining character of the new concerto, with its incisive *tromba* motives and driving Allegro rhythms, was a homophonic texture dominated by the first violin melody – taken to extreme in the unison fanfare opening followed by solo with continuo accompaniment. Clearly this idiom was quite distinct from the more staid and formulaic fugal subjects of the older contrapuntal style. But the ritornello concerto continued to call on more complex textures, both in tutti and solo sections. Fugal ritornellos on more modern subjects are a common feature of

8   Wolf, Introduction to *Antecedents of the Symphony*, pp. xvi–xviii.
9   Solie, 'Aria Structure', p. 43. Further on this issue, see Dubowy, *Arie und Konzert*.

early concertos, highlighting the contrast with lightly scored solo episodes. If, on the other hand, the solo sections thicken out the texture into five-part writing, then a suitable contrast for the tutti may be achieved by doubling the violin parts, resulting in a more transparent three-part texture for the ritornellos.[10]

(c) Complete and closed periods
In the mature phase of the solo concerto, the early part of the movement is divided into separate discrete sections ending with a perfect cadence (i.e. periods). These periods coincide with tutti and solo sections, so that there is a coordination between period structure and textural change. A closed period is one that begins and ends in the same key, as for example with the non-modulatory ritornello. While for Vivaldi this becomes the norm for the opening ritornello (R1) and for the ritornello in a secondary key (R2), neither of these features is by any means standard in the early formative years. The modulatory R1 will be a recurrent feature in the following discussion, and it is too limiting to make tonal stability of ritornellos (even R1) a pre-condition of 'real' ritornello form. R1 may modulate, for example, if a repeat of the motto in the dominant (recalling Corellian and fugal practice) is not followed by a return to the tonic – in which case, the dominant is reached and maintained at a very early stage in the process.

(d) Solo-tutti or the reverse
It is, of course, not a given that the concerto begins with a tutti, raising an important theoretical consideration identified by Norbert Dubowy.[11] If the movement starts solo, it may be perceived as reiterations of solo-tutti, with each solo providing an opening gesture and each tutti a closure. If, on the other hand, as in the prevailing later practice, the movement starts tutti, then the reverse applies – the reiteration of tutti-solo normally requiring an additional tutti to round off the movement. Even then, comparison with the aria, where clearly the vocal entrance presents the essential affect, might suggest that the concerto ritornello movement should be understood as reiterations of solo-tutti *preceded* by the ritornello R1. But in truth, in the concerto the opening ritornello becomes a much more powerful and memorable force, generating the rest of the movement in a quite different way from that in the aria. It is striking that even where there is a solo opening, it is often conceived as a mere introduction, with the primary weight still given to the first ritornello. Our view is therefore that there is a constant interaction between these two concepts, in which each section reacts to the preceding section and anticipates the next in an unfolding set of relationships, with different weightings dependent on a whole range of factors: motive, tonality, texture, separation and duration. In this sense a hierarchy of interlocking but differently weighted relationships between succeeding sections builds up across the movement.

(e) Articulation of the soloist
As has already been suggested, the presence of solo passages is very variable in the early repertoire and (even leaving aside purely ripieno concertos) there are

[10] Talbot, 'The Concerto Allegro', p. 164.
[11] Dubowy, 'Anmerkungen zur Form', pp. 439–42.

examples where solo writing is quite incidental, or sometimes delayed until the second half of a movement, when the music has reached subsidiary keys. Whether the soloist contributes to the early part of the movement – in particular whether the first solo begins in the tonic and then enacts the move to the dominant – is a critical issue. So too is the way the solo is first introduced, whether easing imperceptibly out of an incomplete tutti phrase, or highly dramatized by a bravura entrance or strong thematic statement.

(f) Recurrence of material

Although it is possible to conceive of a ritornello movement in which no material recurs, normally the opening motto returns at least once. In the simplest design it is used simply to articulate each change of key, and the fact that the motto is capable of being used in both major and minor keys is an important element in the rhetorical discourse. More sophisticated possibilities of hierarchization and prediction are engendered when the opening section contains a number of separable motivic elements, which can be selected or reordered for later ritornellos.

Whether the soloist shares material with the ritornello is an important but in historical terms a somewhat problematical area of debate. On the one hand, the simplest echoes between tutti and solo can be seen as recalling older concerto grosso practice; on the other, solo transformation of tutti material can be viewed as an early emergence of motivically integrated rhetorical argument between tutti and solo.[12] But for most of the repertoire under discussion there is simply no consistency of approach that overarches the demands of individual works. An important issue that does warrant more attention is the handling of the recapitulation. Some kind of reprise in the tonic is almost universal, a critical question being how literal a recapitulation it provides: whether it preserves the tutti-solo alternation and especially whether there is a sensitivity to the tonal implications of the opening tonic section (shown, for example, by removing a central passage in the dominant, or by transposing it to the tonic).

(g) Tonal trajectory

A characteristic of ritornello form is the sense of a tonal journey across the available spectrum of keys, most clearly expressed in the circuit process described in Chapter 1. While the pendulum scheme with one return to the tonic represents a variant on this approach, any further central tonics dilute the sense of ritornello form considerably, since they imply an additive structure that could in fact come to a close on any of the tonic cadences. There is a similar loss of the larger picture when other keys succeed each other and return in quick succession. Both of these features may be seen as remnants of the seventeenth-century approach to the newly developing tonal system. The selection and number of keys, their placement in relation to the textural changes, and their establishment by duration and weighting are, therefore, critical issues.

---

12 See Hill, *Veracini*, pp. 146–7, for a discussion of Minos Dounias' apparent inconsistency on this point.

Concertos dating from the years around 1700 by Torelli and Albinoni, long identified as the front-runners in the early development of the concerto, will illustrate
contrasting approaches. Benedetto Marcello and Valentini cannot be regarded as
of such major significance, yet each presents a further perspective. These diverse
works reflect the emerging ritornello concept in various different ways, and
certainly all the elements that were to make up the Vivaldian version of ritornello
form are to be discovered here.

Giuseppe Torelli

The violinist Giuseppe Torelli (*b* Verona, 1658; *d* Bologna, 1709) was based for
most of his life at S Petronio in Bologna, where he was also a prominent figure in
the Accademia Filarmonica (when the S Petronio orchestra was disbanded briefly
from 1696 to 1700, he took a post in Ansbach and also travelled to Berlin and
Vienna). Torelli was famously credited by Quantz, presumably on some kind of
oral authority, with having invented the concerto.[13] Some concept of ritornello
form is clearly evident in Torelli's concertos, which fully develop the textural
alternation of virtuosic solos with simpler tutti materials; the lack of large-scale
tonal planning based on closed periods has, however, led Talbot to identify only
'proto-ritornellos' in his Op. 8.[14]

It has become a commonplace of musical history to associate this development
with the sonata for trumpet and strings in late seventeenth-century Bologna –
especially its diatonic fanfare motives, and its *concertato* alternations between
trumpet and strings in a mosaic structure.[15] In the *sinfonia con tromba* in D (G.9) a
substantial 12-bar opening ritornello is separated from a solo entering in brief
Devise manner (Ex. 3.1). Shortly afterwards the motto appears in the dominant
(R2), followed by departure to vi (in which key the natural trumpet can still
marginally contribute) and by a reprise of both S1 and R1. In the course of this
53-bar miniature, all the principal elements of the ritornello concerto can already
be discerned.

Much more inventive musically, however, are Torelli's string concertos.
Diverse as they are in style and form, the *Concerti musicali*, Op. 6 (Augsburg,
1698) already suggest ritornello form in places, especially in the two concertos
that have solo sections indicated (Nos. 6 and 12). In fact, these three-movement
concertos qualify as the earliest published solo string concertos.[16] All four outer
movements alternate tutti sections (articulated by motto) with clearly differentiated solo passages, using modest string-crossing passage-work. Most striking,
though, is the approach to tonality: of the 13 ritornellos in these four movements,
only two are non-modulatory – and these include none of the opening ritornellos,
which all modulate to the dominant or beyond. The timeline of Op. 6/12 will

---

[13] *On Playing the Flute*, p. 310.
[14] Talbot, 'The Concerto Allegro', p. 169.
[15] For example, Hutchings, *The Baroque Concerto*, pp. 64–88.
[16] For a full discussion of the ritornello procedures in this set see Suess, Introduction to *Giuseppe Torelli: Concerti musicali Opus 6*, pp. viii–xii.

Ex. 3.1. Torelli, Trumpet Sonata in D major, G.9

illustrate the point (Table 3.1). The immediate repetition of the motto in the dominant removes from the soloist the responsibility of the modulation to the dominant, instead enabling a further modulation, which means there is no R2 at all. The solo simply emerges out of the opening ritornello, going straight into Fortspinnung without thematic definition. No key is established firmly, but in constant shifting sands one key slips easily into another, even vi being quickly deserted for an early central return to the opening in the tonic. Thus there is no coordination between texture and tonal structure.

Table 3.1. Timeline of Torelli, Violin Concerto in A major, Op. 6/12

Function	R1 (R2)	S	R3 (RT)	S	R3-R4
Bars	1–11	11–21	22–33	33–53	53–63
Key	I→ V	V→vi	vi // I→V→^{V}/V	→ii→	vi→I
Thematic	M M		M' M M		M M

These are unambiguously ritornello movements, but not on the scale to be found in Torelli's final set of concertos, which has always been regarded as a landmark in the development of the solo concerto. The set of *Concerti grossi*, Op. 8, published posthumously in Bologna in 1709, consists of six concertos for two violins and six solo violin concertos, all in fast-slow-fast form.[17] These are much more developed and impressive works than Op. 6, with a gravity to the tutti sections that reflects Torelli's Bolognese background, especially as six opening ritornellos are well-worked fugal structures. Op. 8/2 illustrates how contrapuntal working may be directly juxtaposed with arresting solo writing of a far more pronounced character than in Op. 6 (Ex. 3.2). In the third ritornello a different idiom intervenes – vividly sonorous semiquaver figuration – which further highlights the contrast between solo and tutti, and adds an overall perspective to the unfolding of the ritornello form.

---

[17] Op. 8/6 (the 'Christmas Concerto') has a slow introduction.

Ex. 3.2. Torelli, Concerto for Two Violins in A minor, Op. 8/2

va omitted

The soloist's status is immediately asserted at the start of the collection. In the opening movement each new section is initiated by the soloists with a leap to the next key, while their own motto remains entirely independent from the tutti material (Table 3.2). This movement has been cited by Norbert Dubowy as a clear example of the solo-tutti conception, reinforced by the separation of tonal blocks derived from seventeenth-century models.[18] While such thematic specialization was never entirely discarded, such an unambiguous solo lead became alien to the later concept of ritornello form.

Table 3.2. Timeline of Torelli, Concerto for Two Violins in C major, Op. 8/1

Function	S1	R1	S2	R2	S3a	R3	S3b	R4a	S4	R4b
Bars	1–9	9–24	25–33	33–48	9–68	68–80	80–93	93–103	103–111	111–116
Key	I	I //	V	V //	iii	iii→vi	→	I	I	I
Thematic	M1	M2	M1 = 1–9	M2 ≈9–24	M1	M2		M2 = 9–19	M1 = 1–9	M2 = 19–24

A completely different effect results when the solo leads directly out of the tutti, emphasising the tutti-solo succession. In eight concertos in Op. 8, the opening ritornello modulates, usually to the dominant, and one never encounters a full-scale solo leading from tonic to dominant; thus in Op. 8/12, a substantial 19-bar solo links R1 and R2, but it both begins and ends in the dominant. The oscillations between tonic and dominant at the beginning of each movement (especially in fugal movements) obviate dramatization of the move towards V.

In general Torelli does not cultivate a strong sense of tonal direction, slipping in and out of keys, and only settling on a final destination at the last moment. In Op. 8/5 in G major, for example, R1 first modulates to the dominant and then suddenly diverts to B minor, only for the contrasting solo to return abruptly to the tonic (Ex. 3.3). The tonal scheme of the movement is very fluid, constantly touching the tonic key only to desert it; yet there is very little dominant, this key

[18] Dubowy, 'Anmerkungen zur Form', pp. 433–5; *Arie und Konzert*, pp. 254–6.

Ex. 3.3. Torelli, Concerto for Two Violins in G major, Op. 8/5

being used largely as a pendant to the tonic in the contrapuntal sections (Table 3.3). A full tonic cadence at bar 61 appears to signal an impending close, but instead the hammer-stroke motto is boldly stated in B minor, initiating a restart, and dividing the movement into two clear halves. Even at the end of the movement the tonic is not clearly established, and indeed the final ritornello diverts to E minor for the ensuing Adagio, without any sense of tonic closure at all.

Such fluidity is not, however, universal. In Op. 8/9 in E minor, for example, the tonal handling shows a more purposeful overall direction: there are the usual modulating ritornellos, but structural returns to the tonic are avoided. The structure is clarified not only by clear differentiation between the fugal tutti and intricate semiquaver solo writing, but also by the strong motto emphasising III and by the reworking of the final ritornello. Still the element of proportion is lacking: very short internal ritornellos are overbalanced by the extremely long final solo, which extends to a full 21 bars out of 78 (Table 3.4).

Torelli's Op. 8 firmly sets out the essential shape of the ritornello movement, with strong contrasts between distinctive tutti material and intricate solo violin writing that would not seem out of place in *L'estro armonico*. Yet there is an occasional sense of strain, as in the heightened contrast in Op. 8/12, where the brilliant second solo in $^9/_8$ rhythm returns uncomfortably to the ritornello in $^3/_4$.

Table 3.3. Timeline of Torelli, Violin Concerto in G major, Op. 8/5

Function	R1a	S	R1b	S	R3a (RT)	R3b	S	R3c (R4)
Bars	1–23	23–31	31–41	41–49	49–61	62–66	66–78	78–98
Key	I →V→iii	iii→I	I →(iii)→	vi→	IV→I //	iii	iii →(I) →	vi → I →vi
Thematic	M a	b	a	b	a	M	b	a

Table 3.4 Timeline of Torelli, Violin Concerto in E minor, Op. 8/9

Function	R1a	S1a	R1b	S1b	R2	S2	R3a	S3a	R3b	S3b	R4
Bars	1–8	9–15	15–22	23–26	27–30	31–39	39–43	43–47	47–49	49–69	69–78
Key	i→v	i	i→v	v→	ii→v	→	III→	V/III→	III	→	i
Thematic	M a		M a		a		M		a		= R1 altered to stay in i

Where one would expect Vivaldi to maintain a proportion and balance in such excursions, here it merely sounds disruptive.

Tutti-solo alternations are used to articulate the larger structure, and there is some sense of overall tonal trajectory. But in general the tonal handling is fluid rather than directional. For Michael Talbot, this is a cause for criticism of Torelli's architectural control,[19] and although we find more to commend in Torelli's handling of ritornello procedures, we agree that the constant tonal flux does not permit the contrast between stable and unstable periods essential to large ritornello forms. Almost all concerto composers eventually came to insist on a long, stable tonic at the beginning and end of every movement. Nevertheless modulating ritornellos persist in the repertoire as a whole, and Torelli's fluid handling of tonality is mirrored in such unlikely places as the early concertos of Tartini.

Tomaso Albinoni

By contrast with Torelli, in whose concertos ritornello form is immediately apparent in the alternation of tutti and solo, the early string concertos of the *dilettante* Tomaso Albinoni (*b* Venice, 1671; *d* Venice, 1751) seem at first to have little to offer to our discussion. It is true that the six concertos in Op. 2 (Venice, 1700) pioneer the modern three-movement form, beginning with a sharply-etched Allegro in homophonic idiom; and the energetic rhythms and diatonic fanfares of the *tromba* style continue into the twelve concertos Op. 5 (1707), which reintroduce fugal writing only in the finales.[20] But the term 'violin concerto' can only be used in its loosest sense here, since it is not the purpose of these concertos to highlight and explore soloistic capabilities at all. Although a

---

[19] 'The Concerto Allegro', pp. 162–3.
[20] Further on the possible Bolognese influence on Albinoni, see Talbot, *Tomaso Albinoni*, pp. 101–5; Selfridge-Field, *Venetian Instrumental Music*, p. 211.

Table 3.5. Timeline of Albinoni, Concerto in G major, Op. 2/8

Function	R1	S	R2-RT-R3a	R/S	R3b-RT-R3c	R/S	R3d- R4a	S	R4b
		(vn)		(vc→vn)		(vc)		(vn)	
Bars	1–7	8–12	13–18	19–29	29–35	35–40	40–46	46–51	51–56
Key	I→V	V	V I vi	vi	vi I V	→	iii ii I	I	I
Thematic	M		M M M		M M M		M M M		

separate part is always provided for the leading violinist, the use of the solo instrument varies across the whole spectrum from those ripieno concertos with no solos, through those with incidental contributions to those where the soloist plays a substantial part.[21]

Not that there is a steady progression from incidental usage to greater consistency: the opening movements of Op. 2 Nos. 8 and 12 contain more solos in semiquaver figuration than many later concertos. Those in Op. 2/8, an early 'motto concerto' in G major, are separated by obsessive recurrences of an incisive tutti motto (Table 3.5). Albinoni shows an awareness not only of the strength of the recurrent motive in articulating the structure, but also of the flux of intensity resulting from the build-up of anticipation. In bars 35–40 a fully accompanied cello solo drives powerfully towards the ensuing motto in B minor (Ex. 3.4).

Ex. 3.4. Albinoni, Concerto in G major, Op. 2/8

This kind of emphasis on the soloist is clearly considered but one option out of many. The defining characteristic of the concerto is not the alternation of solo and tutti in the later Vivaldian sense, nor even the consistent use of contrasting textures in the concerto grosso vein, although both of these elements can be identified. Indeed, some 'solo' passages in semiquavers are entrusted to two or even

---

[21] A useful chart plotting the role of the principal violinist is to be found in Talbot, *Tomaso Albinoni*, p. 104 (where the presence of cello solos is also mapped).

three violin parts; and often the solo parts are 'shadowed' by the tutti, suggesting divisions around a simpler line rather than an accompanied solo.

In general, the use of solo and duet passages is variable and to the modern ear – attuned to consistency and to a regular succession of contrasts – rather unbalanced. Thus while all the opening movements of Op. 5 contain solos, in many cases they are only short sections that emerge unobtrusively out of a tutti, without the dramatized articulation of the later ritornello form.[22] An example from Op. 5/11 will demonstrate how subtly Albinoni engineered this transition, as the unison doublings each drop out in turn (Ex. 3.5a). At the end of the solo, the cadence is reinforced by the tutti and there is a clear separation before the ensuing ritornello – again deliberately weakening the dramatic function of the textural alternation (Ex. 3.5b). Only once, in Op. 5/12, do the solos take the lead, with a duet 'call to attention' introducing each section in the manner of Torelli's Op. 8/1.

Ex. 3.5. Albinoni, Concerto in G minor, Op. 5/11

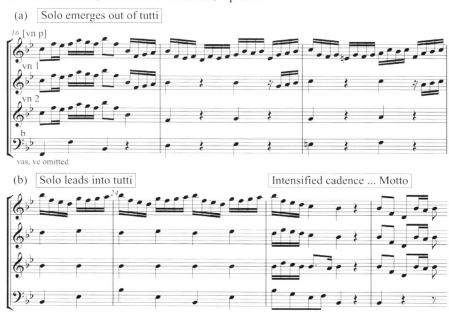

The subordinate function of the solo sections is made explicit in Op. 5/6, where an accompanied duet appears only as an insignificant pendant to each key change. Here, as in many other cases where the solo section is more extended, the modulation has already been achieved in the previous tutti, so that the solo has no dramatic role in driving forward the tonal process. Even in Op. 2/8, the block repetitions of the motto within the ritornellos achieve most of the modulations, while the solos remain static within the keys provided.

Solos can occur at almost any point in the movement – interpolated into the opening tonic section, or delayed until much later – but there is one stage that is

22 See the example in ibid., p. 106.

Ex. 3.6. Albinoni, Concerto in Bb major, Op. 5/1

never entrusted to a solo: the modulation from tonic to secondary key, later to be regarded as the very place where the soloist can assert authority and influence the direction of the movement. Here this move is always left to the tutti, either: (i) already within the opening period, perhaps by immediate repetition of the motto in the dominant in Corellian manner; or (ii) only after a complete ritornello, as in Op. 5/1, where an 8-bar ritornello is immediately followed by further statements of the motto, first in the tonic and then in the dominant (Ex. 3.6).

The variable appearance of solos in Albinoni's string concertos has led Martin Shapiro to reject the terminology of ritornello form altogether in favour of a four-part structure, consisting of opening statement, central section, tonic reprise and coda.[23] Michael Talbot has also striven to avoid ritornello terminology in his five-part scheme for Albinoni concertos, which may be summarized as follows:[24]

(1) closed period ending in I;
(2) open period with motto in I and V, leading to cadence in V;
(3) open period with motto in V and I, leading to cadence in vi (followed by either hiatus or link);
(4) reprise in I;
(5) coda (to emphasize the conclusion, which had in R1 been insufficiently affirmative).

While such a scheme cannot be perceived in all Albinoni's early concertos, it undoubtedly reflects the overall principle underlying his approach. Yet at the same time, we would still maintain that there are elements here that contributed to the emergence of the mature ritornello form, especially with regard to tonal plans and recurring motto. Indeed Talbot's overall scheme is not incompatible with ritornello form at all: the crucial difference from later practice being the avoidance of a modulating solo between tonic and dominant.

Turning now in more detail to the tonal schemes of these early concertos, Albinoni clearly prefers simple and direct patterns, with the dominant the universal first target in major and the mediant in minor (Table 3.6). The pendulum concept prevails, a characteristic of Albinoni's concertos already noted in Chapter 1; and as a result most movements concentrate on the tonic key, with

23 Shapiro, 'The Treatment of Form', pp. 34–52.
24 'The Concerto Allegro', pp. 164–5. For a further similar scheme, expressed in seven sections through an expansion of (2) and (3) into four, see Solie, 'Aria Structure', pp. 36–7.

Table 3.6. Tonal schemes of Albinoni, Op. 2/8, Op. 2/12, Op. 5

Circuit		Pendulum	
Tonal scheme	**Number**	**Tonal scheme**	**Number**
Major			
		I-V-I-vi-I	5
		I-V-I-vi-iii-I	1
		I-V-I-vi-I-iii-ii-I	1
I-V-iii-vi-I	2	I-V-I-iii-vi-I	1
Minor			
		i-v-i-III-i	1
		i-III-i-v-i	2
		i-III-(i)-v-i	1

Table 3.7. Timeline of Albinoni, Concerto in D major, Op. 5/3

Function	R1	R2a		R2b	RT
Bars	1–4	5–8	9–13	13–15	15–17
Key	I	V	V	V	I
Thematic	M	M		M (= 5–6, octave higher)	M (= 1–2)

S2	R3	S4	R4	Coda
17–23	23–25	25–27	28–43	43–47
I→	vi→	(I)	I	I
			M extended (cf. 17)	new

relatively short forays outside, as exemplified in Table 3.7. The most common tonal scheme in major is I-V-I-vi-I, in which the return to the tonic actually initiates the move to the peripheral area. While the variability of texture means that it is difficult to generalize in terms of ritornello structure, the central tonic in pendulum movements is usually articulated in a tutti ('RT'), with the move V-I directly mirroring and reversing the earlier I-V (as in Op. 5/3 discussed below). Albinoni's preference for vi (the relative minor) as the main peripheral key in major also reflects a desire to stay close to the tonic in the latter stages of a movement.

Strongly characteristic of this repertoire is the decisive articulation of the recapitulation by a reprise of the tutti motto (Op. 5/11 being the sole exception here). In six concertos there is a full reprise of the opening tonic ritornello, which is always followed by a separate coda. In the remaining seven, the restatement of the motto similarly expands into a new closing section, perhaps as a consequence of a modulatory R1. In both scenarios Albinoni evidently felt that thematic reprise was not sufficient to emphasize the end of the movement but that additional weight was required for the closing tonic. These closing sections either introduce unconnected new material or else provide a new perspective on earlier motives.

A brief examination of Op. 5/3 will draw together some of these points (Table 3.7). This movement illustrates the early eighteenth-century tendency to slip easily between tonic and dominant, without large-scale articulation of tonal areas. The opening tonic is remarkably short, and an immediate dominant repeat leads straight to a cadence in that key. The process is then reversed, in a neat small-scale symmetry. Only here does a violin solo intervene to influence the musical argument, directing the tonality towards vi before an early return to the tonic. The short opening tonic area notwithstanding, a large proportion of the movement is in the tonic (66%), with only the briefest touch of a peripheral key. While the soloist retains an apparently insignificant position, the change of texture still serves to highlight the tonal process.

Though by no means fully-developed examples of the solo concerto, these early Albinoni works contain many of the seeds of the ritornello concept. They also foreshadow the individual approach that he was to bring to the concerto, including the coda revisiting earlier material and the distinctive use of the central tonic as part of the pendulum scheme.

Benedetto Marcello

Another Venetian *dilettante*, Benedetto Marcello (*b* Venice, 1686; *d* Brescia, 1739), would probably be regarded as a figure of more significance here had the solo violin part survived for his set of 12 concertos, Op. 1, published in Venice in 1708. The set is diverse in form, combining a variety of different genres, and most of the concertos are in four movements with a slow opening. Nevertheless they may justifiably be regarded as solo violin concertos, and strong suggestions of ritornello form can be discerned in the two relevant movements that can be reconstructed. The opening movement of No. 8 in F major is preserved in a hybrid manuscript concerto now in Berlin (C791), while the Vivace forming the second movement of No. 2 in E minor (C788) survives in Bach's C minor keyboard transcription (BWV 981).[25]

The F major concerto provides a direct example of the 'motto concerto', such has already been described in Albinoni's Op. 2/8. The short *tromba* motto is introduced in a Devise pattern on the smallest scale (Ex. 3.7). This goes on to articulate the tonal structure of the movement as in the Albinoni example: but with the crucial distinction that in every case it is the soloist that prosecutes the modulation (Table 3.8). This is true ritornello form, albeit on a diminutive scale and with limited thematic manipulation.

Rather more interesting musically is the movement from Bach's transcription. It begins with a pretence at a fugal movement in *da chiesa* vein, but any fugal implication is immediately abandoned in favour of a more soloistic continuation

---

[25] We are indebted to Richard Maunder for such a reconstruction.

Ex. 3.7. Benedetto Marcello, Violin Concerto in F major, C791 (= Op. 1/8, C790)

Ex. 3.8. Benedetto Marcello, Violin Concerto in E minor, Op. 1/2/II (C788), after Bach BWV 981

(Ex. 3.8). This passage in turn provides the material for a brief closing ritornello that later serves to confirm both dominant and tonic key areas. Thus the fugal implication is rejected in favour of an essentially soloistic movement which contains elements of ritornello form. As will be seen, Vivaldi embraced the challenge of turning this subject into a substantial fugue in RV 565 (Op. 3/11) as if to realize its true implication. In Marcello's hands it remains an insubstantial hybrid, somewhere between a contrapuntal sonata movement and a ritornello structure.

Table 3.8. Timeline of Benedetto Marcello, Violin Concerto in F major, C791 (= Op. 1/8, C790)

Function	R1a-S1a-R1b	S1b	R2-S2a	RT-ST-RT-S2b	R3/S3 x3	R4a-S4-R4b
Bars	1–8	8–16	16–19	20–32	32–41	41–54
Key	I	I→V	V	I →	vi (→ii→V→)	I
Thematic	M M	M	M M	M M	M M M	M

Giuseppe Valentini

The violinist Giuseppe Valentini (*b* Florence, 1681; *d* Rome, 1753) emerged from a quite different milieu.[26] Though born in Florence he studied in Rome with Giovanni Bononcini during the 1690s and it was here that he made a distinguished career as a violinist and composer. The 1700s were as yet a journeyman period, during which he published five sets of chamber music under fanciful titles such as *Bizzarrie per camera* – titles that reflect not only his poetic talents but also a self-conscious tendency towards fantasy and experiment.

The peak of his early achievement resides in his *Concerti grossi*, Op. 7, published in Bologna in 1710. This same year coincided with the beginning of his professional success in Rome, which was reputed to have contributed to Corelli's declining health:

> All these mortifications, joined to the success of Valentini, whose concertos and performance, though infinitely inferior to those of Corelli, were become fashionable, threw him into such a state of melancholy and chagrin, as was thought, said Geminiani, to have hastened his death.[27]

Corelli's dignified contrapuntal idiom still dominated Roman musical taste, as did the four-movement *da chiesa* pattern that he regularized in the Op. 3 sonatas, where a slow opening movement is typically followed by a fugal Allegro.[28] Similarly pervasive was the Roman concerto grosso scoring that alternated a concertino of two solo violins and cello with ripieno strings, in an amplified version of the trio sonata. Yet Corelli's own *Concerti grossi*, Op. 6 (refined over a long period before their publication in 1714) will play only a background role in this book. Only rarely is the alternation of textures essential to the musical argument, notably in the solo figurations in the first Allegro of No. 12, and even here there is no suggestion of ritornello form.

It was surely Corelli's overbearing influence that Valentini had in mind in the preface to the Op. 7 concertos, where he provocatively alluded to their 'new style, thinking that novelties do not usually displease'. Despite this defiant gesture, Valentini has usually been regarded by modern scholars as a neo-Corellian composer. It is true that he generally remained faithful to the scoring and four-movement structure of the Roman concerto grosso. Yet there is a great deal in his concerto repertoire that moves away from Corelli, including a brisk homophonic Allegro idiom and some virtuosic solo breaks for the first violinist. Furthermore, in line with his individualistic temperament (most obviously reflected in harmonic eccentricities), his concertos revel in formal experiment and cross-genre fertilization.

Op. 7 as a whole is too varied to be described fully here. The principal Allegro movements (usually placed second) refer to many different genres, ranging from

---

[26] Careri, 'Giuseppe Valentini'; Careri, 'Per un catalogo tematico'; Talbot, 'A Rival of Corelli'.
[27] Burney, *A General History*, vol. 2, p. 440.
[28] Corelli's concertos Op. 6 are more varied in overall form, although this pattern can be seen in the background of Nos. 1–8.

full-scale fugues to binary and motley through-composed forms. Some movements are ripieno, others have only brief trio passages in the concerto grosso
manner, while still others contain substantial solos. The hybrid No. 3 links a long
solo to a ripieno contrapuntal section; No. 11, though innovatively scored with
four separate violin parts, has a six-part fugue with only incidental solos.

Within this mix, there are some elements that can be clearly allied to ritornello
form. This has precipitated some debate. Michael Talbot has identified an incipient but unrealized ritornello form:

> Vivaldian ritornello form is approached in some fast movements without being
> fully realized . . . Although he reintroduces thematic material diligently,
> Valentini allows his movements in this incipient ritornello form to ramble and
> fails to establish clear focal points. The initial tuttis move too soon to the domi-
> nant, where they dwell too long, so that the later dominant statement of the
> ritornello as a whole loses impact.[29]

By contrast, Paul Everett has argued that Valentini instead developed 'a considered, and unique, adaptation of a sectional approach to the demands of
fast-movement form': one that superimposes elements of binary form on a broad
three-section structure.[30] We shall return to this in more detail when considering
Valentini's later work; for now, let us examine the most relevant movements of
Op. 7, the second movements of Nos. 1, 4, 9 and 12.

Although they are strikingly different, each adopts the driving Allegro idiom,
with clearly defined sections; and where there are solos, these are differentiated
either by distinctive material or by mechanical figurations. Valentini is prone to
piece together extremely long movements by transposing whole chunks to
different keys in a patchwork and rather repetitive manner. The motto itself often
disappears from view as the movement progresses, but nevertheless Valentini
does maintain a strong sense of reprise. In particular he has a predilection for
tonal alteration so as to replace dominant by tonic, in an obvious connection with
end-matched binary form.

Op. 7/1 in A major, though it has only two short solos, will demonstrate something of the quirky individuality with which Valentini pieces together a huge
movement (Table 3.9). While in some senses this is very far from a ritornello
design, it contains elements that suggest it; notably the alternation of changing
textures and the tonal arrivals, as well as block recurrences of material. Furthermore it would appear that Valentini was already aware of certain norms, for in one
particularly striking passage all the listener's expectations are ostentatiously
defeated: after R1 has closed with a fully established tonic cadence, there is no
immediate solo but instead a series of tonal jolts that explicitly negate each arrival
(Ex. 3.9). When the solo does arrive, it is in a deliberately skewed, Picasso-esque
tonality, suggesting both F♯ minor and C♯ minor at the same time. Thus the dominant is not the immediate successor, but is reached only in the middle of the
ensuing ritornello. Striking, too, is the ensuing fugal section, which offers
'soloistic' contrast by beginning with the unaccompanied subject, thus suggesting

---

[29] 'A Rival of Corelli', pp. 362–3.
[30] *The Manchester Concerto Partbooks*, p. 326.

Table 3.9. Timeline of Valentini, Concerto in A major, Op. 7/1/II

Bars	Key	Texture	Material
1–39	I	Tutti	Complete sinfonia movement, with first section I→V reprised IV→I (M throughout)
39–43	→	Tutti	Transition
43–50	vi	Solo	Contrasting, eccentric harmony
50–70	vi→V	Tutti	M in vi, ii and V, followed by closing material from R1
70–82	V→IV	Tutti	New fugal section (derived from M)
82–92	→I	Solo	Unaccompanied arpeggiation
92–113	I→iii→I	Tutti	New chromatic material, and part of fugal section
113–126	I→V	Tutti	Reprise of fugal section etc.
126–131	V	Tutti	M
131–152	I	Tutti	Reprise of first half of R1, adapted to stay in tonic (thus ending same as R1)

an alternative route for the movement. After all this discursiveness, the latter stages include a substantial amount of reprise, involving characteristically extensive rewriting in order to adapt earlier material to the tonic. All in all, there is an undeniable connection with some of the concepts of ritornello structure, but it is handled in a decidedly idiosyncratic way.

Op. 7/4 deliberately sidesteps the ritornello concept: after a closed ritornello the ensuing solo gives every impression that it will take the role of S1. Instead it is immediately absorbed into the full texture, resulting in a ripieno movement in which the pretensions of the soloist are summarily rejected. The two other relevant movements both have much longer solo passages, though within different genres. Op. 7/9 is an extremely long movement in fugal idiom: prominent arpeggiated solos separate fugal tutti sections, in a grafting of virtuosic independence on to contrapuntal tuttis that will be seen in other Roman concertos. On the other hand, Op. 7/12 is a binary movement that would be outside our purview, were it not for its fascinating relationship with other concepts. The first section is short (twenty-seven bars in Presto tempo), including a brief modulatory solo; but the second section is elaborated to eighty bars, with extensive solos articulated by brief references to the motto. The opening and close of each half correspond, in the normal way for late Baroque binary movements (Table 3.10). The movement thus combines the central motto in V – a ritornello form characteristic – with tonal resolution derived from binary form (the transposition of secondary material from dominant to tonic). This adds further weight to Everett's theory about cross-influence between the two; and certainly such tonal resolution was to be a powerful factor in later ritornello movements by Valentini and others.

Ex. 3.9. Valentini, Concerto in D major, Op. 7/1/II

Table 3.10. Timeline of Valentini, Concerto in D major, Op. 7/12/II

Bars	‖: 1–27 :‖	‖: 28–107 :‖
Key	I → V	V → iii → vi → ii → I
Thematic	M close	M close

Early Vivaldi

We may now turn to Vivaldi's earliest concertos, in order to determine whether they shared features with the concertos just considered and to investigate how they relate to Vivaldi's later output, making no apology for this anachronistic way of looking backward from later concertos. We will focus on three groups of early concertos: the cello concertos that Franz Horneck copied in Venice in 1708–09, *L'estro armonico*, Op. 3 (Amsterdam, 1711), and *La stravaganza*,

Op. 4 (Amsterdam, 1716), some of which will of course be considered in more detail during of our overall discussion of Vivaldi.

With *L'estro armonico* we enter familiar musical territory, and most of these concertos feature fully-formed ritornello structures, which in many respects shaped the future direction of the concerto. Yet the set does indeed share many features with the repertoire discussed above, features which were either modified or else abandoned in Vivaldi's later oeuvre. It is organized in a rotation of concertos for four violins, for two violins, and for solo violin, with some solo sections for cello, as with Albinoni. As Talbot has argued, the set shows every sign of having been intended for as wide a reception as possible: it is almost a pan-Italian compendium of varied current practices, and thus cannot be considered typical of Venice around 1710. Indeed, the layout of the eight part-books, with four separate violin parts, reflects Roman practice rather than Venetian.[31]

The concertos for four violins therefore represent a special case in Vivaldi's output, apparently reflecting the influence of the similarly scored Valentini concerto, Op. 7/11. The four violins are used in a kaleidoscope of solos, duets, dialogues, and motivic exchanges. The relevant movements are, in formal terms, outside the limits of our study. While there are some elements of ritornello as a framing device, both RV 549 (Op. 3/1) and RV 580 (Op. 3/10) begin with solos in the manner of Torelli's Op. 8/2, with the tutti acting more as response and cadential confirmation than as initiator or source. RV 580 in particular provides an interesting commentary on ritornello form, for the various tutti sections interpolated between the solos appear together to constitute a complete ritornello, which is never heard in its entirety.[32]

Another special case is RV 565 (Op. 3/11) in D minor, which refers to the concerto grosso directly: both in its broadly four-movement structure and in its fugal second movement. It would, however, be quite misleading to regard this concerto as a primitive stage or as an attempt to imitate the Corellian genre. Indeed it provides a commentary on earlier models, beginning with a D minor fanfare for two violins in concerto-Allegro idiom (compare the opening solo flourish of Valentini's Op. 7/1, itself related to Corelli's violin sonata Op. 5/1). However, any expectation of an ensuing ritornello is thwarted by the interruption of a cello solo and a short chromatic Adagio, leading to a fully-fledged fugue. The similarity of the subject to that found in Marcello's Concerto Op. 1/2 has already been remarked (see Ex. 3.8); usually this is interpreted as a reworking,[33] although the possibility that both composers manipulated a stock opening independently should not be discounted. Vivaldi's subject is considerably longer, as is the substantial movement that he builds from it – a fugue organized according to the broad concepts of ritornello form, reminding us how close the two procedures are. The subject introduces an opening ritornello in the tonic, a central ritornello

---

31 ' "Lingua Romana" ', pp. 312–18. These concertos are clearly intended for solo strings, most modern editions representing an arrangement for orchestral performance: for an accessible accurate score, see the edition by Eleanor Selfridge-Field (Mineola, NY: Dover, 1999), ignoring the solo-tutti emendations.

32 Cf. Dreyfus, *Bach and the Patterns of Invention*, pp. 73–8.

33 For example, Selfridge-Field, *The Music of Benedetto and Alessandro Marcello*, p. 358.

spanning v→i→iv and a final tonic ritornello; short trio sections based on the subject provide the intervening modulations. Thus the powerful frame of the Roman-Bolognese fugal concept is reconciled with an overall ritornello structure: it is a remarkable combination, one that in quite so severe a form is rare in Vivaldi's concerto output.[34]

Although these five concertos from Op. 3 are among Vivaldi's most impressive works, they remain somewhat tangential to our investigation. We will concentrate instead on the solo and double concertos from this period, among which the three early cello concertos have a particular importance as probably Vivaldi's earliest surviving concertos. They also have a claim to be regarded as reflecting the genuine Venetian tradition, devoid of external stylistic considerations such as influenced *L'estro armonico*;[35] although this supposition needs to be set besides their destination for Count Rudolf Franz Erwein von Schönborn, whose preference for conservative musical values has already been remarked (see p. 45). All three are set in the minor mode, with the first movement of RV 402 in C minor emphasizing the emotional intensity by avoiding the major mode altogether (Table 3.11).

Table 3.11. Tonal schemes of Vivaldi's early cello concertos

RV	Key	Tonal scheme
RV 402	c	i-v-iv-i
RV 416	g	i-v-♭VII-III-iv-i
RV 420	a	i-v-III-i

For our purposes, however, the most significant factor is that all three concertos unambiguously use a ritornello structure in the first movement. RV 420 recalls the solo-tutti orientation of Torelli's Op. 8/1: each statement is initiated by the soloist (a long drawn-out cello cantilena with its own motto), the short ritornellos simply confirming each key with figuration over a ground bass (Ex. 3.10). Such a total separation will be found again later (for example, Op. 4/8), but the schematic design is apparently unique in Vivaldi's concerto first movements.

The other two concertos (RV 402 and RV 416) already demonstrate the outlines of Vivaldi's mature ritornello form. It is true that in RV 402 the modulation to the secondary key is not carried out by the soloist, but instead by a second ritornello (R1b, i→v), recalling the procedure in some of the concertos discussed above. But otherwise both movements articulate ritornello form in a manner entirely consonant with Vivaldi's later practice. Both have a clearly rounded R1 ending in the tonic, and in RV 416 the soloist enters with an assertive and distinct gesture, motivically orientated so that the soloist marks his identity by commentary on the ritornello (Ex. 3.11). Subsequent ritornellos always briefly recall the motto, a relatively unsophisticated technique that has been identified in many

---

[34] Furthermore there are motivic connections with the opening fanfare, especially the descending scale passages.

[35] Talbot, ' "Lingua Romana" ', p. 316.

Ex. 3.10. Vivaldi, Cello Concerto in A minor, RV 420

Ex. 3.11. Vivaldi, Cello Concerto in G minor, RV 416

concertos already: yet it is handled here with an assured sense of tonal direction and a particular clarity of function. Furthermore, in RV 416, this clarity already allows for subtle handling of the recapitulation: a solo false reprise in the subdominant is immediately corrected in favour of the tonic (Ex. 3.12). This is a fascinating early example of Vivaldi's instinctive appreciation of the possibilities of tonal rhetoric. Also striking is the use of motivic material in the accompaniment, the comparatively low cello writing allowing the upper strings to develop motivic material over the solo figuration with complex results. In RV 402, this enables a structural blurring such as has been observed in Albinoni – rare in later Vivaldi – whereby the accompanying strings gradually take the lead (Ex. 3.13).

These interesting three cello concertos have been illustrated in some detail as they are both unfamiliar and a crucial test case for assessing Vivaldi's relationship

Ex. 3.12. Vivaldi, Cello Concerto in G minor, RV 416

Ex. 3.13. Vivaldi, Cello Concerto in C minor, RV 402

with his predecessors. Whether the solo concertos from the printed sets were composed at the same time, in the late 1700s, is a matter for conjecture; but certainly the seven remaining concertos from Op. 3 and the twelve in Op. 4 take the outlines of ritornello form into an early maturity. Since they are so well known, they will be illustrated more sparingly, though some detailed discussion of individual examples will be held over for later chapters.

All nineteen concertos begin with full-scale ritornello movements, preceded in two cases by a slow introduction: that in RV 185 (Op. 4/7) leads to a fugal ritornello movement in reference to the concerto grosso. Two concertos begin with the soloist. In RV 204 (Op. 4/11), R1 is preceded by a fanfare for two violins; although, unlike the similar fanfare in RV 565 (Op. 3/11), it is here not subverted, but is incorporated instead into the progress of the movement. The unusual RV 249 (Op. 4/8), on the other hand, recalls Torelli as well as RV 420 in being led by the soloist, with solos and ritornellos maintaining entirely separate thematic identities. On this occasion, however, the ritornellos are all unsettled and modulatory, giving an equal role to both parties in the unfolding of the movement.

The opening ritornellos exhibit many of the motto types that have been suggested in earlier examples, but now expressed so vividly that they represent almost a vocabulary of possibilities: hammer-strokes followed by acceleration, leaping unison octaves, repeated quavers and *tromba* rhythms, broken tonic chords, rushing scales and upbeat patterns. With the widespread diffusion and popularity of these two sets, this vocabulary of direct and memorable motives came to represent such a set of *topoi* that it seems to define the Vivaldian Allegro, and indeed these motives were frequently quoted and adapted by other composers, as will be seen.

In five cases the motto is immediately repeated a fifth higher in the manner described above, one of these being the fugal RV 185/II (Op. 4/7), which serves to remind the listener of the close connection between the two techniques. This remnant of older practice is not a prevailing technique, but one that Vivaldi continues to use occasionally throughout his later output. It does not enforce a monothematic unity, however, for almost all the ritornellos here provide a series of distinct units or motives suitable for extraction and development later in the movement.

The way in which the soloist enters after R1 and the way the move to the dominant is handled have already been identified as critical issues in the early development of ritornello form. Here again Vivaldi betrays some allegiance to older types, while at the same time developing his own rhetorical strategies in their handling. In most of these concertos there is a clear end to the opening ritornello, the soloist entering with some statement of individuality, even a sense of bravura: this in clear distinction from Albinoni, for example. But in three concertos from Op. 4 the opening ritornello is followed by a tutti restatement of the motto, from which the soloist emerges in the unobtrusive and unarticulated manner of Albinoni's Op. 5/1 (see Ex. 3.6). RV 383a (Op. 4/1), illustrated in Ex. 4.18 (p. 102), nevertheless differs in one crucial respect from the Albinoni example: whereas Albinoni repeats the motto again in the dominant, Vivaldi prefers to entrust the modulation to the soloist. Comparison with an earlier version, RV 381, is also instructive. Here S1 begins in much the same way, but the end of S1 is also blurred when the soloist is doubled by the first violin in the closing passage; furthermore both 'S2' and the beginning of 'S4' are similarly doubled, resulting in a kaleidoscopic variety of textures that subtly diminishes the prominence of the soloist. Evidently Vivaldi removed these suggestions of Albinoni's fluid practice in the later (published) version, retaining only the tutti motto to initiate the solo.

Whereas the early move to the dominant was a common procedure in concertos of the 1700s, Vivaldi goes to some pains to avoid this, establishing a substantial tonic base at the opening of the movement. In only one case, RV 265 (Op. 3/12), does the opening ritornello modulate to the dominant, but Vivaldi does not just adopt this key for the ensuing solo: rather, he uses this earlier device to rhetorical advantage, pulling back to the tonic for a ritornello R1b, before a new departure to a quite different key (vi), which in turn delays the eventual establishment of the dominant. This example vividly illustrates how Vivaldi can adapt a particular strategy to suit his own rhetoric, but it is one that he never again employed in a concerto first movement.

The expanded tonic pattern R1a-S1a-R1b occurs in as many as six out of the seven concertos in Op. 3; and even the seventh, RV 230 (Op. 3/9) is highly ambiguous. In three cases the solo resumes as before, the so-called Devise pattern already seen in Marcello's Op. 1/8 (see Table 5.5, p. 121): this scheme, popular with Albinoni later, is one that Vivaldi entirely abandoned.[36] The preference for the pattern R1a-S1a-R1b has already begun to wane in Op. 4, appearing in half the concertos, and in Vivaldi's later output the firm establishment of the tonic is generally achieved by other means.

---

[36] It has been discovered in only one other concerto: RV 276, published in 1714.

Almost always (by contrast with Albinoni) the modulation to the secondary key is entrusted to the soloist, a crucial responsibility that highlights the importance of the soloist in the unfolding of the structure. In only three cases is this modulation carried out by the ritornello R1b, a procedure that Vivaldi hardly ever used later. The tonal schemes of these nineteen concertos are in themselves interesting (Table 3.12). Certainly the relationship between tonal movement and ritornello structure has idiosyncratic features. Two concertos have no peripheral area at all, a real rarity later. One of these, RV 519 (Op. 3/5) in A major, is an example of what we have termed the 'sonority concerto': a concerto in G, D or A major that exploits unison hammered repeated notes and falling octaves or arpeggios in sinfonia manner, along with repetitive brilliant figurations around the sound of the open strings, mostly on tonic and dominant chords with hardly any other harmonic events. In this case even the dominant is not articulated by a ritornello of its own.

Table 3.12. Tonal schemes of Vivaldi's early published concertos

Op.	Key	Tonal scheme	Op.	Key	Tonal scheme
3/2/II	g	i-v-i	4/4	a	i-iv-VI-v-i
3/3	G	I-V-iii-V-I	4/5	A	I-V-I-iii-I
3/5	A	I-V-I	4/6	g	i-v-III-i
3/6	a	i-iv-III-i-v-i	4/7/II	C	I-iii-vi-I
3/8	a	i-III-v-iv-i	4/8	d	i-v-iv-bvii-i
3/9	D	I-V-vi-I	4/9	F	I-V-iii-V-I
3/12	E	I-vi-I-V-I	4/10	c	i-III-v-i
4/1	B♭	I-V-iii-I	4/11	D	I-V-iii-vi-I
4/2	e	i-iv-III-i-v-i	4/12	G	I-V-iii-I
4/3	G	I-V-iii-V-I			

On the other hand, RV 185/II in C major (Op. 4/7/II) has no secondary area, and indeed the entire movement lacks a single cadence in G major. This tour de force is particularly remarkable in a fugal ritornello movement, which disguises the normal subject-answer relationship (tonic-dominant) by an ingenious flatwards harmonization that colours the entire movement (Ex. 3.14). The resultant tonal scheme (I-iii-vi-I) would appear to be a radical experiment for this period; yet, as will be seen, such deliberate avoidance of the expected dominant is a strategy that Vivaldi was to adopt on many occasions later.

In as many as seven concertos R2 is modulatory, an option that was largely eschewed in Vivaldi's later output. In RV 522 in A minor (Op. 3/8) all three possible secondary key areas are tried out, with dramatic shifts of direction (Ex. 3.15). But the motto is conspicuously avoided until the following ritornello, where it emphasizes the subdominant at the end of the search. In RV 310 (Op. 3/3), every internal ritornello is modulatory, this time with each new key

Ex. 3.14. Vivaldi, Violin Concerto in C major, RV 185 (Op. 4/7)

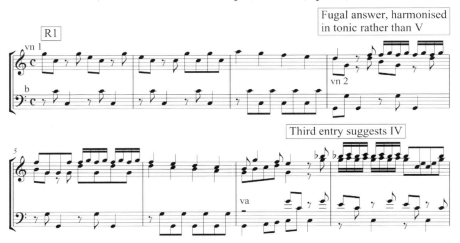

Ex. 3.15. Vivaldi, Concerto for Two Violins in A minor, RV 522 (Op. 3/8)

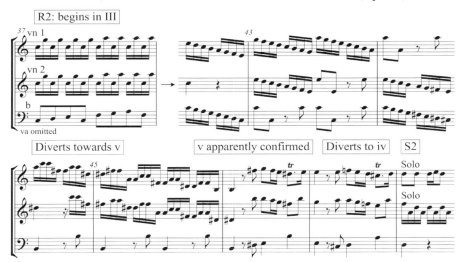

articulated by the motto (Table 3.13). The similarity to Albinoni's Op. 2/8 will be immediately evident (compare Table 3.5). In this case every single solo is tonally stable, filling the gaps between the modulatory ritornellos with essentially static figuration – a procedure found only once again in the Vivaldi sample (RV 220, published in 1717).

Turning now to thematic issues, the usage of the motto in the central ritornellos traverses the entire gamut from this kind of obsessive repetition to constantly new material, as in the comparatively underdeveloped RV 230 (Op. 3/9). As yet there is only limited exploitation of the potential of rearranging motivic segments drawn from R1, although the example of RV 522 reveals that the concept of hierarchization by motivic means was already understood. Neither

Table 3.13. Timeline of Vivaldi, Violin Concerto in G major, RV 310 (Op. 3/3)

Function	R1a	S1	R1b	S2	R2	S3	R3	R4a- S4- R4b	Coda
Bars	1–12	12–16	16–22	22–30	30–37	37–45	45–49	49– 51–55–60	60–64
Key	I	I	I→V	V	V→ iii	iii	iii→V→	I	I
Thematic	M		M		M M'		M M	M	M

does a consistent approach emerge with regard to the thematic material of the solos, and indeed discussion of the significance of connections with the ritornello appears futile at this stage. Two well-known concertos in A minor adopt a diametrically opposite stance: in RV 356 (Op. 3/6) S1 first quotes the motto directly and then reworks the ensuing sequence as part of a tonal debate between secondary keys; while, on the other hand, in RV 522 (Op. 3/8) the soloists develop an entirely new motive of their own.

Recapitulation procedures are also highly variable, and this continues to be an area of much experimentation. In RV 578 (Op. 3/2) the recapitulation is left entirely to the final solo, resulting in no R4 – an almost unique occurrence in Vivaldi's output. But mostly the recapitulation is articulated by the tutti, with segments from R1 presented either in a single ritornello or else spread across two or more sections. In some concertos there is a sense of tonal reworking. In RV 310 (Op. 3/3), for example, the modulation to the dominant in the middle of R1 is omitted in the recapitulation. But there is little cause for the wholesale tonal recasting seen in the concertos of Torelli. Only in RV 265 (Op. 3/12) is there such a clear necessity, since R1a modulated to the dominant: here the final ritornello deliberately seals the process by reversing it, moving from the motto on the dominant back to the tonic.

Even more than Torelli, Vivaldi strongly distinguishes the solo passages by distinctive figuration that, while it does not compare with his later violin writing for intricacy or technical difficulty, belies his reputation for merely routine string-crossing passages. Particularly interesting are the solo passages in the concertos for two violins. Vivaldi follows Torelli in his use of parallel and dialogue passages, but he also includes substantial solos for each violin separately, as well as the texture adopted by Bach where a cantabile melody in one violin part is accompanied by figuration in the other.

All the elements of the 'Vivaldian revolution' are to be found somewhere in the works of his contemporaries during the 1700s: distinctive solo and tutti material, strongly differentiated periods in contrasting textures, a balance of tonally closed and open periods, thematic manipulation and reprise, and an overall tonal trajectory. But they are never coordinated or consistently used in the way that Vivaldi already succeeded in doing in this early group of concertos: this is the essence of his achievement of 'order, connection, and proportion'. For all their unusual and experimental features – signs of a formative stage – Vivaldi had already developed a remarkable sureness of tonal and thematic handling, as well as a clarity of structural unfolding. But this accomplishment implies more than merely assembling the elements together in a well-judged way: rather, Vivaldi began to show how a composer might fully exploit their dramatic and rhetorical potential. The great variety to which each element was susceptible opened the doors to the extraordinary range of options he was to explore in the later concertos.

As Italian concerto composers developed these ideas further in subsequent decades, many different strategies – some of which can be traced back to concertos of the first decade – coexisted within the overall practice of ritornello form. Elements that Vivaldi largely discarded (for example, the imbalance between solo and tutti, or the modulating second ritornello) were preserved in the works of other composers, and these will be considered in later chapters. First, however, we turn to the great corpus of Vivaldi concertos to explore the range of his imaginative response within his own preferred strategies.

CHAPTER 4

'Vivaldi is a Deviant Vivaldian'

Michael Talbot's witty comment, 'Vivaldi is a deviant Vivaldian', focused on the observation that Vivaldi allowed a ritornello to recur in its original form 'far less frequently than the composers who aped his method'.[1] Yet it has far wider ramifications, implying that Vivaldi's followers in general promulgated a much more limited view of his idiom than ever existed in reality; and that this limited view has informed the enduring image of Vivaldi in most modern discussions. The resulting, artificially rigid model does indeed do scant justice to Vivaldi's strikingly diverse invention. Moreover, and ironically, the perception of an allegedly Vivaldian model has done equal injustice to the other concerto composers themselves, as their own individuality can never be fully appreciated when continuously gauged against a supposed Vivaldian norm.

Chapters 4, 5 and 6 will introduce Vivaldi's 'patterns of invention', which were such an important source of inspiration not only for the much studied case of Bach,[2] but also for numerous other Italian and German violinist-composers. One aspect will be the search for a chronological perspective within Vivaldi's own output, which raises the problem of the lack of exact dates for all but a fraction of his work. Even dates of publication are potentially misleading: thus many concertos in Vivaldi's Op. 8 (published in 1725) were apparently written in the mid-1710s.[3] An accurate chronology, relying on purely documentary evidence, therefore represents something of a holy grail for Vivaldi scholarship. Some progress has been achieved, however, through the modern musicological methods developed by such scholars as Everett, Heller, Rasch, Ryom and Talbot.[4] This has enabled us to identify two groups of early and late concertos with some degree of confidence, in order to derive broad conclusions about Vivaldi's changing preferences across his career (these groups are identified in the Catalogue, pp. 344–5).

As soon as Vivaldi triggers a movement with his typically powerful motto, he initiates a complex set of implications for the composer, for the performer and for

---

[1] 'The Concerto Allegro', p. 170, as interpreted in Everett, *Vivaldi: 'The Four Seasons'*, p. 33.
[2] Of most relevance here, Dreyfus, *Bach and the Patterns of Invention*; Wolff, 'Vivaldi's Compositional Art'.
[3] Everett, *Vivaldi: 'The Four Seasons'*, pp. 7–25.
[4] For an overview of these issues, see Everett, 'Towards a Chronology', expanded as 'Towards a Vivaldi Chronology'; see also Kotsoni-Brown, 'The Solo Cello Concertos'; Rasch, 'La famosa mano'; and the chart in Kan, 'The Concerto Adagios', pp. 197–8, with the accompanying discussion.

the trained listener. Yet the outcome is never predetermined: as Leonard Meyer has observed, 'though implicative accounts involve tacit or explicit awareness of if-then relationships, they are not causal but probabilistic'.[5] Certain realizations of the implications will indeed be more probable than others. Our primary purpose will therefore be to identify the range of options that Vivaldi adopted within his overall strategies, and to gauge the frequency of their use – representing his style in general and also reflecting changing preferences as his idiom changed over time. The statistical tables which may apparently disturb our narrative should be read as a fascinating reflection of Vivaldi's rich imagination, as well as of his systematic exploration of implied options. For while in some parameters his preferences are clearly marked, even then the minority options are still of considerable interest, insofar as they represent the limits of his experimentation. In others his preferences are more evenly spread, reflecting the broad range of implications to which each option may lead.

Listening in Three Dimensions

Such implications will, for our experienced listener, extend across large, middle and small dimensions.[6] As Jan LaRue has suggested, the large dimension may expand to include a group of works, in this case the numerous published sets of six concertos or of twelve concertos divided into two volumes. It would appear that they were sometimes intended to be performed as a full set in a musical soirée, as is suggested by the programmatic design of the first volume of Vivaldi's *Il cimento dell'armonia e dell'invenzione* (and not just *The Four Seasons* which begin the set).[7] The same may apply to sets that lay out a calculated succession of contrasting affects, whether selected by the publisher on their own initiative, as in the case of Vivaldi's Op. 6 (with its arresting opening in French overture style), or by Vivaldi himself in *La cetra*, Op. 9.

The next level is that of the individual concerto in the prevailing Vivaldian pattern of fast-slow-fast. Opening with a fast ritornello movement would immediately imply a contrasting slow movement, followed by a brisk finale. This implication must have derived exclusively from listening habits already learned by the early 1710s: a repeated experience of listening to three-movement concertos, whose overall form is not guided by extramusical factors such as a pictorial programme or a religious function. It is true that *L'estro armonico*, Op. 3 (published in 1711) still includes remnants of the older multi-sectional model. But already in this collection seven of the twelve concertos, and all but two of Op. 4 (1716), fall into the three-movement pattern, which quickly became so predominant that later exceptions in Vivaldi's output must be perceived as deliberate deviations from the norm.

Listening in the small dimension starts with the motto and immediately adds a

---

5   *Style and Music*, p. 84.
6   LaRue, *Guidelines for Style Analysis*, p. 6.
7   For discussion of the compilation and design of Vivaldi's Op. 8 see Paul Everett, *Vivaldi: 'The Four Seasons'*, pp. 7–25.

chain of well-articulated motives, eventually building up a perception of the main building blocks of the ritornello movement, namely the periods. But while our discussion will not neglect the nature of the musical material, nor the way in which these periods are built up by connecting motives in relation to one another, it is with the middle dimension that we will be most concerned. The middle dimension implies an awareness of the unfolding of a tonal and thematic argument across an entire movement, an argument enacted by the succession of musical periods and by their textural articulations as ritornellos and solos. Musical recurrences of the motto, of other motives or of entire ritornellos – whether literal or varied – orientate the listener by relating each event to the past and by creating expectations for the future.

The following exposition of Vivaldi's ritornello strategies will introduce 'the actors in order of appearance'. Yet our purpose is not merely to identify the players, but to elucidate their role in the unfolding of the movement, so that a fluid discussion ranging across the entire ritornello structure will inevitably result.

The Actors in Order of Appearance: the Motto

The motto is not only the first event in the ritornello movement, but it is designed to be most easily registered in the listener's memory – with the potential of evoking recall of past events, triggering prediction of future events, and leading a continuous argument. For some readers the mere mention of Vivaldi's mottos may summon up an image of a few worn out clichés. But this is entirely misleading: while it is true that Vivaldi's short, easily memorable mottos inevitably share common rhythmic and melodic traits, in reality they are highly varied.

The profile of the motto is determined by the interaction and fusion of its melodic, rhythmic and textural properties. At first glance, it looks as if Vivaldi's mottos readily lend themselves to classification under a limited number of melodic types, as Walter Kolneder has suggested in his pioneering study of this subject.[8] Yet deeper investigation soon reveals that any decision about motto types is immediately skewed by which parameter is preferred, and any one motto can in fact be classified under several different headings. For example, Kolneder classifies RV 210 (Op. 8/10) under 'Der Einzelton' heading (Ex. 4.1a). Yet the rhythmic structure also suggests the 'hammer-stroke' type, and the overall melodic profile 'scalewise filling of a triad'. Again, the motto of the two-violin concerto RV 522 (Op. 3/8) might be considered a classic 'hammer-stroke', yet Eugene Narmour instead stresses the significance of the octave as its dominating interval.[9] Alternatively, certain mottos may better be described in terms of topics of the kind identified by Leonard Ratner, as with the French overture idiom in RV 324 (Op. 6/1).[10] Any attempt to assemble statistics for Vivaldi motto types would therefore be artificial, even misleading. In general, we will concentrate on a comparative method, identifying where other composers preferred motto types

[8] *Melodietypen bei Vivaldi.*
[9] *The Analysis and Cognition of Basic Melodic Structures*, pp. 242–3.
[10] *Classic Music*, pp. 9–29.

Ex. 4.1a. Vivaldi, Violin Concerto in D major, RV 210 (Op. 8/11)

absent or very rare in Vivaldi. Only a few types are specific enough to be isolated as part and parcel of Vivaldi's melodic vocabulary, including repeated octave leaps, various types of hammer-strokes (amounting to 9%, a surprisingly low figure), trumpet fanfares, or the expressive broken chord with a leap of a sixth exemplified by RV 316a (Op. 4/6, Ex. 4.1b).

Ex. 4.1b. Vivaldi, Violin Concerto in G minor, RV 316a (Op. 4/6)

The motto may function as the entire antecedent of the first period, or it may constitute just the initial sub-component of a longer antecedent. Correlating phrase organization with the motivic parameter reveals two quite different compositional processes:

(1)   The motto comprises a single motivic cell, as in RV 345 (Op. 9/2, see Ex. 1.1), where the entire R1 is spun out from the motto forming the first bar. Such a technique may be referred to as 'synthetic' or 'additive'. In a variant of this technique, a single cell is extended into a longer motto of four bars, which nevertheless retains an irregular internal structure. Thus in RV 239 (Op. 6/6) the cell delineates a D minor triad before returning to the opening note, yet such is the rhythmic impetus that the melody presses on down to the lower octave, then unexpectedly reverses in a powerful drive right up to the highest note of the cell (Ex. 4.1c).

(2)   The motto comprises a regular unit of 2+2 bars. This practice, which was to become the norm in music in *galant* style, 'increased the degree of immediate intelligibility to the listener who quickly grasped paired statements . . . as *units* and was undoubtedly more comfortable in following the continuity of the music'.[11] The compositional technique in this case is 'analytic': the composer first determines the cadential point and then fills in the two motivic sub-units (Ex. 4.1d). Investigation of the entire sample leads to the following conclusions: (i) regular 2+2-bar mottos are in the minority (107 cases or 32%); (ii) sometimes Vivaldi deliberately avoids regularity, as in RV 770 where the melody is expanded from four bars into six by simple repetition. There is no difference in frequency between the earlier and later repertories, with regular mottos appearing in three concertos in Op. 4 and in the same number in Op. 9; although in his very last works Vivaldi does begin to adopt the contemporary fashion for a four-square phrasing with most phrases repeated (aa-bb-cc etc.). This latter development may be illustrated by RV 552, written for the 1740 festivities for the *Kurprinz* of Saxony (Ex. 4.1e).[12]

---

[11]   Ratner, *Classic Music*, p. 35.
[12]   We are indebted to Michael Talbot for this observation.

Ex. 4.1c. Vivaldi, Violin Concerto in D minor, RV 239 (Op. 6/6)

Ex. 4.1d. Vivaldi, Violin Concerto in A minor, RV 357 (Op. 4/4)

Ex. 4.1e. Vivaldi, Concerto in A major for Two Violins, RV 552

Ex. 4.1f. Vivaldi, Concerto in G major for Flute, RV 438, and Cello, RV 414

A four-bar motto immediately raises expectation for an answering four-bar consequent, which may be realized in the simplest way by an immediate repetition of the motto transposed to the dominant, in the older tradition. Yet in fact Vivaldi rarely projects regularity of the motto onto the following phrase, preferring either a shorter answering phrase or, more commonly, a lengthy consequent, extended by Fortspinnung or some other device. These two preferences may be strikingly illustrated by comparison between the mottos of two variant concertos, RV 438 for flute and RV 414 for cello. In the former, the consequent comes to an abrupt halt within bar 7; in the latter, Vivaldi appears to satisfy the listener's expectation for a full cadence in bar 8, but then distorts the regularity by adding another half bar in order to open up the dominant (Ex. 4.1f). Thus regularity of phrase structure was not a central characteristic of Vivaldi's ritornellos.

Turning now to texture, Vivaldi's mottos may be classified in six categories (Table 4.1). Interestingly, the brilliant unison opening so often associated with Vivaldi is limited to a mere 9%. Homophonic textures form much the largest category, yet a significant proportion of mottos still use imitative techniques. Sometimes Vivaldi refers to traditional dissonance-consonance suspensions but mostly imitation is used as sonorous enrichment with no harmonic consequence, as in the constant two-violin exchange in RV 383a (Op. 4/1, see Ex. 4.18). In rare

Table 4.1. Texture of Vivaldi's mottos

Texture	Number	%
Homophonic	169	50%
Imitative counterpoint	67	20%
Free counterpoint	36	11%
Unison	32	9%
Dialogue counterpoint	21	6%
Alternation of unison and homophonic	12	4%

cases the imitation carries on well beyond the head motive, as in RV 316a (Op. 4/6). In those mottos using free counterpoint, two or three equally important motives are superimposed, resulting in such intensive textures as in RV 359 (Op. 9/7), where the two violins constantly interweave in crossing voices. Dialogue mottos, on the other hand, immediately suggest a rhetorical argument on the smallest scale: in the witty motto of RV 228, for example, violins and bass are at first opposed with two contrasting motives, but in bar 3 the violins are immediately won over (Ex. 4.2).

Ex. 4.2. Vivaldi, Violin Concerto in D major, RV 228

The motto, by definition, demands to be reheard. Yet it is not at all necessary that it will be reprised in literal form. Indeed, the very sense of inevitability enables subtle variations to be made to the motto as the movement progresses, revealing the potential of any musical motive to change in certain parameters while being repeated literally in others. Even the absence (or avoidance) of an expected motto can be a powerful tool in articulating the hierarchical structure. Two critical issues therefore arise: (i) how often the motto is reintroduced at crucial structural points in the movement, and (ii) whether it recurs as a literal quotation or in some varied form. Table 4.2 reveals the frequency of various different strategies regarding the articulation of the central ritornellos, strategies which may be grouped together under a number of broad headings.

(1) Motto contributing to unity through repetition at the main structural points
Overall, Vivaldi's preferred strategy was to emphasize two new key areas by heading both central ritornellos with the motto. In the most extreme cases, the motto may be stated literally at the start of every ritornello, including the final

Table 4.2. Vivaldi's articulation of intermediate ritornellos

Melodic articulation	Number	%
Motto contributing to unity through repetition		
Two central ritornellos articulated by motto (R2-R3, or R3a-R3b only)	172	51%
A single intermediate ritornello articulated by motto	34	10%
R2 by motto, R3 by a variant of the motto	9	3%
Motto contributing to hierarchy through selective repetition		
R2 by motto, R3 by another	57	17%
R2 by another, R3 by motto	17	5%
R2 & R3b by motto, R3a by another	5	1%
R2 by variant of motto, R3 by another	2	1%
R3a by motto, R3b by another (no R2)	6	2%
R3a by another, R3b by motto (no R2)	7	2%
R3a & R3b by motto, R3c by another (no R2)	3	1%
Motto marking tonic areas only		
No intermediate ritornello articulated by motto	25	7%

tonic, as has already been illustrated in Chapter 1 with RV 345 (Op. 9/2). Still more intensive are those few cases where the motto also pervades the solos. Albinoni's Op. 9/8 has also been described in Chapter 1 in this connection: a salient Vivaldi example is RV 328, where the motto recurs literally in intermediate ritornellos in v and iv (bars 23 and 52), as well as transformed in S1 and S2, and finally compressed in R4a (Ex. 4.3).

Ex. 4.3. Vivaldi, Violin Concerto in G minor, RV 328

Yet such extreme unity was not Vivaldi's preferred strategy. Indeed, only in eleven cases (3%) do all intermediate ritornellos as well as S1 begin with the motto, and nowhere does Vivaldi go as far as Albinoni in basing every single one of the ritornellos and solos on the motto. His was a dramatic world of transformation and contrast, best represented by the gradual variation of the motto across the ritornellos. Such a procedure has been described in Chapter 1 in connection with RV 317 (Op. 12/1, Ex. 1.12), which is so closely related to RV 328 that they should perhaps be considered as alternative realizations of the rich potential of the beautiful motto. Such gradual variation acts simultaneously both as reference back and as an ongoing process. This is heard still more clearly in a related procedure: increasing stretto as the movement progresses. In the two-violin concerto RV 514, the tightening of the contrapuntal entries across the movement provides both momentum and heightened urgency.

The process of change which the motto, or its absence, effects from one ritornello to the next may be described by Talbot's concept of regression: 'It is, so to speak, development by stripping down rather than by the more usual process of elaboration'.[13] In most Vivaldi concertos the intermediate ritornellos are shorter and less elaborate than the initial ritornello, and in some cases the process of regression includes the final ritornello as well. Still, the term applies specifically to the thematic process, which is frequently balanced by textural and tonal intensification, as in the case of RV 345 (Op. 9/2) discussed in Chapter 1. Here R3a, shorter than R1 by 25%, is nevertheless modulatory and contrapuntal, while the very brief R3b serves to highlight the false reprise and its dramatic rejection.

(2) Motto contributing to hierarchy through selective repetition

If some ritornellos begin with a subsidiary motive from R1 (or with a new motive altogether), while others use the motto, this confirms a hierarchy between the different tonal centres. Vivaldi tends to support R2 with the motto, affording clear priority to the secondary key (usually the dominant). The opposite option of distinguishing R3 with the motto is especially suited for minor-mode movements, which Vivaldi often treated as hovering between two secondary keys. Thus in the A minor concerto for two violins RV 522 (Op. 3/8) the secondary key, C major, is briefly marked in R2 only by neutral figurations (see Ex. 3.15), whereas the motto more powerfully stresses D minor in R3.

Sometimes hierarchy is further emphasized by the selection of a subsidiary motive for one of the ritornellos. Thus in the recorder concerto in A minor RV 445 a well-planned argument between the two secondary centres, C major and E minor, is thematically linked: whereas R2 is strongly linked to R1 by the motto, R3 prefers motive b, with the retention of the original pitch (E minor) realizing the tonal implication from R1 (Table 4.3). Contrast this with the powerful C minor concerto RV 196 (Op. 4/10), where a similar argument is played out, but a different hierarchy results from the deferral of the motto (Table 4.4). This time R2 is based on the secondary motive (the quotation at the same pitch again realizing the tonal implication embedded in R1), but the postponement of the motto to R3 places the dominant on a higher hierarchical level.

---

13   Talbot, *The Finale in Western Instrumental Music*, p. 38.

Table 4.3. Partial timeline of Vivaldi, Recorder Concerto in A minor, RV 445

Function	R1			R2		R3	
Bars	1–6	6–9	9–13	32–34	34–36	49–52	
Key	i	(v)	i	III		v	
Thematic	M+a	b	c	M	c	b	(= 6–9)

Table 4.4. Partial timeline of Vivaldi, Violin Concerto in C minor, RV 196 (Op. 4/10)

Function	R1			R2	R3	
Bars	1–4	5–13	14–24	54–60	75–78	79–85
Key	i	(III)	i	III	v	
Thematic	M	a	b	a (≈5–13)	M	a

(3) The dialectics of two competing mottos
The two main strategies discussed so far are both dependent on the strong realization of the anticipated motto return, or its occasional avoidance in the service of tonal hierarchy. Other strategies reveal Vivaldi's sophistication in rethinking its role so as to create new concepts altogether. One rare option, found in a mere four movements of our sample, is to demarcate ritornello and solo rigorously by allocating each a specialized motto. Thus in RV 249 (Op. 4/8) the solo opens with a motto of its own, quite distinct from the ensuing ritornello motto, and neither contaminates the other as they alternate throughout the movement.

Elsewhere two mottos emerge during the course of a movement, engaging directly in a rhetorical debate. In RV 357 in A minor (Op. 4/4), a brusque opening motto (Ex. 4.4a) is gradually displaced by a more seductive alternative. The motto in powerful unison comprises the entire R2, continuing into the next solo but with a new counterpoint (M2) superimposed (Ex. 4.4b). Gradually this new counterpoint infiltrates the solo until it dominates the ensuing R3a, with the original motto reduced to a subordinate pedal (Ex. 4.4c). M2 similarly opens the next ritornello (R3b) in E minor, but then the principal motto reasserts its personality in forceful unison again, as if confirming that the search for the target key – that is, the dominant minor – has at last been completed. Yet the winner in the argument is still the contrapuntal motive M2 that dominates the recapitulation (Table 4.5).

In the experimental world of Vivaldi's later concertos, it is not surprising to find this idea of dialectical opposition taken to an even further extreme. RV 189 places in stark contrast a portentous Larghetto introduction in C major with a curious ritornello in C minor/major that tensely transforms the repeated quaver motive (Ex. 4.5).[14] It appears that this will be the motto for a separate Allegro movement, and it is indeed used for the next ritornello in A minor (bar 35). Yet the dominant is strongly emphasized in the third ritornello by the reintroduction of the Larghetto material, juxtaposed with the motto in G minor. The recapitulation

---

[14] Included in the autograph collection *La cetra* (1728) and published in 1735.

Ex. 4.4. Vivaldi, Violin Concerto in A minor, RV 357 (Op. 4/4)

Table 4.5. Ritornellos in Vivaldi, Violin Concerto in A minor, RV 357 (Op. 4/4)

Function	R1	R2	R3a	R3b		R4
Bar	1	23	37	52	57	70
Key	i	iv	VI	v		i
Motto	M1	M1	M2	M2	M1	M2

involves the return of the entire Larghetto section, with the Allegro motto reduced to an incidental appearance in the solo (bar 90). Thus what appeared to be a separate introduction has so infiltrated the Allegro as to supplant the motto and at the same time frame the entire movement. The listener is initially invited to question the very essence of how a concerto is expected to start, and, later on, to contemplate the relationship of the opening to the rest of the movement. Material initially presented as unconnected and diverse is progressively integrated into the

Ex. 4.5. Vivaldi, Violin Concerto in C major, RV 189

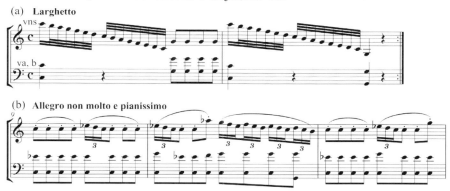

movement's fabric and unfolding argument, in a way that Haydn was to explore later in the 'London' symphonies.

(4) The motto frame and the vanishing motto
The power of the motto's demand to be reheard creates an expectation for the listener which does not have to be fulfilled. Thus the motto may not appear at all in the central part of the movement, as in RV 232, considered in Chapter 1, where the motto marks only the surrounding tonic frame while other motives from R1 articulate the internal ritornellos. Vivaldi used this strategy in only four concertos of the sample, so this option must be considered an interesting experiment that he ultimately deemed unsatisfactory. A more startling option is for the motto to vanish altogether. In general, the listener would surely expect the motto to reappear somewhere in R4, whether at the crucial point of the tonic restatement or later on in R4b (see Chapter 6). However, the statistics of the sample offer a surprise on this issue, since the motto appears nowhere within the final tonic area in as many as 105 movements (31%). Among these are many examples where the motto has already been downgraded, even to the point of extinction.

As has already been suggested, many of Vivaldi's later concertos experiment with the nature of the motto itself, questioning the very concept of the concerto opening and inviting the listener to reflect on how a concerto should begin. In such concertos the opening material is bound to take on a very different function in the movement as a whole. RV 281, for example, begins uniquely with a long cello solo (*forte molto*) under hushed *pianissimo* chords; but clearly this would be quite unsuitable to open subsequent ritornellos, and the cello motive is relegated to brief cadential reminiscences.

Still more radical are those cases where the opening motive never returns at all. Such a strategy undermines the very identification of such a motive as 'motto': perhaps a more appropriate definition in these cases would be the 'affective title' of the movement. Often this strategy reflects the nature of the opening ritornello itself: questioning and probing rather than confidently continuous; or contrasting grandiosity with more lyrical, hesitant responses; or disrupted by rests and fermatas, dissolutions into *pianissimo*, unexpected minorizations, and so on. Such an opening may not be suitable for later ritornellos, which are required to look both ways: to provide both a culmination to the previous solo as well as new impetus for further departures. In any case, it would be normal for Vivaldi to iron out the discontinuities as the movement progresses, as part of a rhetorical strategy for the movement as a whole.

The small group of fourteen concertos (4% of the sample) which fall into this category are among Vivaldi's most individual. All the 'affective titles' have the makings of memorable mottos, yet they never return as such. For example, the presumably late concerto RV 367 ('Allegro, ma poco a poco') begins with a powerful unison declaration;[15] but this impression is dissipated immediately by a nervous echo of the last bar, which is followed by a disjointed succession of discrete and unconnected motives (Ex. 4.6). Ensuing ritornellos are based entirely on motives a and b, eschewing the pomposity of the first bars, which indeed could perhaps not serve as anything other than an opening. A similar collapse of musical coherence occurs in RV 296, where the striking inverse 'Mannheim rocket' breaks off after a few bars and never returns.

Ex. 4.6. Vivaldi, Violin Concerto in B♭ major, RV 367

The virtuoso and capricious bassoon concerto RV 492 begins with an assertive leaping octave figure; but within seconds the momentum has collapsed entirely into a *pianissimo* descending scale, as if the movement is already exhausted after only three bars. This impression of closure is confirmed by the whimsical

---

[15] Regarding the dating of surviving parts (c1737), see Everett, 'Vivaldi's Marginal Markings', p. 253.

reappearance at the end of the movement of the descending scale, lone survivor of the opening motto. The movement's tonal scheme (I-vi-ii-I), lacking any ritornello in the dominant, suits the witty, 'negative' treatment of the motto.

An instructive further example is provided by RV 372 in B♭ (Ex. 4.7). Here there is no such evident musical collapse, and the listener surely expects the opening motive to prove a regular motto throughout the movement. Yet in fact it never recurs, with other motives taking over its structural function. The identity of this motto with that of RV 345 (Op. 9/2), discussed in Chapter 1, raises an important issue. Is there anything inherent in the nature of a motto that will guide its behaviour through the movement? The utterly different treatment in the two concertos – one where the motto is all-pervasive, the other where it is abandoned entirely – provides its own answer.

Ex. 4.7. Vivaldi, Violin Concerto in B♭ major, RV 372

What this example does suggest is that Vivaldi regarded certain stock motto openings as a challenge to his own creative imagination, discovering varied ways in which they could be handled. For example, the opening ritornellos of RV 210 in D major (Op. 8/11) and RV 176 in C major have so much in common that they seem to represent a deliberate exploration of the different possibilities of the same motto. In RV 176 the motto – three hammer-strokes followed by rhythmic acceleration – is presented homophonically over leaping octaves in straight and decorated form (Ex. 4.8a). A homophonic presentation of the motto also occurs in RV 210, but here it is delayed until bar 13 by a complete four-part fugal exposition (Ex. 4.8b; compare Ex. 4.1a). When it does arrive, the motto is disguised within the violin lines in parallel thirds, as if to avoid the simplest 'ideal' presentation. Both ritornellos then lead to similar *minore* phrases in concertino texture, further attesting to the close relationship of the two movements.

Such a contrast also occurs in a further concerto that requires to be brought into the comparison. RV 582 in D major is a grandiose solo concerto with double orchestra, written for Anna Maria to perform at the Pietà in the mid-1720s.[16] Most of the solos are simply purloined wholesale from RV 210, but the motto appears to be quite different, as if to disguise the expedient self-borrowing (Ex. 4.8c). Closer examination, however, reveals a connection here too: the unison motto of RV 582 could be seen as a distended and pompous version of RV 210, which at the same time incorporates the quaver motive from RV 176. Whether the hidden similarity of the motto sparked Vivaldi to incorporate the solo material from RV 210, or whether it was pre-planned, remains unclear. However it does mean that when the actual motto from RV 210 turns up later on in RV 582 (bars 70 and 95, for example), it sounds perfectly at home.

The three concertos are therefore closely linked by shared material, but they are quite different in character. RV 176 is light and evanescent, with solo

---

[16] Talbot, 'Anna Maria's Partbook'.

Ex. 4.8a. Vivaldi, Violin Concerto in C major, RV 176

Ex. 4.8b. Vivaldi, Violin Concerto in D major, RV 210 (Op. 8/11)

Ex. 4.8c. Vivaldi, Violin Concerto in D major, RV 582

evocations of birdsong familiar from the 'Spring' concerto; RV 210 is more serious in its fugal writing, yet this is set against brilliantly virtuosic solos; while RV 582 is an impressive double-orchestra concerto that adumbrates the same virtuosity. This suggests that too many implications flowed from similar material for them to be fully realized in any single concerto.

The Initial Ritornello

Michael Talbot has described the initial ritornello in Vivaldi's concertos as 'a well-rounded musical entity, almost a piece within a piece, whose own pattern of modulation may paraphrase in miniature that of the whole movement'.[17] The 'piece within a piece' implies a number of attributes: an arresting musical personality, with a series of vivid musical characterizations; a self-contained musical entity, made up of discrete units; a well-rounded conception with opening and closing ideas, often surrounding a middle section that gives a foretaste of tonal departure. Paul Everett has defined the basic requirements for the 'right type' of initial ritornello: 'They are modular so that they may be broken apart; they are lengthy so that they may be shortened.'[18] The modular nature of Vivaldi's

---

[17] *Vivaldi*, pp. 110–11.
[18] *Vivaldi: 'The Four Seasons'*, p. 33.

Ex. 4.9. Vivaldi, Violin Concertos in G minor, RV 317 (Op. 12/1) and RV 328

ritornellos is evident in his frequent borrowing of self-contained phrases from one movement to another, as in the G minor concertos RV 317 (Op. 12/1) and RV 328. The similarity of the mottos has already been remarked, and indeed the two concertos actually converge in the consequent phrases (Ex. 4.9; see Exx. 1.12 and 4.3). All but the shortest opening periods link together several modules, which can be reordered and reassembled at will in the later stages of the movement: furthermore these discrete modules are designed to serve equally well at the front, middle or end of a musical period.[19] Both of the consequent phrases illustrated in Ex. 4.9 are fully capable of doing duty as the opening of later ritornellos; and as we have seen in Chapter 1 in connection with RV 232, the choice of which module from R1 is to head each ritornello contributes strongly to the sense of hierarchy.

At the same time, harmonic design plays a major role in building the ritornello as a self-contained musical unit. Vivaldi exploited a diverse array of options, as can be seen in Table 4.6. The most conspicuous outcome of these statistics is that purely diatonic non-sequential ritornellos are in a minority across both early and late groups. Such ritornellos are generally short, such as the festive 10-bar unison that opens RV 519 (Op. 3/5); but despite the harmonic limitations they can be expanded using a variety of techniques. Thus in RV 178 (Op. 8/12), the 2+2-bar motto lands on the dominant, which then becomes a six-bar pedal; and the return of the tonic is obscured by a melodic continuity that carries the entire period to 19 bars altogether. The unusually long opening ritornello of the late RV 207 (Op. 11/1), which spans 27% of the entire movement, is a tour de force of sonorous prolongation of I-V chords in a continuous surface flow of semiquavers (Ex. 4.10).

A more elaborate construction is the tripartite structure identified in Chapter 1, consisting of an opening phrase establishing the tonic (Vordersatz), a passage of harmonic contrast (such as sequential Fortspinnung), and a closing cadential phrase in the tonic (Nachsatz). Comparatively rare in Vivaldi, however, is the further stage of including within R1 a closed area in the secondary key, creating a truly self-contained 'piece within a piece'. The concerto for oboe and bassoon RV 545 has a tripartite R1 that clearly differentiates a central section in the dominant. But this strategy occurs in only 18% of the sample: evidently Vivaldi, while committed to the expansion of R1, was reluctant to dilute the impact of the first directional modulation in S1 by anticipating it here.

---

[19] Michael Talbot has drawn our attention to the *concerto a quattro* RV 156, where the motto is identical with the closing phrase of the ritornello in RV 103.

Table 4.6 Harmonic structure of R1 in Vivaldi

Harmonic structure of R1	Number	%
Contains a middle section with chromatic progressions (such as secondary dominants) or diatonic sequential progressions	181	54%
Entirely in tonic area with diatonic harmony, non-sequential	82	24%
Contains a middle section in another key, perhaps preceded or followed by sequential progressions	61	18%
Ends on non-tonic chord (may be modulatory)	13	4%

Ex. 4.10. Vivaldi, Violin Concerto in D major, RV 207 (Op. 11/1)

Rare but still significant are those opening ritornellos that do not end on the tonic chord, especially those that decisively modulate, requiring the ensuing solo to restart from the tonic. This strategy is intrinsically implicative, for such a unrequited modulation either predicts a later tonal event, or else compensates for an anticipated key that is in fact never realized. In RV 332 in G minor (Op. 8/8), the consequent abruptly shifts to B♭ major, initiating a sequential Fortspinnung towards a strong affirmation of D minor at the close of the ritornello (Ex. 4.11). The ensuing solo, however, selects B♭ major, which is nicely confirmed by R2 through an exact quotation of the consequent of R1, extended this time to cadence in B♭ major. Thus R1 implies two options – relative major and dominant – whereas R2 makes the choice, realizing the former as the principal secondary key.

A quite exceptional and unsettling example of the modulatory R1 is to be found in RV 344, where a solo fanfare in A major is unexpectedly succeeded by an unstable ritornello that settles on C♯ minor. The following solo restarts hesitantly from A major, but the tonal prediction is realized in the next ritornello in stable C♯ minor; and this section then provides the thematic material for all subsequent ritornellos, including even the concluding R4 in the tonic. Such manifest avoidance of any tonal stability in R1 – further emphasized by its lack of a sustainable motto – is unique in our Vivaldi sample.

Ex. 4.11. Vivaldi, Violin Concerto in G minor, RV 332 (Op. 8/8)

Enter the Soloist

The sense of innovation and excitement embodied in the new virtuoso concerto may be difficult for us to recreate now. But we can be sure that the soloist's first individual statement must have been eagerly awaited, so that its timing and character are crucial issues. Still, Vivaldi retained a balance between tutti and solo, and while the soloist outshines the tutti with brilliant figurations, the ritornellos respond by richer thematic material. The statistics show Vivaldi's decisive preference for starting the movement with a ritornello (298 movements, 96%). Nevertheless the small group of movements heralded by the soloist raises interesting issues, for such openings are usually much more than a mere solo flourish, affecting the proportions and tonal/thematic structure of the movement in diverse ways. On four occasions, Vivaldi reverses the ritornello-solo order, the opening solo providing the material for subsequent solos that alternate with ritornellos based on their own motto. The historical background to this reversal of roles has been discussed in Chapter 3 in connection with RV 249 (Op. 4/8). In other cases, the opening solo clearly functions as an introduction, but nevertheless recurs later in the movement. In RV 229, a brilliant showpiece for Anna Maria, the initial solo motive cheekily interrupts R1 but is then lost to view until its return in high relief to mark the recapitulation. The exuberant two-violin elaboration of a D major chord that opens RV 204 (Op. 4/11) provides material for ritornellos as well as solos.

Without such radical means, another way the soloist can make his presence felt before the true first solo (S1) is by an interruption or change of texture within R1. It is rare for Vivaldi to include genuine solo passages here; but in nineteen movements (6%) he includes trio sections in concertino texture. Apparently a reminder of the older concerto grosso tradition, concertino phrases appear occasionally in earlier concertos, but the device persists into later works such as RV 232 discussed in Chapter 1 – and, indeed, it was also exploited in the early symphony. These trios serve not only to extend the ritornello and provide contrasting material for future development, but also to give a foretaste of the new texture to come with S1. Short interpolations flow easily out of the string texture of the violin concertos, but a string concertino passage appears also in a bassoon concerto, RV 481, where it surrounds a brief solo interjection.

An interesting example that deliberately blurs the edges of R1 and S1 is provided by RV 263a (Op. 9/4). Here a set of archetypal hammer-strokes is obsessively reiterated, eight times in all, separated at first by brief concertino passages. But after the fifth time the soloist impatiently interrupts, gradually assuming a more dominating presence until eventually the true S1 begins. In the vast majority of concertos, however, it is not until the first main solo that the soloist is heard as an individual participant, and it is to this dramatic entrance that we now turn our attention.

The Actors Interact

How the soloist enters after R1 and the thematic relationship of this solo with the preceding ritornello are of crucial impact. Indeed this may be seen as the primary rhetorical aspect of the ritornello form, the essence of the engagement between tutti and solo. As to be expected, Vivaldi explored a wide range of thematic relationships (Table 4.7). Much the largest group comprises movements where ritornello and solo are apparently quite contrasting. Yet one must bear in mind that the distinction between 'variant or ornamentation of the motto' and 'different material' is often not clear, as music has an inherent propensity to differ in some parameters while simultaneously concurring in others. Generally Vivaldi retains a certain unity in some parameters, even when ritornello and solo seem unconnected. Thus in RV 244 (Op. 12/2) the expressive tutti motto and the opening motive of S1 sound on first hearing quite distinct (Ex. 4.12). Yet even a superficial analysis suggests that the solo motive is a melodic filling-in of the descending fifth of the motto, while at the same time the entire 5-bar phrase represents an expansion of the original two bars. Even when the solo motive is clearly different from the motto, Vivaldi may relate the two sections through orchestral counterpoint. In the powerful 'Il sospetto', RV 199, the motto presents the two violin parts in counterpoint; S1 replaces the first violin with a new motive, yet the second violin persists (Ex. 4.13).

In merely five movements Vivaldi rejects any shade of thematic affinity between R1 and S1, with each maintaining its own dominating rhythmic pattern. Remarkably, two of these are from *The Four Seasons*, the exceptional and illustrative 'Summer' and 'Winter' concertos. Even in such cases the separation need not persist throughout the movement: in RV 352 (Op. 9/5), for example, the rhythmic dispute between *gavotta* and *giga* rhythms does not continue into the subsequent solos. The cello concerto RV 409, on the other hand, provides the most extreme contrast, with all cello solos in Adagio tempo and all ritornellos in Allegro molto, apparently an experiment in combining elements of the slow introduction with the Allegro ritornello concept – but deliberately disruptively, for the roles are precisely reversed in the following movement.

Table 4.7. Thematic relationship between S1 and R1 in Vivaldi

Thematic material in S1	Number	%
Different material in R1 and S1		
Different thematic material in R1 and S1	182	54%
S1 has figuration only	13	4%
R1 and S1 each have distinct and prevailing rhythmic values	5	1%
R1 and S1 share material		
S1 starts with a variant or ornamentation of the motto, continues with different material	48	14%
S1 starts with the motto unvaried, continues with different material	26	8%
Last motive of R1 repeated as the first motive of S1	20	6%
S1 starts with middle motives of R1	17	5%
S1 starts with the motto, continues with new and other ritornello motives	8	2%
New material in S1 against R1 material in counterpoint	6	2%
S1 starts with an unrelated motive, continues with a variant of the motto	7	2%
S1 starts with figuration, continues with middle or closing R1 motives	3	1%
Different material in R1 and S1, until S1 closes with the motto	1	1%
S1 starts with the motto, continues with new and other ritornello motives, closes with the motto	1	1%

Ex. 4.12. Vivaldi, Violin Concerto in D minor, RV 244 (Op.12/2)

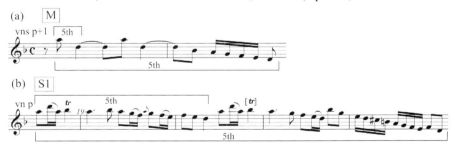

In chronological terms, it is not possible to argue either for a strong trend towards independence of solo from tutti, nor conversely towards an increasing thematic integration between R1 and S1. The two datable groups both show an even fifty-fifty split in this regard. Among those solos that open with a reference to the motto, a literal quotation of the entire motto occurs in only a very small number: these include RV 356 (Op. 3/6) and RV 242 (Op. 8/7), whose familiarity has perhaps overshadowed modern perceptions. In numerous other cases the solo

Ex. 4.13. Vivaldi, Violin Concerto in C minor, RV 199 ('Il sospetto')

Ex. 4.14. Vivaldi, Bassoon Concerto in B♭ major, RV 504

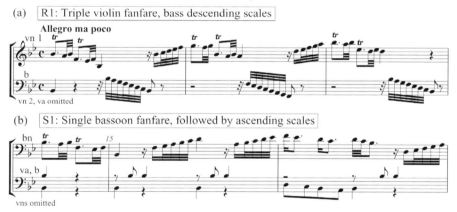

branches off in the course of the motto, as in the imaginative alteration of the harmonic-rhythmic contour in the bassoon concerto RV 504: the solo prefers only a single statement of the fanfare motive, altering the harmonic rhythm and concentrating on an inversion of the bass line (Ex. 4.14).

Much more common is ornamentation or variation of the motto by which the solo comments on the motto not only idiomatically (in terms of instrumental technique) but also rhetorically (in terms of its own individuality). Thus in the dramatic and arresting RV 196 (Op. 4/10) S1 interprets the rhetoric of contrasting rhythms in the motto and decides in favour of the opening rhythm (Ex. 4.15). The emotionally related RV 324, on the other hand, modifies the decisive motto into a lyrical outpouring (Ex. 4.16).

A quite different strategy, used in a substantial twenty cases, is to repeat the

Ex. 4.15. Vivaldi, Violin Concerto in C minor, RV 196 (Op. 4/10)

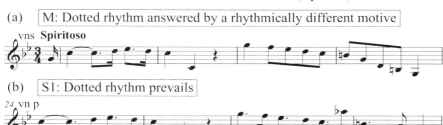

Ex. 4.16. Vivaldi, Violin Concerto in G minor, RV 324 (Op. 6/1)

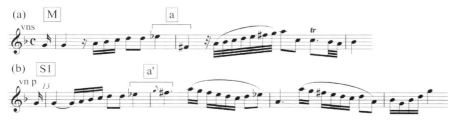

Ex. 4.17. Vivaldi, Violin Concerto in D major, RV 217

last motive of R1 as the first of S1, creating a melodic continuity across the textural change. A sophisticated version of this occurs in RV 217 where R1 closes with a new motive in minor, which S1 immediately transforms into major (Ex. 4.17). A similar blurring of the interface between ritornello and solo is achieved quite differently in those few concertos that repeat the opening tutti motto just where the solo is expected. The historical background to this device, and its usage in Albinoni's Op. 5, have already been described in Chapter 3. Already by the time of RV 383a (Op. 4/1) it may be heard as playing deliberately against the expectation of the powerful and unmistakeable entrance of the soloist. Here R1 reaches a full close, but (instead of allowing the soloist to start) the ritornello intervenes with a restatement of the motto; the soloist belatedly shuts this down with the assistance of the concertino group (Ex. 4.18).

Ex. 4.18. Vivaldi, Violin Concerto in B♭ major, RV 383a (Op. 4/1)

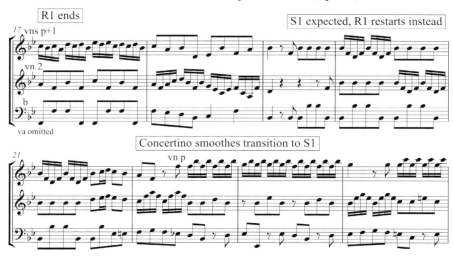

The Solo Unfolds

Vivaldi develops the first solo in myriad different ways. At one extreme is the continuous unified figuration such as dominates every solo in RV 300 (Op. 9/10) – a typical feature of the 'sonority concerto' defined in Chapter 3. At the other extreme are those concertos where the solo changes motivic material every few bars, such as in the late RV 371 in B♭ major. The succession of variants and new motives closely articulates the rhetoric of S1, where the dominant is rejected in favour of a modulation to D minor, which is strongly established well before the ensuing ritornello (Ex. 4.19). In such late concertos, moderate tempo designations (such as Andante molto or Allegro ma poco) allow for highly florid melodies rich with triplets and ornamentation, as well as the possibility of a kaleidoscopic journey through highly contrasting motives.[20]

In some cases Vivaldi explores contrasts and interrelationships between sections in a more complex and sophisticated manner. RV 278 in E minor tosses the listener between stormy outbursts and plaintive, plangent melodies (Ex. 4.20). The mood is set in the opening bars: a ferocious Allegro molto bursts in, but is abruptly cancelled in favour of a *pianissimo* sigh motive, marked Largo. On a second attempt, the storm is succeeded by the main Andantino, a cantabile melody which is, however, prone to tempestuous interruptions throughout the entire movement. As often in the late repertoire, the soloist rises above all this drama, in favour of an elegantly spun melodic line: a long-drawn florid cantabile composed of ornaments, yearning sighs, whimsical plaints and curlicues, and subtly expressive varieties of bowing. Even here, though, there is a brief reference to the storm at bar 29.

---

[20] For discussion of the later style and such tempo designations, together with speculation about dating, see Fertonani, *La musica strumentale*, pp. 85–9.

Ex. 4.19. Vivaldi, Violin Concerto in B♭ major, RV 371

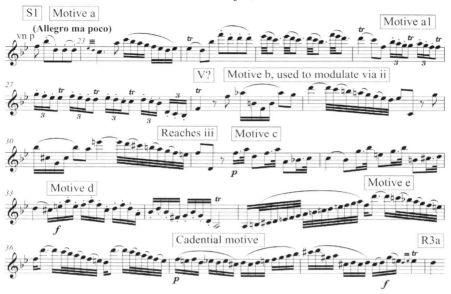

Ex. 4.20. Vivaldi, Violin Concerto in E minor, RV 278

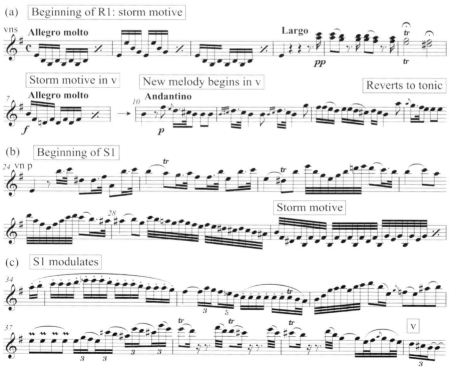

The question immediately arises as to whether the course of the first solo is in some way determined either by the implications of R1 or by a preconceived goal in R2. It is, after all, here that the direction of the movement is ordained, most obviously in the tonal move initiated by the soloist, but also more generally in terms of the way the rhetorical argument is set. In the absence of detailed knowledge of Vivaldi's working methods or of surviving sketches, these are deep waters. Certainly there are many examples where the tonal trajectory of the solo is already foreshadowed by R1; and some evidence suggests that Vivaldi might on occasion work as far as the second ritornello before filling in the intervening solo, or even deciding on the solo instrument. Stavria Kotsoni-Brown's analysis of the autograph of the cello concerto RV 398 indicates that he first completed R1, outlined the bars to make up S1 (twelve, the same number as R1) and then wrote out R2: only then did he settle on the cello as soloist.[21] This does not of itself mean that he had the entire concerto mapped out as he began to write; but it does suggest that he did not simply work from R1 to R2 according to the inspiration of the moment. Rather (as we have proposed in Chapter 1) short-term invention and long-term planning coexisted and nurtured each other.

The Tonal Route of S1

After R1 has established the home key of the movement, and the soloist has asserted his presence in an opening gesture, the essential function of S1 is to execute a modulation to the secondary key. Vivaldi's modulatory processes are extremely varied. In the major mode, modulation to the dominant is natural and easy: in RV 345 (Op. 9/2) the transition from tonic to dominant is almost imperceptible (see Ex. 1.2). Indeed it is so easy that Vivaldi sometimes struggles to prevent a resolution back to the tonic, as we have seen in RV 232 (Ex. 1.9). This can itself be exploited to advantage (as in RV 252) with a series of tentative moves towards the dominant, each of which slides back to the tonic, until eventual confirmation in R2 – the new key being all the more strongly established for being hard won.

But where a peripheral key forms the first target the move is more decisive, since it is less easily reversed; and (lacking the inevitability of the dominant) the establishment of a peripheral key usually involves a more elaborate process through a series of temporary stages. A common procedure is the stepwise sequence. In RV 359 in B♭ major (Op. 9/7) S1 retains the tonic for nearly half of its duration (bars 25–36), before simply raising a solo motive by step to C minor and then D minor, which is confirmed by a cadential passage leading into the next ritornello. Here there is no dominant at all, and indeed the expected secondary key is eschewed altogether in this movement. Another stepwise sequence approaches the dominant from below but then overshoots (IV-V-vi), again resulting in a peripheral key for the second ritornello: in RV 180 (Op. 8/6) this very sequence had already been predicted in R1, which thereby influences the direction of the movement as a whole.

[21] 'The Solo Cello Concertos of Antonio Vivaldi', pp. 215–18.

Ex. 4.21. Vivaldi, Violin Concerto in B minor, RV 390

Such tonal debate within S1 is particularly common in the minor mode, where the option of two or even three possible secondary keys comes into play. Sometimes the solo clearly establishes one secondary key before diverting to an alternative for the ensuing ritornello. The late B minor concerto RV 390, meditative and introverted, features a truly rhetorical debate between relative major and dominant, illustrated in Ex. 4.21. The very short modulatory passages bring into sharp relief the conflict between the two optional secondary key areas.

Vivaldi usually orientates the listener through a motivic change where the modulatory process commences; and sometimes the new direction is reinforced by a change of accompaniment, such as from upper strings to continuo only. Even stronger emphasis results when S1 is bisected by a brief tonic ritornello (R1b): in this case the modulation is introduced not just by a motivic or minor textural change, but by the full force of a ritornello. The resulting pattern reflects two interlocking parameters (Table 4.8). All of these devices are used in the well-known two-violin concerto, RV 522 (Op. 3/8): S1 is interrupted by R1b, heralding the impending modulation, which is then strongly emphasized by a flamboyant solo over a new accompaniment (bar 30).

Table 4.8. The effect of S1a and R1b

R1a	S1a	R1b	S1b	R2
		divided solo		
	I			

A second tonic ritornello (R1b) has a quite different effect when S1a already makes a strong modulation, leading the listener to expect confirmation by R2 in the new key; but instead R1b rejects the first modulation, restating the tonic and forcing the soloist to start a further modulatory process. In RV 259 in E♭ major (Op. 6/2), which follows exactly this pattern, S1a apparently establishes the dominant only for it to be dismissed by R1b at bar 25; only much later at bar 54, after an intervening ritornello in vi, is the dominant finally established with a ritornello of its own. In this case the key originally suggested by S1a eventually proves to be a target later in the movement; alternatively it may never be realized subsequently, as in RV 318 in G minor (Op. 6/3). This movement presents a subtle variant, for it appears at first that B♭ major has been accepted and that R2 already starts in this key at bar 50 (Ex. 4.22). But by cunning reharmonization the ritornello imperceptibly reverts to G minor, and to segments directly quoted from R1. The rhetorical meaning of this tonal process, which is so well supported motivically, is a search for the secondary key in the minor mode. The first choice of the relative major is rejected by the tutti, never to return, while the next solo makes a new departure which successfully confirms the dominant. The whole procedure therefore assumes a significant tonal function, as will be discussed in a broader context in the next chapter.

Ex. 4.22. Vivaldi, Violin Concerto in G minor, RV 318 (Op. 6/3)

The frequency of the various options for S1a and R1b is analysed in Table 4.9. This is one of the few cases where a comparison of the early and late Vivaldi repertoires illuminates a radical change in conception. In the early group Vivaldi strongly favours the textural articulation provided by R1b (60%, including a modulatory S1a in 17%). In the late group its frequency has dropped to a mere 18%, and the modulatory S1a has virtually disappeared.

Table 4.9. S1a and R1b in Vivaldi

Pattern of R1 and S1	Number	%
R1–S1 only (no R1b)	246	73%
R1a–S1a in tonic–R1b in tonic	44	13%
Non-modulatory textural contrast (such as concertino or short solo) contained within R1	21	6%
R1a–S1a (modulates to a key which *is not* realized later in the movement)–R1b in tonic	14	4%
R1a–S1a (modulates to a key which *is* realized later in the movement)–R1b in tonic	12	4%

The actors have thus initiated the drama. The tonic has been established and tonal departure has commenced. The diversity of options that Vivaldi explored in these early stages opens up a whole new array of possible moves, sharply increasing in number at the next stage of the movement. Already the choice of options is highly implicative, with each selection opening up its own range of potential realizations.

CHAPTER 5

Vivaldi Modulando

The presentation of the first ritornello as an enclosed unit leads the listener to expect a contrasting instability, consisting of periods modulating to and establishing secondary and peripheral keys. The firmest establishment of a new key results from a high degree of coordination of parameters, such as when the new key is confirmed by a strongly anticipated perfect cadence, followed by a tonally closed period; supported by a textural change, such as the onset of a ritornello; and articulated by a well-defined motive, typically a restatement of the motto. The new key may then stretch well into an ensuing solo before the modulatory process is resumed. At the other extreme, a more temporary key area may be briefly established by only one or two of these parameters, such as a perfect cadence unsupported by motto or textural change, after which the modulatory process resumes immediately.

Clearly among these parameters the duration of stable key areas, measured in proportion to the full length of the movement, is an important factor. A movement may consist of long stable areas, bridged by only brief modulatory transitions; or alternatively a tonic frame may enclose a highly unstable central section, with many lightly articulated keys soon abandoned. Hierarchy of tonal centres was at the heart of eighteenth-century tonal language. Yet for all that it was soon to be rationalized acoustically by theorists such as Rameau, this hierarchy could not be taken for granted in terms of the listener's aural experience but had to be made manifest by compositional procedures.

The promotion of a key to the status of secondary centre immediately relegates the succeeding keys to the peripheral, possibly with their own internal hierarchy. These harmonic moves assume the role of rhetorical operations, frequently expressing doubt, search, rejection or compensation. Obviously the first new key has the initial advantage of temporal priority in the movement, yet it may be only briefly stressed; and a later peripheral area more strongly privileged by having its own stable ritornello and by motivic emphasis. Thus in the bassoon concerto in G major RV 492, S1 achieves a full modulation to the dominant at bar 18, predicting the arrival of R2 in D major. Yet an interrupted cadence one bar later unexpectedly re-routes the modulation to E minor, which is confirmed by a ritornello (bars 22–25). Consequently the dominant covers a mere 4% of the movement, whereas the submediant spans 14% and is further supported by a ritornello. Vivaldi could expect the listener to predict the dominant as the target of the first departure, not only on the basis of the initial modulation but also by calling on past experience. Instead, the submediant is highlighted by a full ritornello and by long duration –

making it not an alternative secondary degree but, on the contrary, creating a frustration of expectation.

The distinction between the mere suggestion of a key by a secondary dominant and a true tonal centre is intrinsically vague; indeed a more Schenkerian approach would not recognize the significance of what used to be termed 'passing modulations'. Yet it has become clear that short-term tonal articulations can contribute significantly to the overall argument of a ritornello movement. Therefore, in the process of defining tonal schemes, we have considered any degree that receives special support as a new key area, a point of arrival, however brief (while ignoring individual links in a continuous sequential pattern). Simply to subsume brief arrivals within a larger overall tonal progression may cloud the subtle points of the composer's decision-making process, so we always opted for more keys rather than fewer. Indeed, we would suggest that it is an important aspect of the listening experience to recognize that modulations can be identified at several different levels, from large-scale structural goals to more localized moves; and that the constant process of interaction between these levels – including prediction and reminiscence – forms a crucial element of this experience.

Tonal Schemes

As with chess openings, the first move away from the tonic is limited. The composer is faced with seven available degrees, if one includes both raised and flattened sevenths (certain chromatic degrees, such as ♭II, were occasionally used elsewhere, but never as first target). Thereafter the number of possible routes expands at a prodigious rate. Our analysis of the full sample of ritornello movements in the present book has revealed an astonishing array of well over 200 tonal schemes: Vivaldi's immense repertoire alone features ninety-eight of them. Their sheer number suggests that the emerging tonal language, based on progression away from and back to the tonic, encouraged composers to explore and experiment, eventually settling on a few schemes which they regarded as normative, or else continuing to search for new strategies. As will be shown in the course of the discussion, decisions about tonal schemes clearly characterize individual composers.

Table 5.1 analyzes the frequency of tonal schemes in our sample of 337 Vivaldi concertos. The large array suggests several levels of classification:

(1) major (Table 5.1a) and minor (Table 5.1b);
(2) circuit and pendulum (left and right columns, correlating parallel or similar options such as I-V-vi-I and I-V-I-vi-I);
(3) the first move away from the tonic, resulting in large groups such as I-V-x-I;
(4) number of intermediate key areas;
(5) frequency of individual tonal schemes.

The more detailed sub-classifications apply only to the large Vivaldi tables, but the same internal order will be preserved in subsequent smaller tables.

Vivaldi's clear preference for major over minor represented the initial step of a process that was to grant the major mode a normative status in mid- and late-

Table 5.1a. Vivaldi's tonal schemes in major

Circuit		Pendulum	
Tonal scheme	**Number**	**Tonal scheme**	**Number**
Group A: I-V-x-I			
Subgroup A.1: I-V-vi-x-I			
I-V-vi-I	47	I-V-I-vi-I I-V-I-V-vi-I	1 3
I-V-vi-iii-I	17	I-V-I-vi-iii-I I-V-I-vi-V-iii-I	4 1
I-V-vi-ii-I	6		
I-V-vi-IV-I	1	I-V-I-vi-IV-I I-V-I-vi-v-IV-I	1 1
I-V-vi-ii-iii-I	2		
I-V-vi-iii-IV-I	1		
Subgroup A.2: I-V-iii-x-I			
I-V-iii-I	32	I-V-I-iii-I I-V-I-V-iii-I	3 2
I-V-iii-vi-I	24	I-V-I-iii-vi-I I-V-iii-I-vi-I	2 2
I-V-iii-V-I	4	I-V-I-iii-V-I	1
I-V-iii-ii-I	2		
I-V-iii-IV-I	1		
I-V-iii-vi-ii-I	2		
I-V-iii-ii-vi-I	1		
Subgroup A.3: I-V-ii-x-I			
I-V-ii-vi-I	6		
I-V-ii-vi-iii-I	1	I-V-I-ii-vi-iii-I	1
Subgroup A.4: I-V-IV-x-I			
I-V-IV-vi-I	1	I-V-I-IV-vi-iii-I I-V-I-IV-vi-I-iii-I	1 1
Subgroup A.5: I-V-vii-x-I			
		I-V-vii-I-vi-V-I	1

Tonal scheme	Number	Tonal scheme	Number
Subgroup A.6: $I\text{-}V\text{-}^{v}\!/V\text{-}x\text{-}I$			
$I\text{-}V\text{-}^{v}\!/V\text{-}iii\text{-}I$	1		
Subgroup A.7: I-V-I			
I-V-I	6		
Group B: I-vi-x-I			
I-vi-I	1		
I-vi-iii-I	16		
I-vi-IV-I	3	I-vi-I-IV-I	2
I-vi-V-I	1	I-vi-I-V-I	1
I-vi-ii-iii-I	3		
I-vi-iii-V-I	2		
I-vi-iii-vi-I	1		
I-vi-IV-iii-I	1		
Group C: I-iii-x-I			
I-iii-I	1		
I-iii-vi-I	6		
I-iii-ii-I	1		
I-iii-V-I	2		
I-iii-ii-vi-I	1		
I-iii-V-vi-I	2	I-iii-I-iii-V-vi-I	1
I-iii-V-ii-I	1		
I-iii-V-ii-vi-I	1		
Group D: I-ii-x-I			
I-ii-vi-iii-I	1		
I-ii-vi-iv-I	1		
I-ii-vi-V-I	1		
Group E: I-IV-x-I			
I-IV-ii-vi-I	1		

Tonal scheme	Number	Tonal scheme	Number
Group F: I-vii-I			
I-vii-I	1		
Total concertos in major	232		
Number of tonal schemes in major	57		

Table 5.1b. Vivaldi's tonal schemes in minor

Circuit		Pendulum	
Tonal scheme	**Number**	**Tonal scheme**	**Number**
Group A: i-v-x-i			
Subgroup A.1: i-v-VI-x-i			
i-v-VI-i	3	i-v-i-VI-i	1
Subgroup A.2: i-v-III-x-i			
i-v-III-i	10	i-v-i-III-i i-v-i-v-III-i	1 1
i-v-III-iv-i	5	i-v-i-III-iv-i i-v-i-III-i-iv-i	1 1
i-v-III-iv-VI-i	2		
Subgroup A.4: i-v-iv-x-i			
i-v-iv-i	8	i-v-i-iv-i	2
i-v-iv-VI-i	2		
i-v-iv-♭VII-i	1		
Subgroup A.5: i-v-♭VII-x-i			
i-v-♭VII-i	3	i-v-i-♭VII-i	1
i-v-♭VII-III-i	1	i-v-i-♭VII-III-i	1
i-v-♭VII-iv-i	1		
i-v-♭VII-III-iv-i	1		
i-v-♭VII-iv-VI-♭vii-i	1		
Subgroup A.6: i-v-i			
i-v-i	4		

Group B: i-VI-x-i			
i-VI-iv-i	1		

Group C: i-III-x-i			
Subgroup C.1: i-III-v-x-i			
i-III-v-i	10	i-III-i-v-i	1
i-III-v-iv-i	6	i-III-i-v-iv-i i-III-v-i-iv-i	2 1
i-III-v-III-i	2		
i-III-v-♭VII-i	2		
		i-III-i-v-III-iv-i	1
Subgroup C.2: i-III-iv-x-i			
i-III-iv-i	10		
i-III-iv-VI-i	3	i-III-iv-VI-i-VI-i	1
i-III-iv-v-i	1		
i-III-iv-VI-v-i	3		
Subgroup C.3: i-III-VI-x-i			
i-III-VI-i	1		
i-III-VI-iv-i	1		

Group E: i-iv-x-i			
i-iv-VI-i	3		
i-iv-v-i	2		
i-iv-VI-v-i	1		
		i-iv-III-i-v-i	2

Total concertos in minor	105
Number of tonal schemes in minor	41

eighteenth-century music.[1] As will become evident in later chapters, this process was an integral part of the history of the solo concerto, since it endowed the smaller group with a special affective status – immediately suggesting tension, emotional intensity and powerful drama. Individual composers differ only in the extent of their preference for the major.

The scalar degrees are intrinsically mode-sensitive. Table 5.2 indicates a modern view of primary tonal relationships, a concept which (though anachronistic in terms of eighteenth-century theory) will assist the ensuing discussion. In the major mode the dominant is the most directional implicative chord, whereas in the minor it appears both as a directional *major* chord and (in its *minor* version) as a secondary key area. Submediant and mediant keys function quite differently in the two modes: in the major, vi forms the relative minor; while in the minor III forms the relative major. The lowered seventh degree is an integral part of the minor mode, whereas it would be a chromatic (or mixolydian) degree in major. For this purpose, minorization of the tonic is regarded as a chromatic colouring rather than a modulation: it does not as yet hold the potential for initiating structural changes of direction, such as were to be explored later in the century.

Table 5.2. Key relationships

Major			Minor		
	I (vi)			i (III)	
IV (ii)		V (iii)	iv (VI)		v (♭VII)
flatward		sharpward	flatward		sharpward

Relative minor/major keys are given in parentheses

Although the options that command high statistical frequencies are of special importance in indicating preferred trends, this is not the sole purpose of the inquiry. For it is precisely the most unusual and rarely-used options that may turn out to be of special historical and stylistic interest, reflecting not mere caprice but a highly sophisticated development of the concept of tonal implication and frustrated realization.

The First Move

Already in the preferred first move these tables show a marked difference between concertos in major and minor. In major, the move I-V is found in 180 of 232 movements (78%). This so quickly became the normative statistical preference that anything else must be regarded as either a remnant of an older modal practice or as a deliberate critique of this norm. The exceptions are mainly modulations to keys a third away from the tonic: the mediant and submediant. Here an important historical perspective arises. In the sixteenth century Zarlino had

---

[1]   Talbot, *The Finale in Western Instrumental Music*, p. 73.

established the mediant as the tertiary cadential degree, and his prestigious teachings were strictly followed by most leading seventeenth-century Italian and German theorists.[2] But a change had occurred by the early eighteenth century, when Johann David Heinichen presented an innovative and flexible approach to modulations, which he claimed was derived from actual musical practice.[3] In his theory of the 'Musical Circle' the move from tonic to submediant was only a single step, whereas the mediant is a distant four steps away. In other words, the mediant has been replaced by the submediant as the preferred tertiary goal. Bella Brover-Lubovsky has demonstrated Heinichen's close personal affinity with Vivaldi (he was based in Venice from 1710 to 1716), so that his observations were likely to have been influenced by Vivaldi's own attitudes. Indeed, the mediant is the first target in sixteen (7%) of the Vivaldi sample, compared with thirty-one (13%) heading towards the submediant (the 'relative minor' key, in modern parlance). Still, these alternatives pale into insignificance compared with the overwhelming preference for the dominant.

In minor, by contrast, the dominant appears as the secondary key in only 49% of the sample (51 of 105 movements), nearly matched by the selection of the mediant (or 'relative major') in forty-five movements (43%). Again, there is a historical perspective. Talbot has shown that, in Corelli's sonatas and concertos, binary movements in minor move towards the dominant or to imperfect cadences in all but a single movement that reaches the mediant;[4] so that Vivaldi's elevation of the relative major to near equality represents both a historical shift and an expansion of the number of normative options. Heinichen offers some further insight, reversing the priorities from the major mode, by placing tonic and mediant only a single step apart in minor with the submediant four steps away. But clearly there is not an exact equivalence here, because whereas in major the submediant ('relative minor') was an exception to the norm, in minor the mediant ('relative major') is treated as a genuine secondary key. A further complicating factor is the role of the subdominant in minor, the first move in eight movements (8%) – a small group, yet far more significant than the equivalent in major. By virtue of its modal history, the subdominant in minor retains a special status, and its employment in Vivaldi's concertos suggests that it should be considered an equally valid option as a secondary key.

It is clear from these subtle nuances that not only are the choices for the first move inherently different in major and minor, but that the resultant tonal strategies – and therefore compositional strategies for entire movements – are also different in kind. Whereas the listener was expecting the dominant as the first move in major, and might therefore be surprised by any other move, no such single expectation existed in minor key movements.

---

2   See the detailed discussion in Brover-Lubovsky, 'Vivaldi's Harmony', pp. 180ff.
3   See Brover-Lubovsky, 'Vivaldi and Contemporary German Theory'.
4   The Corrente in Op. 4/5 ('Stylistic Evolution in Corelli's Music', p. 147).

Number of Intermediate Key Areas

The number of intermediate keys is an essential factor in describing the trajectory and relative stability of a ritornello movement. As Table 5.3 demonstrates, Vivaldi much preferred tonal schemes involving only two or three intermediate centres. Progression through four or more keys is a marginal strategy: this will be shown later to represent one of the main strategic differences between Vivaldi and certain other concerto composers.

Table 5.3. Number of intermediate tonal centres in Vivaldi

Number of intermediate tonal centres	In major	In minor
1	9	4
2	120	58
3	89	35
4 or more	14	8
Total	**232**	**105**

Central tonic areas in the pendulum schemes are ignored

Tonal Schemes in Major

One intermediate centre
Although small, the group of movements with only a single intermediate centre calls for brief consideration. Only six movements in major adopt the tonal scheme I-V-I, and one of these (RV 175) is a miniature of twenty-nine bars; the other five are 'sonority concertos' as defined in Chapter 3 in connection with RV 519 (Op. 3/5). Vivaldi ventured only once into the experimental scheme I-vii-I, in RV 250 in E♭ major. Throughout the barely sullied alternations of tonic and dominant chords that open the concerto, there is no hint of what is to follow; but in the middle of S1 a move to the dominant is suddenly diverted chromatically to G minor, which is itself rejected in favour of its own dominant, D minor (Ex. 5.1). After the unexpected vii is confirmed in a central ritornello, the process goes into reverse, a touch of G minor initiating a sequential circle of fifths to lead smoothly back to the tonic. Thus instead of merely shocking, the movement in fact illustrates how smooth such an unorthodox move could be. It is surely significant that there is a modal key signature of two flats, rendering the D minor chord an uninflected part of the tonal system.

After the dominant
In the major mode, the move towards the dominant as secondary key creates a strongly directional pull back towards the tonic: indeed one might say that such a resolution is immanent. When the tonic follows directly, it creates the centripetal

Ex. 5.1. Vivaldi, Violin Concerto in E♭ major, RV 250

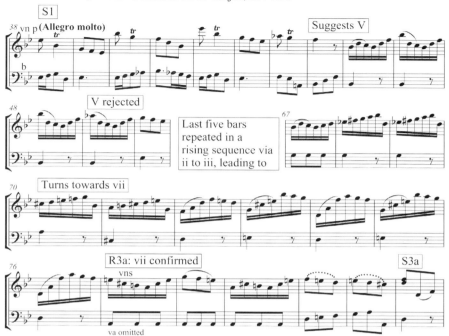

pendulum scheme (I-V-I-x-I); whereas delaying the resolution beyond the entire unstable section creates the centrifugal circuit scheme (I-V-x-I), with the longer-range tension that was later to drive sonata form.

As Table 5.1 indicates, Vivaldi strongly preferred the circuit to the pendulum model, expressly avoiding slipping back into the tonic immediately after the dominant section. RV 252 in E♭ major will serve as an example, though an extreme one, to illustrate the explicit way in which the pull of the tonic may be resisted. The tonic holds its own almost throughout S1, a decisive turn to V being executed only in the last two bars. Yet R2 responds to this challenge by pulling upwards into F major, dominant of the dominant, thus negating any possible chance of immediate resolution to the tonic. A further upward sequence leads to G minor, but the strong directional implication of F major is not forgotten, and the tonal trajectory is replayed in reverse within R3 (Table 5.4). As with the previous example, the two-flat key signature supports the important role of F major as a tonal centre.

Table 5.4. Timeline of Vivaldi, Violin Concerto in E♭ major, RV 252

Function	R1	S1	R2	S3	R3	R4a	S4	R4b
Bars	1–32	32–66	66–79	79–102	102–113	114–117	118–150	150–173
Key	I	I	V→ ᵛ/V	ᵛ/V // iii	iii // ᵛ/V →V→	I	I	I

For the peripheral area immediately after the dominant Vivaldi showed a clear preference for vi (47%) and iii (42%). Yet a comparison between the early and late groups shows a radical increase in the frequency of I-V-vi-I (from 4% to 24%), a change that is especially striking in view of the stability of the pattern I-V-iii-I around 12%. Vivaldi clearly did not consider vi and iii as mutually exclusive, since they appear as two successive peripherals (I-V-vi-iii-I or I-V-iii-vi-I) in 23% of the sample; and sometimes there is a rhetorical argument between the two areas. In RV 204 in D major (Op. 4/11), R2 modulates via a brief tonic chord to iii (established at bar 53); but the ensuing S2 rejects this key abruptly through a sequence of falling fifths, in order to modulate instead to vi (bar 64).

When these two peripheral keys both appear, their relationship automatically reflects on the background tonic-dominant relationship, of which they are the related keys. In the case of I-V-vi-iii-I, the pair vi-iii transposes the tonic-dominant axis to its relative minor, introducing a veiled suggestion of the pendulum tonal scheme. I-V-iii-vi-I, on the other hand, maintains the circuit to the utmost, going out to the point of furthest remove (iii) and back through vi in a single arc. A remarkable example of this is RV 348 in A major (Op. 9/6). R2 ends as usual in the dominant (bar 57), but a hiatus immediately suspends the directional pull of V, with the solo instead presenting new material in C♯ minor. The ensuing ritornello modulates to F♯ minor (bar 76), where there is another hiatus, as the next solo ignores the tonal tension by simply reprising the motto in the tonic. The tonal scheme I-V // iii-vi // I (where // marks a hiatus) involves the complete demarcation of the central peripheral area, with iii-vi reflecting the I-V axis of the first half of the movement.

The peripheral degrees ii and vii almost always function in direct relation to the keys around them. Thus ii never appears as the sole peripheral key, and it is mostly linked with the key a fifth higher, the submediant. In RV 234 in D major ('L'inquietudine'), for example, S2 arrives on a chord of E major as ^{V}/V, which immediately turns into E minor (bar 35); but it is only after an assertion of vi (B minor) two bars later that E minor is permitted to return as the main peripheral area (bars 39–47).

Avoidance of the dominant
A relatively large group of forty movements (22%) not only avoids the dominant as the first target key, but eschews the dominant as a stable key area altogether. The two groups I-vi-iii-I and I-iii-vi-I, together with those adding ii or IV, contribute twenty-eight to this total. This must be counted a significant alternative strategy, as some movements – even the fugal RV 185/II (Op. 4/7/II) – quite explicitly avoid making any reference whatsoever to the dominant. It might be thought that there must be a chronological trend here, with avoidance of the dominant waning through Vivaldi's career; but on the contrary, it is an important strategy in the late group, with twelve movements out of seventy in major avoiding the dominant even as a brief peripheral key.

RV 254 in E♭ major provides a magnificent example, which deserves more detailed discussion. No sooner has the tonic been established by the steady march motto than a chromatic progression with a new triplet countermelody leads sequentially to a cadence in G minor. Though E♭ is immediately restored, the

Ex. 5.2. Vivaldi, Violin Concerto in E♭ major, RV 254

implication of G minor registers in the listener's memory (Ex. 5.2a). The first solo, full of capricious contrasts, appears to lead towards the dominant, yet it overshoots to C minor (Ex. 5.2b). There is therefore no R2, the next ritornello R3a confirming C minor through the march motto. R3b starts in G minor before almost imperceptibly returning to the tonic. However, even then G minor is not forgotten, for it intrudes for a further six bars in the middle of the last solo (bars 86–91). Altogether 50 bars of the total 105 are based on the C minor-G minor axis, whereas the dominant hardly appears save for a few cadential chords.

It is remarkable that the subdominant as an established key area is extremely rare in the Vivaldi concerto repertoire as a whole, and as a first move it appears only in RV 307 in G major. Based on the unique tonal scheme I-IV-ii-vi-I, this movement develops a fascinating process of prediction and delayed, or frustrated, realization. The boisterous R1 is twice cut off by catastrophic disruptions pressing the claims of D major and E minor – in the face of which S1 suggests a conciliatory subdominant, which is adopted as the key of the second ritornello (bars 43–51). D major is never heard again, while E minor is not established until bar 74.

Avoidance of the dominant can even be used as part of a more subtle rhetorical strategy. The exceptional late RV 189 has already been discussed in Chapter 4 in connection with the double motto in contrasting tempos, the one Larghetto in C major and the other Allegro beginning in C minor. Will R2 be in the dominant major or minor? Vivaldi's initial answer is: neither. Instead, he reaches a ritornello in A minor (bars 35–42), creating a very unusual relationship with C minor. Yet this delay provokes still more tension, and Vivaldi does not evade the original question, to which his eventual response is: both. The Larghetto material returns in G major at bar 64, only to be immediately succeeded by the Allegro motto in G minor.

Tonal Schemes in Minor

As we have already suggested, there was no single normative secondary degree in minor, and consequently key areas are much less markedly hierarchized than in major. Both III and v frequently appear in succession: and while one will inevitably be privileged as the first move from the tonic, the second may be more strongly emphasized by other parameters such as duration, motto or texture. Furthermore, the subdominant plays a much more significant role than in major, to the extent that it may be regarded as another possible secondary key. These three secondary degrees dominate the various tonal schemes in minor, with only a small role accorded to VI and ♭VII. It is noteworthy that Vivaldi never used ii in minor. A possible reason could be that its diatonic triad is a diminished chord, yet this could easily have been solved by raising the fifth by a semitone as Vivaldi did with vii in major. A more compelling explanation lies in its lack of a relationship a perfect fifth higher, such as characterized the ii-vi axis in major. In minor, the equivalent key relationship would be ii-VI (e.g. D minor-A♭ major), chords a diminished fifth apart with no harmonic connection.

The concept of rhetorical argument between competing secondary degrees has been described in Chapter 1 with reference to Albinoni's Op. 9/8. A further example from Vivaldi is provided by the cello concerto RV 419 in A minor. The solo moves first to C major for a new cantabile which is itself displaced by E minor with yet another change of motive and texture (Ex. 5.3). The ritornello R2 chooses v by emphatically asserting the motto. Yet the ensuing solo pulls back to III through a circle of fifths, poignantly touching C minor before the next ritornello eventually accepts the new proposed key. The implication of C major suggested in S1 is thus initially rejected in favour of E minor, but is finally realized in R3.

Table 5.3 showed that the number of intermediate keys is similar in major and minor mode movements; yet there is a much larger variety of options in minor, with less concentration on a few favoured choices. As in major, there is a tiny group of concertos with the dominant as the sole intermediate centre, despite the non-directional property of the dominant minor. Any suggestion that the i-v-i pattern might imply the symmetry of binary form (i–v :‖: v–i) is deliberately negated in the G minor concerto for two violins, RV 578/II (Op. 3/2/II). Whereas R2a is a literal transposition of R1, the final ritornello is modulatory, returning with a subsidiary motive from dominant to tonic so that the recapitulation is entrusted to the first violin soloist (Table 5.5).

Ex. 5.3. Vivaldi, Cello Concerto in A minor, RV 419

Table 5.5. Timeline of Vivaldi, Concerto for Two Violins in G minor, RV 578/II (Op. 3/2/II)

Function	R1a	S1a	R1b	S1b	R2a	S2	R2b	S4	Coda
Bars	1–10	10–14	14–20	20–32	32–41	41–57	57–61	61–64	64–70
Key	i	i	i	i →	v	v	v →	i	i
Thematic	M a b	c	a b	c	M a b		b	M	

The minor group also contains Vivaldi's most extended tonal scheme, the unfolding logic of which is of much interest. The pattern i-v-♭VII-iv-VI-♭vii-i in RV 277 in E minor ('Il favorito', Op. 11/2, described by Bella Brover-Lubovsky as 'a unique example of an audacious tonal design'[5]) unusually exploits both forms of the flat seventh. R1 is thematically rich, with four distinct motives, the last of which is coloured by an F major Neapolitan sixth that has important ramifications. The first move is the normal sharpwards turn to B minor, with a stable ritornello (bar 30); but the third ritornello (bar 54) is pivotal in changing the tonal direction of the movement, modulating flatwards from D major to A minor using the memorable Neapolitan colouring. A roving solo reaches the Neapolitan chord once more (bar 75), now en route to an entrance of the motto in C major (Ex. 5.4). This key is rejected immediately in favour of the unique appearance of ♭vii (D

---

5   'Vivaldi and Contemporary German Theory', pp. 66–7, including a detailed timeline.

Ex. 5.4. Vivaldi, Violin Concerto in E minor, RV 277 (Op. 11/2, 'Il favorito')

minor), which is likewise rejected by a continuing ascent to the tonic. In this context D minor is retrospectively heard as an oblique realization of the Neapolitan implications of R1, as is made evident from the bass line. The six key areas are organized in a clear hierarchy, as shown in Table 5.6.

Table 5.6. Proportions of stable tonal areas in Vivaldi, Violin Concerto in E minor, RV 277 (Op. 11/2, 'Il favorito')

Stable area	i	v	♭VII	iv
Proportion	15%	14%	8%	3%
Articulated by	Stable R	Stable R	Modulatory R	Modulatory S
Motto	M	M	M	–

VI	♭vii	i
1%	1%	34%
Modulatory R	Modulatory R	Stable R-S-R
M only	M only	M

The tonal scheme of this movement raises an important issue. The listener may be expected to react to any peripheral key on two levels, recognizing both the long-range tension vis-à-vis the tonic and also its position in the modulatory process away from the secondary key. Which of these two levels predominates will be influenced by other factors. In RV 345 (Op. 9/2, discussed in Chapter 1) each intermediate ritornello is easily perceived in its relationship with the tonic, on account of the powerful restatements of the motto and the neutral figuration of the intervening solos. By contrast, in 'Il favorito' the tonal scheme is more readily comprehensible as a succession of keys that refer to their immediate neighbours: thus D major is heard in a direct relationship with the preceding B minor, whereas the more remote D minor is used disruptively to displace C major en route to the recapitulation.

A particular issue in minor-mode works is the use of modal key signatures (for example, one flat fewer than the modern system). Such key signatures are potential indicators for modally oriented tonal schemes and harmonic treatment, although the linkage is by no means consistent.[6] The intensely dramatic RV 202 in C minor (Op. 11/5), with its two-flat key signature, appears to be dominated by a modal process. Its entire first phrase is based on a pedal point G, with a major triad vaguely pulling towards C minor; and the subsequent phrase is still more enigmatic, leading eventually only to a G major fermata: the tonic is not definitively established until bar 22. The first secondary key is III, which is realized with a full ritornello (bars 47–61). Still, the grounding of R1 on G creates an anxious instability that suggests a relationship with the two-flat key signature; and G minor is indeed the target of the central solo, confirmed in the highly compressed but decisive R3 (bars 87–93). The following solo re-establishes C minor, while nonetheless twice reconciling the tendency towards G by means of an augmented sixth chord on A♭ (bars 106 and 115). This progression brings the earlier focus on G unambiguously into the orbit of the tonic, enabling the final ritornello to reprise the entire R1 in the most compressed form possible, quoting the first two and final seven bars only. Ingeniously this compression replaces all the earlier indecisiveness – the enigmatic implication of both G and C – in a powerfully unambiguous C minor statement. The substantial concluding tonic area (26% of the movement) has resolved the instability: it has taken a long musical argument to come down in favour of C minor.

Vivaldi's Treatment of the Intermediate Tonic

One of the most distinctive personal and group traits in the concerto repertoire will be shown to be the attitude to the pendulum model introduced in Chapter 1. Intermediate tonic areas appear in only 14% of the Vivaldi sample, with a mere touch of the tonic in an additional 9%. Brover-Lubovsky has made the striking observation that in 23% of her own sample (101 movements) Vivaldi meticulously avoided even so much as a single tonic chord between the opening and closing tonic areas – each case a tour de force of heightening expectation for the recapitulation.[7] The pendulum model therefore takes a somewhat marginal role in Vivaldi's output, but he manipulated it in a limited way whenever it suited his strategies, using a variety of rhetorical devices.

Intermediate tonic as a link in a modulatory process
Vivaldi did occasionally allow the dominant to follow its natural path back to the tonic. Typically this occurs near the beginning of S2, with only a fleeting mention that allows rapid onward departure. In RV 347 in A major (Op. 4/5), the dominant resolves immediately on the tonic, which itself leads to its own natural successor – the subdominant – en route to C♯ minor at bar 70 (Ex. 5.5). This is the only passage in the entire movement where the soloist is imitated by a second violin, further highlighting its significance.

Whereas in major the intermediate tonic appears as an anticipated resolution of

---

6   See Brover-Lubovsky, 'Between Modality and Tonality'.
7   'Vivaldi's Harmony', pp. 168–73.

Ex. 5.5. Vivaldi, Violin Concerto in A major, RV 347 (Op. 4/5)

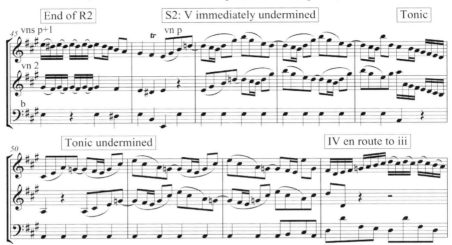

the dominant, no such strong pull exists in minor, because the dominant key is here itself minor. The return to the tonic in minor is therefore more of a strategic event, used to signal a new departure. It is particularly instructive to compare the D minor cello concerto RV 406 and the more elaborate (and presumably later) bassoon reworking RV 481. In the cello version a straightforward S2 modulates from A minor to F major (Ex. 5.6a). But in the bassoon version there is a striking change of direction at this point, with the A minor chord turning major so as to introduce a substantial tonic section with a new mood and texture (Ex. 5.6b); this in turn leads to the unusual submediant for the next ritornello, resulting in the tonal scheme i-v-i-VI-i (unique in the Vivaldi sample).

Early rejection and search for the secondary key
The tonic may return unexpectedly at an early stage in the movement, when R1b rejects the key suggested by a modulatory solo, as we have seen in Chapter 4 in connection with RV 259 and 318 (see Ex. 4.22). In the minor, this is almost inevitably part of a rhetorical argument, the search for the true secondary key. In RV 356 in A minor (Op. 3/6), for example, S1 heads initially towards D minor, and then, more decisively, towards the anticipated C major. Yet here the tutti creeps in *piano* with an inverted version of R1 in the tonic (Ex. 5.7). The next solo begins a new modulation, this time reaching E minor for a full ritornello introduced by the

Ex. 5.6a. Vivaldi, Cello Concerto in D minor, RV 406

Ex. 5.6b. Vivaldi, Bassoon Concerto in D minor, RV 481

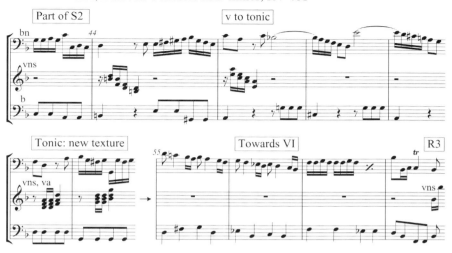

Ex. 5.7. Vivaldi, Violin Concerto in A minor, RV 356 (Op. 3/6)

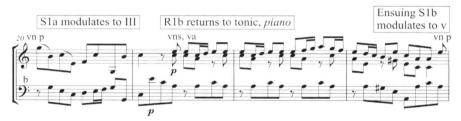

motto (bar 35). The resultant tonal scheme is i-iv-III-i-v-i, with only v articulated by a ritornello.

Intermediate tonic as false reprise, followed by further tonal excursions
Conversely, the intermediate tonic may appear relatively late in the movement in the guise of a recapitulation, which is then succeeded by further tonal exploration. This tonic 'false reprise' can be clearly identified in the light-hearted flute concerto in G major RV 437 (Op. 10/6), where R3 in B minor modulates directly to the tonic for a catchy new cadential section (Ex. 5.8). Suddenly, however, the bass line whimsically diverts to E minor, initiating a new departure and creating the overall tonal scheme I-V-iii-I-vi-I.

Moving in Time: Stability versus Instability

A defining aspect of the concerto concept is the dual role played by ritornello and solo in articulating the structure. How far do the ritornello and solo retain separate, specialized functions during a given movement? And are there other factors that overarch the textural alternations as the movement unfolds in time? One parameter that guides the listener in following the compositional strategy of a

Ex. 5.8. Vivaldi, Flute Concerto in G major, RV 437 (Op. 10/6)

particular movement – sometimes explicitly, sometimes less clearly – is tonal stability. This can be most straightforwardly investigated in relation to the location of modulations, according to both texture and place in the timeline (Table 5.7). The two favoured strategies contrast in their effect. If all ritornellos are stable and all solos modulatory – the alternation resulting in extreme textural specialization – a balance is created between stability and motion. If, however, R2 is stable and R3 modulatory, this balance is disrupted in favour of a gradual intensification. Less common are two other possibilities: modulatory R2 and stable R3, shifting the tonal emphasis towards the peripheral key; and R2 and R3 both modulatory, leading to instability across the entire centre of the movement. That Table 5.7 displays a very wide range of frequencies indicates Vivaldi's understanding of the utmost formal significance of this parameter: his preferences are clear, although (as so often) he experimented with the entire range of possible options. These will now be investigated in more detail.

Stable ritornellos, unstable solos
RV 238 in D minor (Op. 9/8) represents the simplest model whereby solos modulate from one stable ritornello to the next: the model is emphasized here by every stable ritornello being introduced by the motto, and by every modulating solo introducing new material. Even so, it should not be thought that this is an entirely static or architectural process, for a subtle hierarchization imparts a sense of development: R2 and R3 are progressively compressed, and the proportion of each stable key correspondingly reduced from 22% to 16% to 11% (Table 5.8). The seemingly elementary alternation thus hides a highly sophisticated aesthetic conception, one based on three fundamental concepts:

Table 5.7. Location of modulations in Vivaldi

Location of modulations	Number	%
Only in solos	137	41%
In solos and R3[1]	137	41%
In solos, R2 and R3	20	6%
In solos and R2	18	5%
In solos, R1 and R3	10	3%
In solos and R1b	10	3%
In solos, R1, R2 and R3	3	1%
In ritornellos only	2	1%

[1] In 24 of these there is no R2

Table 5.8. Ritornellos in Vivaldi, Violin Concerto in D minor, RV 238 (Op. 9/8)

Function	R1	R2	R3	R4a	R4b
Bars	1–16	35–45	55–62	70–73	81–90
Key	i	v	iv	i	
Thematic	M a b a' c d	M a a' d	M b d	M	b a' c d

(1) regularity of the alternation of stability and modulation, reinforcing antici-
    pation and recall (stable ritornellos with motto reprise versus modulatory
    solos);
(2) progressive modification and intensification (different combinations of the
    R1 motives and abbreviation of ritornellos);
(3) innovation (new thematic material in each solo).

It was central to Vivaldi's concept that the soloist be entrusted with some or all of
the dynamic modulatory process – influencing or controlling the direction of the
tonal argument as a major element in the assertion of authority and individuality.

An important related issue concerns the way in which modulations are
handled. A solo may meander at length through several unrealized centres, as
with the first solo of RV 390 discussed above (Ex. 4.21). Alternatively the solo
may itself consist mainly of long stable areas, connected by economical and
briefly executed modulations. Such is the case with the cello concerto RV 398,
where the solos extend the key of the previous ritornello at length, executing
quick modulations just in time for the next ritornello. Since the ritornellos are
themselves non-modulatory, the total stable areas amount to fully 90% of the
movement.

Stable solos, unstable ritornellos
The inverse option is highly exceptional, and in only two movements are the
modulations restricted entirely to the ritornellos. This would appear to be an early

strategy based on historical precedents, and one soon discarded: in RV 310 (Op. 3/3), illustrated in Table 3.13, the ritornellos based on transpositions of the motto alternate with stable solos in mechanical figurations.[8]

Concentration of instability

In RV 382 the entire unstable area following the dominant is contained within a single continuous tutti that leads from V through iii and vi back to the tonic (thus R2-R3-S4). The fact that this strategy is unique in the Vivaldi sample (though admittedly found elsewhere) may cast further doubt on the authenticity of this concerto.[9]

Tonal hierarchization in the central ritornellos

The presence of a complete ritornello in any single key gives this key a strong prominence, and thus those appearing only in a modulatory ritornello are inevitably of lesser importance in the tonal hierarchy. Table 5.9 amplifies the distinction already suggested by Table 5.7, in distinguishing between the functions of R2 and R3, and in emphasizing Vivaldi's general preference for progression from stable to unstable – whether from R2 to R3, or from R3a to R3b.

Table 5.9. Tonal structure of R2 and R3 in Vivaldi

Tonal structure	R2	%	R3	%
Entirely in a single key area	225	67%	116	34%
Modulatory or harmonically open	47	14%	88	26%
R3a and R3b each stable in a different peripheral key	–	–	63	19%
R3a stable, R3b modulatory	–	–	34	10%
R3a modulatory, R3b stable	–	–	5	1%
R3a and R3b both modulatory	–	–	10	3%
R3a and R3b both stable, R3c modulatory	–	–	3	1%
No R2 or no R3	65	19%	18	5%

Proportion of stable key areas

The overall proportion of stable key areas within the whole will be shown to be one of the salient characteristics of personal idiolects. In the Vivaldi sample, the aggregate of all the stable areas in each movement ranges from the extreme maximum of 99% down to 47%, with an average of 76%. As will be seen, this

[8] RV 220, published in 1717, is the only other concerto sharing this strategy.
[9] Ryom, *Répertoire des Oeuvres*, p. 474.

places Vivaldi at the upper end of the spectrum in generally favouring longer stable areas.

The Thematic Functions of the Intermediate Ritornellos

Vivaldi preferred the intermediate ritornellos to refer to material from R1, as is shown in Tables 5.10 and 5.11. Whereas R2 and R3 are treated differently in their tonal function, they are similarly treated in the thematic parameter. Vivaldi prefers variation over literal repetition of an entire ritornello: the latter occurs in R2 in only nine movements, including RV 578/II (see Table 5.5, p. 121). His main modification technique is the shortening and regrouping of motives and phrases from R1, as we have seen in Chapter 1 in connection with RV 345 (Op. 9/2). In a tiny group of three movements R2 realizes the prediction of the dominant within R1: thus, in the cello concerto RV 411, R2 begins with the motto transposed to V, before immediately quoting the central dominant section of R1 with no need for transposition.

Table 5.10. Thematic relationship between R2 and R1 in Vivaldi

Thematic material in R2	Number	%
All material in R2 taken from R1, modified	239	71%
No R2 (ritornellos in peripheral keys only)	64	19%
Combination of material from R1 and new material	16	5%
R2 a literal transposition of R1	9	3%
Only new material	5	1%
All material of R2 taken from R1, tonic material transposed, material in secondary key area literally quoted	3	1%
All material taken from R1b	1	1%

Table 5.11. Thematic relationship between R3 and R1 in Vivaldi

Thematic material in R3	Number	%
All material in R3 taken from R1, modified	270	80%
Combination of material from R1 and new material	34	10%
No R3	17	5%
Only new material	10	3%
Interjections of specialized motives	3	1%
R3 a literal transposition of R1	2	1%
R3 completes the modulatory process and then introduces the motto	1	1%

The Intermediate Solo – Related or Different?

Whereas the role of S1 is to modulate from the tonic to the secondary key, S2 appears at the height of the unstable stage, performing the modulation from the secondary to the peripheral key area. By the nature of our functional system, S2 may be absent in two situations: either where the first goal is a peripheral key (as in such tonal schemes as I-vi-iii-I), or where R2 modulates directly to the peripheral area. This accounts for the large number of inapplicable cases in Table 5.12, which analyzes the thematic basis of S2. Diversity is the preferred option here, with only a relatively small number of cases where material is derived from S1 or other previous sections. For example, in the delightful flute concerto RV 437 (Op. 10/6) most of S2 (bars 45–51) is a near exact transposition of part of S1 (bars 23–29). In more sophisticated cases S2 presents an imaginative variant of S1: thus, in RV 479, the inversion is evidently designed to exploit the extremes of the bassoon's range (Ex. 5.9).

Table 5.12. Thematic relationships in S2 in Vivaldi

Thematic material in S2	**Number**	**%**
New material	190	56%
No S2	68	20%
Common material in S2 and S1	22	7%
Figuration only (thematic material in S1)	13	4%
Derived from R1	12	4%
Starts with new material, continues with variant of S1	9	3%
Figuration in both S2 and S1	9	3%
Derived from R2	7	2%
Starts like S1, continues with new material	7	2%

Ex. 5.9. Vivaldi, Bassoon Concerto in C major, RV 479

Yet, as with the earlier comparison between motto and opening of S1, it is often difficult to distinguish between similarity and difference. A particularly interesting example is provided by the deeply moving cello concerto in C minor, RV 401. S2 bursts in with a furious scale passage, apparently quite distinct from anything heard before, but on closer examination a division of the second R1 motive; then a new melodic counterpoint sings out over a version of the motto in the accompanying strings (Ex. 5.10). In this way, S2 contrasts strikingly with S1 in rhythm and affect, at the same time invoking earlier motives from R1. Such freedom of invention is further confirmation that there is nothing in the motto that commits the composer to later treatment, an observation heightened by comparison with the quite different treatment of the same material in the central Larghetto of the violin concerto RV 189.[10]

Ex. 5.10. Vivaldi, Cello Concerto in C minor, RV 401

The function of S3 is more diverse. While in the more straightforward cases it is the third solo that leads back from the peripheral area to the tonic, it may also link two different peripheral areas; or, in those concertos with no R2, it will form the second solo (thus R1-S1-R3a-S3-R3b etc.). On the other hand it may be absent altogether in those movements where the return to the tonic is accomplished within a ritornello (R3-R4). As in the case of S2, Vivaldi prefers thematic variety, yet he does experiment with nearly every possible permutation of the relationships between the solos (Table 5.13).

---

[10] For discussion of the sources, with reference to the *sepolcro* idiom, see Kotsoni-Brown, 'The Solo Cello Concertos', pp. 222–5.

Table 5.13. Thematic relationships in S3 in Vivaldi

Thematic material in S3	Number	%
New material	138	41%
No S3	113	34%
Common material in S3 and S1	28	8%
Common material in S3 and S2	21	6%
Figuration only	19	6%
Derived from R1	12	4%
Common material in all solos	4	1%
Derived from R3	2	1%

Occasionally S3 plays a more significant part in the thematic argument than S2, since its later place in the movement gives more weight to the recall of earlier material. Thus in RV 188 in C major (Op. 7/2), S3b at bar 85 very prominently reintroduces the motto but in E minor – the last time the motto is heard, since the following tonic ritornello concentrates on the closing sections of R1. In this way S3b and R4 together provide a thematic recapitulation, which does not coincide with the tonal reprise. The role and thematic handling of the intermediate solos is thus very variable; and indeed Vivaldi introduces three full solos (S1, S2 and S3) in less than half of the sample, suggesting that this pattern was optional from the inception of the ritornello concept.

Separation or Continuity?

The inherently sectional nature of ritornello form carries with it the danger of rupturing the movement into a succession of short sections, something that a composer may nevertheless emphasize by clear breaks between ritornello and solo. Alternatively he may seek continuity by making the final chord of one section function as the start of the next. More rarely there may even be an overlap, whereby one section starts while the previous one is still reaching a cadence, in the manner of *stile antico*. As will be seen later, preference for marked separations over continuity varies considerably from one composer to another.

In 66% of the sample Vivaldi separates at least one ritornello from the ensuing solo, although a consistent separation of all ritornellos (as in RV 436) is much less frequent (5%). Usually a common chord retains a sonorous connection over the rhythmic break, or else the solo provides a resolution to the final chord of the ritornello: although there are examples of more extreme hiatus at the point of recapitulation, as will be seen in the next chapter. Such separations naturally emphasize the importance of the soloist in making a new beginning. By contrast, Vivaldi preferred solo sections to gather momentum towards the culminating ritornello, with only 28% of the sample including any separation between solo and ritornello. When combined with harmonic disjunction, the effect is dramatic, as in RV 324 in G minor (Op. 6/1), where S1 reaches the dominant only for the following ritornello to negate the arrival with an abrupt shift to the subdominant (Ex. 5.11).

Ex. 5.11. Vivaldi, Violin Concerto in G minor, RV 324 (Op. 6/1)

In the course of the excursions to peripheral keys the listener constantly antici-pates the unavoidable restatement of the tonic, with the expectation of a stable tonic area to follow. Whereas after the opening gestures of the movement the tonal options widened dramatically, at this point the tonal options inevitably narrow to one. Yet the selection of the actor to be honoured with this crucial gesture (whether ritornello or solo), the nature of the process leading back to the tonic, and the relationship between the opening and the closing tonic areas, once more open up a broad array of options, which require detailed discussion in the next chapter.

CHAPTER 6

Vivaldi and the Recapitulation

Almost all first movements in the Vivaldi concerto repertoire end with a section in the tonic and with a strong sense of closure that emphasizes the separation from the second movement. Only 3% of our sample preserved a remnant of the early concerto by leading *attacca* to the next movement. But beyond this consistency lies an almost infinite variety of procedures for restating the tonic and organizing the section that follows. It will come as no surprise at this stage in our argument that this closure offers much scope for experimentation and invention in its handling; and that the different parameters are frequently not coordinated. Indeed the closing section almost always plays an active role in the overall strategy of the movement, whether by direct manipulation of earlier motivic material, or more subtly by revisiting earlier tonal arguments, or still more imperceptibly by redressing tonal proportions.

In our discussion of the final tonic area of the ritornello form we will therefore adopt the term 'recapitulation', traditionally reserved for the mature sonata form. The Medieval Latin word *recapitulare* signifies 'to go over the main points of a thing again', *recapitulatio* 'a summing up, restatement by heads, recapitulation'.[1] The *Oxford English Dictionary* adapts similar definitions to English usage: 'recapitulate: to go over or repeat again, properly in a more concise manner; to give the heads or substance of (what has been already said); to summarize, restate briefly'; 'recapitulation: a summing up or brief repetition'. Thus a musical recapitulation might be expected to review and reinterpret some of the main elements of the movement up to that point. The loaded term 'recapitulation' is all the more appropriate here, precisely because the large array of options explored in the Italian concerto shares a number of thematic and tonal strategies with contemporary binary-form practice – strategies that were to become enshrined in mature sonata form.

The recapitulation is a realization of two expectations:

(1) anticipation of the tonic return itself, focusing the listener's attention on the very point of arrival (where on the timeline of the movement it occurs, how it is reached, and whether parameters are coordinated);
(2) anticipation of a stable area in the tonic following the point of return, focusing attention on the motivic, harmonic and temporal relationships between the opening and the closing tonic areas.

---

[1] Charlton T. Lewis and Charles Short, *A Latin Dictionary* (Oxford: Clarendon, 1880).

These two expectations act semi-independently of each other and will therefore be considered separately, although they will naturally interweave in the course of the chapter.

Section 1: The Re-establishment of the Tonic

Following the culmination of the centrifugal process in the last peripheral area (the 'point of furthest remove'), a reversal sets in with the tense approach towards the anticipated restatement of the tonic. How the recapitulation is reached has a forceful influence on the listener's perception: contrast, for example, the smooth modulation via a circle of fifths, inevitably weaving back to the expected return, with the shock tactics of an abrupt hiatus to the tonic, the return forced upon an unprepared listener. Table 6.1 demonstrates the different types of harmonic transition in the Vivaldi sample. Not unexpectedly, smooth retransitions predominate (a total of 70%). Yet the remaining 30%, where there is a harmonic disjuncture or hiatus, still represents a highly significant proportion, and the various procedures represented here will form an important part of subsequent discussion. Table 6.2 indicates where the hiatus occurs in these 102 movements.

Table 6.1. Types of harmonic retransition in Vivaldi

Harmonic retransition	Number	%
Sequential retransition	128	38%
Hiatus	88	26%
Non-sequential retransition	63	19%
Retransition leading to pedal-point	23	7%
Exact transposition of a phrase from peripheral key to tonic, without hiatus	21	6%
Exact transposition of a phrase, peripheral key to tonic, with hiatus	9	3%
Hiatus from peripheral key to dominant, leading to tonic	5	1%

Table 6.2. Point of hiatus at the recapitulation in Vivaldi

Point of hiatus	Number
Coincides with beginning of S4	58 (of which 12 by motto)
Within R3-R4	27 (of which 25 by motto)
Within S3-S4	7
Coincides with beginning of R4	5
To dominant within R3-R4	5

True or False?

Another issue that relates to the point of recapitulation is the concept of false
reprise. This term, more commonly associated with Haydn and the classical
period, requires some clarification. It is used here in two different senses:

(1) for the tonic motto appearing in the middle of the movement, before new tonal
explorations (such cases are described here as RT or ST);

(2) for a deceptive recapitulation that reprises the motto in a peripheral key.

We are concerned here only with the latter sense. Clearly the term 'false reprise'
should only be used in very particular circumstances, for it cannot refer indiscrim-
inately to every appearance of the motto in a peripheral key, the normal preserve
of R3. Rather it is reserved for those specific cases where the listener is led to
expect the return of the tonic, but instead the solo diverts to an unexpected peripheral key for the ensuing ritornello; the error is then immediately 'corrected' by
reversion to the tonic for the true recapitulation. An example of such preparation,
diversion and correction has already been seen in Chapter 1 in connection with
RV 345 in A major (Op. 9/2, Ex. 1.6): here the false reprise in F♯ minor is
followed by a hiatus that sharply distinguishes the tonic recapitulation. But in RV
386 in B minor a sideslip from the intrusive E minor back to the tonic disguises
the recapitulation altogether (Ex. 6.1).

Ex. 6.1. Vivaldi, Violin Concerto in B minor, RV 386

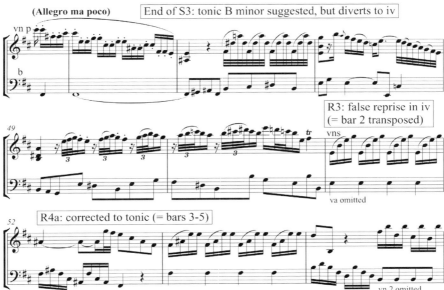

Articulation of the Recapitulation

Given that the tonic return is the primary element of expectation for the listener, how strongly it is articulated and whether it is reached by solo or by tutti are crucial compositional decisions. Yet, perhaps because this is the one feature common to every single concerto, it is also subject to the greatest variety and invention. The most straightforward option – a solo modulating from the last peripheral key to a ritornello that reasserts the tonic – is but one of several choices, as demonstrated in Table 6.3.

Table 6.3. Point of re-establishment of the tonic in Vivaldi

Point of re-establishment of the tonic	Number	%
At the beginning of S4, after a modulatory ritornello	100	30%
At the beginning of R4, after a modulatory solo	96	28%
Within a ritornello (R3-R4)	96	28%
Within a solo (S3-S4)	45	13%

The first striking feature of this table is the even spread across the range, with only the weakest articulation (within a solo) significantly less frequent. Vivaldi shows a slight preference towards ritornello rather than solo; and towards change of texture rather than continuity. But these two preferences are coordinated in only 28% of the sample: the strongest articulation of the tonic return where S3 is succeeded by R4. Further analysis shows a striking chronological shift away from the ritornello preference; and where the recapitulation does coincide with textural change, there is a marked swing away from ritornello R4 towards solo S4 (Table 6.4).

Table 6.4. Point of re-establishment of the tonic in Vivaldi's early and late concertos

Point of re-establishment of the tonic	Early %	Late %
At the beginning of R4, after a modulatory solo	52%	24%
Within a ritornello (R3-R4)	20%	30%
At the beginning of S4, after a modulatory ritornello	17%	31%
Within a solo (S3-S4)	11%	15%

The listener's sense of the strength of the tonic articulation is also significantly affected by the thematic parameter: whether the tonic is introduced by the motto, by other earlier material, or by a new motive altogether. Table 6.5 adds this parameter to Table 6.4, in a hierarchical matrix ranging from the strongest articulation (upper left cell), where R4 initiates the recapitulation with the motto, to the weakest (lower right cell) where it occurs in the middle of a solo with new

Table 6.5. Textural and thematic articulation of the recapitulation in Vivaldi

	By motto	By other ritornello material	By S1 material (not motto)	By new material	TOTAL
By R4	63	32	0	1	**96**
By S4	17	32	30	21	**100**
Within ritornello R3-R4	64	29	0	3	**96**
Within solo S3-S4	5	23	6	11	**45**
TOTAL	**149**	**116**	**36**	**36**	**337**

material. In between are many different combinations, including a sizeable group where the tonic motto appears in the middle of a ritornello. Another striking conclusion to be drawn from this table is the extreme rarity of a recapitulation introduced by R4 with new material (only four cases). By contrast, S4 initiates the recapitulation with new material in a significant number of instances, suggesting that the ritornello was inherently linked to repetition of material, whereas the solo was associated with flexibility and change.

Having laid out a range of issues connected with the point of recapitulation, we will now investigate in more detail how it is handled in each category in Table 6.4.

(a) Recapitulation at the beginning of R4, after a modulatory solo
As Table 6.5 indicates, in only sixty-three movements in the sample (19%) is the start of the recapitulation supported by all parameters at their strongest: textural change to tutti, allied to reprise of the motto. In the rare five cases where harmonic hiatus is added, the effect is startling and unambiguous, a violent disruption that forces the return. This practice may be a reference to another genre, the Da Capo aria, where the contrasting middle section typically ends in a peripheral key before an abrupt return to the opening ritornello; it is also often to be found in sinfonias of the period, including those of Vivaldi. The most striking example in the concerto sample is the disjuncture in RV 350 in A major, where S3 ends in B minor, only for the ritornello to begin immediately with the motto in the tonic (Ex. 6.2).

Ex. 6.2. Vivaldi, Violin Concerto in A major, RV 350

Ex. 6.3. Vivaldi, Violin Concerto in G major, RV 306

At the other extreme, the tonic ritornello may be well prepared and smoothly approached by a long chain of solo sequences, much the most common procedure in Vivaldi, as Table 6.1 indicates. This strategy has the effect of a strong drive towards the tonic release, through the combination of obsessive motivic repetition with powerfully directed sequential progressions. In RV 306 in G major, the final solo leads directly from the peripheral B minor to the tonic, first via a rapid sequence round the circle of fifths, and then with a much more definitive chromatic ascent (Ex. 6.3): here the preparation is so strong that the tonic can withstand a temporary diversion at the start of R4. Anticipation for the eventual tonic can be heightened by a dominant pedal, the significance of which is not so much that it leads from a remote key to the tonic, as that it confirms an earlier unfulfilled move towards the tonic. In RV 242 in D minor (Op. 8/7) the tonic is already implied at the end of R3 but not fully established: and the entire ensuing solo is built around a dominant pedal that eventually resolves into R4.

(b) Recapitulation within a ritornello (R3-R4)
Where the recapitulation occurs in the middle of a modulatory ritornello (R3-R4), the textural parameter is no longer relevant and it therefore requires special treatment to make a dramatic point of the recapitulation. The most arresting device is again that of harmonic hiatus, which combines with the motto in an impressive sub-group of twenty-five concertos. One example has already been mentioned in connection with false reprise: in RV 345 (Op. 9/2, Ex. 1.6) the violent lurch back to the tonic rudely interrupts the musical flow so as to highlight the 'correction' of the false reprise. The resultant pattern is typical of concertos in this group: R3a S3 **R3b-R4a** S4 R4b.

Yet the mid-ritornello tonic can also be highlighted by more subtle means than hiatus. In the A minor flute concerto RV 440, a rapid sequential modulation is followed not by the strong opening motto but by a later *piano* variant, which highlights the return in a deliberate understatement. Alternatively, the tonic return can

Ex. 6.4. Vivaldi, Cello Concerto in G major, RV 413

Ex. 6.5. Vivaldi, Violin Concerto in C major, RV 190

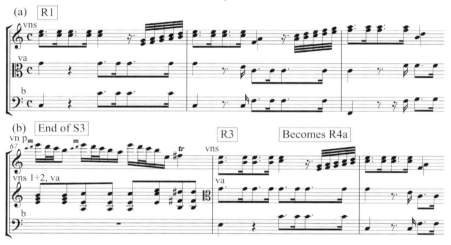

be downplayed altogether. In twenty-three concertos, the exact sequential transposition of a motive from peripheral key to tonic disguises the return of the tonic;
and even where there is a harmonic hiatus, the dramatic effect is entirely vitiated
by a continuity of texture and rhythm, as in the cello concerto RV 413 (Ex. 6.4).

Still more sleight of hand is displayed in a variant of this procedure, where the
motto starts in a peripheral key but translates mid-stream into the tonic – while
maintaining the rest of the musical content intact. This results in something of the
same harmonic dislocation as that caused by hiatus, but it is only experienced by
the listener after the event. The most extreme example must be RV 190 in C
major, where only a single chord remains in the old key of E minor and the note E
acts as a pivot that enables the melody to be preserved exactly (Ex. 6.5).

(c) Recapitulation at the beginning of S4, immediately after a ritornello R3
Many of the same considerations apply when the tonic return is entrusted to the
soloist, in that it may be either strongly articulated and dramatized, or passed over
without comment. Yet a solo recapitulation inherently makes less impact than a
tutti ritornello, requiring a hiatus or striking thematic reprise to give special
emphasis. This strategy increases the demands on the listener, who is required to
appreciate secondary parameters – tonality, solo motives – in order to appreciate
the workings of the compositional argument.

Ex. 6.6. Vivaldi, Violin Concerto in D major, RV 217

In RV 232 (discussed in Chapter 1), the solo recapitulation is highlighted by the combination of hiatus and the forceful return of the principal solo motive. Often, though, the effect is more subtle, as with the disguised return to the tonic in RV 217 in D major (Ex. 6.6). Here F♯ serves as the usual common note across the hiatus, reinforcing the listener's pleasure in discerning the reinterpretation by which the soloist eases unobtrusively into the new key. The solo melody is in fact a reprise of the opening of S1, the melodic contour of which had already suggested an ambiguity between D major and F♯ minor.

(d) Recapitulation within a solo (S3-S4)
The fourth option, intrinsically the weakest in terms of articulation, is the least common in Vivaldi's output. Even here, however, the recapitulation can be pointed up by harmonic means, motivic returns, and changes of register or accompaniment. Thus in RV 316a in G minor (Op. 4/6), the tonic is highlighted by a change of texture: the first violin recalling a secondary motive from R1 (bar 17), the soloist introducing a new, heterophonic counter-melody (Ex. 6.7).

Ex. 6.7. Vivaldi, Violin Concerto in G minor, RV 316a (Op. 4/6)

But in a few cases Vivaldi avoids motivic or textural emphasis of the recapitulation altogether: indeed the returning tonic may be only hinted at before further explorations. It is intrinsic in our method that the point where the tonic is first reasserted by a strong perfect cadence is regarded as the start of the recapitulation.

But the tonic may not yet be fully re-established. A common strategy is for the tonic to be gradually reconfirmed, so that the final ritornello represents the culmination of an extended process; thus, avoiding the motto at the moment of recapitulation does not necessarily mean it is omitted altogether. An interesting example of this procedure is provided by RV 204 (Op. 4/11), where the tonic is extremely weakly articulated within a solo (bar 71). A mild diversion initiates a new build-up of tension, leading with ever increasing energy to a tutti-solo dialogue at bar 94 and then finally to the return of the unison motto at bar 107. In this way the tonal recapitulation is placed well ahead of the thematic and textural reprise; and fully 41% of the movement is taken up with the process of confirming the final tonic.

Section 2: Temporal, Motivic and Harmonic Relationships between the Opening and Closing Tonic Areas

The fact that the tonic return may occur in either solo or ritornello has important ramifications for the larger structure of the movement. Table 6.6 distributes the Vivaldi sample across all the various permutations possible within the recapitulation. The first remarkable conclusion from this table is that only 6% correspond to the simplest textbook model, where the final tonic is confined to a single R4 following a modulatory S3. In the vast majority, the tonic is either introduced in the immediately preceding section (usually S4-R4) or else spread over a ritornello-solo complex such as R4a-S4b-R4b.

Temporal Relationships

An immediate issue arising from Table 6.6 is the proportion of the recapitulation within the movement as a whole. A simple comparison between the proportions of opening and final tonic areas immediately suggests that the latter tends to be longer than the former (this obtains in 61% of the whole sample). More detailed analysis of the early and late groups reveals that there is a clear chronological trend in favour of lengthening the final tonic, as Table 6.7 dramatically demonstrates. There is thus no universal balance between opening and closing tonic areas, such as could have been achieved by simply hanging identical ritornellos at each end of the movement: the symmetry of the Da Capo aria is alien to Vivaldi's conception of the ritornello form.[2] With the complex ritornello-solo patterns already described, the tonic is usually established well before the final ritornello.

The tonic thus appears to be pushed back further into the movement; and certainly in later concertos the last peripheral key is often quitted by a deliberately abrupt return to the tonic, which is then greatly prolonged. In the flamboyant 'echo' concerto RV 552, composed in 1740, the final peripheral key takes only 8% of the movement, as compared to 42% for the recapitulation and 33% for the

---

[2]   In this respect he differs from some of his contemporaries, such as Telemann, who favoured the symmetrical frame as well as simple transpositions for internal ritornellos.

opening tonic. This trend appears to be matched by the diminishing role of R3: thus in the late RV 386 in B minor, the final peripheral E minor is only touched upon as a false reprise before the tonic is reasserted (see Ex. 6.1), resulting in a very strong hierarchy and an overwhelming preponderance of the tonic (Table 6.8).

Table 6.6. Structure of the recapitulation by texture in Vivaldi

End of peripheral area	Recapitulation	Number	%
R3	R4a-S4-R4b	93	28%
R3	S4-R4	79	23%
S3	R4a-S4-R4b	77	23%
S3	S4-R4	35	10%
S3	R4	19	6%
R3	S4a-R4a-S4b-R4b	19	6%
S3	S4a-R4a-S4b-R4b	10	3%
R3	S4	2	1%
R3	R4-S4	2	1%
R3	R4	1	1%

Table 6.7. Proportion of final tonic against opening tonic in Vivaldi

Final tonic divided by opening tonic	All	Early	Late
0–80%	23%	43%	17%
81–100%	16%	19%	12%
101–120%	13%	9%	16%
121%–	48%	29%	55%

Table 6.8. Proportions of stable tonal areas in Vivaldi, Violin Concerto in B minor, RV 386

Stable area	i	III	v	i	iv	i
Proportion	19%	15%	2%	5%	1%	43%

Diversity and Reinterpretation

If the closing tonic is indeed to convey a sense of recapitulation – of reinterpretation or summing up of earlier events – it must involve more than a mere reprise of the opening ritornello. Two contrasting approaches to the recapitulation will be evident in the following discussion. On the one hand, the return of the tonic may be used as a point of departure for fresh flights of fancy, and frequently S4 introduces not only new material but also the most extravagantly soloistic excursions and capriccios. On the other hand, the recapitulation may represent a powerful stabilizing force, firmly rooted in the tonic and integrating earlier material into a unified whole. This effect is all the more strengthened when it involves active reworking, lending a sense of culmination or *peroratio*, in a way that a simple Da Capo cannot. Such reworking might involve linking together thematic material from R1 and S1; or reinterpreting and resolving an earlier tonal argument; or generally picking up loose threads and bringing them to a new resolution. A striking example of such a reinterpretation occurs in RV 479, where in the middle of R1 the bassoon contributes an entirely unexpected *minore* flourish; this is left as an unresolved question mark until the corresponding point in the recapitulation (bar 80), where it is extended into a long solo interpolated between R4a and R4b.

One powerful strategy is tonal reinterpretation, especially the omission of material originally in the dominant or its transposition to the tonic so as to strengthen the sense of resolution. Another related theme is compression, a transformation in itself that also allows space for further reordering and reworking. The frequent motivic repetitions needed to establish the tonic at the beginning were no longer necessary later; and indeed, because the sense of time passing alters as a movement progresses, the leisurely unfolding of the opening might seem mechanical and prolonged at the end. Admittedly, not every composer of the period adopted this approach, so it cannot be regarded as a universal perception. Nevertheless for Vivaldi such compression was clearly an important and very deliberate part of the compositional process. His working manuscripts explicitly demonstrate a strategy of excising bars from versions that started out with a more evenly proportioned structure; this applies especially to the later ritornellos in a movement.[3] It is certainly quite possible for him to give the impression of a complete ritornello in a few bars. In RV 371, R4a reduces the essential elements of R1 from twenty-two to seven bars. This is indeed a summing-up, a 'restatement by heads', allowing the interpolation of a long and florid solo section before a snatched R4b close.

The Ritornello R4

Although a ritornello movement unfolds in time through both ritornellos and solos, there is always a sense that the ritornellos themselves constitute an overarching narrative across the concerto. The closing tonic ritornellos form the final stage in this argument. The extent to which the material of R1 is retained,

---

3 We owe this observation to Michael Talbot.

Table 6.9. Relationship of R4 and R1 in Vivaldi (when no R4b)

R4 in relation to R1 (when no R4b)	Number	%
Most of R1 without motto	37	27%
Da Capo of R1	35	26%
Closing section only	32	24%
Motto and closing section	11	8%
Compressed or rewritten R1	9	7%
Other, including new material	9	7%
Motto only	3	2%
Total	**136**	

shortened or reorganized at this stage varies enormously, no doubt in response to the larger demands of each concerto. This variety can be most simply demonstrated in those concertos where there is only a single tonic ritornello R4 (Table 6.9).

Vivaldi is highly consistent in his intensive use of material from R1; yet in only 26% is R4 a simple Da Capo, with the remainder consisting of various compressions or reorderings of material from R1. Particularly interesting are those cases where the central modulatory (or unstable) section of R1 is omitted, for this clearly represents a strategic decision to reinforce the tonal stability of the recapitulation. A subtle and telling example is provided by RV 242 in D minor (Op. 8/7), where a single phrase emphasizing the dominant is deliberately excised (Ex. 6.8).

Ex. 6.8. Vivaldi, Violin Concerto in D minor, RV 242 (Op. 8/7)

An entirely different strategy emerges when the motto itself is omitted, as in over half the present selection. In 1752 Quantz advocated this as a matter of principle:

> The ritornello [R1] must be of suitable length. It must have at least two principal sections. The second, since it is repeated at the end of the movement, and concludes it, must be provided with the most beautiful and majestic ideas . . .

Finally, the Allegro must be concluded as briefly as possible in the last tutti with the second part of the first ritornello.[4]

Vivaldi frequently identified the omission by writing 'Da Capo al segno' at the end of the last solo and placing the Segno somewhere in the middle of R1. This notational practice may have been imported from the operatic aria: the expansion of the aria ritornello in the early eighteenth century called for abbreviation of the returning ritornello at the end of the A-section. Yet, since concerto movements are invariably short and not part of a long opera act, it would appear that the frequent omission of the motto in R4 stemmed from deeper compositional considerations.

In such movements the second part of R1 is given the full weight of a tonic ritornello. Sometimes the motto is omitted precisely because it lacks this weight, as has already been seen in certain concertos with hesitant openings, where the second phrase assumes the role of a replacement motto. At the furthest extreme, the closing section alone may be reprised, implying an acceptance that the tonic has already been sufficiently emphasized by the soloist, and that the essential function of the final ritornello is to provide closure rather than to suggest a new beginning.

The Ritornello R4a-R4b

The situation is much more complex where there are two tonic ritornellos, R4a and R4b. Table 6.10a analyzes the thematic relationship between R4a and R1 in the relevant 199 concertos; Table 6.10b does the same for R4b. But even leaving aside the intervening solo for the moment, R4b cannot be considered in isolation from R4a. Where R4b begins with the motto (31%), a section entirely independent of R4a is implied; but the two tables indicate that R4a is much more likely to begin with the motto, R4b with a later section of R1. This suggests a possible relationship between R4a and R4b: might the two ritornellos together replicate R1 around an intervening S4?

Certainly there is some correlation. Yet this does not mean that the whole of R1 is thereby reprised, as occurs in RV 522 in A minor (Op. 3/8), where all the material of R1 is dispersed across the final ritornellos. The prominence of this concerto as an example of ritornello form has resulted in this procedure becoming enshrined as a typical model, and it is indeed a compelling concept. Yet it is in fact quite a rarity, occurring in only thirteen Vivaldi movements. The relationship between R4a and R4b turns out to be very fluid indeed, and Vivaldi experiments with myriad combinations, selecting and varying motives such that they appear in quite a different light. A common pattern, found in forty-two concertos, is for R4a-R4b together to present an overview of R1, consisting of the motto and closing phrase only. In this way the tutti selects the most stable tonic material, omitting a modulatory or sequential central section of R1.

---

[4] *On Playing the Flute*, p. 312.

Table 6.10a. Relationship of R4a and R1 in Vivaldi (when both R4a and R4b present)

R4a in relation to R1	Number	%
Motto or opening section	109	55%
Compressed or reordered R1	56	28%
Motto and closing section	13	7%
Closing section only	11	6%
Other, including new material	5	3%
Da Capo of R1	3	2%
Most of R1 without motto	2	1%
Total	**199**	

Table 6.10b. Relationship of R4b and R1 in Vivaldi (when both R4a and R4b present)

R4b in relation to R1	Number	%
Closing section only	108	54%
Da Capo of R1	37	19%
Motto and closing section	16	8%
Other, including new material	16	8%
Most of R1 without motto	14	7%
Compressed or reordered R1	5	3%
Motto only	3	2%
Total	**199**	

A handful of concertos offer a more wide-ranging tonal reinterpretation. This may take the form of transposition of non-tonic material into the tonic, as in RV 196 in C minor (Op. 4/10), where the second phrase of R1 is transposed from E♭ into C minor for the final ritornello, substituting for the motto, which is omitted altogether from the recapitulation (Ex. 6.9). This transposition powerfully pulls earlier 'deviant' material back into line, reinforcing the resolute mood of the concerto, and leading directly into the severe C minor Adagio. A quite different kind of tonal reinterpretation occurs in RV 237 in D minor. Here – and this may be a unique example – a passing tonal implication in R1 is taken up and more fully explored in the recapitulation. The motto is reprised at bar 98, but a touch of G minor in the fourth bar inspires an entirely unexpected tonal diversion to which both soloist and tutti contribute, before the previous course of events is restored. This flight of tonal fancy results in a sizeable 10-bar interpolation of G minor (bars 103–12), quite the opposite of the more normal omission of tonal

Ex. 6.9. Vivaldi, Violin Concerto in C minor, RV 196 (Op. 4/10)

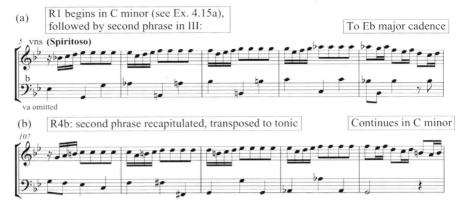

Ex. 6.10. Vivaldi, Violin Concerto in D minor, RV 246

excursions. The listener first understands the return of D minor at bar 98 as the recapitulation, then as a central false reprise leading to further tonal departures, and finally as a false 'false reprise', since it initiated the recapitulation after all.

The Solo S4

It will already have become clear that Vivaldi accords the soloist a major role in the recapitulation, with only twenty concertos lacking a final solo in the tonic. The solos taken together may also develop a separate argument across the movement, and in the recapitulation the integration of the soloist into the whole becomes a prime issue, focusing around the possible recurrence of earlier tonic material.

Least integrated are those strongly individualized solos with new displays of virtuosity, as in the extraordinarily complex and vivid RV 246 (Ex. 6.10). This is also the place where Vivaldi may include an elaborate solo capriccio (the term is used here to denote a separate passage of the most brilliant figuration, either without accompaniment or else underpinned only by a long pedal) or the

Table 6.11. Thematic structure of S4 in Vivaldi

Thematic structure of S4	Number	%
S4 consists of new material or figuration	119	38%
S4 uses earlier material in other ways	108	34%
S4 starts as S1, diverges where S1 moves towards secondary key	69	22%
S4 contributes to the reprise of R1	9	3%
S4 starts as S1, later transposes some secondary key material from S1	5	2%
S4 starts with new material, later transposes some secondary key material from S1	4	1%
S4 based on solo introduction	3	1%
Total	**317**	

opportunity for an improvised cadenza.[5] In such cases, the tonic is typically undermined by far-ranging harmony, requiring a further build-up towards an explosive climax when the tonic finally returns in the closing ritornello. The excitement may be intensified by a long dominant pedal – a device that almost always succeeds, rather than precedes, the initial return to the tonic. By contrast, other solos maintain a reflective character over a static bass, with minorization perhaps adding a lingering wistfulness before the inevitable return of the buoyant tutti and final closure. The ambitious RV 210 in D major (Op. 8/11) extends this idea in a particularly subtle way, by drawing out a poignant solo from the *minore* concertino section in R1.

With regard to thematic integration and reworking, the solo S4 displays as wide a range of practice as we have seen in the closing tonic ritornellos (Table 6.11). Clearly the final tonic solo is under no imperative to make an integrated contribution, with only 3% directly reinterpreting R1 and 26% revisiting earlier solo material in a way that can be seen as a reassessment. Nevertheless both of these strategies are highly significant. To begin with the latter, in sixty-nine cases (22%) S4 reprises the opening material from S1, but diverges at the point of modulation to the secondary key, as can be seen in RV 329 (Ex. 6.11). This forms an explicit tonal reinterpretation, a deliberate negation of the directional pull towards the secondary key in favour of the tonic, which is thereby emphatically asserted and maintained. A still stronger reinterpretation occurs in those five cases where some of the ensuing material in the secondary key is also transposed to the tonic. In RV 331 the motive may be only transitory, but it is still memorably distinctive and used specifically to define the relative major in S1 and the tonic in S4 (Ex. 6.12). This concept – reprising tonic material and then transposing secondary-key material to the tonic – is of course fundamental to later

---

[5] Further on capriccios and cadenzas see Whitmore, 'Towards an Understanding of the Capriccio', and Grattoni, ' "Qui si ferma à piacimento" '.

Ex. 6.11. Vivaldi, Violin Concerto in G minor, RV 329

Ex. 6.12. Vivaldi, Violin Concerto in G minor, RV 331

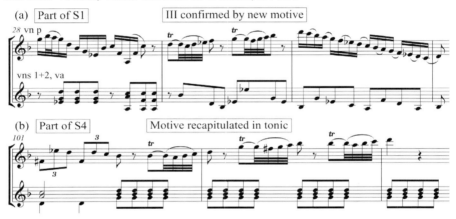

eighteenth-century principles of tonal resolution, as exemplified in sonata form. It may occur in only in a handful of Vivaldi concertos, and by no means extensively even there; but the fact remains that it was one of the numerous possibilities open to him.

Integration of Ritornello and Solo

In a few important cases, Vivaldi explores the possibility of a different kind of resolution, integrating the disparate and opposing forces of solo and ritornello. One option was to entrust the ritornello material to the soloist, thereby transforming its function and directly resolving the dialectic between the two modes. In two cases, S4 reworks the entire R1. RV 248 in D minor had preserved up to this point a clear distinction between the severe contrapuntal style of the ritornellos and the freer, often virtuosic idiom of the solos. At the point of tonic return, however, the soloist claims ownership of the contrapuntal style, with the solo S4 transforming the contours of R1 in a striking concertino texture. The ensuing ritornello picks up the latter part of R1, unaltered, but omits the motto, which had been so memorably entrusted to the soloist.[6]

The most sophisticated reinterpretations involve both ritornello and solo sections. In seven movements the recapitulation of R1 spans both ritornello and solo, with material spread across two or more sections. Only once, in RV 401, is the motto accorded to the soloist (a strong assertion of role again) leaving the remainder of R1 to the tutti. In the remaining six cases the soloist develops subsidiary material from the middle of R1. Most straightforwardly, R1 is simply distributed across R4a-S4-R4b, without any other structural changes. In RV 299 (Op. 7/8) the sequential second phrase of the ritornello is entrusted to the soloist in a lightly disguised figuration. This change not only serves to integrate the ritornello/solo functions, but also neatly hierarchizes them, with the tutti entrusted only the most diatonic and stable material in the recapitulation.[7]

More complex in its reinterpretation of R1 material is RV 318 in G minor (Op. 6/3). This tightly integrated movement is permeated by no fewer than five principal motives, which are used intensively as the basis of the solos. As Table 6.12 shows, the soloist contributes to the recapitulation first with motive b, but then interpolates a more extended discussion of the sequential a before a final allusion to the motto. Now R4b supplies the missing unison c, but no longer needs to refer to the motto or to motive b in the light of the previous solo.

Table 6.12. R1 and recapitulation in Vivaldi, Violin Concerto in G minor, RV 318 (Op. 6/3)

Function	R1				
Bars	1–6	7–12	13–16	17–20	20–24
Thematic	M	a	b	c	d
Notes	and tail	sequential	around V	unison	cadence, variant of M

R4a		S4 (all slightly varied)				R4b
141–144	145–152	153–156	157–173	174–175	176–179	180–193
M	a' extended	b	a extended	b (part)	d'/M	a' c d

Perhaps the richest example of integration is provided by RV 277 in E minor (Op. 11/2, 'Il favorito'). The unusual tonal scheme and the manner in which the recapitulation is approached have already been discussed (see Ex. 5.4). Equally unusual is the elaborately recomposed recapitulation, where the soloist both reprises S1 and contributes to the recapitulation of R1, thus establishing a new

---

[6]   The second case is the more subtle paraphrase in the flute concerto RV 434 (Op. 10/5).

[7]   Compare RV 356 (Op. 3/6), where the soloist does not precisely contribute to the recapitulation of R1 but instead alludes twice to the sequential consequent of R1, a passage not otherwise reprised.

Ex. 6.13. Vivaldi, Violin Concerto in E minor, RV 277 (Op. 11/2, 'Il favorito')

relationship between solo and tutti (Ex. 6.13, Table 6.13). Such integration of R1 and S1 in free alternation between tutti and solo is certainly highly unusual in Vivaldi's time, and indeed such possibilities were seldom explored again until their highest manifestation in Mozart's piano concertos.

Table 6.13. R1, S1 and recapitulation in Vivaldi, Violin Concerto in E minor, RV 277 (Op. 11/2, 'Il favorito')

Function	R1	S1
Bars	1–14	15–30
Thematic	M a → b c	d etc. (→ v)

R4a	S4a	R4b	S4b	R4c
83–84	85–90	90–92	92–106	106–117
M	a'	b	d etc. (in i)	M' a → b c [= R1 D.C. abbreviated]

Conclusion: Compositional Choices and Strategies

Since it addresses a universal issue – the way in which the recapitulation is handled and its relationship with the earlier parts of the movement – this chapter has revealed particularly clearly the extremely wide range of choices available to Vivaldi. The question immediately arises as to why Vivaldi should select one option rather than another. Comparison of movements with similar mottos, such as the G minor concertos RV 328 and RV 317 (Op. 12/1), reveals quite different ways of approaching the tonic and of relating S4 to earlier sections. The conclusion must be that the recapitulation is in no way determined by the material and must instead reflect broader issues of implication and realization in each movement.

A further look at RV 210 (Op. 8/11) will illustrate this point vividly. The

Table 6.14. Ritornello structure of Vivaldi, Violin Concerto in D major, RV 210 (Op. 8/11)

Function	Key	Texture of opening	Motives
R1	I	Fugal	M a b c (*minore*) d
R2	V	Fugal with bass accompaniment	M b
R3	vi	Unison	M a
R4a-S4a-R4b	I	Fugal with solo figuration	M c (extended) b d

Ex. 6.14. Vivaldi, Violin Concerto in D major, RV 210 (Op. 8/11)

similarity of motto and R1 to RV 176 has already been noted (Ex. 4.8); and indeed there is a correlation in the recapitulation also, in that the *minore* concertino phrase is extended as a central interlude. But its purpose is quite different, and in RV 210 it forms part of an overarching strategy for the movement as a whole (Table 6.14). In the first part of the movement the fugal ritornello material is kept distinct from the brilliant or cantabile solo writing (see Ex. 4.1a). Yet, as the concerto progresses, the two modes come together: first the motto underpins the virtuosic figuration in S2, and then at the point of the recapitulation, the soloist (instead of retiring in triumph) perseveres with figuration against the fugal reprise (Ex. 6.14). This highly unusual procedure finally reconciles the two personae, as well as providing a necessary continuity above the static fugal motto. Furthermore, since the momentum of the solo line needs eventually to be dissipated and resolved, some distinctive outcome is required at the end of the figuration; and this is provided by extending the original concertino *minore* from five bars into a wistful solo of twelve bars. There is then a typical sense of second arrival as the tonic is again prepared by the soloist and finally reaffirmed in R4b, which fuses two disjunct sections from R1 together.

In this way two strategies for the whole movement interlock: firstly, the clear hierarchization of tonal areas by texture, and secondly the progressive integration and eventual reconciliation of solo and tutti. Despite all the changes in the recapitulation, the length of the final tonic (25 bars) almost precisely matches that of R1. This is a fine example of *ars combinatoria*, reorganizing and reordering the material from R1 in response to a strong overarching musical concept.

Thus we have interpreted each Vivaldi ritornello movement as a rhetorical oration, proceeding from the affective proposition enshrined in its motto and initial ritornello to further statements that comment on the proposition through a rich array of similarities, variants and contrasts. For Vivaldi the unitary musical statement embodied in the ritornello is sufficient to unleash this complex musical argument without the need for textual connotations (other than the occasional programmatic rubrics that merely stimulate the imagination). The soloist, whether adopting an entirely separate persona or commenting on the proposition more directly, is equally a part of the argument, with contrast of texture and musical manner providing one of the strongest ways of articulating it.

In order to project his oratory most effectively, Vivaldi took the numerous and disparate elements available to him in the early concerto repertoire and organized them in 'order, connection, and proportion', thus pioneering the first large-scale autonomous instrumental form in musical history. He developed the concise, directional, clearly ordered yet flexible ritornello model as a rhetorical argument, exploring a range of contrasting affects within a single movement, rather than as the static mould it has sometimes been dubbed.

Vivaldi's immense repertoire laid open a broad array of options in all parameters, some general to music of the time, others specific to ritornello form. His contemporaries, whether embedded in traditions and habits of their own as with the Roman school, or younger followers in Venice and elsewhere, reacted directly to the options he offered: selecting some, eliminating others, and exploring new ones, thus multiplying not only the size but also the diversity of the concerto repertoire.

CHAPTER 7

Rome: Renovating Tradition

The Roman musical environment, described in Chapter 2, was quite different from that of Venice, being based around the often ostentatious patronage of cardinals and princes such as Ottoboni and Ruspoli, and around the church performances that attained an elaborate scale on the most important feast days. Roman concertos, whether written for private *accademie* or for more public occasions, also lie in a distinct tradition of their own. Constantly in the background was Arcangelo Corelli (1653–1713), the dominant figure in Roman musical life until his later years, whose five sets of sonatas, published between 1681 and 1700, provided the classic formulation of the early eighteenth-century solo and trio sonata. His *Concerti grossi*, Op. 6, scored for concertino two violins and cello plus ripieno strings, may not have been published until 1714, but they were evidently circulating in some form many years before then, perhaps even as early as the 1680s.

This dominating influence must have laid a heavy burden of responsibility on his pupils and successors. Yet they were hardly reticent in asserting their own musical individuality, and indeed it would be a mistake to assert that the younger Roman concerto composers were simply conservative followers of Corelli – just on the basis of their continuing allegiance to a four-movement structure (beginning with a slow movement) and to the traditional seven-part scoring. This Roman scoring may indeed hide fully-fledged solo concerto movements such as have already been described in Chapter 3 in connection with Valentini's Op. 7 (1710); and Valentini in particular seems to have gone out of his way to set himself up as a modern rival to Corelli within the confines of Roman convention.

The other principal Roman concerto composers were Valentini's contemporaries Antonio Montanari (1676–1737) and Giovanni Mossi (*c*1680–1742), whose surviving works similarly date from the 1710s and 1720s. The repertoire survives in a variety of sources. Ottoboni's library naturally contains some examples, although it is surprisingly patchy in this regard, the best-represented composer being Valentini, who was not in fact among Ottoboni's favoured violinists.[1] Concertos by all three composers survive in Pisendel's hand, in scores apparently copied on his visit to Rome in 1717.[2] And after a somewhat slow start there were several Amsterdam publications during the 1720s: it would appear,

---

[1] Everett, *The Manchester Concerto Partbooks* and 'A Roman Concerto Repertory'; La Via, 'Il Cardinale Ottoboni'. Further on the Roman environment see pp. 36–7.
[2] Pozzi, 'Il concerto strumentale italiano'.

however, that Roman concertos were regarded as too old-fashioned for publication thereafter, for a large number of concertos by these composers remained unpublished among Le Cène's effects on his death in 1743.[3]

One further composer who should be mentioned here is Pietro Antonio Locatelli, whose years in Rome (1711–23) culminated in the Amsterdam publication of his Op. 1 *Concerti grossi* in 1721. But since his only set of solo concertos, (*L'arte del violino*, Op. 3) derives from a different phase of his life, they will be considered in Chapter 9.

While certain Corellian practices are clearly in evidence in the Roman repertoire, both Mossi and Montanari work against this background in an innovative way: indeed because the Corellian tradition was so strongly established, they are able to use it rhetorically, by creating expectations for the listener that can be explicitly rejected. Valentini goes still further, developing an entirely individual idiom that eventually moves away from anything recognizably Corellian. It should not therefore be thought that the Roman concerto took on a new lease of life only in Germany and England, while remaining statically tied to Corellian practices in Rome itself.[4] This chapter will demonstrate that elements of newer concerto styles, and indeed of ritornello form, infiltrated the Roman repertoire to produce a distinctive synthesis.

Giovanni Mossi

Giovanni Mossi (*b* ?Rome, *c*1680; *d* Rome, 1742) was active as a violinist in Rome from as early as 1694, and he established a position as one of the regular violinists at the musical performances given by Ottoboni, Pamphilj and Ruspoli, as well as at church festivals.[5] Between 1716 and 1733 six sets of instrumental music were published in Amsterdam, including concertos Op. 2 (*c*1720), Op. 3 (*c*1720)[6] and Op. 4 (1727). During his own lifetime Mossi was regarded as a pupil of Corelli – though without direct evidence – and his music was certainly influenced by his mentor. But the concertos present a fascinating picture of a composer at the crossroads between continuing practices of an older Corellian world and more modern melodic and formal innovations.[7]

Op. 2 is firmly in the Corellian concerto grosso tradition, and will therefore not be considered here. But while Opp. 3 and 4 retain the Roman seven-part layout, both sets contain many solo violin movements (the second solo part entirely

---

3   So too were concertos by the Roman violinist Domenico Ghilarducci (Rasch, 'I manoscritti musicali', pp. 1067–8). It is true that Le Cène's general lethargy during the 1730s resulted in a decline in publication across the entire repertoire, but Roman composers seem to have been particularly affected.

4   As implied in 'Concerto (ii)', *NG2*. Elsewhere Talbot has gone so far as to suggest that Valentini provided a more potent model than Corelli for other Roman composers ('A Rival of Corelli', p. 365).

5   Sgaria, 'Giovanni Mossi'.

6   No. 5 survives in a copy by Pisendel, perhaps deriving from his 1717 visit to Rome.

7   This point is elaborated in Sgaria, 'Giovanni Mossi', pp. 1162–7.

doubling the ripieno); others are conceived as double concerto movements, while Op. 4/12 rotates four solo violin parts in the manner of Valentini's Op. 7/10 and Vivaldi's Op. 3/10.

Mossi also experiments with the number and type of movements, mostly retaining the traditional four-movement outline, but dispensing with the opening slow movement in a few concertos (especially in Op. 4).[8] Fast movements, whether placed first or second, often suggest ritornello form, as Table 7.1 demonstrates.

Table 7.1a. Structure of movements from Mossi, Op. 3

Number/ movement	Key	Substantial solos	Texture of R1	Elements of ritornello form
1/II	D	Vn	Fugal	Yes; central modulatory R
2/II	F	Vn	Fugal	Partially, but very long R1 (54%), only brief central R
3/II	d	Vn	Solo, then homophonic	Yes
4/II	B♭	–	Fugal	–
5/I	B♭	Vn	Homophonic	Yes
6/II	A	Vn	Fugal	Yes

Table 7.1b. Structure of movements from Mossi, Op. 4

Number/ movement	Key	Substantial solos	Texture of R1	Elements of ritornello form
1/I	D	Vn/2vn	Homophonic	–
2/II	G	Vn	Homophonic	Yes
3/II	B♭	2vn	Imitative	Yes
4/I	E	Vn/2vn	Homophonic	Yes
5/II	c	Vn	Homophonic	Yes
6/I	A	–	Homophonic	–
7/II	F	One for vn	Contrapuntal	–
8/I	C	2vn	Homophonic	Yes
9/I	b	–	Imitative	–
10/II	d	Vn	Imitative	–
11/I	e	2vn	Homophonic	Yes
12/II	g	4vn	Homophonic	Opening ritornello never recurs

---

8   Ibid., pp. 1152–3.

Table 7.2. Timeline of Mossi, Violin Concerto in A major, Op. 3/6/II

Function	R1a	S1a	R1b	S1b	R3a	RT	S3	R3b	R4
Bars	1–19	19–31	31–37	37–51	51–55	55–64	64–70	70– 74–84	84–90
Key	1 →	V → I	I	I →	vi →	I →	V →	iii → V →	I
Thematic	M fugato	M	M	M		M	M	M M	M

It will be apparent from these tables that Mossi is trying out an array of different approaches to the concerto concept, drawing on elements from the concerto grosso as well as the publications of Valentini and Vivaldi (the succession of solo violin → two violins → four violins at the end of Op. 4 suggests *L'estro armonico*). Yet within those movements that broadly draw upon the ritornello concept, there is a wide variety of strategies, many of which would seem decidedly unorthodox if viewed in a Vivaldian context.

In Op. 3, five movements are relevant here, of which three are fugal second movements in the *concerto da chiesa* tradition. Yet even these contain extensive solos, recalling Torelli's Op. 8, and the effect is as much one of contrapuntal ritornellos surrounding brilliant solos as of fugues with solo episodes. The example of Op. 3/6 in A major will illustrate both these strong contrasts and Mossi's apparently fluid approach to tonality (Table 7.2). The movement begins in strict fugal idiom, a texture rigorously maintained in the later ritornellos (Ex. 7.1a). Even the first solo begins similarly in Corellian double stops, but it then breaks into Mossi's customary violinistic figurations (Ex. 7.1b). The regular alternation between counterpoint and figuration gives the movement a clear design, with the fugal subject providing a strong framework and the free-flowing solos imparting a certain improvisational character.

At first sight, Mossi handles tonality flexibly in the old manner, with frequent returns to the tonic and peregrination around related keys – sometimes establishing them firmly, at other times rejecting immediate harmonic goals by means of Corellian suspensions across cadences. Yet the movement unfolds a more sophisticated overall tonal strategy than this might suggest. The opening fugal complex by necessity fully explores the dominant, which is confirmed by the strong cadence at bar 19 as well as the entrance of the soloist. A return to the tonic initiates a new departure to vi (F♯ minor) and an entry of the subject in R3a. This implies a fugal answer in C♯ minor, but instead the tonic surprisingly returns to frustrate this expectation; and C♯ minor is in fact delayed until R3b. In this way Mossi exploits techniques very familiar from early eighteenth-century fugal writing in the service of a larger tonal plan. The movement was likely to communicate equally well with listeners versed in the older traditions as with those already cognizant of the new ritornello idiom. Whether as a deliberate ploy to combine the two concepts, or simply as a natural development of a virtuoso violinist's contrapuntal background, the movement demonstrates how closely fugal procedures interlock with ritornello form.

The coherence offered by the fugue subject is less apparent in the other two concertos. Op. 3/5 begins with a Allegro in a brisk homophonic idiom, playing against fugal expectations by deliberately inviting but not realizing such

Ex. 7.1. Mossi, Violin Concerto in A major, Op. 3/6/II

Ex. 7.2. Mossi, Violin Concerto in B♭ major, Op. 3/5

treatment (Ex. 7.2). While this bold motto is cleverly varied in the ensuing solo, in a striking adoption of the modern concerto manner, it disappears during the two central ritornellos, which instead present vague reminiscences in similar rhythms. Mossi is again reluctant to lose contact with the tonic: S1 starts a modulatory process but soon reverts, so that the main central ritornello of the movement begins in the tonic and modulates to vi. This perhaps suggests that Mossi was aware that he had started a movement in Vivaldian ritornello form but then went out of his way to avoid following the normal pattern.

The concertos of Op. 4 are more diverse, and in some ways they revert to the concerto grosso tradition, with more active roles for second violin and cello. On the other hand, of the six ritornello movements with substantial solos, none is in a fugal idiom: indeed Mossi seems deliberately to parade a direct modern style in the opening mottos, with Vivaldian arpeggiated motives and simple homophonic textures – so much so, in fact, that one is tempted to see this as a deliberate ploy to attract attention and court popularity. More subtly, though, it could represent a commentary on style change: Op. 4/6 in A major begins with an unmistakably Vivaldian unison motto, but this is immediately transformed into a fugato trio, much closer to Mossi's older idiom (Ex. 7.3). A couple of brief violin solos interrupt the flow, and the listener is led to expect a full solo entry to follow. But it never happens: the movement continues as a ripieno movement in fully-worked three-part counterpoint, with only fleeting appearances of the motto. As if to emphasize the rejection of modern ritornello form, the next movement is a severe D minor fugue.

Ex. 7.3. Mossi, Concerto in A major, Op. 4/6

All six movements retain the contrast seen in Op. 3 between tutti material and thematic solo figuration. The distinction is now less dramatic because of the more modern-sounding mottos, yet there is still no highly directed sense of thematic or tonal development. The motto again plays a very variable part, appearing directly in R2 in only three movements, never in peripheral keys, and only twice in the recapitulation. Mossi's rather neutral melodic style does, however, suggest profuse motivic allusions in a loose network of connections. In Op. 4/8, for example, no single bar from R1 ever recurs later, yet the patchworking of tiny fragments into new melodies results in a much less diffuse movement than this might imply.

A major element of this hidden unification is a persistent leaning towards counterpoint: indeed, Corellian textures typically infiltrate as the movement progresses, suggesting that this is perhaps Mossi's natural home. Thus in the fine C minor concerto Op. 4/5, the energetic homophonic motto (Ex. 7.4a) is used in R2 to introduce a whimsical stretto, which, twenty bars later, has been transformed into intense three-part imitation (Ex. 7.4b). By this time the motto itself has disappeared for ever, but the aural memory of related counterpoint still manages to create a strong perception of unity.

Ex. 7.4. Mossi, Concerto in C minor, Op. 4/5/II

(a) [R1]

Allegro moderato

vn 2 omitted

(b) [Part of R3/RT]

Such free transformation suggests an improvisatory approach towards structure, and indeed an unshackled approach to tonality persists from Op. 3. Interim
returns to the tonic are common, and in manifold ways Mossi avoids the strategy
of modulating within a solo and confirming the new key with a well-articulated
ritornello. Hardly ever do the different parameters absolutely coincide, resulting
in a dislocating effect on the listener. The opening of Op. 4/4 in E major illustrates
this in a particular vivid way (Table 7.3). First of all the entrance of the soloist is
blurred by the reprise of the tutti motto after R1 (in the manner of Vivaldi's Op.
4/1); then, after a very clear move to the dominant with the strongest possible
cadence, the expected ritornello R2 is ostentatiously replaced by a rest (Ex. 7.5).
The solo instead re-establishes the tonic for a further ritornello (R1c), and only
then does the anticipated motto in the dominant intervene, smack in the middle of
this ritornello.

Table 7.3. Timeline of the opening of Mossi, Concerto in E major, Op. 4/4

Function	R1a	R1b	S1a	S1b	R1c	R2a	S2	R2b
Bars	1–9	9–13	13–20	20–26	26–31	32–34	34–41	41–48
Key	I	I	I → V	V → I	I	V	V	V
Thematic	M	M				M	cf. 20	new

Rather than demonstrating an insecurity with ritornello form, this last example
suggests a strong awareness on Mossi's part, a deliberate rhetorical play with
implications that comments on Vivaldian ritornello form. The apparently cavalier
approach to motivic recall in his concertos, together with the unorthodox succession of keys, results in a type of ritornello form that sounds strange to the listener
attuned to Vivaldian procedures. Yet Mossi certainly develops a highly individual concept for the concerto, one that both draws on his Corellian background
and simultaneously refers to the new.

Ex. 7.5. Mossi, Concerto in E major, Op. 4/4

Antonio Montanari

The most celebrated violinist working in Rome was Antonio Montanari (*b* Modena, 1676; *d* Rome, 1737), variously employed by Ottoboni, Pamphilj and the Borghese family over a long period from 1692 onwards.[9] He seems first to have been employed on a permanent basis by Ottoboni around 1712, and on numerous occasions he led Ottoboni's public musical celebrations, ranked ahead of Ghilarducci and Mossi.[10] He was clearly a considerable virtuoso, and his concertos reflect a violinistic technique well in advance of his colleagues, while always remaining within the bounds of Roman propriety.

Montanari was not a prolific composer, but the collection of eight concertos published as Op. 1 in Amsterdam is one of the most ambitious and elaborate sets of the period. Though the set did not appear until *c*1730, it is likely that the concertos were composed considerably earlier.[11] At first glance these also appear to be Corellian concerti grossi, not only in the seven-part layout and predominant four-movement structure, but also in melodic and contrapuntal idioms. Indeed Nos. 2–4 are clearly in traditional mould and are thus outside the scope of this study. But the other five concertos turn out quite differently.

No. 5 is the only concerto in three movements, and the only one to begin with a homophonic Allegro. As with Mossi's Op. 3/5, the long homophonic opening ritornello refers to the fugal technique of a dominant answer, but this time it is extended almost to breaking point by a continuous spinning-out that reaches the dominant motto only at bar 12. The movement as a whole hints at a ritornello

9   La Via, 'Il Cardinale Ottoboni', p. 494.
10 In view of this connection, it is surprising that hardly any of Montanari's music survives in the Ottoboni collection.
11 No. 8 survives in a score in Pisendel's hand, perhaps copied in 1717 while he was studying with Montanari in Rome. A further violin concerto in Dresden (D-Dl, Mus. 2767-O-1, in the hand of a copyist) is in a more straightforward ritornello form, with a modulating R2 that unexpectedly takes wing in a fine passage of chromatic counterpoint. Less persuasive is a curiously structured violin concerto in B♭ major in Lund (S-L, Saml. Engelhart, No. 382), whose authorship remains in doubt.

Ex. 7.6. Montanari, Violin Concerto in E♭ major, Op.1/6/II

structure, but remains loose-limbed, with a succession of solo figurations across the concertino group, separated by brief allusions to the motto.

Much more elaborate are concertos Nos. 1, 6, 7 and 8, all solo violin concertos in four movements, with only occasional participation by the second violin. The solo violin writing is often intricate, whether in ornate Adagio fantasies or in the advanced technical requirements of Allegro movements (Ex. 7.6). The second movements of Nos. 6–8 are all fugal in the manner of Mossi, but on a larger scale, with the fugue subject again articulating a ritornello structure around solo episodes. As with Mossi, the neutrality of the solo figuration blends naturally with the somewhat formulaic nature of the surrounding contrapuntal material. Yet, as this example shows, the figuration is more inventive and challenging than

Table 7.4. Timeline of Montanari, Violin Concerto in E♭ major, Op.1/6/II

Function	S/R1	S1	R3a	S3a	R3b	S3b	R4	S4 (coda)
Bars	1–15	15–19	20–28	28–39	39–41	41–47	48–59	59–67
Key	I (V) → iii	→	vi (iii) →	ii → vi	^{V}/vi →	ii → ^{V}/iii //	I	I
Thematic	M fugal		M fugal				M fugal	

that of Mossi – indeed, the conjunction of really virtuosic violin writing with serious contrapuntal style strongly suggests the possibility of an alternative concerto idiom, one leading in quite a different direction from Vivaldi.

In both Nos. 6 and 7, with their full-scale fugal expositions, the dominant receives its customary early prominence and the exposition is soon followed by departure to a peripheral key, avoiding the need for R2 altogether. In Op. 1/7, the move away from the tonic is achieved in a single crotchet, almost by hiatus. The result is a strongly ternary harmonic framework, with the outer sections concentrating entirely on I and V, and the inner sections focused on peripheral areas. Even more precipitate is the departure in Op. 1/6 in E♭ major, occurring already in R1 (Table 7.4). Again the centre of the movement intensively explores all available minor keys; and here the separation at the point of recapitulation is highlighted by perhaps the most extreme articulation in the entire repertoire (Ex. 7.6). The return of the E♭ major exposition is prepared by a D major chord, playing upon the harmonic ambiguity of the first few notes of the subject. The disjuncture is further accentuated by a long silence: a highly dramatic gesture.

Montanari seems to have deliberately begun the set with the least forbidding and most modern work. Once the opening florid Adagio is over, Op. 1/1 is certainly the closest to a Vivaldian concerto, the main Allegro prominently exploring such *galant* traits as syncopations and triplets. The homophonic motto is explicitly derived from the preceding Adagio, in a way that is evidently designed to highlight the transformation of style (Ex. 7.7a). The first solo, too, affects a soloistic swagger, while alluding to the motto in the walking bass accompaniment (Ex. 7.7b). Yet Montanari has a surprise in store for the unsuspecting Venetian listener. R2 fails to provide the expected confirmation of V with the motto, but instead modulates vertiginously to IV. This key dominates the central part of the movement, reflecting the two-sharp key signature and resulting in a tonal scheme (I-V-IV-ii-I) never used by Vivaldi.

These four works are exceptionally well crafted, the alliance of virtuosity with solid contrapuntal writing suggesting the possibility of a lineage of post-Corellian solo concerto such as no other composer attempted. Hitherto almost completely ignored, Montanari's concertos rank amongst the most impressive achievements in the Italian repertoire.

Ex. 7.7. Montanari, Violin Concerto in A major, Op. 1/1

Giuseppe Valentini

Giuseppe Valentini (*b* Florence, 1681; *d* Rome, 1753) has already been encountered in Chapter 3 in connection with his highly individualistic Op. 7 concertos,
published in Bologna in 1710.[12] This collection was dedicated to Michelangelo
Caetani, Prince of Caserta, and his wife Anna Maria Strozzi, who continued to be
Valentini's principal patrons until at least 1727. Also in 1710 Valentini began to
play at the church of S Luigi dei Francesi, where (after leading for nearly thirty
years) Corelli had been succeeded by his pupil Matteo Fornari. On Corelli's death
in 1713, however, Valentini took over the post, confirming both his high status
among Roman violinists and his long-sought succession to Corelli's mantle. Over
the next forty years he maintained numerous other church positions, sometimes as
maestro di cappella, and his reputation as musician and poet was confirmed by
the rare honour of membership of the Arcadian Academy. In this light it is difficult to understand his relationship with Ottoboni: while his works figure prominently in Ottoboni's library, suggesting at least some private contact, he appeared
only sporadically among the *ripieno* violinists at the Cardinal's public musical
functions.

Once he had established himself in Roman musical life, Valentini was less
concerned with making his name as a published composer. Three concertos
appeared in Amsterdam anthologies during the 1710s, but his only other major
concerto publication was the set of ten concertos Op. 9, published by Le Cène in
1724. Valentini's music is, however, well represented in manuscript collections.
Dresden possesses five concertos, of which three were copied by Pisendel,

---

[12] Careri, 'Giuseppe Valentini (1681–1753)'; Careri, 'Per un catalogo tematico'; Dunning, *Pietro
Antonio Locatelli*, vol. 2, pp. 207–34; Talbot, Michael, 'A Rival of Corelli'.

Table 7.5. Timeline of Valentini, Concerto in F major, Op. 9/4/II

Function	R1 – R2a	S2	R2b – R3	S3	R4a	S4	R4b
Bars	1–23	23–30	30–51	51–62	62–79	79–90	90–94
Key	I → V	V	V → vi	vi V	I I	I	I
Thematic	M M	a	M M	a a	M M (≈ 1–23)	a (≈ 23–30)	coda

presumably in Rome in 1717: one of these is identical with Op. 9/9, suggesting that the printed set may well contain works from the same period. The Ottoboni collection includes eight concertos, again with concordances among the printed works.

As we have seen in Chapter 3, Valentini's Op. 7 retained the outline of the Roman concerto grosso in its scoring and overall four-movement form, but developed it in diverse directions, sometimes referring to the ritornello concept. In general his later concertos follow along much the same lines, although with a more melodic emphasis and fewer wild flights of fantasy. In Op. 9, solos are used even more sparingly than before. None of the second movements contains a long virtuoso 'break' like that in the Op. 7/9 fugue, and solo passages are largely restricted to subordinate passages for two violins and cello.

Two broad formal strategies can be discerned in the later collection. Binary form sinfonia movements press strongly towards the central secondary key, with 'second subject' material later recapitulated in the tonic in an embryonic sonata form.[13] Often this subsidiary material is entrusted to the soloists. On the other hand, three concertos (Nos. 4, 8 and 9) contain substantial ritornello movements, beginning with a closed homophonic R1 and articulating tonal stages with the motto in the normal way. Even these movements recall the ripieno concerto, since solos appear incidentally and are not the driving force behind the music. Thus in Op. 9/9 a two-violin solo starts immediately after R1 to differentiate the new section, but it is subsumed into the tutti texture after only a few bars.

In Op. 9/4 in F major the solos have a quite different role, with a distinctive melody returning to confirm each tonal stage: V, vi and final tonic (Table 7.5, Ex. 7.8). Such highlighting of the dominant and subsequent transposition to the tonic – the 'second subject' of sonata form again – mirrors the sinfonia movements in the set, providing striking confirmation of the influence of binary form on Valentini's ritornello structures. Such a strong sense of tonal recapitulation is a highly distinctive feature of Valentini's concertos.

Seven manuscript string concertos may also be presumed to date from c1710–25, and they reflect a similar diversity both in form and in the usage of soloists.[14] Manchester 25 in D major includes the most substantial relevant

---

13 Talbot, 'A Rival of Corelli', p. 363.

14 These comprise Manchester Nos. 25, 26, 30 (also published in 1716), 31 and 65 (ed. Geerb, 1998); and Dresden Mus. 2387-O-2 and 2387-O-3. Everett regards Nos. 25, 26 and 30 as dating from the middle of the period 1710–1724, Nos. 31 and 65 from around 1724 (*The Manchester*

Ex. 7.8. Valentini, Concerto in F major, Op. 9/4/II

Table 7.6. Timeline of Valentini, Concerto in D major, Manchester 25/II

Function	R1	S1 (trio → vn1)	R2	S2 (trio → vn1)	RT	R3a	S3a (vn1)
Bars	1–34	34–41	41–51	51–58	58–68	68–69	70–80
Key	I	I →	V	V →	I //	vi	vi
Thematic	M		partly from R1		= R2		

R3b	R3c	S3b (vn2)	R3d	R4a	S4	R4b
80–94	94–96	96–107	107–121	121–149	149–153	153–172
vi →	iii	iii	→	I	I	I
partly from R1	= R3a		≈ R3b	≈ R1	≈ S1	≈ R2 (cf. RT)

movement, which introduces a significant new strategy to its blend of binary and ritornello forms (Table 7.6). Paul Everett has asserted in connection with this movement that 'any resemblance to ritornello form is, of course, superficial'.[15] Valentini's individual structures can be interpreted in many different ways, but we would still maintain that this movement may be heard against a background knowledge of ritornello procedures, with a substantial R1 that feeds subsequent ritornellos. Everett has divided the movement into a ternary form with new sections beginning at bars 68 and 121, reflecting the tonal scheme. But such an interpretation denies the listener's perception of bars 58–68 as a tonic interruption (RT), a premature closure that thwarts the expected confirmation of the dominant. That bar 68 is not in fact a genuine tonic closure is emphasized by the way it is forcefully rejected in favour of the delayed submediant (Ex. 7.9).

The new strategy explored in this movement is an extension of the influence of binary form, which goes a stage further than the process we have identified in Op.

Concerto Partbooks, pp. 310–11). There are concordances with Op. 9 in both Dresden and Manchester.

[15] Everett, *The Manchester Concerto Partbooks*, p. 324.

Ex. 7.9. Valentini, Concerto in D major, Manchester 25/II

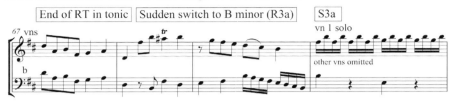

9/4. Here R2 provides not a new start but merely a culmination to the brief solo drive towards the dominant. While it does use motives from R1, its function is to end the dominant section and to confirm a temporary closure at bar 51. In the recapitulation, the entire complex R1-S1-R2 is reprised, adapted to remain in the tonic – just as if there had been a binary-form double-bar at bar 51. This complex movement therefore combines a whole series of implications at different levels (Table 7.7).

Table 7.7. Analytical options for Valentini, Concerto in D major, Manchester 25/II

Bars	1–51	51–68	68–121	121–172
Key	I → V	→ I	vi → iii →	I
(a) Ritornello	R1-S1-R2	S2-RT	R3a to R3d	R4a-S4-R4b
(b) Binary with reprise	A	→	B	A'
(c) Ternary (Everett)	A		B	A'

The discussion of this movement reveals again how closely ritornello form – an overall concept rather than an inflexible mould – may be related to other musical genres of the period. It can easily turn into a version of binary form, as will be explored further in Chapter 14 in connection with Tartini; it was easily reconciled with fugal procedures; and it may occasionally be interpreted in the context of an overall ternary form. We are by no means assuming that every listener always anticipated pure ritornello form at the start of each concerto, but rather that the ritornello concept was flexible enough to accommodate and inter-lock with other prevalent idioms; and conversely that other genres may some-times be fruitfully experienced against a ritornello background. This is especially true of centres like Rome, which did not fully succumb to the spell of the 'Vivaldian revolution'.

A special preface to the *Allettamenti per camera*, Op. 8 (1714) – written by the dedicatee – refers to *Un'Opera di Concerti grossi con Trombe, Obue, e diversi altri Stromenti* as nearly finished and ready for publication.[16] It was never published in this form, but (to judge from surviving manuscripts) Valentini was particularly interested in writing for wind instruments, which were indeed prominent earlier in Rome than elsewhere. Inevitably his wind concertos develop new formal designs, since wind instruments cannot dip in and out of the texture in the same way as

16   Talbot, 'A Rival of Corelli', p. 353.

strings. The two agreeable oboe concertos published in *Concerti a cinque* (1717) both use small-scale ritornello form, with solo-tutti exchanges in chamber manner and frequent returns to the tonic. No. 4 strongly resembles the oboe concertos in Albinoni's Op. 7 (1715), with a clear Devise opening and a full recapitulation of both R1 and S1, extended into a coda referring to the central section.

Much more ambitious are the two remaining concertos in Dresden, which may perhaps be linked with the unpublished *Opera di Concerti grossi*. Both contain large-scale ritornello-type movements, but they are hybrids that avoid consistent use of solo instruments. Mus. 2387-O-1 begins like a regular concerto for two oboes, but changes course with the introduction of two trumpets and timpani shortly after R2. Mus. 2387-O-5 is essentially an oboe concerto, but in the Allegro second movement a virtuosic solo violin unexpectedly intrudes, just at the point where R3 in the submediant is expected.[17]

Apparently the latest surviving concertos by Valentini are the two wind concertos in the Ottoboni library: Manchester 28, scored for two oboes doubling recorder, and Manchester 51, scored for two recorders with optional horns.[18] Everett has placed these works in the mid- to late 1720s, calling attention to their *galant* melodic inflexions and experimental structures. Both the second movements are indeed individual and even progressive, with a flexible relationship between soloists and tutti in the sinfonia manner. Nevertheless these movements may again be perceived against ritornello form, which enhances the listener's appreciation of their surprising features. Certainly Manchester 28 in A major has a unique tonal scheme, which is linked to the replacement of oboes by recorders for the central episode. R2 diverts quite unexpectedly from E major to C major (Ex. 7.10), and the recorders enter in seductively pastoral thirds, hovering between C major and F major in sensuous contrast to the surrounding sharp keys. When the oboes return, they introduce a false reprise in D major, eventually corrected, resulting in the remarkable overall scheme I-V-♭III-♭VI-IV-I.

Ex. 7.10. Valentini, Concerto in A major, Manchester 28/II

---

[17] Curiously, the oboe part is written in the score in C major, as if intended for trumpet, but the compass indicates that this is not a practical interpretation.

[18] Both ed. Everett (2001, 2000). See also Everett, *The Manchester Concerto Partbooks*, pp. 311, 331–42, where these movements are somewhat differently viewed against a three-section design.

We have dwelt on Valentini's concertos at some length, because they lie in a particularly interesting relationship with ritornello procedures. They have sometimes been airily dismissed as essentially Corellian concerti grossi by virtue of their scoring and four-movement form, but this interpretation does scant justice to Valentini's individuality in adapting and commenting on ritornello procedures. Particularly striking is his innovative incorporation of binary-form concepts. In distinguishing the secondary key with contrasting melodic material and later reprising this in the tonic, he brought to the concerto a foretaste of 'sonata form' decades ahead of its widespread acceptance. Charles Burney's offhand dismissal of Valentini's concertos ('they have been long since consigned to oblivion, without any loss to the public, or injustice to the author')[19] seems entirely inappropriate. They may not burn with the inspirational fire of the concertos of his greatest contemporaries, but they certainly deserve the attention they are only now beginning to receive.

[19] Burney, *A General History*, vol. 2, p. 437.

CHAPTER 8

The Venetian Orbit

Though on the decline as a political and economic power, Venice continued to provide an attractive environment for composers during the first half of the eighteenth century, hosting the largest group of concerto composers across two generations. Six were trained in Venice and active there for many years: Gentili, Albinoni, the Marcello brothers, Tessarini and Vivaldi. Though not himself Venetian, Bonporti from nearby Trent is included here for convenience and comparison. Others (to be discussed in the next chapters) studied, performed and composed in Venice for extended periods before crossing the Alps for more lucrative positions. Among these, Platti was probably born in Venice and he certainly trained there before taking up a post in Würzburg in 1722. Three outstanding violinists made more fleeting visits: the Florentine Veracini in 1711 and intermittently over the next five years; the Bolognese Brescianello in or before 1715 (when he was recruited to Munich); and Locatelli during the mid-1720s, during his travels between the Rome and Amsterdam periods of his life. Finally, Tartini (the subject of Chapter 14) was also closely connected with Venice, apparently hearing Veracini there in 1716 and becoming a frequent visitor after he was appointed to S Antonio in Padua in 1721.

It cannot be argued that this large group projected a unified conception of the concerto, and it would be quite misleading to regard these composers as representatives of a single Venetian school in the shadow of Vivaldi. Indeed Gentili stands largely outside the development of the ritornello concerto. The others, however, in their individual ways show an awareness of the developing potential of the Vivaldian concerto form: sometimes adapting older procedures to take it into account, sometimes mirroring Vivaldi's own practice, and sometimes leading it in directions that he never pursued.

Giorgio Gentili

The oldest of the Venetian concerto composers to be considered here is Giorgio Gentili (*b* Venice, *c*1669, *d* Venice after 1731). Appointed as a violinist to the ducal church of S Marco on 10 July 1689, he remained in this post at least until 1731. His first set of concertos, published as Op. 5 in 1708, is very much in the Corellian concerto grosso tradition discussed in the previous chapter, with multi-movement structures and generally full contrapuntal textures. Only occasionally are there virtuosic flourishes, and these again are Corellian in inspiration:

No. 9 in D major opens with solo arpeggiation clearly modelled on Corelli's violin sonata Op. 5/1.

Gentili's Op. 6 therefore comes as a considerable surprise. The set survives only in a manuscript dedicated to the Elector of Saxony in 1716, and though the manuscript is laid out in the format of a printed edition, it never attained a wider circulation. The twelve concertos are diverse in structure and idiom, and there are vestiges of concerto grosso textures throughout. Yet sometimes Gentili is clearly attempting to come to terms with the new solo concerto: hammer-stroke mottos open Op. 6/2 and Op. 6/9 (the latter in triple time like Torelli's Op. 8/5), and there are extended passages of virtuosic solo figuration for the *violino principale*. Yet Gentili is none too successful in his new guise. The material itself is undistinguished and he is unable to sustain the ritornello designs with a convincing coherence. In the ambitious opening movement of Op. 6/12, for example, a brief motto of repeated semiquavers articulates the rambling tonal scheme outlined in Table 8.1. More successful are shorter movements such as the opening of Op. 6/11 in C minor: here the poignant unison motto (Ex. 8.1) acts as a simple refrain between short solo sections, outlining a much more persuasive tonal scheme (i-v-ii-♭VII-III-i).

Table 8.1. Ritornellos in Gentili, Concerto in D major, Op. 6/12

Key	I	I	vi → V	I → V/V/V	I → V	iii	I	V	vi	I	I
Thematic	M	M	M	M	M	M	M	M	M	M	M

Ex. 8.1. Gentili, Violin Concerto in C minor, Op. 6/11

Doubled at the lower octave

Clearly the new idiom posed considerable challenges to a composer steeped in the older manner. Others who might also been seen as relatively conservative in outlook reacted to the 'Vivaldian revolution' in different ways and with considerably more success.

Tomaso Albinoni

Tomaso Albinoni (*b* Venice, 1671; *d* Venice, 1751) considered himself a musical *dilettante*, at least until his father's death in 1709, after which he asserted his independence from the family playing-card business as an opera and instrumental composer of European reputation.[1] He continued to publish major sets of concertos regularly until the mid-1730s, transferring allegiance to the firm of Roger and Le Cène in Amsterdam, and developing a speciality of concertos for

---

[1]   Talbot, *The Instrumental Music of Tomaso Albinoni*; Talbot, *Albinoni: Leben und Werk*; Talbot, *Tomaso Albinoni*.

one or two oboes. One of the pioneers in the early history of the Venetian concerto (as we have seen in Chapter 3), he continued to maintain a certain independence of mind, developing his own conception of the concerto while showing awareness of the emerging Vivaldian ritornello form.

If one adopts a teleogical stance, however dangerous that may be, it is easy to trace a line of development from the incipient ritornello features of Op. 2 (published in 1700), through the expanded dimensions of Op. 5 (1707), to the mature ritornello form that emerges in the oboe concertos of Op. 7 (1715) and especially Op. 9 (1722). The string concertos in these two sets, as well as most of those in Op. 10 (1735–36), broadly continue the lines laid down in the earlier publications, but in Op. 10 Nos. 8 and 12 Albinoni finally espoused full-scale ritornello form in the solo violin concerto. His contribution to the concerto, spanning a period of at least thirty-five years, suggests a continuous process of searching for better, or at least alternative, strategies. It would appear that he reached the apex of his identification with ritornello form precisely at the height of his creative inspiration in Op. 9. The fact that in Op. 10 he partly turned away from ritornello form, at the same time as his imaginative powers shone less brightly, highlights the very high quality of the concertos in which he came closest to the influence of Vivaldi.

Oboe concertos
The concertos for solo oboe (four in Op. 7, four in Op. 9) and for two oboes (four in each set) demand separate treatment, because it is here that Albinoni developed his individual version of ritornello form in the most sophisticated way, inspired not only by the sound of the oboe as a vocal soloist, but also by the new textural possibilities it opened up. For whereas a solo violin could move in and out of the texture relatively unobtrusively, the entrance of the solo oboist and its subsequent role in the movement required a different approach.

The oboe, essentially a French creation, was already well known in Venice by the end of the seventeenth century, and there were several outstanding players there during Albinoni's lifetime, including Ignazio Sieber, who taught at the Pietà between 1713 and 1716.[2] Possibly he was the inspiration behind Albinoni's concertos: those in Op. 7 were the first oboe concertos to appear in print, heading a sizeable corpus of published Italian works for the instrument. The following discussion will be based on fifteen concertos, omitting Op. 7/5 which, in its succession of sections in varying sonorities and close adherence to the tonic, is more akin to the concerto grosso.

As Talbot has observed, the oboe concertos of Vivaldi are closely modelled both in structure and even in instrumental idiom on his violin concertos.[3] With Albinoni, however, the oboe is distinguished much more noticeably as a quasi-vocal soloist, through the cantabile melodic writing and narrow-gauged figuration appropriate to the instrument. This is particularly evident in solo entrances, which almost universally adopt a device from the earlier operatic aria, the Devise described in Chapter 1. The single statement of the solo Devise after a

[2]   Bernardini, 'The Oboe in the Venetian Republic'; Talbot, 'Albinoni's Oboe Concertos'.
[3]   *Tomaso Albinoni*, pp. 164–5.

closed ritornello functions as an announcement that explicitly draws attention to the individuality of the soloist, like the entrance of the singer on stage, and it also clearly separates the roles of tutti and solo, whether or not they actually share material. The second statement of the Devise, following R1b, then has a different structural role, which is to lead away from the arena of the opening into something new, expressed in tonal terms by the move to the dominant. It will be immediately evident that this is a quite different strategy from that adopted in Albinoni's early string concertos.

In nine cases the solo begins with the motto, perhaps in a slightly varied form. Even in the other cases, there is no strong differentiation between material, and Albinoni's concertos in general continue to show a high cohesion in terms of common rhythms and diatonic patterns. In the case of the double concertos, the two oboes always work as a pair, either in parallel or in close imitation (not as two separate soloists, as is often the case with Vivaldi's double concertos). The lack of clear thematic differentiation, together with the limited potential of the oboe for virtuosic figuration, encourages a greater integration of tutti and solo than in many a violin concerto of the period. Indeed, paradoxically, the contrasting timbre of the oboe permits it to take part inside a contrapuntal texture in a way that would be meaningless in a violin concerto. Certainly the imaginatively varying textures of the double oboe concertos are a constant delight, compensating for Albinoni's somewhat repetitive diatonic material and sequences.[4]

The concerto for two oboes Op. 7/2 illustrates Albinoni's experimentation with the relationship between texture and motive as a means to develop a musical argument. Tutti and soloists have their own distinct motives at first – the one an angular unison, the other in mellifluous thirds – but as the movement unfolds they start to interact in diverse ways, resulting in four principal textures:

(1) duet for two oboes, sometimes with accompaniment;
(2) strings only;
(3) strings dominating, with two oboes enriching the sonority;
(4) dialogue between oboes and strings.

While a ritornello scheme can be perceived in the background, the movement is not based purely on an opposition of solo and tutti but rather on a fluidity of textural interactions, culminating in the final section, where the superimposition of the oboes over the unison ritornello produces a sense of harmonious resolution.

In Op. 9/6 and Op. 9/12 the oboes even play a full part in a kaleidoscopic rotation of textures within R1 itself. A common technique within the ensuing solo is for the string accompaniment to start lightly but acquire an increasing importance through counterpoint and dialogue as S1 leads up to R2, at which point the oboes drop out. The ritornello is therefore not distinguished by a fuller and more complex texture, as in most Vivaldi concertos, but rather by a uniformity of string sound.[5]

We have already mentioned the connection of the Devise with the contemporary aria, but the analogy with vocal forms should not be taken too far. While up to

4   Talbot, *Tomaso Albinoni*, pp. 158–60.
5   See also the discussion of Op. 9/6 in Chapter 1.

the arrival of R2 there is a close correspondence with the first section of an operatic aria, Albinoni's conception does not reflect the overall shape of a Da Capo
aria, nor in any detailed sense the structure of the A-section alone.[6] Albinoni
rather adopts the general principles of the Vivaldian ritornello form – sectional
and subdivisible ritornello, articulation of tonal areas by texture, thematic integration and manipulation – leading to an expanded structuring of instrumental
form. Yet he develops this out of his own earlier practices, maintaining a concentrated and buoyant sonority, in which shifting patterns reflect new images of the
same material rather than the highly dramatic or sensitive fantasy of Vivaldi.

Albinoni's selection of tonal schemes also differs markedly from that of
Vivaldi, with a continued preference for the pendulum pattern around a central
tonic (compare Table 8.2 with Table 5.1). Two essential features of the early
string concertos are maintained: a universal adoption of the dominant or relative
major as the first target – always emphasized by R2 – and an immediate reversion
to the tonic. Now, however, the tonic does not normally recur within the tutti
section (for R2 is hardly ever modulatory) but is instead transferred to the ensuing
solo. The natural tendency of the dominant to return to the tonic at this point has
been discussed in Chapter 5: but where Vivaldi usually avoided this temptation,
Albinoni embraced it as his preferred strategy, as has already been illustrated in
connection with Op. 9/6 (see Ex. 1.7).

Table 8.2. Tonal schemes of Albinoni's oboe concertos

Circuit		Pendulum	
Tonal scheme	**Number**	**Tonal scheme**	**Number**
Major			
		I-V-I-vi-I	3
		I-V-I-vi-iii-I	4
		I-V-I-vi-I-iii-I	4
I-V-vi-ii-IV-I	1		
		I-V-I-iii-vi-(ii-v)-vi-I	1
Minor			
		i-III-i-v-♭VII-iv-i	1
		i-III-i-iv-VI-i	1

The length of the central tonic varies considerably. In Op. 7/9, it can scarcely
be regarded as a tonal centre, being treated rather as a springboard on the way to
the subdominant (compare the similar procedure seen in Vivaldi, Ex. 5.5). In Op.
7/6, on the other hand, it extends to a full 23% of the movement: here (exceptionally) a tutti restatement of the motto in the tonic acts as a very persuasive false
reprise before a new departure to vi. This is an extreme example of tonal

---

6   Solie, 'Aria Structure', pp. 43–5 (and see above, p. 54).

Table 8.3. Proportions of stable tonal areas in Albinoni, Oboe Concerto in D major, Op. 7/6

Stable area	I	V	I	vi	I
Proportion	27%	10%	23%	2%	30%
Motto	M	M	→ M		M

Table 8.4. Average proportions of stable tonal areas in Albinoni's oboe concertos

Stable area	Opening tonic	Secondary	Intermediate tonic	First peripheral	Second peripheral	Closing tonic
Average proportion	26%	12%	6%	5%	4%	29%

proportions favouring the tonic (a total of 80%), with the motto articulating a rondo-like structure (Table 8.3).

Another striking continuity from the earlier period is Albinoni's strong commitment to vi as his preferred peripheral key in major. Usually this key is succeeded by iii, with a further intermediate tonic perhaps continuing the sense of tonal debate (I-V-I-vi-I-iii-I). Albinoni maintains a powerful tonal hierarchy in almost every case. This is reflected firstly in the matter of modulatory central ritornellos. While R2 is stable in the secondary key in every case but one, there is never just a single stable R3, and twelve concertos have at least one modulatory peripheral ritornello. Tonal hierarchy is also reflected in the strong contrasts in duration of stable tonal areas (Table 8.4). These two factors, taken together, indicate a high degree of instability in the peripheral area, which is taken to an extreme in Op. 7/3 in B♭ major. Here the arrival at D minor is short-lived, an immediate move to G minor initiating a circle of falling fifths (D-G-C-F-B♭) before the final confirmation of G minor, all within 11 bars (Ex. 8.2 shows the beginning of the process).

As already suggested above, Albinoni explores more complex textures than are normally found in concertos of the period, even within the opening ritornello. While R2 is almost always stressed by the tutti motto without soloists, this section is usually followed by much more fluid textures, so that solo and ritornello sections intermingle or even transform from one to another. In Op. 9/9 in C major, for example, the solo passage following R3a is gradually taken over by the strings, culminating in a strong tutti cadence in iii at bar 66, which serves as R3b. In Op. 9/12 this process is taken so far that most of the 'solo' after RT (bars 43–51) is in fact dominated by the tutti violin line. Conversely the following section – structurally, R3 – is overlaid by a cantabile oboe line. Such deliberate ambiguity of roles reveals Albinoni's compositional subtlety at its most ingenious, in which he was scarcely matched by any composer other than Bach. Like Bach, Albinoni was undoubtedly influenced by Vivaldi at this point of his compositional activity, and he adopted certain traits from Vivaldian concerto procedures; yet this influence was blended into his own conception of the concerto, which involved a certain reluctance to differentiate ritornello and solo.

Ex. 8.2. Albinoni, Oboe Concerto in B♭ major, Op. 7/3

It was surely the meeting between these two different approaches that spurred Albinoni to some of the most imaginative concerto writing of the period.

Albinoni's recapitulations take the idea of reinterpretation to its furthest extreme, resulting in some of the most complex passages in his concertos. Following the pattern set in the early string concertos, the point of recapitulation is always strongly articulated, in almost every case by the motto (Table 8.5). But thereafter Albinoni explores a variety of procedures, amply justifying the contention that the recapitulation provides an opportunity for the most creative manipulation of material. Frequently he brings together sections of R1, S1 and ST/RT in new juxtapositions and rescorings that may reverse the earlier functions. In this kaleidoscopic whirl of textures – a fluid mix in which now the soloists, now the strings come to the fore – concepts of ritornello and solo become redundant.

Table 8.5. Articulation of the recapitulation in Albinoni's oboe concertos

Articulation of the recapitulation	Number
Within a ritornello (R3-R4), articulated by motto	4
Coincides with the beginning of S4, articulated by motto	4
Coincides with the beginning of R4, articulated by motto	3
Within a solo (S3-S4), articulated by motto	2
Within a ritornello (R3-R4), articulated by a previous motive other than motto	1
Coincides with the beginning of S4, articulated by a previous motive other than motto	1

The role of the coda remains forceful, and in a few cases it can be easily distinguished from the preceding reprise of R1 – as in Op. 9/6 (discussed in Chapter 1). In more complex cases, however, the recapitulation unfolds continuously with yet more reworkings of material and a strong feeling of closure, as if the very concept of coda were infiltrating the ever-varying reprise. This may be best illustrated by Op. 9/9, especially as solo and ritornello had been so clearly differentiated earlier. The recapitulation includes not only tonic material from R1, S1 and ST, but also dominant material transposed – all reworked, in *ars combinatoria* fashion. Table 8.6 outlines the relationship between the two sections: particularly striking is the way the unsettling function of bars 3–5 is delayed until the tonic has been securely re-established.

Table 8.6. Derivation of the recapitulation in Albinoni, Concerto for Two Oboes in C major, Op. 9/9

Recapitulation bars	Quoting	Original bars	Taken from
73–75	literally	1–2	R1
75–78	literally	6–9	R1
78–84	literally	19–24	S1
84–89	transposed from V	25–30	S1
89–94	literally	41–45	ST
94–97	2ob added	3–5	R1
97–100	recast with 2ob leading	6–9	R1
100–103	transposed	30–33	S1
103–104	literally	10–11	R1

The later violin concertos

Clearly the particular demands and possibilities presented by the oboe inspired Albinoni to his own engagement with Vivaldian ritornello form. The violin concertos of this period are better viewed as successors to Op. 5, albeit with some reference to the newer ritornello procedures. Only one of the four string concertos in Op. 7 (No. 10) contains violin solos, but all four in Op. 9 do so. Also in this group are the concerto published in *Concerti a cinque* (1717, Co2), and two concertos surviving only in Dresden manuscripts, copied by Pisendel, presumably in Venice in 1716–17 (Co4, Co5).[7]

These eight concertos perpetuate by now familiar Albinoni characteristics: the predominance of the pendulum tonal pattern (Table 8.7); the articulation of the recapitulation by the motto, followed by a complete or partial restatement of R1; the separate closing section which may be described as a coda. The violin is given

---

7   Four concertos survive in Pisendel's hand, including his adaptations of Co2 and Op. 7/10 (Talbot, *Tomaso Albinoni*, pp. 161, 168–72).

Table 8.7. Tonal schemes of Albinoni's later violin concertos (including Op. 10/8 and Op. 10/12)

Circuit		Pendulum	
Tonal scheme	**Number**	**Tonal scheme**	**Number**
Major			
I-V-vi-I	1	I-V-I-vi-I	1
		I-V-I-vi-iii-I	2
		I-V-I-vi-I-iii-I	3
		I-V-iii-I-vi-I	1
I-V-ii-vi-I	1		
Minor			
		i-III-i-v-i	1

greater prominence in this late group than in Op. 5, as well as more virtuosity in passages of high solo figuration (even if some of the brilliance of Co5 may be attributable to Pisendel's intervention). Solos are spread much more evenly throughout each movement, and all of these works can be regarded as violin concertos in the broad sense of the term. But again Albinoni retains his own conception of the role of the soloist, who often glides into and emerges from the string texture with none of the bravura associated with Vivaldi.

One important structural feature of Op. 5 remains in evidence. In half of these eight concertos, the modulation to the dominant is accomplished in a tutti by direct repetition of the motto a fifth higher (compare Ex. 3.6). Yet those four concertos that entrust the first modulation to the soloist show how Albinoni's newer conception of ritornello form could be transferred to the violin concerto. Co2 and Co5 even draw on the Devise idea, introducing the solo with duet passages that directly recall the two-oboe concertos just discussed. Op. 9 Nos. 4 and 7 instead modify Albinoni's earlier practice of following a complete R1 with a further motto in tonic and dominant:[8] here there is just the single tonic motto, leaving the soloist to assert the move towards the dominant in the manner of Vivaldi's Op. 4/1 (see Ex. 4.18).

As in the oboe concertos, there is a clear contrast between stable tonic/dominant areas and unstable peripheral areas. Op. 9/7 marks the well-prepared vi with only a brief tutti cadence, the sole remnant of R3 (Ex. 8.3); while R3 is avoided altogether in Op. 7/10, as S3 rushes through ii-iii-vi-iii-ii with just a couple of tutti interjections. Albinoni thus essayed an option that was to prevail in the classical concerto, in which R3 was reduced to a brief tutti articulation of the main peripheral key or even abandoned altogether.[9]

Despite the continuance of idiosyncratic procedures of his own, it is clear that

---

[8] The significance of these two concertos has also been highlighted by Shapiro, 'The Treatment of Form', p. 163.

[9] Simon, 'The Double Exposition', pp. 115–17.

Ex. 8.3. Albinoni, Violin Concerto in D major, Op. 9/7

vn 2, va omitted

Albinoni is working here against a background of Vivaldian ritornello form. Talbot has observed that 'Albinoni [imitates] Vivaldi only very selectively, almost grudgingly'.[10] Yet it is always possible to identify clear ritornellos, which are usually marked by Albinoni's preferred statements of an unaltered motto. Where a solo does not culminate in a ritornello, there is a strong sense that it is missing – implying that Albinoni has developed techniques to manipulate the listener's expectations within a shared knowledge of ritornello form.

With the late string concertos Op. 10, we move into a quite different sound world. Here Albinoni radically modernized his melodic style to match the new *galant* idiom of Tartini or Locatelli, with triplet figurations, decorative trills and ornaments, and separate phrases that can be immediately repeated. Albinoni's forthright diatonicism survives the change, but it is enriched with small-scale *minore* contrasts. Most noticeable of all, perhaps, is the simplified texture that places direct emphasis on the upper melodic line. The loss of the textural variety that so distinguished the oboe concertos is not compensated by the sophisticated thematic manipulation that elevates the concertos of Tartini, nor indeed by the melodic invention of Albinoni's early concertos. As a result these concertos have received a bad press from modern critics; yet they are good examples of their type, and make for our purposes a stimulating commentary on the marriage of older procedures with newer melodic idioms.

Six of the twelve concertos include brief violin solos in a return to the variable and often sporadic use of the soloist remarked earlier. Only Nos. 8 and 12 adopt full-scale ritornello form for their first movements, with clearly separated violin solos. In both movements, the first modulation is allotted to the soloist, and in Op. 10/8 – an unambiguous solo violin concerto – S1 at last achieves the final stage. Here the solo motto (accompanied only by violins) is immediately transposed to the relative major: a version of the tutti procedure developed in Albinoni's works of thirty years earlier (Ex. 8.4). After a stable R2, the ensuing solo now mirrors the oboe concertos in stating the motto first in III and then in the tonic. Thus both modulations are displaced into the solo, a major change from the earlier violin concertos. The recapitulation also shows an awareness of newer tonal thinking: instead of the full Da Capo found in nearly half of Albinoni's concertos, this movement uniquely omits the modulatory phrase (bars 4–7) in the reprise. At the same time Albinoni retains his own idiosyncrasies – the overt pendulum scheme,

10   Talbot, *Tomaso Albinoni*, p. 158.

Ex. 8.4. Albinoni, Violin Concerto in G minor, Op. 10/8

the reliance on a pervasive motto, the articulation of the recapitulation by R4, the subsequent coda. Thus he blends in a single movement older structural principles with newer aspects of ritornello form and an unashamed attempt to ape the most up-to-date melody and texture.

A comparison between the two Venetians reveals their differing attitudes towards ritornello form. Vivaldi turned it into his axiomatic choice and then dedicated the rest of his life to exploring the innumerable options implicit within it. By contrast, Albinoni had already developed his own ways of constructing large-scale instrumental movements and he dipped into Vivaldian ritornello form only when it suited him, interpreting its implications in his individual way. His final set of concertos, on first impression the most modern, blithely returns to older models in all but two concertos, as if to emphasize that ritornello form was only one path of many and that solo display was not the principal essence of instrumental music.

The Marcello Brothers

Alessandro Marcello (*b* Venice, 1669; *d* Venice, 1747) and his brother Benedetto (*b* Venice, 1686; *d* Brescia, 1739) had, as Venetian noblemen in high public office, even less reason than Albinoni to pursue a commercial agenda in developing the concerto; and since neither was writing for their own performance – Alessandro preferred to collect musical instruments – soloistic display was certainly low on their priorities. Indeed, after publishing his pioneering Op. 1 in 1708 (considered in Chapter 3), Benedetto turned away from instrumental composition altogether, perhaps regarding the concerto as a symptom of that shallowness that he sought to counter in his psalm settings and attacks on modern opera.[11]

Alessandro was a figure of much greater significance in the later development of the concerto, although his works lie only on the periphery of this study, since their relationship with ritornello form is somewhat tangential. He was the composer of one of the best-known concertos of this period, the oboe concerto in D minor D935, published in Amsterdam in 1717 (in one source in C minor). This concerto, made famous through Bach's keyboard transcription (BWV 974), has also been attributed to Benedetto,[12] and indeed there is a striking similarity with

[11] Surviving in Dresden are a rather routine concerto (C784) apparently derived from the sinfonia to *Spago e Filetta* (1719) and another for two violins (C797), probably copied in 1716–17 by Pisendel and on the miniature scale of Op. 1/8.

[12] Selfridge-Field, *The Music of Benedetto and Alessandro Marcello*, p. 365.

Ex. 8.5. Alessandro Marcello, Oboe Concerto in D minor, D935

the opening of Benedetto's Op. 1/8 (see Ex. 3.7). In both, a short motto in two halves is played by upper strings, and the soloist enters in Devise manner, accompanied by continuo (Ex. 8.5). The oboe concerto is, however, much more assured in its varied use of the motto across a short-breathed ritornello form; and Alessandro's authorship is not necessarily in doubt.

More musically developed are Alessandro Marcello's concertos with two oboes (D936–944): six in *La cetra*, a set published in Augsburg in 1738 under the Arcadian pseudonym Eterio Stinfalico, and three in manuscript in Venice.[13] The preface to *La cetra* leaves considerable flexibility to the performers with regard to instrumentation,[14] but in essence they may be regarded as concertos for two soloists, the solo parts being variously distributed around oboes, violins and cello. But these are not full-scale virtuoso works, with only occasional violin figuration; some opening movements lack solos altogether, while others are reminiscent of the concerto grosso. No doubt this attitude reflects the restrained Arcadian ideals of the Accademia degli Animosi.

The main emphasis is less on developing new approaches to Vivaldian ritornello form (though there are hints of this) than on experimenting with colouristic textures and musical idioms. Indeed the most straightforward common-time Allegro is eschewed altogether, in favour of either triple-time Allegro or gentler rhythms that suggest the opening of a trio sonata. D941 (*La cetra*/6) makes explicit the whole question of metre: though written in $^3/_4$, it sounds at first like $^2/_4$ with its fugal subject in hemiola. Possibly the German destination of *La cetra* inspired a more cosmopolitan embracing of a variety of idioms. In this same movement there is an unexpected Lento episode where 'reverse dotting' seems to echo a delicate French minuet; while the very opening movement of the set combines suggestions of the French overture style with Italianate concerto figuration (Ex. 8.6).

It is hardly surprising therefore that ritornello procedures remain in the background here. Typically, the motto introduces just one central ritornello beginning in the dominant around which the movement revolves, as illustrated by D939 in E

13 The concerto for seven recorders (D945) is irrelevant to this study.
14 Selfridge-Field, *The Music of Benedetto and Alessandro Marcello*, pp. 35–6.

Ex. 8.6. Alessandro Marcello, Concerto for Two Oboes in D major, D936 (*La cetra*/1)

Table 8.8. Timeline of Alessandro Marcello, Concerto for Two Oboes in E minor, D939 (*La Cetra*/4)

Function	R1	S1 (vn1)	R2	S2 (vn2)	R4
Bars	1–10	11–27	28–37	38–54	55–64
Key	i	i → v	v	v → ii	→ i
Thematic			= R1 transposed (vn parts reversed)	= S1 transposed	new

minor (*La cetra*/4, Table 8.8). Here bars 1–27 are simply repeated a fifth higher with the parts redisposed, ending, rather strangely, in F♯ minor. Only by sleight of hand does the final ritornello pull back to the tonic.

Clearly the concertos of Alessandro Marcello have features in common with those of Albinoni, in their reluctance to abandon older textures and methods of construction at the same time as they incorporate elements of the Vivaldian ritornello into a flexible mixture of idioms. Something of the same can be said of the much more strongly individual concertos of our fourth *dilettante* composer.

Francesco Antonio Bonporti

The Trent priest, Francesco Antonio Bonporti (*b* Trent, 1672; *d* Padua, 1749) was a prolific composer of chamber music, mostly published in Venice. His reputation was formerly based on the misattribution of his inventions Op. 10 to J.S. Bach, but his single set of concertos Op. 11 (Trent, *c*1727) has latterly received special prominence as a result of Arthur Hutchings' encomium in his influential 1959 book on the concerto.[15] Bonporti sometimes retains a Corellian turn of phrase and even vestiges of his technique of extending long musical paragraphs through dignified suspensions. As a consequence, Hutchings and others have understandably placed Bonporti outside the Venetian orbit altogether. Nevertheless this is an appropriate place to consider his concertos in the light of those of Albinoni and Alessandro Marcello, which are similarly askew to the main development of the Venetian concerto.

Op. 11 is certainly a highly distinctive collection, displaying a rare degree of fantasy in terms of harmonic exploration and rhythmic experiment. Fantasy

---

[15] *The Baroque Concerto*, pp. 305–14.

Ex. 8.7. Bonporti, Violin Concerto in D major, Op. 11/8

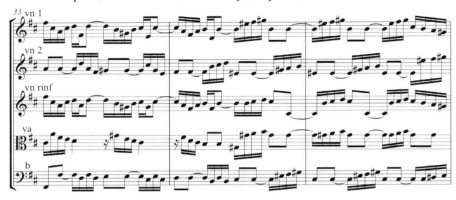

Ex. 8.8. Bonporti, Violin Concerto in F major, Op. 11/6

extends to the forms too: indeed the set resembles a disquisition on the many ways in which the concerto as a whole – and the ritornello movement in particular – might be approached. Although all ten concertos are in three movements, the idioms are highly varied, as are the textures: indeed four of the opening movements are not written in solo ritornello form at all. The remaining six range from the relatively straightforward violin concerto movement that opens Op. 11/9, to those with much more complex interactions between solo and tutti. Partly this variety results from the scoring for two violins, 'violino di rinforzo', viola and continuo. The third part is in fact much more than a doubling ripieno, diving in and out of the first part and often providing a new third line, as in the intensely Bachian motivic working in Op. 11/8 (Ex. 8.7). It seems evident from this interweaving five-part counterpoint that single strings are intended, so that Bonporti can exploit a whole range of shifting textures besides the homophonic violin solo with continuo and the four-part string tutti.

In general, Bonporti strives towards a tightly organized integration, by repeating whole sections or by reworking earlier material in different contexts. This taut compositional approach is sometimes reflected in complex thematic manipulation: thus in Op. 11/6, a Corellian sequence is transformed in a diminution that is again suggestive of Bach (Ex. 8.8). Yet if this might appear a rather severe compositional ethos, in reality these concertos are remarkable for their experimental range, as is immediately apparent from the unusual tonal strategies of four of the six concertos (Table 8.9).

Particularly striking here is the frequent avoidance of the dominant as the first target. In three concertos vi is preferred, delaying the dominant until later: thus in Op. 11/9, S1 moves decisively to vi, but this is immediately 'corrected' by reversion to V for R2. In Op. 11/3, by contrast, the multi-sectional R1 itself comes to a

Table 8.9. Tonal schemes in Bonporti's Op. 11, Nos. 2, 3, 4, 6, 8, 9

Circuit		Pendulum	
Tonal scheme	**Number**	**Tonal scheme**	**Number**
Major			
I-V-iii-vi-I I-V-iii-vi-ii-I	1 1		
I-vi-V-iii-I	2		
		I-vi-I-iii-V-I	1
		I-IV-vi-I-V-iii-I	1

Table 8.10. Timeline of Bonporti, Violin Concerto in B♭ major, Op. 11/3

Function	R1	S1	R3a	RT	R3b	S3a
Bars	1–23	24–30	31–50	51–54	54–58	59–65
Key	I → (V) → vi	vi	vi →	I	→	iii

R3c	R4a	S4	R4b
66–103	103–118	119–129	129–180
iii → V →	I	I	I (IV) I

halt on vi, which is then treated as the first target key: only after a lengthy exploration of peripheral keys is the dominant reached and articulated by the motto (Table 8.10). Bonporti intensifies the directionality of this fascinating movement through long-range rhythmic acceleration. The movement starts with syncopations suggesting quaver motion, soon shifts into a *giga* and finally arrives, within R3, at semiquaver passage-work (Ex. 8.9).

Ex. 8.9. Bonporti, Violin Concerto in B♭ major, Op. 11/3

Highly unusual for a different reason is the strategy in Op. 11/6, which reverses the normal balance by beginning with a flatward move to IV en route to vi. It takes a forceful hiatus to restore the tonic so as to initiate the customary sharpward move (Table 8.11). Even where the dominant is the first goal, the second ritornello may be complex and modulatory: Op. 11/4 contains a very extended central ritornello with three clear sections in V, iii and vi. In this way

Table 8.11. Timeline of Bonporti, Violin Concerto in F major, Op. 11/6

Function	R1a-S1a-R1b	S1b	R3a	S3a	RT	S3b	R4a-S4a etc.
Bars	1–13	13–18	18–25	25–31	32–36	36–45	46–67
Harmony	I →	IV	IV	→ vi //	I →	V → iii → V/vi //	I
Motto	M		M		M		M

Bonporti underlines the contrast between the stable tonic areas and the more rest-less intermediate section.

Op. 11/9 in E major appears to adhere to a much more Vivaldian concept, in its alternation of closed tutti periods with modulatory solos. Despite the feint towards vi within S1, the second ritornello is a stable period in the dominant – indeed, a complete transposition of R1. But all this security is suddenly under-mined when, near the end of the recapitulation, there is a change of direction, revisiting the hitherto unrealized key of C♯ minor (Ex. 8.10). This constitutes an almost Beethovenian catastrophe in the context of the early eighteenth-century concerto, requiring a substantial 18-bar coda to resolve the new tension. Charac-teristically, this coda introduces an Adagio ornamental fantasy for the soloist – a dissolution of rhythmic drive and preparation for the slow movement found in several of these concertos.

Ex. 8.10. Bonporti, Violin Concerto in E major, Op. 11/9

All six concertos explore unusual strategies, following some of the broad lines of Vivaldian form, but rethinking the ritornello concept in novel ways. Rather than simply taking elements of ritornello form where he chose, Bonporti requires the listener to hear these innovative procedures as commentaries on norms that were already (by the late 1720s) well established. Thus the originality of his concertos lies as much in the way they question these norms and challenge the listener's expectations as in more obvious marks of individuality and expressive fantasy.

Carlo Tessarini – in the Wake of Vivaldi?

The principal representative of the younger Venetian generation was Carlo Tessarini (*b* Rimini, *c*1690; *d* Netherlands, *c*1767), whose concertos are much closer to those of Vivaldi, on which they were presumably modelled. Tessarini's increasingly restless international career has been outlined in Chapter 2.[16] After some fifteen stable years in Venice, where he was violin teacher and *maestro de' concerti* at the Ospedaletto, his employment at Urbino Cathedral (1731–57) was punctuated with forays north of the Alps, including extended visits during the 1740s to Paris, London and the Netherlands.

The concerto was a constant feature of Tessarini's diverse career. The earliest surviving works are probably those copied by Pisendel, perhaps in Venice in 1716–17.[17] No doubt Tessarini wrote concertos for the Ospedaletto, just as Vivaldi did for the Pietà; and others for his own performances at Urbino Cathedral. In 1724, Le Cène's unauthorized edition of the Op. 1 concertos was published in Amsterdam, and swiftly pirated by Walsh in London. Tessarini's growing fame was attested by his inclusion in Walsh's second anthology entitled *Harmonia Mundi* (1728): 'Collected out of the Choicest Works of the most Eminent Authors viz Vivaldi Tessarini Albinoni Alberti never before Printed'. Similarly indicative of his esteem is the programming of his concertos at the 1725 première of Telemann's comic intermezzi *Pimpinone* in Hamburg (see p. 48). Further Amsterdam publications include two volumes entitled *La stravaganza* (Op. 4, 1736–37), in which concertos alternate with ripieno works. The title is a clear homage to Vivaldi's own Op. 4; two more volumes remained unpublished on Le Cène's death in 1743.[18]

By this date, however, Tessarini's focus had shifted to Paris, where instrumental publications dedicated to members of the Parisian nobility were available from the main music-sellers as well as from his own publishing business: these include six *Concerti a cinque* (*c*1745) and three entitled *Contrasto armonico*, Op. 10 (*c*1748). Reflecting his high international prestige and travels around Northern Europe, his concertos were still widely advertised in London and the Netherlands into the 1750s, and as late as 1762 'recently arrived works by the great composer C. TESSARINI' were on sale in the Hague.[19] A willingness to absorb diverse musical influences is one of the most impressive features of Tessarini's career, and the fact that he had new symphonies published in Paris in the 1760s is indicative of his continued engagement with the latest genres and idioms.

---

[16] Dunning, Albert, 'Some Notes on the Biography of Carlo Tessarini'; Hirshberg and McVeigh, Introduction to Carlo Tessarini, *Twelve Violin Concertos Opus I*.

[17] Tes15, 17 and 23 (Op. 1, Nos. 1, 2 and 5), the last of these also in a variant version.

[18] Rasch, 'I manoscritti musicali', pp. 1050–1.

[19] See pp. 32–3, and Hirshberg and McVeigh, Introduction to Carlo Tessarini, *Twelve Violin Concertos Opus 1*.

Tessarini's preserved concerto output includes thirty-six solo violin concertos, a single flute concerto, and five for two violins. These forty-two concertos provide us with the largest available repertory by any single composer other than Vivaldi and Tartini. Some indication of chronology is given by the publication dates of the main printed sets: from 1724 to the late 1740s; other sources include manuscripts in most of the principal collections, as well as a small group now in King's College, Cambridge, whose provenance is unknown.

Many of fine quality, Tessarini's concertos explore a broad range of affects, from sensitive Empfindsamkeit in minor to brilliant confidence in major, as well as light and airy *galant* writing, rich with the typical semiquaver triplets associated with this style. In the large dimension, there is a special interest in the organization of Op. 1 – possibly Le Cène's initiative. Each of the two volumes exploits a diverse array of moods, beginning in lyrical minor vein and moving through *buffo* and exuberant affects to festive celebration: the extrovert virtuosity of the final A major concerto is underlined by a brilliant unaccompanied capriccio in the last movement.

Any study of Tessarini's style and strategies cannot avoid a comparison with Vivaldi, since it is inconceivable that Tessarini would not have used every opportunity to benefit from the experience of working in Venice so close to the master, who was some twelve years his senior. By the time the Op. 1 collection was published in 1724, he could certainly have heard and studied Vivaldi's Opp. 3, 4, 6 and 7, as well as numerous concertos played at the Pietà, and probably the concertos to be published a year later as Op. 8, even though their programmatic elements apparently made no impact on him. At the same time, any comparison between Tessarini's forty-two concertos and Vivaldi's immense repertory should be handled with great caution. Our discussion of Vivaldi's concertos has revealed his experimentation with myriad options in every parameter, and it can surely mean very little that certain options only rarely used by Vivaldi are entirely absent from Tessarini's much smaller repertory. Real significance attaches to salient statistical preferences common to both – all the more so when certain preferred options are even more prevalent in Tessarini than in Vivaldi, suggesting a process of selection. Conversely, an option strongly present in Vivaldi but missing from Tessarini may reflect a process of elimination.

Surviving variants of Tessarini's concertos allow a rare glimpse into the composer's workshop. The concerto published in 1724 as Op. 1/5 in G major (Tes23) also survives in a set of parts copied by Pisendel (apparently in Venice in 1716–17), which differ in significant aspects. Similarly a concerto in D major preserved in Cambridge (Tes9) appears to be an earlier version of Op. 1/10 (Tes8).[20] If the suggested chronology is correct, an important aspect of Tessarini's revision is the heightened contrast between ritornello and solo. In Tes23 an intermediate tonic ritornello is immediately followed by R3 in vi in the Pisendel copy; whereas in Op. 1/5 a brief solo is inserted between the two ritornellos. Even more strikingly, in the manuscript of the finale, R1b is succeeded immediately by R2 with the motto, but they are separated by a long

---

[20] For a detailed discussion and music examples which will not be replicated here, see Hirshberg and McVeigh, 'The Making of a Ritornello Movement'.

solo in the published version. These heightened articulations certainly reflect Vivaldi's practice, and perhaps represent an attempt to 'modernize' concertos initially conceived in an older vein. Similarly, whereas in Tes9 the final ritornello simply presents R1 Da Capo, the recapitulation in Tes8 omits the dominant version of the motto at bars 4–7, reflecting an increasing preference for a modified recapitulation.[21]

The motto
Two of Vivaldi's favourite melodic types are prominent in Tessarini's output (see Catalogue). Six movements begin with traditional hammer-strokes, but much more distinctive are the octave leaps that Tessarini develops in ways all his own. One is to tap the kinetic energy of the octave leap so as to aspire higher with larger leaps, as can be seen simply in Tes12 and, more interestingly, in Tes33. The other is the 'gap-fill melody' identified by Leonard Meyer: 'Gap-fill melodies consist of two elements: a disjunct-interval – the gap – and conjunct intervals which fill the gap.'[22] In Tes9 the octave leap is immediately filled by a rising scale, in Tes26 by a falling one; and there are many extensions of this pattern, as in Tes40 (Op. 1/11) where a typical upward thrust precedes both the octave leap and the consequent gap-fill. It is clear that Tessarini uses octave leaps not as a convenient cliché, but as a springboard for invention; and the extrovert exuberance of his major-mode concertos often seems to stem from the way in which his mottos arch beyond a single-octave frame.

Thirty of Tessarini's mottos appear in homophonic textures, with only three in unison. Where there is imitation, it is more a case of textural enrichment from a delayed second violin entry than intrinsic contrapuntal working (see Ex. 8.12). Tessarini inclined towards regular phrasing slightly more than Vivaldi: 45% of his mottos adopt a 2+2-bar structure, as against 32% for Vivaldi. Yet a comparison of two variant concertos shows that the regular motto of the (presumably earlier) Tes9 was then modified in Tes8 into a three-bar phrase. Moreover, regularity is only rarely (in eight cases) passed on to both the next ritornello motive and the opening of the solo.

The initial ritornello
Tessarini's conception of R1 took its lead from Vivaldi's 'piece within a piece', yet went much further, in that half enclose a stable section in another key, compared with only 18% in Vivaldi (compare Table 4.6). Tessarini's second preference is for a middle section with chromatic progressions or diatonic sequences (36%, compared with 54% in Vivaldi). Most significantly of all, while 24% of Vivaldi's opening ritornellos are entirely rooted in the tonic, this applies to a mere three by Tessarini (7%).[23] Even these three cases contain *minore* contrasts: thus in Tes2 (Op. 4/10) a plaintive solo follows a theatrical interruption of brilliant tonic and dominant sonorities (Ex. 8.11). Tessarini's preference for a

[21] Tes3 and Tes5 are also closely related, as will presently be discussed.
[22] *Explaining Music*, p. 145. For a comprehensive analysis of the implications of this device see Narmour, *The Analysis and Cognition of Basic Melodic Structures*, pp. 220–32.
[23] Or, indeed, only two, since Tes3 and Tes5 are so closely related.

Ex. 8.11. Tessarini, Violin Concerto in C major, Tes2 (Op. 4/10)

Ex. 8.12. Tessarini, Violin Concerto in G major, Tes27

Table 8.12. Thematic relationship between S1 and R1 in Tessarini

Thematic material in S1	Number	%	% in Vivaldi
Different thematic material in R1 and S1	24	57%	59%
S1 starts with a variant or ornamentation of the motto, continues with different material	8	19%	14%
S1 starts with the motto unvaried, continues with different material	7	17%	8%
Last motive of R1 repeated as the first motive of S1	3	7%	6%

more elaborate tonal trajectory within R1 reflects his contribution to the early sinfonia. The similarity is clearly evident in Tes27, where the tonal stages are marked by sharply distinguished material (Ex. 8.12).

The first solo
Tessarini closely matched Vivaldi in preferring to characterize the first solo with its own thematic material (compare Table 8.12 with Table 4.7, and see Catalogue). However he displays his best rhetorical art when allowing the soloist to elaborate the motto, with subtle alterations of phrase rhythm and harmonic movement. Three of the finest examples appear in Op. 1. The five-bar motto of Tes40, with its pounding octave leaps, is modified into a graceful two-bar solo motive; while the solo of Tes15 makes a delicate commentary on the apparently quite unrelated sighing motto. By contrast, in Tes23 the soloist enters with a powerfully individual statement, yet this too turns out to be a variant of the motto, wittily preceded by the hammer-strokes that are normally the preserve of the ritornello (see Catalogue).

Just as Tessarini used marked contrasts within R1 to highlight the tonal argument, so too in the solos. In Tes17 (Op. 1/2) he signals the modulation by means of a distinct semiquaver passage and then marks the arrival of the dominant with its own theme (Ex. 8.13). Only in one concerto, Tes5, does S1 consist of the mechanical figurations used occasionally by Vivaldi (4%). In its twin Tes3, with its closely related R1, the solo soon departs from these figurations to introduce a new cantabile melody, suggesting a later and more advanced conception.

Ex. 8.13. Tessarini, Violin Concerto in F major, Tes17 (Op. 1/2)

Both Tessarini and Vivaldi showed an overall preference for a single continuous S1 unbroken by R1b (71% and 73% respectively). Still, a significant group

Table 8.13. Tessarini's tonal schemes

Circuit		Pendulum	
Tonal scheme	**Number**	**Tonal scheme**	**Number**
Major			
I-V-vi-I	19	I-V-I-vi-I	7
		I-V-I-V-vi-I	1
I-V-vi-iii-I	1		
		I-V-I-iii-I	1
I-V-iii-vi-I	1	I-V-I-iii-vi-I	1
I-V-I	3		
		I-ii-vi-I-V-I	1
Minor			
i-III-i	1		
i-III-v-♭VII-i	1	i-III-i-v-i	1
i-III-iv-III-i	1		
i-III-iv-VI-i	1		
i-III-iv-VI-♭II-III-i	1		
i-III-VI-iv-i	1		

of twelve movements adopts the pattern R1a-S1a-R1b, five of these modulating to the secondary key in S1a before reverting to the tonic in R1b. Comparison between the variants Tes8 and 9 suggests that one purpose was to create a longer opening tonic area. Whereas in Tes9 S1 modulates directly to the dominant for R2, in the apparently later variant Tes8 (Op. 1/10) the solo is rewritten to return unexpectedly to the tonic for a further R1b. As a result the opening tonic area spans 38% of the movement rather than the 26% of the manuscript version.[24] This example suggests that whereas Vivaldi used the pattern R1a-S1a-R1b mostly in his earlier concertos, Tessarini instead adopted it later as a deliberate strategy to extend the opening tonic area.

Tessarini's tonal schemes
The increasing preference for the major mode during the eighteenth century is well illustrated in Tessarini's output, with thirty-five concertos in major and seven in minor. Table 8.13 summarizes his tonal schemes, showing that he adopted and strongly confirmed Vivaldi's emerging preferences (compare Table 5.1). Thirty-four concertos have only a single peripheral key. Within the major group, the dominant is the first target in all but Tes39 (Op. 1/8), where R1b

---

[24] Hirshberg and McVeigh, 'The Making of a Ritornello Movement', pp. 48, 67.

modulates to ii and the dominant is delayed until the very last ritornello in a uniquely experimental scheme (I-ii-vi-I-V-I). For the first peripheral key vi is decisively preferred, with twenty-eight cases (80%), as against a mere three selecting the mediant.

The small group of minor-mode concertos shares no tonal scheme with the major. Whereas Vivaldi considered v and III to be alternative secondary key areas, Tessarini made the definitive choice of the relative major, anticipating the universal preference of the later eighteenth century. Of special interest is his treatment of the dominant in the one concerto with the scheme i-III-v-♭VII-i, the engaging Tes35 in A minor (Op. 1/7). Whereas Vivaldi might have explored a rhetorical argument between two secondary degrees, Tessarini ensures that the dominant is heard as a peripheral area. R2 boldly articulates III with the motto (bars 33–36), whereas R3 begins with a modulatory section based on a new motive (bars 48–52); only then does the motto articulate v, which is however immediately quitted for G major, negating any sense of firm arrival.

An especially lucid illustration of tonal planning is provided by Tes14 in D minor, with the tonal scheme i-III-iv-VI-i. At first glance, it might appear a textbook example, with all four ritornellos dominated by the 'Adeste fidelis' motto.[25] In reality, the treatment is much more subtle, since each of the internal ritornellos describes a modulatory process of its own. Already III breaks into the opening period after a hiatus, dividing R1 into a ternary i-III-i pattern (Ex. 8.14).[26] R2 realizes the suggested F major, reworking the same thematic ideas, yet this time with a smooth move to its own dominant (C major) and back. By contrast, R3 is modulatory, emulating R1 in the hiatus from G minor to B♭ major, but ending inconclusively on an F major chord. R4 is simply a Da Capo reprise of R1. Tessarini thus creates a clear tonal hierarchy by both harmonic and thematic means, supported by the proportionate durations of the stable centres: opening tonic 34%, III 17%, iv and VI 3% each, and final tonic area 21%.

Tes16 in E minor explores the exceptional scheme i-III-iv-VI-♭II-III-i, which sounds, however, much less idiosyncratic than it looks on paper. The stable frame of i-III. . .III-i surrounds an intensely unstable area, with ritornellos and solos sharing the modulatory role. The unusual Neapolitan key of ♭II (F major) is reached directly from C major, and it is just as easily quitted by a step-wise sequence to the mediant G major.

This unique case notwithstanding, Tessarini generally followed Vivaldi closely in his preference for long stable areas. The aggregate of stable areas in each movement ranges from the extremely high 95% down to 41%, with 80% as the average – slightly above Vivaldi's 76%. Tessarini was also highly consistent in his emphasis of tonal hierarchy through duration. The initial tonic is longer than the secondary key area in thirty-two movements; and the two are roughly equal in duration in a further seven. The secondary is longer than any of the peripheral areas in thirty-two of the thirty-eight relevant movements. The relationship between the outer tonic areas, on the other hand, does not reflect any

---

[25] As defined in Meyer, *Style and Music*, pp. 51–4.
[26] A similar hiatus within R1 (from i to III) occurs in all but one of Tessarini's concertos in minor.

Ex. 8.14. Tessarini, Violin Concerto in D minor, Tes14

consistent planning, since the final tonic area is longer than the initial in only twenty-four movements (57%).

The intermediate ritornellos and solos

Tessarini continued on the path paved by Vivaldi in the specialization of R2 and R3 in terms of tonal stability (compare Table 8.14 with Table 5.9). The strong preference for stable R2 as against modulatory R3 is self-evident; and in only nine cases is there a separate stable R3, reflecting Tessarini's liking for the modulatory combination R3-R4. As a result of its unique tonal scheme (I-ii-vi-I-V-I), there is of course no R2 in Tes39 (Op. 1/8). Also exceptional is Tes20, where R1b modulates to the dominant and the ensuing solo (instead of remaining there) pushes straight on to the peripheral vi.

Considering Tessarini's preference for simple and strongly directed tonal schemes, it is perhaps surprising that he adopted the pendulum concept in as many as twelve concertos (29%, as against only 14% in Vivaldi). But these brief intermediate tonic areas enact subtle rhetorical interpretations in other parameters. In Tes23 in G major (Op. 1/5), with the tonal scheme I-V-I-vi-I, S2 is apparently heading for the expected peripheral ritornello, only for this to be negated by a sudden switch to a quirky syncopated motive in the tonic (Ex. 8.15). vi is finally asserted and eventually confirmed by the motto in R3 (bar 73), only for the syncopated motive to re-emerge so as to lead back to the tonic for the recapitulation proper.

Tessarini carried Vivaldi's mild preference for a unifying motto one stage

Table 8.14. Tonal structure of R2 and R3 in Tessarini

Tonal structure	R2	R3
Entirely in a single key area	38	9
Modulatory or harmonically open	2	27
R3a modulatory, R3b stable	–	1
No R2 or no R3	2	5

Table 8.15. Thematic relationships in S2 and S3 in Tessarini

Thematic material	S2	S3
New material	19	7
Material derived from S1 or R1	14	11
Figuration only	3	2
No S2 or no S3	6	22

Ex. 8.15. Tessarini, Violin Concerto in G major, Tes23 (Op. 1/5)

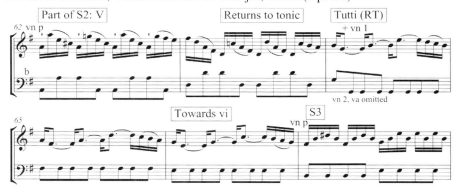

further. Whereas the motto heads both R2 and R3 in 54% of the Vivaldi sample, this obtains in twenty-eight movements by Tessarini (67%). The same unifying tendency does not extend to S2 and S3, although there is a closer thematic relationship between these and earlier sections than in Vivaldi (compare Table 8.15 with Tables 5.12 and 5.13).

The recapitulation
The location of the re-establishment of the tonic is one of the most significant choices in the composition of a ritornello movement (Table 8.16). Tessarini's obvious preference for tonic reprise within a modulatory ritornello (R3-R4) might seem designed to downgrade the recapitulation, especially as the motto is absent in half these cases. But this is mitigated considerably where the motto is forcefully reasserted in the tonic after a hiatus, with powerfully dramatic effect, as

Table 8.16. Point of re-establishment of the tonic in Tessarini

Point of re-establishment of the tonic	Number	%
Within a ritornello (R3-R4)	18	43%
Within a solo (S3-S4)	9	21%
At the beginning of S4, after a modulatory ritornello	8	19%
At the beginning of R4, after a modulatory solo	7	17%

Ex. 8.16. Tessarini, Violin Concerto in D major, Tes8 (Op. 1/10)

in Tes9 (Op. 1/10, Ex. 8.16). The use of the pattern R3-R4 has two opposite consequences in Tessarini's repertory. One is towards conciseness and economy. In this last example the opening tonic area comprises thirty-seven bars spread over R1a-S1a-R1b, whereas the closing tonic is limited to a single R4 lasting seventeen bars.[27] The opposite strategy obtains in Tes41 (Op. 4/2), a long movement extending to 231 bars in *alla breve*. Here a similar hiatus leads to a highly curtailed reprise of R1, but this is followed by a very long roving solo (fifty-five bars), an Adagio cadenza and a full Da Capo. Consequently the final tonic area is more than twice the length of the opening.

Tessarini's least favoured option is to reassert the tonic with R4 after a solo; only in two such cases is R4 a straight Da Capo of R1, one of these being Tes16 described above, where Tessarini must have felt that the progressive hierarchization of dominant and peripheral keys needed to be balanced by a firm stability. A witty and unusual manipulation of the listener's expectations is found in Tes17 in F major (Op. 1/2). Here R2 and R3 are both based on the motto, leading the listener to anticipate yet another restatement in the tonic; but the brief R4 presents a remarkable transformation, amounting to only ten bars as against the twenty-five bars of R1 – and mostly in F minor.

Those recapitulations initiated by the soloist range widely in sophistication. In Tes38 (Op. 1/6) six bars of mechanical figurations in the tonic merely delay the

---

[27] In this respect it is diametrically opposed to its variant Tes9 (Hirshberg and McVeigh, 'The Making of a Ritornello Movement', pp. 47–50).

Ex. 8.17. Tessarini, Violin Concerto in B♭ major, Tes42

Ex. 8.18a. Tessarini, Violin Concerto in G major, Tes22 (Op. 1/3)

Ex. 8.18b. Tessarini, Violin Concerto in G major, Tes28

entrance of the Da Capo ritornello. At the other extreme are subtly conceived reinterpretations, where the tonic is re-established by a variant of the first motive of S1
– as in Tes42, where both S1 and S4 briefly debate tonic and dominant, with S1
moving to the dominant and S4 affirming the tonic (Ex. 8.17). As a result of this
explicit resolution of tension, the full Da Capo that follows has no tonal significance, its role being simply to round off the movement with a thematic reprise.

   Where the recapitulation takes place within a solo (S3-S4), it is never articulated by the motto, but, as with R3-R4, there are two clear strategies. Either a
smooth transition disguises the return through only the weakest possible articulation, as in Tes22 (Op. 1/3) where the tonic is reached sequentially at bar 52 in
seamless continuity. Alternatively, a hiatus forces the return by more drastic
means: in Tes28, also in G major, the powerful solo motive is wrenched from E
minor in order to reaffirm the tonic (Ex. 8.18).

   In a significant fourteen cases (of which the last example is one), S4 provides a
tonal reinterpretation of S1, beginning with a restatement of the tonic opening,
but departing at the point of modulation in order to remain in the tonic. Tessarini

thus followed Vivaldi in treating the emerging concept of recapitulation as a principal area for exploration, almost totally avoiding the textbook device of leaving the tonal resolution to a Da Capo of R1.

Venice was a cauldron of musical experimentation for professionals and *dilettanti* alike. Only in their enthusiasm for the development of the solo concerto and a broadly shared conception of the instrumental Allegro can the Venetian composers considered here be regarded as a unified group. Older composers such as Albinoni and Alessandro Marcello retained an allegiance to their own musical background, and each composer developed a strongly individual response to the emerging Vivaldian ritornello form – imaginatively rethinking and even challenging these rapidly established norms. So too did other Italian composers who left Venice on their way to lucrative posts and new influences across the Alps.

CHAPTER 9

From Venice across the Alps

The glory of Venice attracted so many Italian violinists for brief visits or longer sojourns that it would be meaningless to attempt to group them all together, and the concept of a unified Venetian school of concerto composers following in the wake of Vivaldi is something of a chimera. Hardly any violinists were left untouched by the 'Vivaldian revolution', yet it is striking how rarely they simply aped the master. Indeed one of the most remarkable outcomes of this study has been to identify the many innovative and individual ways in which composers adapted what could have seemed a ready-made mould. The composers discussed in this chapter, as well as Platti in the next, all spent significant periods in Venice before moving north for long-term posts or a more peripatetic virtuoso career.

Giuseppe Antonio Brescianello

The violinist Giuseppe Antonio Brescianello (*b* Bologna *c*1690; *d* Stuttgart 1758) was in Venice in 1715 when he was invited to Munich by the Elector of Bavaria. The following year he took a post at the Württemberg court at Stuttgart, where he remained for his entire career, although with one interruption (1737–44) when the court opera was temporarily disbanded. It was during this period that his Op. 1 appeared: a collection of six concertos and six symphonies, published in Amsterdam in 1738. A further eight concertos survive in manuscript, including two double concertos in the Wiesentheid collection: one for bassoon and violin, the other for oboe and violin (perhaps intended for the oboist Giovanni Platti).

Brescianello's violin writing is soloistic but never especially demanding (even in the manuscript concertos), and he relies considerably on routine sequential figuration. Yet in other respects his highly individual approach to the concerto and to ritornello form seems to refer outside Venice, perhaps to his Bolognese upbringing. Two characteristics stand out: the richness and variety of texture, and a prevailing tonal instability. Typically the energetic quaver movement of a short motto is enhanced by loose imitation or rhythmic activity in the inner parts (Ex. 9.1); the motto is then repeated, and succeeded by strongly contrasting material. These characteristics are consistently maintained in his repertoire across changing melodic idioms. Bre12 (Op. 1/3) opens with a Vivaldian motto and sequence that would not be out of place in *L'estro armonico*, while at the other extreme Bre2 turns the immediate dominant response into the grandiose opening of a 'classical' symphony, before an attenuated sequential consequent (Ex. 9.2).

Ex. 9.1. Brescianello, Violin Concerto in C major, Bre3

Ex. 9.2. Brescianello, Violin Concerto in C major, Bre2

Taking this textural variety further, four concertos have significant solos or trios within R1. Thus in the double concerto Bre10, the violin already asserts a presence in R1, even though S1 is essentially an oboe solo. Bre4 (Op. 1/9) even begins with a substantial solo, the succeeding tutti carrying out the first structural modulation in the manner of Vivaldi's Op. 4/8.

This last example hints at the tonal instability that is characteristic of Brescianello's concertos. Even within R1 this restlessness is always reflected in an early departure from the tonic, such as the immediate transposition of the motto to the dominant, or the exceptional move to ii and iii in Bre1. Instability is naturally most evident at the centre of the movement, a feature highlighted by the tonal schemes (Table 9.1): after the customary dominant several peripheral keys typically provide a compendium of available tonalities. Particularly unusual is Bre9 in G major, where an innocuous enough minorization at the end of R1 affects the course of the movement as a whole (Table 9.2). Both R2 and R3 select

Table 9.1. Brescianello's tonal schemes

Circuit		Pendulum	
Tonal scheme	**Number**	**Tonal scheme**	**Number**
Major			
I-V-vi-IV-iii-ii-I	1		
I-V-vi-iii-ii-I I-V-vi-iii-ii-IV-I I-V-vi-iii-vi-v-IV-I	1 1 1		
I-V-iii-vi-ii-I	1	I-V-I-iii-vi-I	1
		I-V-I-iii-V-I	1
I-V-v-ii-iv-v-VI-iii-I	1		
I-V-^{V}/V-vi-iii-I	1	I-V-^{V}/V-vi-I-iii-V-ii-I	1
Minor			
i-v-III-v-III-iv-i	1		
		i-v-i-III-iv-VI-III-i	1
i-v-iv-VI-III-i	1		
		i-III-i-v-iv-VI-♭vii-i	1

Table 9.2. Ritornello structure in Brescianello, Violin Concerto in G major, Bre9

Function	R1a	R1b	R2	R3/S	R4
Bars	1–15	33–38	42–48	58–63	98–114
Key	I (V i)	I → V	v → ii	iv → v → VI	I (V, i) I
Thematic	M a b c d	M a	d c	d	= R1 + Coda

the minor-mode motive d, while S3 wittily continues this reversal of norms by insisting on E major rather than E minor; and the major-minor ambiguity persists through both S4 and R4 (Ex. 9.3). When, as here, R2 is modulatory, the instability is especially evident; indeed in only three cases is R2 entirely closed in the secondary key (this trait will be further explored in Chapters 11 and 12). Similar insecurity is found in the peripheral area, with a modulatory R3 in eleven concertos. Often the rapid tonal succession is emphasized by a block construction, piecing together short phrases in different peripheral keys. Still more unsettling is the avoidance of a full period after a well-prepared modulation, leaving the new key frustratingly unrealized. In the large-scale Concertone in E♭ major, Bre5, several key-changes are heralded by long pedals (over which the violin weaves in free fantasy), but each new key is only briefly confirmed before a fresh departure (Ex. 9.4, Table 9.3).

Brescianello compensates for this apparent tonal waywardness through a high

Ex. 9.3. Brescianello, Violin Concerto in G major, Bre9

Ex. 9.4. Brescianello, Violin Concerto in E♭ major, Bre5

Table 9.3. Proportions of stable tonal areas in Brescianello, Violin Concerto in E♭ major, Bre5

Stable area	I	V	V/V	vi	I (false reprise)	iii	V	ii	I
Proportion	28%	4%	2%	6%	6%	3%	3%	1%	24%

Ex. 9.5. Brescianello, Violin Concerto in C major, Bre2

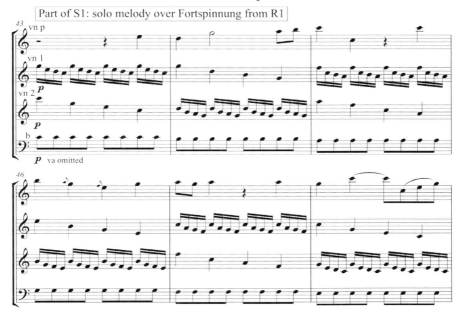

degree of thematic consistency across ritornellos. Never does he introduce new material not previously heard in R1, and in eight concertos both R2 and R3 begin with the motto. The same melodic consistency does not extend to the solos, which indeed show hardly any connections with each other. There are, however, some interesting links between ritornello and solo. Of the five examples where S1 uses the motto, one is an extremely distant variant (Bre5, see Catalogue), while in Bre7 the entire first half of R1 underpins a new solo line. The same technique occurs more startlingly in Bre2, where the Fortspinnung from R1 is used to accompany a cantabile *galant* melody quite unlike Brescianello's customary idiom (Ex. 9.5).

   In view of Brescianello's general avoidance of motivic manipulation, it is hardly surprising that the recapitulation holds no special interest. As many as eight concertos have just a single tonic ritornello derived from R1, of which two present a full Da Capo. In most cases, however, the tonic return has already been foreshadowed in the previous solo, even if weakly articulated and immediately undermined, in line with Brescianello's characteristic roving manner.

Francesco Maria Veracini

Despite his reputation and carefully maintained image as a performer of outstanding virtuosity, Francesco Maria Veracini (*b* Florence, 1690; *d* Florence, 1768) gave scant attention to the violin concerto during his long career as a solo violinist, which was outlined in Chapter 2.[1] Only five concertos survive (three of

---

[1]   Hill, *The Life and Works of Francesco Maria Veracini*, especially pp. 139–52; White, 'The Life of Francesco Maria Veracini'.

which were printed during his lifetime), and it cannot be said that they represent the composer at his most creative. His energies were more imaginatively channelled into the violin sonata, and it would appear from an anecdote related by Charles Burney that this was the genre he preferred:

> And being called upon [at a festival in Lucca c1723], would not play a concerto, but desired the hoary old father [Girolamo Laurenti] would let him play a solo at the bottom of the choir, desiring Lanzetti, the violoncellist of Turin, to accompany him; when he played in such a manner as to extort an *e viva!* in the public church.[2]

It is possible too that Veracini's later comments about the superficiality of modern instrumental music were as much directed at the concerto as at the symphony.[3] Certainly it would appear that he had abandoned concerto composition by the mid-1730s.

Veracini's first concerto (Hill D1) is very much a special case. Written in 1712 for a celebratory Mass in Venice (see p. 33), it is a highly elaborate and richly orchestrated *concerto a otto stromenti*. The festive opening ritornello is conceived on the grandest scale, building up from a single repeated note into cascades of D major scales and incorporating lively episodes for oboes and for trumpets and timpani. The movement then unfolds as an expansive ritornello form in the latest Venetian manner, with lightly accompanied violin solos in virtuosic figuration (fourteen bars of Veracini's own 'à capriccio' left blank in the manuscript); the festive idiom continues into a fanfare for violin solo at the end.[4]

Concerto D2, published in *VI concerti à 5* (Amsterdam, c1719) can scarcely be described as being in ritornello form at all, despite the clear solos in standard string-crossing patterns; and it appears to reflect earlier models. The first ten bars consist of rapid alternations of tutti and solo, moving immediately to the motto in the dominant in the manner of Albinoni. Peripheral area and tonic reprise follow a normal course, but then Veracini extraordinarily reprises the first eight bars a fifth higher, ending unambiguously in E major (^{V}/V). This perilous procedure – a remnant of seventeenth-century practice – requires a strenuous pull back to the tonic; and such a tonal scheme (I-V-vi-I-V-^{V}/V-I) has not been encountered anywhere else in our repertoire.

Concertos A1 and B♭ begin with regular ritornello movements. The former, published in *Concerti a cinque* (Amsterdam, 1717) could pass for a rather dull Vivaldi pastiche, with unmistakeable premonitions of 'Spring' and torrents of routine figuration. Ex. 9.6 illustrates the Vivaldi reference in the context of an unusual false recapitulation, where the rare hiatus to the dominant uses a progression more characteristic of the return to the tonic.

The remaining Concerto A2 presents an intriguing experiment: a movement in anti-ritornello form (Table 9.4). Written in a thoroughly up-to-date melodic idiom, with syncopations and *galant* figuration embellished with trills, it cannot possibly pre-date Vivaldi's solidification of ritornello form. But after a regular R1

2   *A General History*, vol. 2, p. 450.
3   Hill, 'The Anti-Galant Attitude', pp. 168–72.
4   Musical example in Hill, *The Life and Works of Francesco Maria Veracini*, pp. 140–3.

Ex. 9.6. Veracini, Violin Concerto in A major, Hill A1

Table 9.4. Timeline of Veracini, Violin Concerto in A major, Hill A2

Function	R1	S	R (not R2?)	S (trio)	R (not R3?)	S	R
Bars	1–18	19–40	40–47	48–51	52–56	57–73	74–91
Key	I (V) I	I → V → I	I → V	V	I	I	I
Thematic	M	M	new			new	= R1

and a solo leading from tonic motto towards V, the norms fall away: the solo reverts to the tonic, the key in which all three succeeding ritornellos begin, and only in the final Da Capo does the motto finally return. Such an explicit avoidance of ritornellos in distant keys must be a deliberate strategy, to be heard against the norms of established practice. Certainly the unexpected return to the tonic at bar 32 is given special prominence by a translucent 'halo' effect (Ex. 9.7).

Ex. 9.7. Veracini, Violin Concerto in A major, Hill A2

Pietro Antonio Locatelli

The career of Pietro Antonio Locatelli (*b* Bergamo, 1695; *d* Amsterdam, 1764) bears some similarity with that of Veracini: both were acknowledged as virtuosi of the highest distinction, both spent much of their lives in Northern Europe, and both only briefly engaged with the solo concerto before returning to older genres. But the importance of Locatelli's concerto output is of a quite different order.

Locatelli's early years were spent training and working in Rome, where he befriended Valentini and played frequently for Ottoboni at S Lorenzo in Damaso (1717–23).[5] This period culminated in the *Concerti grossi*, Op. 1, published in Amsterdam in 1721 with a dedication to his patron, Monsignor Camillo Cybo. But after he left Rome in 1723, Locatelli's life changed completely: for several years he adopted the lifestyle of a travelling virtuoso, visiting Mantua, Venice and several German courts before eventually settling in Amsterdam in 1729.

It was in Venice that he wrote, or at least began, the concertos to be published in Amsterdam in 1733 as Op. 3: *L'arte del violino: XII concerti . . . con XXIV capricci ad libitum*. The set was dedicated to the Venetian nobleman Girolamo Michele Lin (or Lini), who was Locatelli's patron there at some time during the period 1723–27. The grateful letter of dedication implies that Lin had gone out of his way to hear Locatelli's concertos, 'when they were performed by me at those celebrated events, with such a fine and incomparably large orchestra'. This statement has been the subject of much speculation, since no documentary evidence has supplied the missing information about Locatelli's performances of these or indeed any other works in Venice. Some grand public occasion seems to be suggested, but at the same time Lin's own involvement must surely be implied behind the customary obsequious tone, and it remains possible that they were put on at the Palazzo Lin on the Grand Canal.[6] After Locatelli's arrival in Amsterdam, where he eschewed public performance, there was little need for him to produce more violin concertos; and only two others survive in Dresden manuscripts (Wo03, Wo04), perhaps reflecting a hitherto undocumented visit there.

Most of the attention given to the famous Op. 3 has revolved around the truly sensational virtuosity of the capriccios inserted into the fast movements, their extraordinary showmanship unparalleled until the later antics of Lolli and Paganini.[7] Yet this obsession has diverted attention from the concertos themselves, which are not only beautiful and distinctive examples of the genre, but also explore the potential of ritornello form in an unusual way. Indeed nine of the fourteen concertos by Locatelli begin with a gentle, affecting Andante,[8] in which cantabile melody and *galant* pleasantry are allied with delicate rococo

---

5   Calmeyer, 'The Life, Times and Works of Pietro Antonio Locatelli'; Dunning, *Pietro Antonio Locatelli*; Dunning, ed., *Intorno a Locatelli*; Dunning, ed., *Pietro Antonio Locatelli: Catalogo tematico*; Eynard, *Il musicista Pietro Antonio Locatelli*.

6   See the full discussion in Dunning, Introduction to Opera omnia, 3, pp. lxvii–lxxiv. All Locatelli's concertos are now available in the modern collected edition.

7   See, for example, Cantù, 'I tre Locatelli e Paganini'; Porta, 'La tecnica violinistica'. Further on Locatelli's performing style, see pp. 40–1.

8   In three cases after a short introduction.

Ex. 9.8. Locatelli, Violin Concerto in F major, Op. 3/3

ornamentation (Ex. 9.8a). The main technical challenge for the soloist here lies in exceptionally high and ornate melodic lines (Ex. 9.8b). These two examples show the conjunction of short phrases typical of Locatelli's idiom, spinning out a long *galant* melody by linking and repeating single-bar units; the equally characteristic ABB melodic construction can be found in the opening Andante of Op. 3/4.

The solo entry illustrated in Ex. 9.8b betrays only loose connections with the motto in contour and rhythm; and thematic working in solo sections is generally limited to such family resemblances, similar *galant* ideas that give an illusion of integration. Only four movements introduce S1 with the motto, and half do not even have a final solo in the tonic. The two manuscript concertos are exceptional in Locatelli's output in reprising the opening of S1 in S4; equally unusual is the tonal recapitulation in Op. 3/3 where the closing phrase of S1 is transposed from dominant to tonic.

At first glance, Locatelli's manipulation of ritornello form seems entirely in line with three contemporary trends.[9] A secondary key is clearly articulated in the middle of R1 in all cases; R2 is strongly emphasized by the motto in the dominant; and the peripheral ritornello is weakened by short duration, modulation or new material (indeed it is absent in five movements). Yet if everything said so far might suggest a rather restricted response to the form, these unpromising outlines in fact conceal a highly imaginative approach.

As many as eight concertos have a modulatory R2, which, combined with the absence or instability of R3, gives a restless feel to the centre of the movement. This rich harmonic exploration functions as a strongly rhetorical device, as is reflected in the tonal schemes (Table 9.5). In Op. 3/2 in C minor, for example, there is an explicit debate about the secondary key. First, in a passage of exquisite tenderness, the relative major is strongly prepared and apparently established

---

[9] The following analysis omits the exceptional Op. 3/6, described below.

Table 9.5. Locatelli's tonal schemes

Circuit		Pendulum	
Tonal scheme	**Number**	**Tonal scheme**	**Number**
Major			
I-V-vi-ii-iii-I I-V-vi-ii-vi-I	1 1	I-V-I-vi-iii-ii-I	1
I-V-iii-I	2		
I-V-iii-vi-I	1	I-V-I-iii-vi-I	1
		I-V-ii-I-vi-I I-V-I-ii-vi-I	1 1
I-i-♭III-(v)-V-^{V}/V-♭VII-IV-(i)-I	1		
I-V-^{V}/V-iii-ii-I	1		
Minor			
		i-III-v-♭VII-i-ii-i	1
		i-III-♭VII-i-iv-v-i	1
i-iv-v-iv-III-i	1		

Ex. 9.9. Locatelli, Violin Concerto in C minor, Op. 3/2

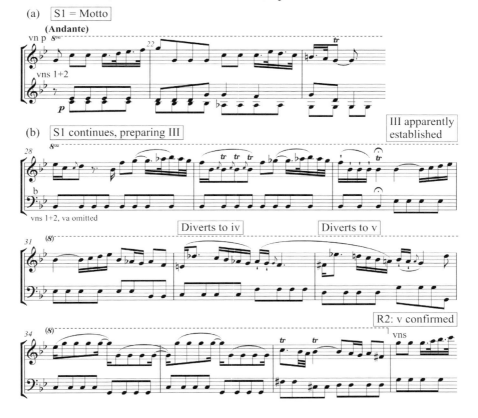

Table 9.6. Timeline of Locatelli, Violin Concerto in C minor, Op. 3/2

Function	R1	S1	R2	R3	S2 (ST)	R4a	Capriccio	R4b
Bars	1–21	21–37	37–38	39–49	50–53–57–78	79–82	83–167	168–184
Key	i	i → III (iv) v	v //	♭VII	→ i → ii →	i		i
Thematic	M	M	M	M		M		= R1 abbrev.

with a new melody; but it is immediately rejected by F minor, itself to be undermined by the dominant, which is finally confirmed by R2 (Ex. 9.9). The pattern of rising thirds (C minor, E♭ major, G minor) is then further extended to B♭ major and D minor, with the unusual appearance of ii in the minor mode being facilitated by the two-flat key signature (Table 9.6).

Locatelli's expressive sensitivity derives from an essentially vocal conception, with subtle shades of feeling being reflected not only in delicate ornamental filigree and rhythmic intricacy but also in harmonic colouring. In Ex. 9.9 a poignant shadow passes across the melody in the touch of E♭ minor at bar 29: such incidental minorization appears frequently in Vivaldi for moments of harmonic contrast and even pathos, but here it reflects a later sensibility, a fluidity of emotional nuance that marks mid-eighteenth-century sentiment at its most compelling. The way in which Locatelli side-slips into the minor mode foreshadows Mozart's ability to write in major and minor at one and the same time: Op. 3/8 in E minor, for example, tints each turn to the relative major with a touch of G minor.

This predilection for the minor mode is taken to its ultimate degree in Op. 3/5 in C major, where the soloist's entrance is a real *coup de théâtre* (Ex. 9.10). The solos proceed as if the movement were in C minor, following an independent harmonic trajectory that emphasizes the lack of emotional connection between tutti and solo. S1 moves towards its relative major, which is diverted to G minor using the very same progression as Ex. 9.9. R2 reaffirms the major mode, modulating to D major – at which point the next solo calmly begins in B♭ major, as if untouched by the interruption.

Ex. 9.10. Locatelli, Violin Concerto in C major, Op. 3/5

Several movements include textural contrasts within R1, in the form of solo and concertino passages, while Op. 3/12 presents the entire ritornello twice: the first time a bare continuo line, the second a harmonization in full tutti. Op. 3/6 in G minor is particularly complex in textural terms, beginning (after a short introduction) with a plaintive quartet passage that suggests the concerto grosso in the background. This passage acts as a refrain throughout the movement, resulting in an unusual hybrid structure which is further highlighted by the use of hiatus. R1

Ex. 9.11. Locatelli, Violin Concerto in A major, Op. 3/11

ends inconclusively on a D major chord, only for S1 to begin in B♭ major, a device without precedent at this point in the movement (although harmonically fore-shadowed in Op. 3/5, just described). The solo then modulates to its own domi-nant (F major) for the second ritornello, avoiding R2 altogether; at this point another hiatus restores the quartet refrain in G minor, initiating a new start.

It will be apparent from these examples that there is much more to Locatelli's solo concertos than the virtuosity for which they are famed: indeed some move-ments such as Op. 3/12 make minimal violinistic demands, outside the notori-ously difficult capriccio. Only one concerto introduces Locatelli's new levels of virtuosity into the first movement itself: Op. 3/11 combines the most brilliant figuration with a driving symphonic idiom in the ritornellos, resulting in the most bravura concerto to date (Ex. 9.11a). The capriccio also develops a much closer relationship than usual, not only recalling the pattern of the first solo, but also weaving in a hand-breaking reference to the opening of R1 (Ex. 9.11b).

In most concertos the impact of the capriccio is deliberately heightened by independent figuration in a contrasting metre, and by the preceding ritornello ending on a perfect cadence. In such cases it might be inferred that the movement could be performed perfectly well without the capriccio and tutti coda.[10] Two factors suggest that this was not the primary intention, and that the capriccio and coda formed an integral part of the conception: (i) in three movements the capriccio is preceded by an extended dominant pedal; (ii) the tutti coda some-times makes a distinct and by no means formulaic contribution to the composition as a whole. Thus in Op. 3/4 the coda comprises an ingeniously compressed reca-pitulation of the R1 tutti-solo complex, with the central dominant material trans-posed to the tonic.

Locatelli's concertos, or rather the capriccios associated within them, remained enormously influential for the next hundred years – Paganini was famously inspired by them in his own caprices – yet they remain highly exceptional for the period. Other composers continued to explore the rich potential of the Vivaldian concerto in no less interesting but certainly less ostentatious ways.

---

[10] This issue is discussed in Whitmore, 'Towards an Understanding of the Capriccio', pp. 47–8. Similar considerations apply to the finales.

CHAPTER 10

Platti and d'Alai – the Common Taste

A unique mark of homage at the head of one of Giovanni Platti's violin concertos has prompted us to separate Platti from Chapter 9 and instead link him with the sole Parma composer, Mauro d'Alai. In the Dresden manuscript of Platti's Concerto in A major (I18) the solo violin part carries the rubric 'Giov. Platti / Su'l gusto di Niauro'. If there are any doubts whether Niauro is indeed d'Alai, these are dispelled by comparison with the first movement of Dal10 in the same key, apparently Platti's direct model, as will be shown at the end of this chapter.

Giovanni Platti (*b* Padua or Venice, before 1692; *d* Würzburg, 1763) was trained in Venice, where his father was a member of the orchestra of S Marco; and in 1722 he was engaged with a group of Italian musicians for the court of the Prince-Archbishop of Bamberg and Würzburg, where he worked for the rest of his life. Though primarily known as an oboist, he was also a singer and played a range of string, wind and keyboard instruments: it is for his forward-looking harpsichord sonatas, published in 1742, that he has become best known (beginning with Faustino Torrefranca's exaggerated claims for his invention of the classical style).[1] Yet almost all of his surviving concertos are for cello, no doubt written for the bishop's brother in nearby Wiesentheid, Count Rudolf Franz Erwein von Schönborn, whose musical enthusiasms were described in Chapter 2.

Twenty-two cello concertos survive in complete form at Schloss Wiesentheid, as well as one oboe concerto and the violin concerto already mentioned.[2] This substantial and significant group of solo concertos, little studied as yet, is one of the outstanding pearls of our survey. Yet it reveals Platti in a quite different light from that in which he is normally presented. Rather than being purely in the vanguard of the development of newer styles, these concertos display his mastery of an astonishing range of idioms. At the one extreme are concertos that do indeed contain delightfully *galant* melodies and light orchestral textures; yet at the other are certainly the most severe and intricately contrapuntal movements of our entire repertoire, all in the minor mode. These latter concertos mirror the contrapuntal tendencies of the Zani cello concertos in the Wiesentheid collection (and, at a

---

[1] *Le origini italiane*. Further on Platti, see Dangel-Hofmann, ' "Der guthe Houboist" '; Freeman, 'The Earliest Italian Keyboard Concertos'; Iesuè, 'Le opere a stampa e manoscrittee'; Iesuè, *Le Opere di Giovanni Benedetto Platti*; Torrefranca, 'Prime ricognizioni dello stile violoncellistica'.

[2] A further six cello concertos lack one or more parts (I33, I39, I41, I43–45) and are not analysed here.

Ex. 10.1. Platti, Cello Concerto in D minor, I26/II

lower artistic level, those of Perroni), evidently reflecting the Count's attachment to the older Italian idioms.[3]

Five minor-mode concertos lead from a substantial slow introduction into a full-scale fugal ritornello movement. Usually the solo cello participates as a fourth voice in the fugal exposition before joining the continuo part, as in I26/II (Ex. 10.1). These well-crafted movements all suggest *stile antico*, whether in the subject itself or in chains of sequential suspensions: the obsessively tight imitative working in the minor mode creates an intense atmosphere far removed from the normal run of eighteenth-century concertos.

Other movements maintain a strongly contrapuntal conception without such an austere fugal framework. In two concertos this intricacy extends to the solo sections as well, with the soloist participating as an equal voice in four-part counterpoint. In I30, S1 simply recasts the imitative opening of R1, the soloist being subsumed in the undifferentiated texture (Ex. 10.2a). Only gradually does the semiquaver figure eventually inspire some more distinctive solo figuration, so that by the recapitulation the soloist has largely broken free from contrapuntal constraints: the principal motive now functions merely as a backdrop (Ex. 10.2b).

These highly contrapuntal concertos bring to the forefront the question of the relationship between tutti and soloist – between counterpoint and homophony, thematic consistency and individuality, austerity and virtuosity. This question is all the more potent for being played out against the partially obscured background of ritornello form, for in I30 Platti makes the dichotomy between contrapuntal and soloistic writing the very essence of the musical argument: the individuality of the soloist only slowly emerging from the unified, continuous string texture.

Even among movements outside this severe idiom, several begin with lively imitation, interspersing canonic or *antico* passages within a more homophonic idiom. Only rarely does Platti essay a simpler and more direct musical language, as in I22, which goes so far as to suggest the contemporary sinfonia (Ex. 10.3). Despite the apparently stark differences of idiom, however, the overall approach to ritornello form shows a remarkable consistency, with some elements almost uniform across the entire repertoire. Particularly consistent is Platti's modulatory

---

[3] See Chapters 2 and 12.

Ex. 10.2. Platti, Cello Concerto in E minor, I30

(a) [S1]

(b) [S4]

Ex. 10.3. Platti, Cello Concerto in A major, I42

(a) [R1]

(b) [S1]

strategy across the ritornello structure. Opening ritornellos are on a large scale: all but six enclose a clear modulation to a secondary key and many include an internal reprise to produce a substantial 'piece within a piece'. Every concerto contains two or more central ritornellos, with R2 articulating a secondary key. Yet in sixteen movements (70%) this R2 is modulatory, and the change of direction is often forcefully highlighted; while in all but three concertos the final

Table 10.1. Platti's tonal schemes

Circuit		Pendulum	
Tonal scheme	**Number**	**Tonal scheme**	**Number**
Major			
		I-V-I-vi-I	1
		I-V-I-vi-I-iii-I	1
		I-V-I-V-vi-iii-V-I	1
I-V-iii-vi-I	2	I-V-iii-I-vi-I	1
I-V-iii-V-iii-vi-I	1		
I-V-iii-ii-vi-I	1		
I-V-iii-ii-vi-V-I	1		
Minor			
		i-v-i-iv-III-v-i	1
		i-v-i-iv-♭vii-iv-VI-i	1
i-III-v-iv-i	3	i-III-i-v-iv-i	2
i-III-v-iv-VI-i	1	i-III-i-v-iv-i-III-i	1
		i-III-v-i-iv-i	3
i-III-v-III-iv-VI-i	1	i-III-v-i-III-VI-iv-i-v-i	1

peripheral ritornello is modulatory. Taken together, these preferences give a highly unstable character to the central part of the movement.

It is hardly surprising, therefore, that Platti's tonal schemes tend to be roving and exploratory – indeed around a third are unique to him (Table 10.1). To some extent this reflects the antique cast of some of the concertos, and the more contra-puntal movements are indeed responsible for the longer and more volatile schemes here. But elsewhere, too, Platti imaginatively experiments with the listener's expectations, pulling the musical argument in unpredictable directions. The table reflects five minor-mode movements where S1 appears to establish III as the secondary key, only for it to be rejected in favour of the alternative domi-nant. In other cases the tonal argument twists and turns, debating keys in alterna-tion or realizing earlier predictions. As many as thirteen (57%) are pendulum schemes, which reflect either a change of direction initiated by a central tonic or else a later false reprise in the tonic. It is also very striking that all minor-mode movements reach iv somewhere in the peripheral area en route back to the tonic.

The impression of instability in the middle of the movement is reinforced by Platti's approach towards the motto. Although his thematic manipulation is generally highly integrative, it does not rely on recurrences of the motto (Table 10.2). Rather he makes free reference to other motives from R1, according each motive a status in the musical argument. In I31 in E minor, for example, the second ritornello eschews the anticipated motto in III: instead it begins in a quite unexpected and subtly dramatic way with a subsidiary motive from R1, now ambiguously reharmonized to suggest G major before returning immediately to

Table 10.2. Use of the motto in central ritornellos in Platti

Use of motto	Number
Both R2 and R3	4
R2, not R3	5
R3, not R2	4
R2 and R3b, not R3a	5
Neither	5

Ex. 10.4. Platti, Cello Concerto in E minor, I31

the tonic (Ex. 10.4a-b). The selection of subordinate, hesitant material from R1 completely undermines the long-prepared G major: only a decisive harmonic thunderbolt eventually leads towards an alternative secondary key, confirmed here by the soloist strongly reaffirming the motto.

This last example has already demonstrated the way in which the soloist plays a dynamic part in Platti's musical argument. Typically, the solo sections are tightly integrated, in line with his predilection for free-ranging recall of earlier material, and for imaginative recombination of motives. The relationship of S1 to R1 will demonstrate some of the possibilities near the start of the movement (Table 10.3). The high proportion of solos beginning with the motto is immediately evident, but also striking is the number that refer to R1 towards the end –

Table 10.3. Thematic material of S1 in Platti

Thematic material of S1	Number
M → new material → motives from R1	10
M → new material	4
New material → motives from R1	5
New material only	4

sometimes with the motto transposed into the secondary key, and sometimes with subordinate motives.

Further into the movement, Platti likes to integrate different strands by translating material from ritornello to solo, and vice versa. It is commonplace for solos to draw extensively on R1; but much more unusual are quotations from solos within a ritornello. Thus in I19, R3 appropriates the opening of S1, just as, at the start of S3, the soloist had transformed the motto (Ex. 10.5). Such reconciliation of thematic and textural parameters naturally reaches its zenith in the recapitulation. No uniformity can be detected in Platti's approach, except that there is always a substantial amount of recasting and that it usually involves both solo and ritornello. Exchange of material remains characteristic: thus in twelve cases the solo reprises elements of R1 different from those heard already in S1. It is certainly not essential to Platti's thinking that the recapitulation is headed by the motto, for this only occurs in eight movements – even if the motto always recurs subsequently in some form or another.

Ex. 10.5. Platti, Cello Concerto in C major, I19

In addition to the thematic argument, Platti brings to the recapitulation a strong tonal consideration, for he consistently seeks to avoid any suggestion of a secondary key here. His simplest technique is just to omit modulatory passages when reprising earlier sections. More complex are those movements involving transposition of material from the secondary key into the tonic, whether taken from the end of S1 (eight cases in S4, one in R4) or from R1, as occurs twice in R4 and twice in S4. The latter represents a highly unusual form of tonal recapitulation.

Since each movement responds differently to the demands of its musical material, it would be impossible to select a typical example of such recomposition, but one concerto lying between the extremes of Platti's contrasting styles will illustrate some of these concepts. I38 in G minor builds a complex structure out of

Table 10.4. Timeline of Platti, Cello Concerto in G minor, I38 (Wiesentheid 665)

Function	R1	S1	R2	R3a
Bars	1 – 10 – 13 – 18 – 22	22 – 29 – 36 – 42– 45	45 – 50 – 54 – 58	59 – 63
Key	i	i→ III→v	v →	III
Thematic	M a M b	c d e b	M b M	f

S3	R3b	R4a	S4	R4b
63 – 68 – 73 – 80 – 84	84 – 92	93 – 97	97 – 115	116 – 127
III→iv → VI	VI→	i	i	i
g h f	M	g	h d→e'	M' a M b

several contrasting motives (Table 10.4), beginning with the arresting motto and its continuation shown in Ex. 10.6a-b. The climax of the movement is reached in R3b, with an unusually strong assertion of VI by the motto, its regularity modified into a continuous modulation from E♭ major to F minor en route to the tonic (Ex. 10.6c). The recapitulation, by contrast, sneaks in imperceptibly via an augmented sixth chord and a subsidiary motive (Ex. 10.6d). Thereafter the tonic is gradually established in the following solo by the transposition of S1 motives from both secondary keys; and finally reconfirmed by the new conjunction of motto and closing section to form R4b (Ex. 10.6e). Particularly striking in the movement as a whole are two features: first, the careful integration of diverse material into a persuasive whole by subtle recall and reminiscence across both tutti and solo sections; and second, tonal aspects of the recapitulation, with almost all the earlier motives returning in the tonic in some form or other.

Platti's little-known cello concertos are among the most interesting of the entire repertoire considered in this book. Not only are the musical ideas and their development of a high order, but Platti displays in addition an impressive coherence in his handling of ritornello form. In particular, each concerto unveils new relationships between solo and tutti, with the handling of thematic and tonal aspects of the recapitulation proving especially revealing.

Mauro d'Alai: the Sole Concerto Composer in Parma

Mauro d'Alai (or d'Alay) (*b* Parma, late 17th century; *d* Parma, 1757) was apparently an outstanding virtuoso violinist, though little is known of his career. His name appears first among the performers at Parma Cathedral on 15 August 1712, and there are similar references until 1739; he also played at major festivals of the Chiesa della Steccata in 1729 and from 1731 to 1739.[4] During the late 1720s he visited Spain and London, on the latter occasion as Faustina Bordoni's accompanist, 'minder' and perhaps more. He must surely have met Vivaldi when the latter

---

[4] Pelicelli, 'Musicisti in Parma', pp. 32–3.

Ex. 10.6. Platti, Cello Concerto in G minor, I38

visited Faustina's Venetian house around 1728; a stronger indication of their relationship is provided by the fact that two of d'Alai's concertos were included in
Anna Maria's part-book, which dates from *c*1723–26.[5]

Fifteen violin concertos ascribed to Mauro d'Alai have reached us, one of them
(Fonds Blancheton, No. 15) with a dual ascription which we have considered as
more likely by Zuccari (Zuc6, see Chapter 12); a further concerto is for two
violins. On the title page of the set of twelve concertos, Op. 1 (Amsterdam, 1727)
the composer's name is given as 'Signor Mauro d'Alay detto il Maurini',
evidently a commonly used nickname: the variety of names under which d'Alai
was known has given rise to considerable confusion.[6] No. 6 is in fact a sinfonia
with no solo part, so it has been excluded from consideration here. Four other
concertos have survived in manuscripts in Dresden and Manchester.

D'Alai's concertos reveal an avid disciple of Vivaldi in every aspect, from the
selection of mottos and solo material to deeper layers of long-range structure. The
similarity of Dal2 (Op. 1/5) to Vivaldi's RV 277 (Op. 11/2) goes beyond the
cliché of the hammer-stroke motto to its subsequent handling, suggesting that
d'Alai might well have known the Vivaldi concerto in manuscript before its
publication in 1729. Similarly, Dal9 in G minor (Op. 1/12) is so close to Vivaldi's
RV 317 (Op. 12/1) and the related RV 328 that it should perhaps be considered a
homage to Vivaldi, in the same way as Zani's concerto Zan15 (illustrated in
Chapter 1). D'Alai's concerto begins with a beautiful transformation of Vivaldi's
motto, and the consequents are also closely linked (compare Ex. 10.7 with Ex.
4.9). The similarity continues into the initial solo motive, which (unusually for
d'Alai) is a close variant of the motto.

Ex. 10.7. D'Alai, Violin Concerto in G minor, Dal9 (Op. 1/12)

Like nearly all the composers discussed so far, d'Alai tended to avoid regular
phrase structures. A glance at the mottos in the Catalogue will reveal that his few
four-bar motives are, with one exception, continuously spun out; the exception is
the 2+2-bar phrase of Dal8 (Op. 1/3), and even here he adds a motto tail to blur the
regularity. D'Alai's mottos are mainly presented in homophonic textures or in
unison: indeed of the three concertos that start with imitation, only Dal12 (Op.
1/11) carries its elegant two-part imitation into later ritornellos. A much more
striking textural effect introduces Dal3, the Vivaldian dialogue counterpoint
being inverted later in the ritornello (Ex. 10.8) and recurring throughout the
movement.

---

5   Fourés and Talbot, 'A New Vivaldi Cantata', pp. 103–4; Talbot, 'Anna Maria's Partbook'. One
    of the concertos is Dal14 (= RV Anh. 75).
6   Date kindly communicated by Rudolf Rasch.

Ex. 10.8. D'Alai, Violin Concerto in D major, Dal3

The proportion of minor-mode concertos is as high as 27%, close to the figures for Vivaldi (31%) and Zani (32%), and clearly contrasting with the domination of the major mode in other repertoires. Moreover, the four concertos in minor express serious and dramatic affects, similar to those of Vivaldi and Zani. D'Alai's tonal schemes are presented in Table 10.5. Particularly striking here is his preference for tonal schemes based on ascending fifths (I-V-^{V}/V or i-v-^{v}/v, found in nine of the fifteen movements). This tonal strategy is highly unusual in the repertoire as a whole, and deserves closer attention. As suggested in the discussion of its rare appearance in Vivaldi, the dominant of the dominant (a more directional term than 'major supertonic') is not a 'related key' in conventional parlance: the extreme sharpward move decisively prohibits the natural tendency of the dominant to fall back to the tonic in the Albinoni pendulum manner. D'Alai even uses the same strategy in two of his minor-mode concertos, resulting in the still more unusual minor dominant of the dominant (or 'minor supertonic'). This is a key never used at all in the Vivaldi sample.

The rhetorical implications of the modulation to ^{V}/V may be illustrated by Dal2 in D major (Op. 1/5, Table 10.6). R2 is announced by the hammer-stroke motto in V, modulating to E major in d'Alai's usual manner (Ex. 10.9). The ensuing solo initiates a roving tonal debate by immediately turning flatwards, but any suggestion of the tonic is dismissed as premature, with R2b finally reconfirming V and picking up the ritornello where it left off. As a consequence of this extended section, the dominant area amounts to 21% altogether, the same as the initial tonic. It is the nature of this centrifugal process around the dominant that propels the argument here. The minor-mode peripheral area is of little consequence: a mere touch of F♯ minor, separated by hiatuses on both sides.

A similar strategy, albeit on a grander scale, is enacted in Dal7 in F major (Op. 1/8, Table 10.7). The entire movement again comprises a tour de force essay on tonic-dominant polarity. Its essential concept is inherent in the motto (see

Table 10.5. D'Alai's tonal schemes

Circuit		Pendulum	
Tonal scheme	**Number**	**Tonal scheme**	**Number**
Major			
I-V-iii-I	2	I-V-I-V-iii-I	1
I-V-^{V}/V-V-I	2	I-V-I-V-^{V}/V-I	1
I-V-^{V}/V-vi-I	2	I-V-I-V-^{V}/V-iii-I	1
I-V-^{V}/V-iii-I	1	I-V-I-vi-I-iii-I	1
Minor			
i-v-iv-i	1		
i-v-^{V}/v-i	1		
i-v-^{V}/v-v-i	1		
i-v-iv-VI-♭vii-i	1		

Table 10.6. Timeline of d'Alai, Violin Concerto in D major, Dal2 (Op. 1/5)

Function	R1	S1	R2a	S2	R2b	S3	S4	R4
Bars	1–14	15–27	27–33	34–43	44–51	52–55	56–73	73–87
Key	I (V) I	→ V	V → ^{V}/V	V	V //	(iii) // (V)	I	
Thematic	M		= 1–6	I rejected	= 7–14		→ capriccio	= R1 D.C.

Ex. 10.9. D'Alai, Violin Concerto in D major, Dal2 (Op. 1/5)

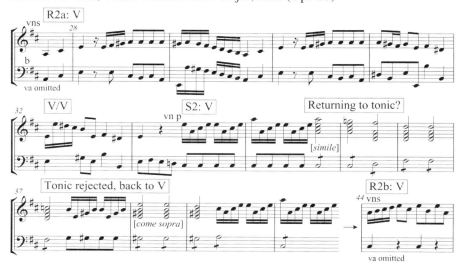

Table 10.7. Timeline of d'Alai, Violin Concerto in F major, Dal7 (Op. 1/8)

Function	R1a	S1a	R1b	S1b	R1c	R2
Bars	1–24	25–35	36–43	44–83	84–91	92–101
Key	I → V	→	I	I (V vi) I	I	V
Thematic	M		M¹		M	

S2	R3	S3	R4a	S4	R4b
102–129	130–135	136–156	157–164	165–187	188–195
(vi) →	V/V	V	I	I	I
	M¹		= 1–8	cf. S1b	= R1b

Catalogue), which by ending on a dominant chord immediately seeks a response: either to return to the tonic or to adopt the new key. R1a takes the second option and strongly asserts the dominant, yet the first solo straightaway pulls back to the tonic; the next solo S1b at first seems to be moving away decisively in a long roving modulatory section, but once again in vain. Only the inherent tendency of the motto to end on the dominant eventually loosens the power of the tonic in the third ritornello (R1c-R2). The following solo heads towards D minor, a key already presaged in S1b; yet this peripheral area never materializes and D (turned to major) instead leads directly to G major (^{V}/V), the only peripheral key to be accorded a full ritornello (R3). The return via the dominant completes the symmetrical tonal arch, in which ^{V}/V is the point of furthest remove. Altogether the initial and closing tonic areas, including the roving solos S1a and S1b, take up an amazing 71% of the movement; the dominant amounts to 15% and ^{V}/V to 3%. Thus 89% of the movement consists of stable areas arranged in a powerful hierarchy.

D'Alai also uses the dominant of the dominant as the sole peripheral area in two of the four minor-mode concertos. In Dal1 in C minor (Op. 1/10),[7] d'Alai clarifies his unusual tonal process by using the same thematic material in all four ritornellos: R1a, R1b-R2 (i-v), R3 (^{v}/v) and R4. Yet he subtly differentiates the section in the dominant by recasting the second motive over a pedal in order to give the secondary key sufficient emphasis (Ex. 10.10a). Being privileged with a ritornello of its own, ^{v}/v is simply accorded an exact transposition of R1, with the same descending chromatic bass for the second motive (Ex. 10.10b).

Renowned as a virtuoso violinist, d'Alai composes long and elaborate solos with minimal accompaniment, showing a particular liking for E-string melodies and chordal arpeggiation. Solos consisting of continuous figuration appear in four of the concertos (Dal1, 2, 14 and 15); frequent changes of grouping and harmonic rhythm lend them an effervescence and ebullience very much in Vivaldi's manner. But most of the solo sections develop a characterful melodic profile of their own. D'Alai mirrored Vivaldi's preference for thematic independence in the

---

[7]   Ed. Everett (1998).

Ex. 10.10. D'Alai, Violin Concerto in C minor, Dal1 (Op. 1/10)

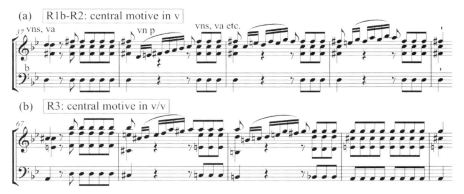

Ex. 10.11. D'Alai, Violin Concerto in B minor, Dal15 (Op. 1/9)

initial solo, only referring distantly to R1 in four cases: in Dal9, 10 and 11 the soloist subtly embellishes the contour of the motto (see Catalogue), while in Dal2 the solo is loosely derived from the second bar. Subsequent solos show a similar lack of concern with thematic integration, S2 being related to S1 in only six movements, S3 in just a single case.

In the recapitulation, faced with the diversity of options developed by Vivaldi, d'Alai preferred strong articulation of the tonic arrival by R4, although not necessarily with the motto. Of special interest is the approach to the recapitulation in the beautiful Dal15 (Op. 1/9), which has the tonal scheme i-v-iv-i. Here d'Alai as usual resists the pull of the dominant to the tonic within S2: on this occasion it is bluntly averted in favour of the subdominant (Ex. 10.11). R3 consists only of the motto in iv, leaving the ensuing solo to lead back to a weakly articulated recapitulation (S3-S4). Eventually R4 picks up where R3 left off, so that the two combined comprise a full thematic Da Capo of R1. Since d'Alai had so obviously rejected the tonic en route from v to iv, the listener is led to perceive R3 as a false reprise, yet it turns out to play a crucial part in the thematic argument, since the motto is not restated when the tonic arrives. At the same time, it results in a balance between the opening i-v progression and the lower fifth relationship of iv-i.

For d'Alai, the structure was taken care of by the powerful progression of ritornellos, strongly dependent on material from R1 and often nearly complete restatements. The freedom thereby released to the soloist allowed an improvisational fantasy to the solo sections, where rhythm is often flexible and normal harmonic decencies go by the board. This harmonic waywardness is allied to a highly idiosyncratic approach towards tonality, revolving around tonic-dominant debate and an extension of this polarity a further fifth higher towards $^V/V$. It is this first characteristic that is so clearly mirrored in Platti's homage.

Platti's Homage to d'Alai – the Personal 'Gusto'

We have already identified the model for the first movement of Platti's violin concerto I18 in d'Alai's concerto in A major Dal10. The latter starts with a jaunty motto over the simplest harmony, yet all expectations are immediately negated by an intrusive diminished seventh chord leading to the dominant, which is later confirmed by a full cadence (Ex. 10.12a). When the motto returns at the end of R1, however, the distortion is corrected, confirming the original expectations (Ex. 10.12b). The implications of this striking opening are to be realized later. The long S1 moves firmly to the dominant, preparing for R2 at bar 28, yet this is explicitly rejected by a surprising reversion to the solo opening in the tonic (Ex. 10.12c). The second ritornello at bar 39 thus restarts from the tonic motto, yet this time accepting the implications of the diminished seventh and ending in the dominant. Now the sharpward movement sets in in earnest. The following solo arrives at B major ($^V/V$), only for R3 to use the diminished seventh procedure to move up another fifth to the distant region of F♯ major; and thence in the following roving solo by a further fifth to C♯ minor, an extremely unorthodox way of arriving at the mediant. The recapitulation starts as a literal reprise of R1, yet the insistence in R1 on the dominant raises an immediate question about the role of that key, which d'Alai answers by interpolating a new solo that starts from a C♯ chord and reverses the entire tonal trajectory of the movement down the circle of fifths (Ex. 10.12d).

A timeline presenting this distinctive movement alongside that of Platti will clarify how he interpreted d'Alai's strategy (Table 10.8). Platti not only borrows from d'Alai's motives, but he poses exactly the same harmonic questions in the opening bars, albeit on a more condensed timescale (Ex. 10.13a). Again a short solo passage within R1 leads to a recall of the opening with all tonal ambiguities removed. Unlike his model, Platti chooses to reintroduce the diminished seventh to initiate the solo modulation (Ex. 10.13b). Yet just at the moment where the dominant is reached, he also returns unexpectedly to the opening of S1 in the tonic, such a distinctive procedure as to provide extremely compelling evidence for the connection. Significantly Platti's strategy diverges at the point where

Ex. 10.12. D'Alai, Violin Concerto in A major, Dal10 (Op. 1/1)

Table 10.8. Timeline of d'Alai, Violin Concerto in A major, Dal10 (Op. 1/1); and Platti, Violin Concerto in A major, I18

Function	R1	S1	ST	RT	R2	S2
D'Alai Bars	1–18	18–28	29–39	39–44	45–46	48–60
Keys	I (* V) * I	I → V	I	I *	V	V →
Thematic	M solo M	a	a	M		a
Platti Bars	1–17	18–39	39–48	48–52	52–62	63–82
Keys	I (* V) * I	I * V	I	I *	V	V →
Thematic	M solo M	a	a	M	incl. solo	a

R3(a)	S3a-R3b-S3b	S4a	R4a		S4(b)	R4b
60–64	65– 78		79–87		87–97	97–101
v/V * (v/v/V)	→ (ii) → iii		I (* V) *		→ I	I
			= 1–9			= 14–18

82–92		93–105	105–111		111–113	114–116
iii *		→ I	I *		I	I
			= 1–12 omitting V		= 12–14	= 15–17

* = diminished seventh chord

Ex. 10.13. Platti, Violin Concerto in A major, I18

d'Alai presses on further to ^{V}/V: instead Platti more conventionally prefers to begin R3 in iii. He was evidently impressed by the device of the diminished seventh, and by the debate between tonic and dominant that it initiated, whereas the strategy of ascending fifths did not affect him at all.

We may conclude from this not only that Platti knew d'Alai's concertos and appreciated them well enough to divert from his own individual style in order to emulate his contemporary, but also that d'Alai established a recognized 'gusto' which we may distinguish in his small surviving repertoire.

CHAPTER 11

Bologna: Overthrowing Tradition

The principal institutions of Bologna – the basilica of S Petronio and the Accademia Filarmonica – created a favourable environment for violinist-composers, providing more cohesion than the many diverse locales in Venice.[1] Giuseppe Matteo Alberti and Girolamo Nicolò Laurenti must have played their concertos together at the regular musical gatherings of the Accademia, alongside (from 1725) Lorenzo Gaetano Zavateri. Concertos may well have been performed at S Petronio and on civic occasions, as well as at aristocratic houses, which was certainly the case with Alberti's Op. 1. These three composers stayed in their home city for more extended periods than their itinerant Venetian colleagues, and thus there is every reason to consider them – together with Gaetano Maria Schiassi, who moved away from Bologna around 1727 – as a 'second Bolognese school' of concerto composers, exploring the newly emerging ritornello form in the wake of Torelli. Yet, as the forthcoming discussion will demonstrate, personal idiolects proved stronger than local identity.

Giuseppe Matteo Alberti

Giuseppe Matteo Alberti (*b* Bologna, 1685; *d* Bologna, 1751) was active in the city throughout his professional career. Elected a member of the Accademia Filarmonica in 1705, he was chosen as president in 1721 and in five subsequent years. From 1709 he was a violinist in the orchestra of S Petronio, and he gained a number of important posts in Bologna, for example as *maestro di cappella* of S Giovanni in Monte from 1726 until his death.

Alberti is an important figure in our study, not only as a prolific concerto composer but also as a useful touchstone of our comparative method. Michael Talbot has observed that 'so far as we can tell, he was the first Italian composer living outside Venice to imitate Vivaldi closely and consistently . . . [yet] in matters of melodic construction he perhaps follows Albinoni more closely than Vivaldi, and there are also strong elements of Bolognese academicism and the *stile tromba*'.[2] Talbot added the thoughtful observation that 'from the historian's point of view Alberti is likely to remain more important as a type of composer than as one in his own right'. Little has changed since this assessment was

---

[1]   Gambassi, *L'Accademia Filarmonica di Bologna*; and *La cappella musicale di S Petronio*.
[2]   Talbot, 'A Thematic Catalogue', pp. 1–2.

published in 1976, and it will be the purpose of the present discussion to turn Alberti from a mere type into an individual composer with his own personal style.

Alberti's preserved solo concerto output consists of twenty violin concertos and one concerto for two violins. Five solo concertos are included in his Op. 1, composed – according to the title page – to be played at concerts at the house of his patron Count Orazio Bargellini and published in Bologna in 1713. Three further concertos were published: T21 in the anthology *VI concerti* (Amsterdam, *c*1719); the double concerto T1 in the unauthorized Op. 2 (Amsterdam, 1725); and T12 in Walsh's second set entitled *Harmonia Mundi* (1728). The remainder survive only in manuscript, especially in Vienna (the Estensischen Musikalien), in Paris (the Fonds Blancheton) and in Manchester (the Ottoboni library, reflecting the Cardinal's position as protector of the Accademia Filarmonica).[3] T13, ascribed to Alberti in the Fonds Blancheton, is attributed to Ghignone in a Dresden manuscript partly copied by Pisendel. Flimsy stylistic grounds provide no sound basis for adjudication, especially since only one other Ghignone concerto is known; nevertheless, we have preferred the ascription to Ghignone (see Chapter 13), limiting the discussion of Alberti to twenty concertos.

Alberti's Op. 1 comprises ten concertos, a feature shared with Bonporti's Op. 11 that contrasts with the six or twelve compositions typical of contemporary practice. Half of the set are ripieno concertos, but the odd-numbered works are solo violin concertos opening with fully fledged ritornello movements. Published only four years after the posthumous Op. 8 by Torelli, they are roughly contemporary with the earliest solo concertos of Vivaldi, raising a fundamental historical question: how far do they reflect Alberti's individual innovation and how far are they indebted to the works of his slightly older contemporaries? Although there are evident connections with the concertos of Torelli, Alberti's close colleague in Bologna, they are only loosely related in terms of the handling of ritornello form at a deeper level. Neither do they adopt the Roman scoring for four violins favoured by Valentini and copied in Vivaldi's *L'estro armonico* (1711), preferring instead the emerging Venetian norm of the *concerto a cinque*.

This does not, of course, mean that Alberti was uninfluenced by the ritornello form developed in *L'estro armonico* and other Vivaldi concertos circulating in manuscript; nor by the style of Albinoni concertos such as Op. 5 (1707), for all their much less advanced formal characteristics. But a more fitting approach would surely be to study Alberti in his own right as one of the originators of ritornello form rather than to place him *a priori* in the shadow of Vivaldi. In the ensuing discussion a distinction will therefore be kept between Alberti's Op. 1 and the remaining, presumably later, concertos.

Motto and texture

Although his mottos may be heavily dependent on standard clichés, Alberti's concertos nonetheless maintain an individual character and a buoyant rhythmic vitality that proved especially popular in England.[4] T14 is a 'sonority concerto'

[3] Further on the concertos now in Manchester, see Everett, *The Manchester Concerto Partbooks*, pp. 393–409.

[4] Talbot, 'A Thematic Catalogue', p. 1.

Ex. 11.1. Alberti, Violin Concerto in F major, T8

Table 11.1. The texture of Alberti's mottos

Texture	Number
Homophonic	8
Imitative counterpoint	6
Free counterpoint	3
Unison	3

enjoying the brilliant G and D major figurations that extend across most of the movement; while T8 is a witty concerto in *buffo* idiom that anticipates the world of *La serva padrona* (Ex. 11.1). Even Alberti's three minor-mode concertos are far from melancholic or deeply affecting. The influence of Bolognese trumpet music, a genre to which Alberti himself contributed, is apparent in many of the mottos – in fanfares, dactylic rhythms and a generally brisk diatonic melodic idiom (a characteristic he shares with Albinoni).

The scholarly environment of the Accademia Filarmonica is reflected in a predilection for contrapuntal textures (Table 11.1). Imitative openings in fugal manner make clear reference to the Bolognese/Corellian trio sonata tradition, in which respect there is a certain connection with Torelli. This type of opening has a direct implication for the second ritornello: in T21 the tonic-dominant imitation that opens the movement is mirrored by a dominant-tonic resolution en route to the peripheral area (Ex. 11.2). The simple figurations of S1 replace the traditional episode between the two fugal expositions. In such movements Alberti consistently maintained the fugal motto within the fifth-related orbit, never once transposing it to a peripheral key – and thus remaining loyal to a long tradition of fugal practice. In a single case, he expanded the relationship to the fifth below: in T1, R3 states the subject in the subdominant, so that the fugal answer in the tonic can then form the recapitulation.

Even when the motto itself is homophonic, counterpoint sometimes swiftly supervenes, and indeed Alberti frequently marks a structural division or tonal arrival by means of an abrupt textural and rhythmic change. T6 opens with a homophonic motto in repeated semiquavers, whereas the Nachsatz introduces an animated contrast; the tonic resolution is confirmed by a more solemn passage

Ex. 11.2. Alberti, Violin Concerto in B♭ major, T21

with Corellian suspensions, which sets off in sharp relief the ensuing homophonic solo (Ex. 11.3).[5]

Yet these examples will already have indicated that it would be misleading to label Alberti as an essentially contrapuntal composer. The diminutive ritornello in T21 may begin like a *stile antico* fugue, but the anticipated third entry in the viola or bass never arrives, the exposition instead dissolving via Corellian counterpoint straight into solo figuration – by contrast, for example, with the fully fledged fugue in Vivaldi's RV 565 (Op. 3/11). To be sure, Alberti followed the trend initiated by his mentor Torelli, who in Op. 8/9 and Op. 8/11 limits the imitative entries to only two violins; but he goes further in tilting the proportion in favour of homophony, emphasizing contrasts of texture with frequent articulations. Rather than being embedded in *stile antico*, Alberti uses counterpoint as one of several different approaches, acting like an outside observer in the same way as Andrea Zani, to be discussed in the next chapter.

Tonal strategies
Alberti retains a conservative attitude towards modal key signatures, which occur in as many as eight concertos; yet this usage appears to be of little harmonic

---

5   The edition by Ettore Desderi (1955) adds a spurious second violin part to the first fifteen bars, which exaggerates these contrasts still further.

Ex. 11.3. Alberti, Violin Concerto in E minor, T6 (Op. 1/7)

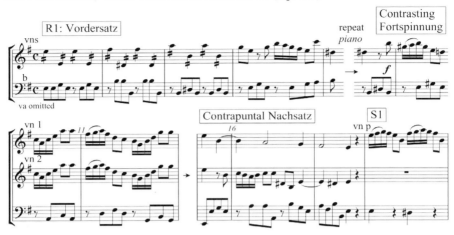

Table 11.2. Alberti's tonal schemes

Circuit		Pendulum	
Tonal scheme	**Number**	**Tonal scheme**	**Number**
Major			
		I-V-I-vi-I	7
		I-V-I-vi-iii-I	2
		I-V-I-vi-iii-ii-I	1
		I-V-vi-I-iii-IV-I	1
		I-V-I-vi-IV-I	1
		I-V-vi-I-IV-iii-I	1
		I-V-I-iii-I	1
I-V-^{V}/V-vi-I	1		
I-V-I	1	I-V-I-V-I	1
Minor			
		i-v-i-v-III-i	1
		i-III-v-i-III-i	1
		i-III-iv-i-v-i	1

consequence. Entirely modern is Alberti's distinct preference for major over minor (which he shared with the other Bolognese composers): only three concertos are in the minor mode (two of these in the early Op. 1). Alberti's tonal schemes resemble those of Albinoni in the strong preference for the pendulum concept, the universal selection of the dominant as the first target in major, and the preference for vi as the first peripheral key (compare Table 11.2 with Tables

Table 11.3. Average proportions of stable tonal areas in Alberti

Stable area	Opening tonic	Secondary	Intermediate tonic	First peripheral	Second peripheral	Closing tonic
Average proportion	25%	13%	6%	10%	5%	25%

3.6 and 8.2). The pendulum partly results from the mirroring of the fugal opening I-V with V-I entries in R2, a procedure comparable to that identified in Albinoni's early concertos; and again the preference for vi is not coincidental in this context, since (as the relative minor) it remains closely within the tonic orbit.

Yet at the same time Alberti matches Vivaldi in his preference for long stable periods alternating with very short modulatory passages, which sometimes last no more than a single bar. The average total duration of stable areas in Alberti's concertos is 81%, and, in the two most extreme cases, the stable areas amount to as much as 98% of the movement. These stable areas are used to maintain a clear tonal hierarchy, as is demonstrated in Table 11.3. An example from T19 in A major will illustrate the precipitous way in which Alberti modulates between stable areas. After R2 resolves into the tonic in Alberti's usual fashion (apparently closing the first stage of the movement), there is a dramatic leap across a hiatus to F♯ minor; and the return to the tonic is similarly achieved by hiatus, so that the peripheral area is entirely isolated from the surrounding tonic on both sides (Ex. 11.4).

Ex. 11.4. Alberti, Violin Concerto in A major, T19

It might appear that such brusque modulations would leave little opportunity for complex tonal debate. Yet the section immediately following R2 does offer some scope for more sophisticated treatment. One strategy concerns the search for a peripheral key. In the well-planned T12 in G major, the overall tonal scheme is Alberti's favourite I-V-I-vi-I. R2 is followed by a neatly organized unstable section: an immediate return to the tonic introduces a search for the desired peripheral area, trying first IV and again V, each approved by a tutti unison (a characteristic feature of the Bolognese concerto),[6] before finally settling on vi, which is confirmed by a long stable area (Ex. 11.5). Another type of search involves the return to the intermediate tonic itself: thus, in T3 in C major, the dominant area is followed by a touch of D minor, which is immediately rejected in favour of a temporary tonic en route to further explorations (Ex. 11.6). The striking resemblance to Vivaldi's 'Il favorito' (RV 277, Op. 11/2) reaches beyond the common motto to the similar strategy of tonal search.

[6]   Everett, *The Manchester Concerto Partbooks*, p. 396.

Ex. 11.5. Alberti, Violin Concerto in G major, T12

Ex. 11.6. Alberti, Violin Concerto in C major, T3

Alberti's usage of the intermediate tonic is, therefore, more than just an instinctive response to the habitual pull of the dominant. In eight movements it lasts far beyond a single cadence, spanning 4–10% of the movement (in one case, even 16%). The concertos in the minor mode are also revealing, for here the pendulum scheme can only be achieved by the deliberate majorization of the dominant key. This process is strongly highlighted in T16 in G minor (Op. 1/9), where R2 is not allowed to close definitively in D minor but turns at the last moment to D major so as to resolve onto the intermediate tonic.

The general reliance on the tonic-dominant axis is heightened by other parameters. R2 is always based on material from R1 and is usually stable in the secondary key: furthermore, of the five cases where R2 is modulatory, four are propelled by the arrival of the central intermediate tonic within the ritornello. By contrast, the peripheral R3 quotes R1 material in only three cases, never starting with the motto; indeed, in three movements R3 is reduced to a brief tutti interjection, and it is absent altogether in six. While the avoidance of a strong peripheral area may to some extent reflect the Bolognese trumpet sonata heritage, at the same time it reveals an emerging sense of hierarchy that was fundamental to large-scale tonal planning.

The recapitulation
Unlike Vivaldi, Alberti preferred to articulate the restatement of the tonic through a powerful R4: a hiatus from the peripheral key (another Bolognese character-istic)[7] emphasizes the point in as many as eight out of fifteen cases. The recapitu-lation consists solely of a full Da Capo of R1 in nine movements; in a tenth (T4) the original fugal exposition is simply filled out with additional counterpoint. Yet there are examples of a more complex reinterpretation. T17 in G minor has the only modulatory R1 in Alberti's repertoire, requiring special treatment in the recapitulation.[8] The opening extends the early model described in Chapter 3 in connection with Albinoni's Op. 5/1: after a short and apparently complete R1, the ritornello restarts with the motto but here continues further into the Fortspinnung section so as to lead to B♭ major, where the solo emerges unobtrusively out of the tutti texture. In order to balance this bipartite structure, the recapitulation not only reprises the complete R1, but also contrives a new sequential Fortspinnung as a coda to replace the modulatory second period.

The most sophisticated tonal recapitulation occurs in the substantial concerto T12, published in 1728 in Walsh's anthology *Harmonia Mundi*, and therefore possibly a later work. The recapitulation again starts with a Da Capo of R1; but then, as if by inertia, the soloist reprises S1 almost in its entirety, including the full modulation to the dominant as if to lead into R2 once more. At this point the error is rectified and the dominant immediately resolves to the tonic, with R4b balancing the recapitulation through a literal repetition of the closing section of R1.

Alberti the violinist
In view of Alberti's varied and imaginative treatment of the ritornello, his solo writing is puzzling and rather disappointing. In eleven movements the solo mate-rial is limited to figuration of a mechanical cast, lacking the virtuosic brilliance that renders Vivaldi's solos so breathtaking. In others, figuration of this kind is prefaced by more interesting melodic material, loosely related to the motto. In the exceptional T10 Alberti takes flight in imaginative cantabile melodic lines, such as the plaintive D minor cantilena given in Ex. 11.7. While dry figuration predominates in the early Op. 1, as well as in T21 (published in 1717), the more interesting solo lines all appear in the Ottoboni concertos now in Manchester, suggesting that they may be later works dating from the early 1720s.

Ex. 11.7. Alberti, Violin Concerto in F major, T10

7   Ibid., pp. 396–7.
8   Ed. Hirshberg, *Ten Italian Violin Concertos*, No. 1.

Despite reservations about his solo writing in general, Alberti's contribution as one of the early pioneers of ritornello form deserves to be recognized. His idiom retained some of the characteristics of the Bolognese concerto developed by Torelli and his contemporaries; yet at the same time he appreciated the structural force of ritornello form – and, in particular, the tonal hierarchization that it expresses so powerfully.

Girolamo Nicolò Laurenti

Girolamo Nicolò Laurenti (*b* Bologna, 1678; *d* Bologna, 1751) was also a violinist at S Petronio for his entire career, rising to the post of leader in 1734. He became a member of the Accademia Filarmonica as an instrumentalist in 1698, and was admitted as a composer in 1710 in recognition of his instrumental music ('un *Concerto* a quattro') – an unusual accolade, since sacred vocal music was normally submitted (see p. 35). His concertos must have figured in both contexts, and may well have been selected for the 'sinfonia' that he contributed (for most years until 1748) to the academy's annual festival mass.

Laurenti was a member of a large family of Bolognese musicians, which included his father, Bartolomeo Girolamò Laurenti, and three brothers, Pietro Paolo, Angelo Maria and Lodovico Filippo. This has resulted in considerable confusion, and also to occasional difficulty in attributing individual works, a situation that may apply to the small repertoire of ten concertos studied here.[9] Lau9 (in the Manchester collection) and the set of six concertos Op. 1 (Amsterdam, 1727) do carry specific attribution to Girolamo Nicolò Laurenti and to Girolamo Laurenti respectively. But the three Dresden concertos ascribed to 'Signor Laurenti' (Lau2, 6 and 8) are significantly different and the question arises as to whether they might have been written by another member of the family. In the absence of any further evidence, however, the Laurenti repertoire will be discussed *in toto*.

Most of the opening ritornello movements of Op. 1 are laid out on a small scale. Lau1 and 10 are miniatures comprising fifty-two and forty-three bars respectively, harking back to Vivaldi's exceptional diminutive RV 175 with its mere twenty-one bars. Lau1 combines an extremely clear and balanced ritornello form with a textural mixture of solo, grosso and ripieno traits. The style suggests a sinfonia with some concertino contrasts; yet both R1 and R2 lead to prominent violin solos and similar cello figurations, contributing the textural contrast expected of the solo concerto. This borderline movement will therefore still be included in our discussion.

The set is carefully organized so as to close with the longest and most elaborate concerto, as with Tessarini's Op. 1, although Laurenti's range of affects is more limited than those explored there. Many of the concertos begin with some hint of contrapuntal writing, the second violin shadowing the melody of the first in some way; but any suggestion of a fugue (as in Lau4) is quickly dissipated in favour of

---

[9]   An autograph concerto in Bologna was unavailable for consultation; a concerto supposedly in the Österreichische Nationalbibliothek (Vienna) is in fact a sonata.

Ex. 11.8. Laurenti, Violin Concerto in A major, Lau10 (Op. 1/2)

more homophonic textures in the manner of Alberti. Indeed a light, *buffo* spirit prevails, as in the boisterous opening concerto (Lau3) where the energetic sinfonia opening provides a foil to a graceful solo replete with *galant* triplets; even the single minor-mode concerto (Lau5) does not venture into any deeply expressive affect, despite some quirky harmonic inflections.

If Laurenti's motivic materials are related to the newly emerging *galant* style, he goes to some lengths to disguise their inherent regularity. In Lau1 this is achieved by attaching a short transitional motive or 'motto tail' to the end of the motto (see Catalogue).[10] A more subtle manipulation appears in Lau10, where the essential four-bar phrasing is on one level emphasized by the new, syncopated violin motive in bar 5, as well as by the repetition of the opening bass line underneath; yet at the same time regularity is disguised by the anticipation of this new motive in the lower parts at the end of bar 4 (bracketed in Ex. 11.8).

The Bolognese contrapuntal heritage is also evident in the manuscript concerto Lau9, yet it does not go beyond the most token acknowledgment, for the movement turns out to be highly experimental, not to say eccentric. It starts in the manner of Torelli as if to imply a fully fledged fugue, yet viola and bass merely go through the motions and the fugue soon dissipates into a loosely contrapuntal idiom. Then the soloist enters in a completely different vein, ignoring the $^{12}/_8$ metre in favour of a boldly assertive $^4/_4$, and the movement unfolds a free juxtaposition of the two metres, which are even at one point combined (Ex. 11.9).[11] There is some attempt to accommodate the soloist to the prevailing rhythms yet the lasting impression is one of deliberate dislocation, as the final solo, after starting in $^{12}/_8$, eventually reverts to $^4/_4$.

Unlike the Op. 1 concertos, the three Dresden concertos (Lau2, 6 and 8) were conceived on the grand structural scale of Vivaldi's most elaborate works; and they are indeed among the finest in the entire repertoire discussed in the present book. The magnificent E minor concerto Lau6 combines Laurenti's intricate contrapuntal mastery with Vivaldian tonal rhetoric. A short *Largo e spicco* in French overture style leads to the main Vivace movement. The opening ritornello, a substantial 'piece within a piece', brings immediate contrapuntal intensification to the forceful hammer-stroke motto, not only in the interweaving

---

[10] This device is discussed in Ramot, 'The Organization of the First Ritornello', pp. 36, 59.
[11] See also the examples in Everett, *The Manchester Concerto Partbooks*, p. 291.

Ex. 11.9. Laurenti, Violin Concerto in G major, Lau9

accompaniment but also in the counterpoint in the second violin. After a contrasting burst of semiquaver figuration, further intense elaboration of motives from the motto brings R1 to an impressive climax (Ex. 11.10). The overall structure is illustrated in Table 11.4. The tonal argument is heightened by the striking use of hiatus, such as has already been remarked in Alberti. III is first introduced by an abrupt hiatus within S1, but this unprepared key is soon supplanted by the dominant; only after a new start does G major eventually win its case in a long solo confirmed by R3. The movement consequently has unusually proportioned stable areas: 27% (tonic), 4% (III), 4% (v), 2% (intermediate tonic), 20% (III) and 33% (final tonic). As a result of the two hiatuses, the stable areas together span 90% of the movement, with modulation limited to the tonal argument between III and v.

Laurenti shares with Alberti a marked preference for the major mode, but a comparison of his tonal schemes with those of Alberti reveals little else in common (compare Table 11.5 with Table 11.2). Laurenti prefers the circuit model, and even in the three cases of pendulum the intermediate tonic areas are very brief, mere touches propelling the modulatory process forwards. Moreover, Laurenti makes little use of vi, Alberti's favourite peripheral key. A modal conception is evident in two concertos. Lau6 in E minor, illustrated in Ex. 11.10, adds C♯ accidentals to an unusual degree, in line with Laurenti's propensity for chromatic colouring. More structurally, Lau10 (Op. 1/2) in A major, with a key signature of two sharps, gravitates towards IV, as is common in such cases. The central resolution of V to I overshoots to D major; but the subdominant remains stable for only a single bar before the tonal swing that inevitably settles on the tonic, resulting in the overall scheme I-V-(I)-IV-I.

Ex. 11.10. Laurenti, Violin Concerto in E minor, Lau6/II

Table 11.4. Timeline of Laurenti, Violin Concerto in E minor, Lau6

Function	R1	S1	R2	S2a	RT	S2b	R3	S4a-R4a-S4b-R4b
Bars	1–23	23–37	37–40	40–43	43–44	44–64	64–67	67–99
Keys	i	i // III →	v	→	i	→ III	III //	i
Thematic	M		M		M'			

Where Laurenti's practice most clearly resembles that of Alberti is in the handling of the recapitulation. In eight concertos the recapitulation is strongly articulated by a ritornello (R4) following S3, and in four of these he heightens the effect of the tonic arrival by a harmonic hiatus. Yet in only three cases is R4 merely an exact Da Capo of R1. Thus in Lau2, just as the Da Capo approaches its final cadence, three bars are inserted from the intermediate tonic ritornello (bars

Table 11.5. Laurenti's tonal schemes

Circuit		Pendulum	
Tonal scheme	**Number**	**Tonal scheme**	**Number**
Major			
I-V-vi-I	1	I-V-I-vi-I	1
I-V-iii-I	1		
I-V-iii-vi-I	1		
I-V-iii-IV-I	1		
I-V-iii-V-♭VII-I	1		
I-V-IV-I	1		
I-V-ii-IV-I	1		
Minor			
		i-v-i-III-i	1
		i-III-v-i-III-i	1

67–69 = 29–31), nicely tying together loose ends in the manner of Albinoni and overtly strengthening the tonic confirmation.

Laurenti concentrates his compositional invention on the overall tonal structure and on the thematic elaboration of stable ritornellos. Diversity is the keyword for his solos: S1 only elaborates the motto once (Lau4), while the remainder present entirely new material. He does, however, avoid Alberti's dull figuration in favour of well-shaped and idiomatic violin writing, as a glance at the solo entrances in the Catalogue will show; his more brilliant solos traverse varied rhythmic and melodic patterns in the manner of Vivaldi. Furthermore, the soloist plays an active role in the rhetorical argument, as we have seen in Lau6 (Table 11.4), where the soloist first suggests the intermediate tonic – approved by the tutti through the motto – and then switches to the victorious tonality of G major.

A comparison with Alberti, admittedly complicated by the extreme diversity of Laurenti's repertoire, suggests that they shared a predilection for the *buffo* spirit set against the Bolognese contrapuntal backdrop. There are certain features in common, notably their handling of the recapitulation; but overall their tonal and structural preferences differed to such an extent that one cannot consider them as representing any unified Bolognese approach. Similarly divergent in many respects are the concertos of their two younger contemporaries, Zavateri and Schiassi.

Zavateri *the* Galant

Lorenzo Gaetano Zavateri (*b* Bologna, 1690; *d* Bologna, 1764) studied the violin in Bologna with Torelli and composition with Predieri. He was active at S Petronio from 1713, joining the *cappella* as a viola-player twelve years later, and he became a member of the Accademia Filarmonica in 1717. Although he was

well-known as a violinist in Northern Italy, his career as a player and teacher
remained focused on Bologna for the rest of his life. Only six concertos by
Zavateri have been preserved, as the even-numbered works in a set of twelve
Concerti da chiesa e da camera published in Bologna in 1735 (the remainder are
for ripieno). They span a broad range of affects, providing in a handful of works a
conspectus of Zavateri's vivid orchestral imagination and highly idiomatic
violin-writing.

The two concluding concertos pay tribute to venerable traditions. Zav10
continues in a line of Christmas Concertos, following Corelli's Op. 6/12 in
placing the traditional $^{12}/_8$ pastorale as the last of four movements, rather than
second as in Torelli's Op. 8/6. The second movement here is a joyous Allegro
featuring two solo violins: its instrumentation reflects the concerto grosso tradition suggested by the solemn opening Grave, yet the idiom and ritornello form are
entirely modern. On the other hand the concluding concerto Zav12 ('a Tempesta
di Mare') pays unquestionable tribute to Vivaldi, both in its title and in its vivid
depictions of nature.

The *galant* style focused on short-range aspects of melody and rhythm associated with the emerging opera buffa and sinfonia. New ideas of melodic construction and texture, transforming the entire musical sonority, could be readily
absorbed by ritornello form, yet *galant* penetration into the well-established
concerto was gradual and cautious, as we have seen in connection with Laurenti
and others. Zavateri was among those who embraced the *galant* wholeheartedly,
favouring light semiquaver triplets, Lombardian snaps and slides, semiquaver
syncopations, and short-term chromatic inflexions and switches of mode. The
same spirit even permeates the sole concerto in minor. Zavateri emphasizes the
well-articulated sectional structure associated with the *galant* by systematically
separating ritornello and ensuing solo. The opening of S1 is usually an elegantly
turned melody that loosely varies the motto so as clearly to differentiate the 'sing-
ing' violin soloist.

Yet Zavateri did not associate his *galant* style with a regular phrase-structure,
following Laurenti in deliberately preventing regularity by means of extensions
or overlaps. Thus in Zav6 the motto itself – beginning with hammer-strokes in
French overture style – is compressed into an irregular phrase of 1½+2 bars (see
Catalogue). Furthermore, Zavateri explores an especially varied palette of
textures, shifting fluently between homophony, free counterpoint and short-range
imitations. Zav4 begins with the kind of loosely contrapuntal motto we have seen
in Laurenti, before sequential imitations lead seamlessly into pure homophony
(Ex. 11.11); the profusion of grace-notes and trills is the epitome of *galant* style.
Corellian suspensions add a further textural contrast a few bars later. Even where
the motto is indeed just a simple two-bar melody, as in Zav8, Zavateri adds a
disjunct counterpoint that not only enriches the texture but also provides tension
and energy to propel the movement forward (Ex. 11.12). By such means, Zavateri
goes to some lengths to disguise the essentially *galant* nature of his musical
language, providing an interesting Bolognese perspective on changing musical
styles.

Zavateri shared with Laurenti a preference for circuit schemes (Table 11.6),
and with Alberti a strong thematic unity between R1 and R2: indeed, in two

Ex. 11.11. Zavateri, Violin Concerto in C minor, Zav 4 (Op. 1/4)

Ex. 11.12. Zavateri, Violin Concerto in E♭ major, Zav 8 (Op. 1/8)

Table 11.6. Zavateri's tonal schemes

Circuit		Pendulum	
Tonal scheme	Number	Tonal scheme	Number
Major			
I-V-vi-I	2		
I-V-iii-vi-I	1	I-V-I-iii-I	1
		I-V-iii-I-vi-I	1
Minor			
i-v-III-iv-i	1		

movements R2 is a literal transposition of R1. But in other respects his treatment of the intermediate ritornellos is quite different, since R2 is modulatory in three concertos and R3 unstable in all five where it is present. The result is more fluid than the concertos of either Alberti or Laurenti, reflecting the restless and changeable character of Zavateri's idiom.

Ex. 11.13. Zavateri, Violin Concerto in G major, Zav12 (Op. 1/12)

Where he does fall in line with the practice of his Bolognese contemporaries is in the handling of the recapitulation, which in four movements is entrusted to the ritornello following a solo; five end with a full Da Capo. The final ritornello is always dramatically set off from the preceding solo by a blunt change of character or tempo. Thus in the common-time Allegro in Zav2 the last solo unexpectedly accelerates into $^{12}/_8$, and there are equally brilliant figurations and capriccios in the other concertos – sometimes leading directly into the Da Capo as a triumphant resolution of a dominant pedal (Zav10), sometimes delaying the inevitable return with a sentimental Adagio (Zav4). The dislocation is particularly clear in the programmatic Zav12 ('a Tempesta di Mare'). The opening ritornello depicts the beginning of the storm ('principio di cativo tempo'), and increasingly tumultuous rain and thunder eventually lead to an exhortation by 'voci al cielo' (voices to heaven), expressed in a plaintive B minor Adagio solo – only for an apparently unmoved deity to insist upon the return of the storm in the manner of a Da Capo aria (Ex. 11.13).

Gaetano Maria Schiassi

Gaetano Maria Schiassi (*b* Bologna, 1698; *d* Lisbon, 1754) was active in Bologna for the first half of his career: as an instrumentalist member of the Accademia Filarmonica from 1719, as a violinist at the ducal court of Alderano Cybo Malaspina during the early 1720s, and also as a prolific opera composer. Probably from 1727 he was employed by the Landgrave of Darmstadt, and by 1734 he had moved to Lisbon, where he spent the remainder of his career in the service of the royal court.

Schiassi was mostly active in the opera house and his surviving concerto repertoire is limited to a single set of concertos published in Amsterdam in 1727.[12] The set is strongly in the Bolognese tradition, with eleven violin concertos followed by a Christmas pastorale. Schiassi seems to be asserting his serious Bolognese credentials by starting with a C minor concerto with a *stile antico* finale; and passages of interlocking suspensions turn up in other concertos, especially in minor-mode sections. Sch2 also makes direct reference to the Bolognese *tromba*

---

[12] Rasch, 'I manoscritti musicali', p. 1056. On Le Cène's death in 1743 many Schiassi concertos remained unpublished (ibid., p. 1068).

Ex. 11.14. Schiassi, Violin Concerto in C minor, Sch1 (Op. 1/1)

idiom in its brilliant unison fanfare opening. But these traits are in fact exceptional, and the prevailing style is strongly in line with Vivaldian practice around 1720: Sch8 even draws on the stock motto found in RV 345 (Op. 9/2, Ex. 1.1) and in RV 372, also in B♭ major. Only occasionally does Schiassi venture into the more *galant* idiom of Zavateri, in syncopated solo episodes or in the linked motivic fragments that open Sch6.

The eleven solo concertos vary considerably in both length and violinistic difficulty. Several of the opening movements are comparatively undeveloped, and none makes extravagant demands on the soloist, although Sch10 does contain a lengthy capriccio in changing metres. For the most part Schiassi distinguishes the solo part in other ways, most obviously by deliberate surprises – such as the Adagio Cantabile solo entrance in Sch7, or the 13-bar minor-mode Andante that initiates the recapitulation in Sch2. More subtly, every one of the solo entrances begins with either a direct transformation of the motto or with some allusion to its shape or key elements. Thus in Sch1 the soloist expressively transforms not only the motto but also subsequent phrases, so as to achieve a poignantly balanced eight-bar phrase (Ex. 11.14). Later solos revisit this same material, which emerges in a different perspective each time.

At first sight Schiassi seems to rely on a fairly standardized approach towards ritornello form. All eleven concertos move first to the dominant, whether major or minor, and in all but one R2 opens with the motto, usually extended to a substantial quotation from R1. The peripheral area receives a short third ritornello, yet it is often tonally unstable and deprived of the motto. In accordance with the usual Bolognese preference, ten concertos end with a complete Da Capo of R1, although in every case the tonic is anticipated in the previous solo and sometimes articulated by a strong thematic statement.

Yet closer examination reveals rather less uniformity than this summary might suggest. The exceptional cases are themselves worthy of note: thus in Sch9 the dominant is surprisingly reasserted in the third ritornello, which then whirls with solo interventions through iii to vi in the space of five bars, as if in panic at the mistaken direction. By contrast, the dominant is expressly downgraded in Sch11. R2 eschews any thematic statement in the dominant but instead modulates

Table 11.7. Schiassi's tonal schemes

Circuit		Pendulum	
Tonal scheme	**Number**	**Tonal scheme**	**Number**
Major			
		I-V-I-vi-I	1
		I-V-I-vi-i-I	1
I-V-vi-iii-I	2		
		I-V-I-iii-I	1
I-V-iii-vi-I	2		
I-V-^{V}/V-iii-vi-I	1		
I-V-^{V}/V-IV-vi-I	1		
Minor			
i-v-III-i	1	i-v-i-III-i	1

Ex. 11.15. Schiassi, Violin Concerto in A major, Sch7 (Op. 1/7)

immediately, and the two peripheral keys vi and iii are both privileged in ensuing ritornellos by reference to the motto.

Schiassi's tonal schemes also reveal his inventive handling of these funda-mental patterns (Table 11.7). Two movements go out of their way to avoid the central return to the tonic by stressing ^{V}/V at the heart of the movement; and in Sch7 in A major this results in a unique tonal scheme, I-V-^{V}/V-IV-vi-I. Schiassi ingeniously moves flatwards to IV via a sequence that avoids establishing the tonic en route (Ex. 11.15), before he eventually reverses the process in favour of vi, the main goal.

In three of the pendulum movements S2 uses the tonic to initiate new tonal departures in the normal way: but in a fourth (Sch5 in G major) a quite excep-tional strategy occurs near the beginning of the movement. The ritornello at bar 16 gives every impression of being R2 in the dominant (Ex. 11.16a-b), but this turns out to be deceptive as it quickly reverts to the tonic as R1b. This procedure

Ex. 11.16. Schiassi, Violin Concerto in G major, Sch5 (Op. 1/5)

somewhat resembles Vivaldi's RV 374 (Op. 7/6): yet in the Schiassi movement there is no eventual confirmation of the dominant, but instead an early move towards iii, the key of the next ritornello (Ex. 11.16c). This strategy creates an issue for the recapitulation, which exceptionally for Schiassi extends beyond the reprise of R1 to incorporate the whole of S1. The solo reaches as far as the dominant cadence, as in Alberti's T12 described above. But now the false R2 is replaced with an unambiguous affirmation of the tonic, a striking reworking that serves to confirm the tonal resolution (Ex. 11.16d).

A Bolognese Group Style?

Our analysis has clearly shown that regular encounters at the Accademia Filarmonica and at S Petronio did not forge a cohesive and unified approach towards the developing violin concerto. All four composers do draw to some degree on traditional features of the Bolognese idiom: the brisk Allegro in *stile tromba* with fanfare rhythms and a forthright diatonicism; the contrapuntal textures, ranging from suggestions of fugal openings in the Torellian manner to passages of Corellian suspensions. Yet these idioms are increasingly replaced by more arresting Vivaldian mottos and by intimations of the new sinfonia manner. The neutral figurations favoured by Alberti are supplemented by more *affettuoso* solo writing, with *galant* mannerisms making inroads as elsewhere. In this respect the Bolognese group is simply following general trends in the wake of Vivaldi, suggesting that Venetian influence overpowered most local idiosyncrasies, and that the differences between their concertos principally reflect the compositional and soloistic idiolects of each of the four composers.

At the same time, they held in common certain attitudes towards ritornello form. A strong preference for the major mode is evident, and in both major and minor the first destination is normally the dominant (92%). R2 is usually privileged by the motto, and the status of R3 is downplayed – indeed the fact that Alberti so often avoids R3 is a reminder that this remnant of older practice links with the newer trend towards hierarchization. Also shared is the preference for new material in the solos, which, if related to the ritornello at all, usually present a distant transformation; thematic reference across the solos is a rarity. This factor gives weight to the ritornellos in the structure overall, a factor exaggerated by the consistency with which the Bolognese composers favoured a full Da Capo of R1 (68%). Furthermore, in 70% of cases the recapitulation is initiated by a ritornello after a solo, the strong articulation of R4 sometimes even dramatized by a hiatus. Even where the tonic is established in the preceding solo, it is rarely emphasized; and R4a-S4-R4b patterns are comparatively unusual (28%, over half of these in Alberti).

Although the Bolognese turned most of their inventive skills to the ritornellos, only Alberti relegated the solos to a secondary position. The three other composers present engaging solos that skilfully juxtapose brilliant passage work with expressive cantabile lines. Their combination of sensitive solo writing with intricately crafted ritornellos is both rewarding and distinctive.

CHAPTER 12

A Tale of Two Cities: Milan and Vienna

In 1706, during the War of the Spanish Succession, the duchy of Lombardy came under the rule of the Viennese imperial court, a shift of power ratified by the Peace of Utrecht in 1713. As well as political exchange between Milan and Vienna, this resulted in strong musical links, which extended to other parts of Lombardy. Thus Andrea Zani, from a small town near Cremona, spent a decade in Vienna, with significant influence on his style and output; while Giovanni Perroni took up a permanent post there after a successful career in Novara and Milan. All the other composers considered in this chapter – Scaccia, Brivio, Zuccari and the two Sammartini brothers – were members of the ducal orchestra in Milan and active in Milan's rich musical life, allowing ample opportunity for interaction between them. Some worked alongside each other for many years, while others can have interacted only briefly as a result of travels elsewhere.[1] We begin our discussion with Zani, before focusing on those composers who may be more legitimately grouped together as a 'Milanese school' of concerto composition.

Andrea Zani – between Casalmaggiore and Vienna

Andrea Zani (*b* Casalmaggiore, 1696; *d* Casalmaggiore, 1757), one of the finest concerto composers of the period, was never employed in Milan, working in his home town for most of his life. Here in 1729 he published a set of symphonies and concertos as Op. 2 (reissued *c*1737 in Amsterdam as Op. 1); the six concertos were also copied for the large Dresden orchestra under Pisendel. During the 1730s Zani was in Vienna, at the invitation of Antonio Caldara, vice-Kapellmeister at the imperial court. Here he must have met the cello-playing Count Rudolf Franz Erwein von Schönborn, to whom he dedicated his second published set of concertos, Op. 4 (Vienna, *c*1733; as Op. 2, Amsterdam, *c*1741).[2] A set of twelve cello concertos written for the Count survives in manuscript, a magnificent addition to the twenty-six cello concertos by Vivaldi and twenty-two

---

[1] Another significant Lombard violinist-composer was Gasparo Visconti, the Cremonese nobleman who (as Gasparini) was lionized in London in the 1700s; back in Cremona by 1713, he made a profound impression on Tartini (Monterosso, 'Gasparo Visconti'). The sources of concertos attributed to Visconti are, however, too diffuse for secure attributions to be made at this point, and they are therefore excluded from the present study.

[2] Lindgren, 'Count Rudolf Franz Erwein von Schönborn', pp. 269–70. Further on Zani, see Monterosso, *Musicisti cremonesi*, pp. 79–82; and 'Medaglioni di musicisti lombardi', pp. 51–4. Three Zani concertos are available in modern editions.

by Platti, together offering a welcome variety to the limited concert repertoire for the cello. Further concertos survive in manuscript in Dresden, Karlsruhe, Manchester and Paris, resulting in a total preserved repertoire of thirty-seven concertos: twenty-three for violin, twelve for cello and two for flute.

Zani's instrumental writing, while not rivalling the taxing demands of Vivaldi's hardest concertos, is highly idiomatic and technically varied. His concertos embrace a wide range of idioms. A small group of *galant* concertos is marked by decorative solo material rich in semiquaver triplets and affective sighs, as in the flute concerto Zan9 (see Catalogue). Here both motto and solo entry exceptionally fall into the regular phrase structure later associated with *galant* writing (compare the deliberate avoidance of regularity in the solo entry of the flute concerto Zan25). At the other extreme, Zani shows a clear propensity for contrapuntal writing in *stile antico*, possibly reflecting his years in Vienna as well as the Count's predilection for music in older idioms.

Mottos

Zani's selection of mottos has much in common with Vivaldi, yet his preferences are different. Six suggest the hammer-stroke pattern, but all are modified in some way into a more continuous melodic statement, as in the rhythmic acceleration out of the third crotchet that so energetically propels the motto of Zan7. A significant ten mottos lean expressively on the middle of the first bar or else on the first beat of the second, giving the opening notes a feeling of anacrusis quite opposed to the effect of hammer-strokes or fanfares. This emphasis is particularly poignant when coupled with a yearning leap or appoggiatura to the dominant, both of which combine in the motto of Zan32. For the most part Zani shares the contemporary preference for homophonic opening textures, with four movements announced by bold Vivaldian unisons. Yet even essentially homophonic openings can be infiltrated by contrapuntal activity, even hints of *stile antico,* as in Zan 29 (Op. 4/12, Ex. 12.1). In two cases the motto initiates a fugal texture with far-reaching implications, as will be considered presently.

Ex. 12.1. Zani, Violin Concerto in A major, Zan29 (Op. 4/12)

The issue of Zani's relationship to Vivaldi has already emerged in the discussion of their different strategies in handling a common motto (Chapter 1). A mere thematic resemblance is of little significance in a repertoire based on a common vocabulary and stock melodic patterns. More is needed to suggest a direct influence,[3] and Zan1 (Op. 2/8) provides just such evidence, in its apparent reworking

---

[3]   Cf. Jan LaRue, 'Significant and Coincidental Resemblance'.

Ex. 12.2a. Vivaldi, Violin Concerto in C major, RV 184

Ex. 12.2b. Zani, Violin Concerto in C major, Zan1 (Op. 2/8)

of the *galant* concerto RV 184. Zani modifies the unison hammer-stroke fanfare into a light imitative texture (Ex. 12.2). His indebtedness is further evinced in the overall structure of R1, with a brief concertino phrase taking on the same role in both movements. Likewise, the similarity between the motto of Zan27 and that of Vivaldi's RV 316a (Op. 4/6) is so striking as to suggest a deliberate homage. Zani avoids the close imitation that distinguishes Vivaldi's motto, yet out of this homophonic opening he builds an intensively contrapuntal ritornello (Ex. 12.3). Thus, while there is no evidence of any personal contact between Vivaldi and Zani, it appears that Zani was well acquainted with Vivaldi's concertos, commenting on some of them in his own individual way.

Ex. 12.3a. Vivaldi, Violin Concerto in G minor, RV 316a (Op. 4/6)

Ex. 12.3b. Zani, Cello Concerto in G minor, Zan27

Ex. 12.4. Zani, Cello Concerto in C minor, Zan5

The initial ritornello

Most of Zani's ritornello movements are structured on a grand scale, calling for long and elaborate initial ritornellos. About half contain a middle section in a secondary key, and in the remainder the ritornello is considerably expanded through extensive sequential passages. The beautifully structured R1 of Zan5 exemplifies Zani's expansive musical thinking (Ex. 12.4). The concise motto is rich in potential, with three distinct elements in as many bars: Vivaldian arpeggio and pounding octaves contrasting with an emollient concertino effect. The middle section of the ritornello links a new cantabile idea to the concertino motive in an imitative texture, with bar 2 now providing the bass. Yet it is the ensuing expressive melody that the first solo selects as its principal motive, in preference to the energetic motto.

Texture

As has already been suggested, Zani's propensity for counterpoint and rich harmonic textures often leads to imitative writing in R1. He even draws on the *da chiesa* tradition in one case, the grandly conceived Zan4 (Op. 4/11). The slow first movement, based on plangent sigh motives, leads to an unusually long Allegro of 307 bars. This promises to be a full-scale fugal movement; yet it quickly becomes clear that there is to be a more subtle debate, for there is no third entry of the

Ex. 12.5. Zani, Violin Concerto in C minor, Zan4/II (Op. 4/11/II)

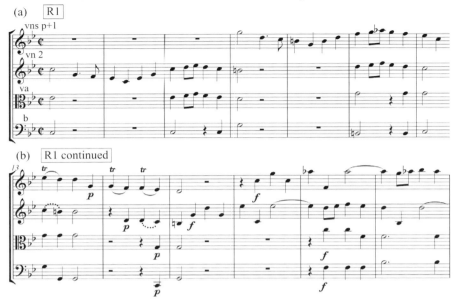

subject, and the earnest contrapuntal texture soon evaporates in a flurry of trills (Ex. 12.5). The contrapuntal dialogue is resumed with a new subject and renewed intensity and purpose, only for this too to dissipate into a light coda. The solo is thus enabled to emerge from an apparently contrapuntal movement without jarring disruption (see Catalogue), and indeed all the extremely long solos are scored in airy homophonic textures, which contrast with the fugal central ritornellos and full Da Capo. This single *stile antico* concerto reveals Zani as a commentator on the older style, a style which he could readily embrace at the same time as he observed it from the outside.

Tonal schemes

With twenty-five concertos in major and twelve in minor, Zani's preferences resemble those of Vivaldi; yet he departs from Vivaldi in his penchant both for the pendulum scheme and for multiple peripheral keys, resulting in an extremely diverse array of tonal schemes (Table 12.1). In his choice of secondary key in minor-mode concertos, Zani gives clear priority to the dominant over the relative major, preserving the older practice much more consistently than Vivaldi.

The exquisite cello concerto in A major, Zan30, takes the rare route to the subdominant as the first target in major (Table 12.2). As it is so unusual, this option is of special interest in the history of tonal thought. R1 does include a short dominant area, which is highlighted in two bars without continuo; yet the implication is not realized in S1, which immediately succumbs to the natural tendency of the tonic chord to resolve to IV, initiating an immediate modulation to D major. The stable subdominant area takes up 25% of the movement, whereas the peripheral keys F♯ minor and C♯ minor, though strongly articulated through perfect cadences, are swiftly abandoned. Vivaldi adopted this rare option only once, in RV 307 in G major, and for a different reason (see p. 119).

Table 12.1. Zani's tonal schemes

Circuit		Pendulum	
Tonal scheme	**Number**	**Tonal scheme**	**Number**
Major			
I-V-vi-I	1		
I-V-vi-iii-I	2	I-V-I-vi-iii-I I-V-I-V-vi-I-iii-I I-V-I-vi-I-iii-IV-I	1 1 1
		I-V-I-vi-I-ii-iii-I	1
I-V-iii-vi-I I-V-iii-vi-ii-I I-V-iii-vi-v-IV-I	5 1 1	I-V-I-iii-vi-I I-V-iii-I-vi-IV-I I-V-I-iii-vi-I-IV-I I-V-I-iii-V-vi-I	1 1 1 1
		I-V-IV-I-vi-I	1
I-V-^{V}/V-vi-v-IV-I I-V-^{V}/V-vi-iii-ii-I	1 1	I-V-^{V}/V-vi-I-iii-I	1
		I-V-^{V}/V-I-iii-vi-I-IV-I	1
		I-V-^{V}/V-I-♭VII-vi-iii-I	1
I-IV-vi-iii-I	1		
Minor			
i-v-III-i i-v-III-VI-i i-v-III-VI-iv-♭vii-VI-i	1 1 1		
		i-v-III-i-iv-i	1
i-v-VI-iv-iii-♭II-i	1		
		i-v-i-♭VII-v-iv-VI-i	1
i-v-iv-VI-i	2		
		i-III-i-v-III-i	1
i-III-v-iv-♭vii-VI-i	1	i-III-i-v-♭VII-iv-i i-III-v-♭VII-i-♭VII-III-i	1 1

Table 12.2. Timeline of Zani, Cello Concerto in A major, Zan30

Function	R1	S1	R3a	S3a	R3b	S3b	S4	R4 D.C.
Bars	1–18	18–24–38	38–46–49	49–61	61–64	64–67	67–77	77–94
Key	I (V) I	I → IV	IV →	vi →	iii	→	I	I

Table 12.3. Zani's articulation of intermediate ritornellos

Melodic articulation	Zani number	Zani %	Vivaldi %
R2 by motto, R3 by another	25	68%	19%
Two central ritornellos articulated by motto (R2-R3, or R3a-R3b only)	10	27%	54%
A single intermediate ritornello articulated by motto	2	5%	10%

Table 12.4. Tonal structure of R2 and R3 in Zani

Tonal structure	R2	R3
Entirely in a single key area	12	6
Modulatory or harmonically open	24	19
R3a and R3b each stable in a different peripheral key	–	4
R3a stable, R3b modulatory	–	6
R3a and R3b both modulatory		1
No R2 or no R3	1	1

The intermediate ritornellos and solos

Zani and Vivaldi differ markedly in their preference with regard to the thematic articulation of the intermediate ritornellos (compare Table 12.3 and Table 4.2). Zani uses the motto as a powerful means to enhance hierarchy, as we have seen in Chapter 1 in connection with Zan15 (Op. 2/12). While R2 is consistently related to R1 and always headed by the motto, this is much less often the case with R3. Zani's favoured strategy is to emphasize tonal hierarchy by avoiding the motto here, while, at the same time, retaining thematic unity by selecting a later motive from R1. In this way the potential of a seemingly unimportant idea from R1 may eventually be explored and realized, as in Zan31 in A minor (Op. 2/2), where a brief central motive from R1 (bars 8–10) provides the sole material for R3 in an extended sequence (bars 162–173).[4]

Zani's overall tonal strategy also differs crucially from that of Vivaldi (compare Table 12.4 and Table 5.9). The high number of movements where R2 is unstable is of particular significance, contributing to the overall impression of fluid progress through a variety of keys. This fluidity is not, however, allied to a breakdown in the ritornello framework: indeed Zani articulates the peripheral area by R3 in every case but one (Zan35). Zani's predilection for a long succession of briefly articulated tonal centres naturally tends to call for modulatory solos: all but two movements contain a modulatory S3, either between two

---

[4]   Ed. Hirshberg and McVeigh (2001).

peripherals or else leading back from the final peripheral to the tonic. Such expansive unfolding of ritornello form contrasts with Vivaldi's approach (a third of the Vivaldi sample lacks S3 altogether).

Zani prefers to assert the character of the soloist in a cantabile vein, avoiding both the neutral figurations that prevail in Alberti's concertos and more assertive bravura gestures. As a result, in only four cases does S1 begin with a direct quotation of the motto (see Catalogue). Others begin with a variant (such as the particularly elegant melodic transformation in Zan13, Op. 4/9), or else refer to different motives from R1 – as in the deliberate selection of an expressive melody in Zan5, discussed above. But in twenty-three cases there is no connection with the ritornello at all, and indeed thematic unity is in general a low priority in Zani's solo sections.

The intermediate tonic

An intermediate tonic appears in about half of Zani's output, reflecting the generally fluid nature of his tonal argument; and on several occasions the tonic is strongly reasserted twice in the course of the movement. In Zan8 the tonic return assumes a crucial rhetorical role within the tonal scheme I-V-I-vi-I-iii-IV-I.[5] Here the intermediate tonic first appears as a surrender to the pull of the dominant (bar 116), leading via a smooth sequence to the anticipated vi for R3. The ensuing solo then returns to the tonic with a hiatus, which is somewhat mollified by a block transposition, the technique frequently used by Tessarini. The listener is in no doubt that this is the recapitulation, especially when the tonic is confirmed by an apparent R4 at bar 170. Yet, just as the movement seems to be about to close, a sudden chromatic modulation lurches away to iii (bar 197), and a further solo reaches IV (bar 234), before the true recapitulation finally arrives in bar 266. Such a double statement of an intermediate tonic might appear merely to recall the less directed practices of early ritornello form; yet here the second appearance is clearly a false recapitulation that leads instead to new departures, a massive extension that results in a huge movement of 328 bars.

The recapitulation

Also distinct from Vivaldi are Zani's preferences for the point of re-establishment of the tonic, especially his total avoidance of the option of reaching the tonic within a ritornello (compare Table 12.5 and Table 6.3). In only five cases does R4 introduce the recapitulation, and in every case Zani makes some play with the concept. Even in the sole example where the final tonic is simply a Da Capo of R1 (Zan2), he conspicuously weakens the effect by preceding it with a totally unexpected solo in the tonic minor. In Zan13 (Op. 4/9), where the return of the tonic is strongly articulated by the tutti motto (bars 199–202), the ritornello is brusquely cut off by a virtuosic and tonally unstable solo that delays the Da Capo for a further fifty-seven bars. In the remaining three cases, the motto is supplanted by other motives, even (in the charming *galant* flute concerto Zan9) by the variant that opened S1.

Zani strongly preferred to reach the tonic within a solo S3-S4, a preference that

---

5   Ed. Hirshberg, *Ten Italian Violin Concertos*, No. 7.

Table 12.5. Point of re-establishment of the tonic in Zani

Point of re-establishment of the tonic	Zani number	Zani %	Vivaldi %
At the beginning of R4, after a modulatory solo	5	14%	28%
Within a ritornello (R3-R4)	0	0%	28%
At the beginning of S4, after a modulatory ritornello	9	24%	30%
Within a solo (S3-S4)	23	62%	13%

raises a fundamental question: since he avoids the most easily available tools for a strong articulation – textural change and restatement of the motto – does he place any weight at all on the point of restatement of the tonic? Indeed he does, in his own refined manner. Though the motto is only once used to strengthen the arrival, the tonic is always marked by motivic and textural change; and it is here that Zani's individuality is revealed at its most remarkable. In Zan31 (Op. 2/2),[6] the tonic is approached by modulatory figurations over a spare violin accompaniment, but its arrival at bar 204 is delineated both by the entrance of the continuo and by a new, expressive melody. A more subtle example is provided by Zan26 (Op. 2/6), a particularly elaborate movement with the extended tonal scheme i-v-III-VI-iv-♭vii-VI-i. After all the roving instability of the central part of the movement the return of the tonic is extremely powerfully prepared with virtuosic arpeggiations over a dominant pedal; yet Zani avoids the immediate resolution in R4, replacing it instead with a plangent, contrasting motive developed out of S1 (Ex. 12.6). The effect is to reserve this critical moment for the soloist in advance of the full force of the tutti entrance; and the eventual Da Capo, delayed by twelve bars, is thus of no tonal consequence.

While fully cognizant of Vivaldi's strategies and paying homage to the Venetian master through direct quotations, Zani nevertheless retained his distinct individuality. His numerous well-crafted and memorable concertos for violin and for cello are among the most rewarding discoveries to come out of this book.

We turn now to Milan itself, where (as we have seen in Chapter 2) the ducal court maintained a large orchestra for opera and other court music, an orchestra that achieved European fame after the new opera house was completed in 1717. While Milan is certainly more celebrated for the development of the symphony by G.B. Sammartini and his followers, concertos must often have been heard at court, at private concerts during Lent or outdoors at the Castello. A substantial repertoire of concertos by Milanese instrumentalists survives, concertos that (with the exception of those by the Sammartini brothers) have so far been entirely neglected.[7] Though stylistically diverse in many respects, this repertoire shows

---

6   Ed. Hirshberg and McVeigh (2001).
7   See Hirshberg and McVeigh, 'The "Virtuosi Instromenti" ', on which the remainder of this chapter is based (by kind permission); the article includes some additional examples. An essential

Ex. 12.6. Zani, Violin Concerto in G minor, Zan26 (Op. 2/6)

striking consistencies in terms of underlying attitudes towards ritornello form, even among those composers who moved away from Milan; and some similarities with the concertos of Zani can also be identified.

Details of Milanese orchestras during the period remain scanty, but three well-known lists of personnel provide essential reference points. In 1711 a large contingent of Milanese instrumentalists took part in the festivities at Novara surrounding the transfer of the relics of S Gaudenzio. By 1720 the opera orchestra was both sizeable and securely established, to judge from a list of thirty-two 'Virtuosi Instromenti nell' Orchestra'; while a similar list dating from 1748 indicates that the orchestral complement had risen to forty-six (see p. 34). Each of the composers to be discussed here appears in at least one of these three lists.

Permanent in Milan: Angelo Maria Scaccia

The concerto composers with the most consistent presence in Milanese musical life over several decades were Giovanni Battista Sammartini and Angelo Maria Scaccia. The violinist Scaccia (*b* Milan, *c*1690; *d* Milan, 1761), whose father was a regular member of the large ducal ensemble, was among those named at the 1711 festivities. On 31 March 1719 he became a supernumerary member, appearing in the list of 1720 and again (heading the second violins) in 1748. He was the first Milanese violinist to publish a major set of violin concertos; and when he finally took over his father's regular orchestral position on 16 January 1751 his stature was recognized with the award of the first ducal *patente di violinista*.

source is Barblan, 'La musica strumentale e cameristica'; for a recent catalogue, see Brusa and Rossi, 'Sammartini e il suo tempo'.

Apart from the set of six concertos published as Op. 1 (Amsterdam, *c*1730), and a single concerto published in an anthology of 1736, Scaccia's surviving repertoire is scattered across several manuscript collections. Of the fourteen concertos in all, two (Sca5 and Sca8) have dual attributions. No external evidence has been found that could confirm either attribution, yet on the admittedly flimsy grounds of stylistic analysis we have accepted that Sca8 (also attributed to G.B. Somis) is consistent with the remainder of Scaccia's output, whereas Sca5 (also attributed to Hasse) displays certain traits that appear nowhere else in his concertos: Vivaldian repeated quavers, the tripartite construction of R1 and its close relationship with S1, along with the very large proportion of stable sections (totalling 93%, as against an average of 68%).[8] This latter fundamental difference in overall harmonic conception is particularly persuasive, and the ascription to Scaccia must be regarded as extremely doubtful.

Excluding Sca5 from the present discussion, therefore, all of Scaccia's output is in the major key. One concerto (Sca10) is in A♭ major, the only example of this key yet discovered in the entire contemporary concerto repertoire; it must normally have been avoided because of the serious tuning problems it presents, whether for the strings or for the normal harpsichord temperaments (see Ex. 12.9). This experimental work lies mostly in a low tessitura, the solo line requiring the E-string in only five of seventy-nine bars; especially unusual is the opening of the first solo on the G-string.

As the Catalogue shows, Scaccia makes a varied selection of motives from the common stock of the day: hammer-strokes, Vivaldian leaping octaves, broken tonic chords and scalic patterns. Often the melodic line is focused around the fifth degree of the scale, implying a descending line to follow. In six concertos the first main solo starts with new material; in the remaining seven, the solo ornaments and reinterprets the motto without ever literally repeating it. Sca4 provides an example of a reinterpretation of the stock hammer-stroke motive: in this way the soloist asserts his individuality while still commenting on the ritornello material.

Scaccia's tonal schemes reflect a balance between circuit and pendulum patterns, similar to that of Zani's concertos in major (Table 12.6). The dominant is accorded a ritornello in every case except Sca4, where it is clearly rejected as part of the tonal strategy: S1 prepares the dominant only to divert instead to vi for the second ritornello. For peripheral keys Scaccia prefers iii and vi in various combinations, frequently engaging in a tonal progression that involves a rhetorical weighing up of alternatives. In Sca2, the tonal scheme I-V-iii-V-vi-I results from two quite separate departures from the dominant: the first from V to iii through a hiatus and change of texture within R2, the second from V to vi through a chromatic interruption within S3, leading to R3 (Ex. 12.7).

Vivaldi markedly preferred to base ritornello movements on stable sections, frequently limiting the modulations to single bars or else to shifts by hiatus. In our sample, the aggregate of stable areas averages 76%: by contrast, the average for Scaccia is 68%. The long passages of instability in Scaccia's concertos contribute strongly to the creation of a tonal hierarchy, as in Sca7, where the opening and

---

8   See Hirshberg and McVeigh, 'The "Virtuosi Instromenti" ' for a more detailed discussion of
     Sca5, which in the nineteenth century was also attributed to Vivaldi (RV Anh. 64).

Table 12.6. Scaccia's tonal schemes

Circuit	Number	Pendulum	Number
Major			
I-V-vi-I	1	I-V-vi-I-vi-I	2
		I-V-vi-iii-I-iii-v-IV-I	1
I-V-vi-iii-I	2		
I-V-vi-vii-iii-I	1		
I-V-iii-vi-I	1	I-V-iii-I-iii-vi-I	1
I-V-iii-V-vi-I	1	I-V-iii-vi-I-iii-I	1
I-V-vi-IV-vi-I	1		
		I-V-I-II-V-I	1

Ex. 12.7. Scaccia, Violin Concerto in C major, Sca2 (Op. 1/3)

closing tonic areas together take 42% of the movement, the stable dominant area 11%, and each of the peripheral degrees (vi-IV-vi) only 3%.

An important factor here is Scaccia's clear preference for modulatory intermediate ritornellos, including R2 (Table 12.7) – in contrast with Vivaldi (Table 5.9) and still more with Tessarini's strong differentiation between stable R2 and unstable R3 (Table 8.14). In Sca3 in D major, R2 starts in V but the flow is soon disturbed, and the instability continues into the ensuing solo (Ex. 12.8). In the passage following the example, the modulatory progression restarts from F♯ minor, with the falling fifths this time pulling towards an anticipated restatement of the tonic. But it overshoots by two fifths (F♯-B-E-A-D-G♯-C♯), cadencing instead on the remote degree of vii. The circle-of-fifths progression returns for a third time, finally resolving into a strongly articulated F♯ minor at bar 74, at which point a hiatus emphasizes an abrupt reassertion of the tonic. Thus Scaccia creates a tense balance between the centripetal urge to return to the tonic and the

Table 12.7. Tonal structure of R2 and R3 in Scaccia

Tonal structure	R2	R3
Entirely in a single key area	3	2
Modulatory or harmonically open	9	4
R3a and R3b each stable in a different peripheral key	–	2
R3a modulatory, R3b stable	–	1
R3a and R3b both modulatory	–	3
No R2 or no R3	1	1

Ex. 12.8. Scaccia, Violin Concerto in D major, Sca3

contrasting centrifugal pressures. The entire unstable section is shaped as a rhetorical argument in the subjunctive, offering diverse implications and delayed
realizations. Despite the seemingly trivial motivic material, the movement
displays a sophisticated manipulation of the resources of tonal syntax.

In the ritornello sections, Scaccia favours a rapid turnover of musical material,
with short contrasting phrases following in quick succession, and R1 can never

Ex. 12.9. Scaccia, Violin Concerto in A♭ major, Sca10

Ex. 12.10. Scaccia, Violin Concerto in C major, Sca1

be considered monothematic in the use of the opening motto. Scaccia's liking for contrasts is also reflected in the mixing of the functions of solo and tutti: indeed in seven concertos he includes one or more brief solos within R1, serving no larger tonal function. His thematic manipulations thrive on light airy textures, with only occasional touches of counterpoint – as in Sca6, where a new motive is presented in the violins as counterpoint to the motto in the bass (bars 1–4), or Sca10 in A♭ major, where simulated imitation enriches an unusual sonority (Ex. 12.9). Had it been a D major concerto by Vivaldi, a brilliant unison and octave texture would surely have been expected. The rare passages of strict contrapuntal working are set in sharp relief to the surrounding contexts (for example, Sca6, bars 107–20).[9]

Scaccia's quirky capriciousness leads to an originality of musical idiom that is far from the conventional understanding of baroque continuity and (apparent) inevitability. His concertos thrive on contrasts, interruptions and extremes of rhythmic variety, as in Sca1 (Ex. 12.10). Though not reaching the limits of

[9]   Ed. Hirshberg, *Ten Italian Violin Concertos*, No. 6.

Table 12.8. Point of re-establishment of the tonic in Scaccia

Point of re-establishment of the tonic	Number
At the beginning of R4, after a modulatory solo	8
Within a solo (S3-S4)	3
Within a ritornello (R3-R4)	2

Table 12.9. Opening and recapitulation in Scaccia, Violin Concerto in B♭ major, Sca13 (Op. 1/1)

Function	R1a	S1a	R1b
Bars	1–13–22	23–28	29–43
Key	I (V)	I	I
Thematic	M a	b	c M

S4a	R4a	S4b	R4b
145–172	173–184	185–210	211–215
I	I	I	I
M' b c' etc.	M = 1–12		M = 39–43

virtuosity, such violin writing projects a rugged bravura character, in line with Scaccia's generally assertive manner. For striking intrusions he favours brusque three-note chords, and thematic material is characteristically presented in double stops, the dominant pedal amounting almost to a mannerism. Harmonically the propensity for contrasts is reflected in the occasional spicing of his usually diatonic idiom with capricious chromatic lines and harmonic surprises. On the broader scale, diminished seventh chords or turns to the minor are used to undermine stability and thus initiate broader tonal excursions.

Scaccia's conception of the recapitulation contrasts with that of Zani (compare Table 12.8 with Table 12.5). In four movements the strong textural articulation of the recapitulation is enhanced by a full Da Capo of R1. Yet in other cases Scaccia explored a more subtle strategy of tonal recapitulation: in Sca4 (Op. 1/5), for example, R1 includes a middle section in the dominant, predicting the secondary key, but in the recapitulation this five-bar section is seamlessly removed. Much more complex is the recapitulation in Sca13 (Op. 1/1, Table 12.9).[10] The strong anticipation of V that dominates R1 would be superfluous in the final tonic area, so the recapitulation again pointedly avoids the dominant section, while at the same time reordering the themes and textural functions so as to reintegrate solo and tutti.

It is true that Scaccia's concertos lack the melodic distinction and the

---

[10] See the fuller analysis and musical examples in Hirshberg and McVeigh, 'The "Virtuosi Instromenti" ', pp. 207–12.

Table 12.10. Timeline of Brivio, Violin Concerto in G major, Bri2

Function	R1a	S1a	R1b	S1b	R1c	S1c
Bars	1–16	17–26	27–28	29–38	39–40	40–54–66
Key	I (V)	i–I	I	i–I	I	I → V
Thematic	M			= 17–26	= 27–28	M

R2a	S2	R2b	R3	S3	S4a	R4a etc.
66–73–82	83–89–117	117–124–133	133–137	138–145	146–176	176–217
V →	iii →	V →	vi	vi →	I	I etc.
M	M	M = 66–73	M			= 1–40+

contrapuntal richness of those of Zani. Yet there is some compensation in his long-range handling of the implication-realization process, and manipulation of the listener's expectations is enhanced by sophisticated control of tonal resources and by subtlety of motivic working.

Giuseppe Brivio

Giuseppe Ferdinando Brivio (*b* Milan, ?; *d* Milan, *c*1758) is included as a violinist only in the 1720 list of the Milan orchestra; he may perhaps be identified with the prolific opera composer and impresario. Although his instrumental output was small, one concerto was included in the prestigious French collection of Italian music assembled for Pierre Philibert de Blancheton, alongside concertos by Scaccia and Zuccari.

The only other violin concerto by Brivio to have survived (Bri1) opens with a brief first movement that appears to be an awkward arrangement of a trio sonata.[11] By contrast, the violin writing in the Fonds Blancheton concerto (Bri2) is fluent and idiomatic, with Vivaldian figurations and passage work (mostly in a high register) that contrast markedly with Scaccia's more forthright idiom. The concerto also displays some of the finest formal planning in the repertoire. The most salient rhetorical device is that of two departures from the dominant (R2a and R2b in Table 12.10). A similar pattern of two departures from the dominant has been described in Scaccia's Sca2. Brivio presents the alternatives even more explicitly. Starting from the motto in the dominant in both cases, the two options are highlighted by the sudden change to Corellian counterpoint (Ex. 12.11).

Carlo Zuccari

The violinist Carlo Zuccari (or 'Zuccarini', *b* Casalmaggiore, 1704; *d* Casalmaggiore, 1792) came from the same town as Zani, and he received his training in Northern Italy; but after travelling to Vienna in 1723 in the suite of Count Pertusati 'his restless temperament induced him to continue his wanderings

---

[11] An oboe concerto in D-ROu, lacking ritornello form, has not been included here.

Ex. 12.11. Brivio, Violin Concerto in G major, Bri2

around Europe'.[12] Eventually in 1736 he settled in Milan, where he played an important role as a teacher and orchestral musician, playing for Sammartini on many occasions. His name is included among the first violins in the 1748 list. Eight of Zuccari's concertos are known to have survived in manuscript: of these one is also attributed to Mauro d'Alai, yet it has been included in the following analysis for reasons to be discussed.

Zuccari's concertos display little of the thematic and tonal manipulation seen in Scaccia's music. His strength lies in his attractively *galant* melodic idiom, direct and tuneful without elaborately decorative solo writing. That sometimes tiresome mannerism of the period – a tendency to paste together short two-bar units with repeats – is mitigated by some adroit extension and linking of phrases.

[12] Monterosso, *Musicisti cremonesi*, p. 83.

Ex. 12.12. Zuccari, Violin Concerto in D major, Zuc3

Table 12.11. Zuccari's tonal schemes

Circuit	Number	Pendulum	Number
Major			
		I-V-I-vi-I	2
		I-V-I-V-vi-I-i-♭III-i-I	1
I-V-vi-iii-I	2	I-V-I-vi-iii-I	1
I-V-iii-I	1		
I-V-iii-vi-I	1		

Zuc3 avoids the simplest regular phrase structure: the opening motto has five bars, while the solo answer, which might have consisted of four bars, is extended to six by the insertion of bars 9–10 (Ex. 12.12). Taken together with the ensuing motto transposed into the dominant, the overall period is still sixteen bars long, yet divided into three balanced phrases (5+6+5).

Zuccari joins Scaccia in his absolute preference for the major mode. As the tonal schemes indicate (Table 12.11), Zuccari selects only iii and vi as peripheral degrees in diverse combinations, preferring (by comparison with Scaccia) longer stable tonal areas reached by direct modulations. The aggregate of stable areas averages 79% – similar to Vivaldi – by comparison with 68% for Scaccia. Zuccari does not share Scaccia's preference for the modulating R2, with only two concertos using such a strategy.

One of the most interesting features of Zuccari's concertos is the textural treatment of R1. In seven concertos the opening ritornello includes one or more solos. These solos serve different purposes. In Zuc3 the opening orchestral march is immediately interrupted by a solo consequent in cantabile *galant* manner (Ex.12.12) – as if to distinguish the 'voices' of the two participants at the very beginning. In four concertos, Zuccari integrates two separate solos into the unfolding of R1, presenting a complete and rounded structure. But solos within R1 create a certain ambiguity for the listener, who is after all not aware of the larger formal dimensions until much later. The delightful Zuc8 makes

Ex. 12.13. Zuccari, Violin Concerto in A major, Zuc8

entertaining play with this ambiguity (Ex. 12.13). A short solo section in trio texture highlights the dominant, which is enhanced by a strong tutti cadence. Here, however, the soloist reasserts the tonic, rejecting the suggested dominant. This defiantly soloistic entrance might be heard as the start of a whole new section, indicating that the ritornello was complete. In the end, however, it turns out to be a 'false solo' interpolated within the opening tonic area, merely a foretaste of the translucent E-string solo writing that characterizes the movement.

Zuc7 is quite exceptional, both within Zuccari's output and more generally (Table 12.12).[13] Just when a tonic ritornello, based on variants of R1 motives, appears to have concluded the movement at bar 105, a self-contained tutti in the minor mode is interposed; a full Da Capo is needed to resolve the interruption and to round off this long movement. An analogous procedure occurs in Sammartini's Symphony in C major (J-C 7).[14]

Zuc6 has been ascribed to both Zuccari and Mauro d'Alai. It would again be dangerous to make a firm attribution on stylistic grounds alone, but the concerto is within the bounds of Zuccari's style, while in some ways atypical of d'Alai. The most striking feature that allies it to Zuccari's practice is the very long opening ritornello (seventy bars), which includes two substantial solos, one of

[13] Ed. Hirshberg, *Ten Italian Violin Concertos*, No. 9.

[14] *The Symphonies of G.B. Sammartini, i: The Early Symphonies*, ed. Bathia Churgin (Cambridge, Mass.: Harvard Publications, 1968): Symphony No. 1 in C major, bars 48–73.

Table 12.12. Timeline of Zuccari, Violin Concerto in G major, Zuc7

Function	R1a	S1	R1b	S2a	RT	S2b	R2	R3
Bars	1–13	14–23	24–38	38–41	41–42	42–46	46–57	58–76
Key	I	I	I → V	V →	I	I →	V →	vi →

R4a	S4	R4b	Interpolation (Tutti)			R4c
77–86	86–97	98–105	106–113	114–132	133–150	150–163
I	I	I	i // ♭III // i			I

them an ethereal 'solo rossignol', recalling the birdsong also found in Zuc2 (see Catalogue). This entire multipartite section is repeated Da Capo at the end, a practice also found in Zuc2, 5 and 8.

Giovanna Battista Sammartini

The celebrated symphonist Giovanni Battista Sammartini (*b* ?Milan, 1700/01; *d* Milan, 1775) never placed the concerto at the centre of his musical concerns, but he developed a distinctive approach to the challenges posed by the confluence of ritornello form with his developing symphonic idiom. Since Sammartini's concertos have already been extensively studied by Ada Beate Gehann, we do not intend to give a comprehensive overview, but rather to highlight points of comparison with the other composers already discussed.[15] Table 12.13 gives the details of the concertos studied here, extending across his early and middle style periods up to *c*1755.

Table 12.13. Solo concertos by G. B. Sammartini to *c*1755

Concerto	Instrumentation	Key
J-C 69	Vc piccolo or vn	C
J-C 77.1	Vn	A
J-C 74	Vn	F
J-C 72	Fl	D
J-C 75	Vn	G
J-C 71 (both versions)	Fl	D
J-C C-8 (D-Rtt, Mappe Marcello 15d)	Vn [bass part missing]	G

---

[15] Gehann, *Giovanni Battista Sammartini*, and Introduction to *Giovanni Battista Sammartini: Four Concertos*. We are most grateful to Ada Beate Gehann for her generous advice regarding matters of authenticity and dating, and for making copies of her scorings available to us. See also Gehann, 'Merkmale der Konzertsatzform', in Cattoretti, ed., *Giovanni Battista Sammartini and his Musical Environment*.

Table 12.14. G. B. Sammartini's tonal schemes

Circuit	Number	Pendulum	Number
Major			
		I-(IV-vi)-I-V-I	1
		I-V-I-vi-I	1
		I-V-vi-iii-I-ii-I	1
		I-V-I-vi-iii-I	1
		I-V-I-vi-I-iii-I	1
		I-V-iii-I-vi-I	1
		I-V-I-V-I-ii-vi-I	1

In terms of compositional strategy, these concertos share a number of characteristics with the Milanese repertoire already discussed. Sammartini's ritornellos show a high degree of melodic consistency. The longer opening ritornellos even present the thematic material twice, with the first half leading to a central caesura on the dominant, and the second half returning early to the tonic. This kind of 'symphony within a concerto' is clearly seen in the opening ritornello of J-C 72, where the second half both reprises the motto and transposes the earlier dominant material into the tonic.[16] The same thematic material is spread across the central modulatory ritornello, while the tonic return is articulated by the motto and the closing ritornello presents a full Da Capo. Three of these concertos include solo sections within the opening tonic ritornello, in the manner seen frequently in the concertos of Scaccia, Zuccari and his brother Giuseppe.

The central instability associated with the modulatory R2 is found in five cases, and the ensuing solo typically engages in a process of tonal debate involving the rejections and realizations already discussed in the music of Scaccia and others. This feature is accentuated by Sammartini's consistent avoidance of a separate ritornello in a peripheral key. The resulting ritornello structure is simple overall (tonic ritornello–modulatory ritornello–tonic ritornello(s)), yet the instability and diversions en route to the tonic are reflected in complex tonal schemes, with a universal preference for pendulum patterns (Table 12.14).

The pendulum model is used in three ways:

(1)   Return to the tonic in the middle of the second ritornello, following the dominant and initiating a new departure to peripheral areas. Even where the tonic key is not fully articulated, Sammartini always touches on a tonic chord before moving away.[17] Furthermore in one of the two cases where R2 does not modulate (J-C 71), Sammartini plays with the suggestion of a 'false' tonic return: R2 begins as usual in the dominant (bar 80), the tonic is strongly reasserted with the distinctive motto, but it is then rejected in favour of the dominant again.[18]

---

[16]   Further on the two-section ritornello see Gehann, *Giovanni Battista Sammartini*, pp. 151–63.

[17]   Further on Sammartini's tonal schemes and the modulatory second ritornello, see ibid., pp. 8–9, 74–80.

[18]   Ed. Gehann (2002).

Table 12.15. Timeline of G. B. Sammartini, Violin Concerto in A major (J-C 77.1)

Function	R1	S1	R2 RT R3	S3	R4a S4 R4b (D.C.)
Bars	1–48	49–78–92	92–100–105–112	113– 117– 131–141–167	167–171–180–227
Key	I	I → V	V I → vi	vi // I roves I → iii →	I

(2) Return to the tonic at an early stage in the ensuing solo. Sammartini frequently creates a strong sense of anticipation, the return to the tonic suggested or implied well before it is achieved, in a continuing dialogue with peripheral keys. This constantly shifting focus – an ambiguous interplay of suggestion, frustration and eventual realization – is a technique of tonal roving distinct from Vivaldi's clear-cut linear approach, where the tonic is generally avoided until its eventual point of arrival. J-C 77.1, with its rondo-like tonal scheme, provides an example of such roving (Table 12.15). In this instance the tonic is used in a rhetorical manner: the two appearances in S3 both seem to be the final tonic return, but instead prove to be springboards for new departures. Only after a long preparation does R4a eventually confirm the tonic.

(3) False reprise, as in J-C 74, where the well-prepared tonic return at the expected place (bar 111) is exploded by a dramatic diversion to ii, followed by a full Da Capo 15 bars later.[19]

Even the one case of an apparently elemental scheme of I-V-I contains a more complex tonal argument. In the early concerto J-C 69 there are no peripheral keys in the main course of the movement, yet the opening ritornello strongly articulates IV (bar 20) and vi (bar 31).[20] These articulations of IV and vi are conspicuously avoided in R4, thus accentuating the recapitulatory function.

Giovanni Perroni

Whereas the composers discussed so far spent much of their creative lives in Lombardy, Perroni's successful career as a virtuoso cellist reached its peak in Vienna. Giovanni Perroni (or Peroni; *b* Oleggio, Novara, 1688; *d* Vienna, 1748) worked at Parma from 1704 to 1714, and contributed (with his brother) a major oratorio to the 1711 celebrations in Novara. In 1712 he played a concerto at the festive Mass in Venice honouring the ambassador of the newly elected emperor, Charles VI.[21] Six years later he was working in Milan, and his name appears in the 1720 orchestra list; but the following year he was appointed cellist at the court in Vienna. The five cello concertos now in the Wiesentheid collection were presumably intended for Count Rudolf Franz Erwein von Schönborn, in common with Zani's fine set of cello concertos discussed above.

Perroni's earliest concerto (Per6), performed after the Te Deum at the Venice ceremony, displays strong Corellian traits in its alternation of slow and fast sections: the first Allegro contrasts imitative writing with solo passagework,

---

[19] Ed. Gehann (2002).
[20] Ed. Jenkins (1956).
[21] Haas, *Die Estensischen Musikalien*, p. 31; Hill, *The Life and Works of Francesco Maria Veracini*, p. 11.

Ex. 12.14. Perroni, Cello Concerto in D major, Per1

within only an incipient ritornello framework.[22] The five Wiesentheid concertos are much more fully developed. Brilliant and very demanding, they clearly reflect Perroni's superb technical mastery of the instrument. The solos sparkle with fast passagework, triple stops and large leaps, as well as some extremely high figuration, reaching up to f♯" on one occasion (Ex. 12.14; see also Catalogue, Per1).

For all this virtuosity, the proper title for Perroni's concertos would surely be 'contrapuntal obsession', perhaps reflecting the Count's taste for older idioms. Dense imitation, double counterpoint, inversions and rhythmic dislocations crowd the texture, often masking the distinction between ritornello and solo. Per4 even opens with tutti and solo exchanges. Such contrapuntal weaving limits the number of motives used in each movement, giving a highly consistent thematic flavour. In Per2 two motives are presented both horizontally and in counterpoint; and in an early contribution to the ritornello, the soloist presents the lower motive against distorted versions of the other (Ex. 12.15).

Perroni's contrapuntal leaning is revealed in the nature of his subjects. Per5 is even based on a fugal theme in *stile antico*, which is extended in a continuous stream to last a full eighteen bars, a manner of construction that has a direct effect on how the movement is structured. When the soloist enters with a bravura flourish spanning the entire range of the cello, this is pitted against the full 18-bar theme in counterpoint. Even when Perroni introduces a *galant* four-bar phrase in Per3 the interweaving counterpoint extends it to a continuous 10-bar unit (Ex. 12.16). Here a crucial difference emerges between the premises of Perroni and Scaccia. While Scaccia combines diverse brief motives into a planned succession of alternating stable and unstable periods, Perroni's motto determines the unfolding of the entire movement.

Perroni's tonal schemes concentrate on iii and vi as peripheral keys, like those of Zuccari (Table 12.16, p. 272). Yet, notwithstanding his contrapuntal penchant, Perroni's concertos remain prone to unexpected chromatic inflections. Per3, just mentioned, introduces chromaticism already at the very start. This eccentric colouring is used throughout the movement, so that G major chords are frequently inflected with A♭ in neither a modulatory nor a Neapolitan context.

---

[22] We are grateful to John Walter Hill for kindly making available to us a copy of this beautifully written score.

Ex. 12.15. Perroni, Cello Concerto in E major, Per3

Ex. 12.16. Perroni, Cello Concerto in G major, Per4

Table 12.16. Tonal schemes of Perroni's Wiesentheid concertos

Circuit		Pendulum	
Tonal scheme	Number	Tonal scheme	Number
Major			
I-V-vi-I	1		
I-V-iii-vi-I	3	I-V-iii-vi-I-V-I	1

Giuseppe Sammartini

The oboist Giuseppe Sammartini (*b* Milan, 1695; *d* London, 1750) participated at Novara in 1711 and played alongside his brother in the ducal orchestra (his name appeared in the 1720 list), before settling permanently in London in 1729.[23] He achieved a reputation as one of the leading soloists of his time, yet few solo concertos by him were published. Most of the publications were posthumous, so the surviving repertoire cannot be securely linked to his Milanese period: indeed it is likely that manuscripts in the Royal Music Library, now in the British Library, reflect the period of his service to Frederick, Prince of Wales. Unlike the other Milanese composers discussed here, Giuseppe Sammartini displays an extreme stylistic diversity in his concertos, no doubt reflecting his move from one powerful musical centre to another. The London reverence for the Corelli tradition and the example of Geminiani and Handel may account for the small number of solo movements in ritornello form in his concerto output. Indeed, the three oboe concertos in the set published posthumously as Op. 8 have no movements in ritornello form at all.[24] Nevertheless it has proved surprisingly revealing to consider his works in the Milanese context.

Only one work can be securely dated to the Milanese period, the oboe concerto in F major SamG7 (published in 1717), and, though the second movement of this *da chiesa* concerto is diminutive in scale, it shares the Milanese propensity for instability in the central section. The tonal scheme, however, is unique to Giuseppe Sammartini: after the strong sharpward pull of the first half of the movement, a single tonic chord functions as an axis turning towards the subdominant, a balancing of sharpward and flatward movement that will be seen again in the concertos of the Turinese violinist G.B. Somis.

Whether the remaining ritornello concertos were written in Milan or London (and stylistic references to the concerto grosso idiom point to the latter in some cases), it is striking that a central harmonic instability obtains across Sammartini's repertoire. Table 12.17 presents the tonal schemes of the concertos included in the present study (once again, all in major), and his preference for unstable sections touching briefly on at least two peripheral keys is obvious, as is his proclivity for pendulum schemes. Eleven out of twelve concertos include a modulatory R2. Such distinctive tonal handling, taken together with a characteristically flexible

---

[23] Lance, 'The London Sammartini'.
[24] Kirakowska, 'Giuseppe Sammartini's Concertos, Opus 8'.

Table 12.17. Giuseppe Sammartini's tonal schemes

Circuit		Pendulum	
Tonal scheme	**Number**	**Tonal scheme**	**Number**
Major			
I-V-vi-I	1	I-V-vi-I-V-I	1
I-V-vi-iii-I	1	I-V-vi-I-iii-I	1
I-V-vi-iii-vi-I	1	I-V-I-vi-I-iii-I	1
		I-V-vi-I-ii-I	1
		I-V-I-vi-ii-iii-vi-I	1
I-V-iii-ii-vi-I	1	I-V-I-iii-ii-I-vi-IV-I	1
		I-V-I-ii-iii-IV-V-vi-I	1
		I-V-^{V}/V-I-IV-I	1

Table 12.18. Timeline of Giuseppe Sammartini, Oboe Concerto in G major, SamG9

Function	R1a	S1a	R1b	S1b	R2 (S)	RT
Bars	1–21	21–33	34–45	46–65–86	87–100	101–111
Key	I (V)	I	I (V) I	I → V	v–V	I
Thematic	M		M		(no continuo)	M

R3	S3	S4	R4
112–115–122–130	131–137–143–149–156	156–197	197–212
→ ii → iii	→ IV →V → vi →	I (IV–V–v–IV) I	I
			M = 34–39, 9–12, 40–45

treatment of the tutti-solo alternation, suggests that Sammartini's Milanese experience continued to exert a strong influence in the background.

The oboe concerto in G major SamG9, surviving in the Dresden collection, will serve as an example of how Sammartini develops an individual rhetorical strategy around the pendulum scheme (Table 12.18). Only the tonic is articulated by the motto. Once the dominant has been finally secured (after two earlier false moves, marked as (V)), a full ritornello is expected at bar 87. Yet instead the mode switches to minor, with new material, and although this section acts functionally as a ritornello (R2), its light texture – oboe and upper strings – retains a solo character. Such harmonic and textural ambiguity significantly weakens the dominant. The immediate return to a tonic ritornello with motto presents an extreme example of a particular rhetorical strategy. The tonic initiates a new beginning and a different form of argument: a process of interruption and ambiguity that briefly articulates each degree of the scale (ii-iii-IV-V-vi) in turn. The full cadence on iii, for example, leads to an ambiguous chord that could stay in B minor, return to the tonic, or (as actually happens) lead to C major (Ex. 12.17).

Ex. 12.17. Giuseppe Sammartini, Oboe Concerto in G major, SamG9

The subdominant here functions as a scalar degree in a continuous sequential process, rather than in its polar function in relation to tonic and dominant. The succession of briefly articulated intermediate keys recalls Scaccia's practice, as does the extreme hierarchization between the well-established tonic and brief areas of stability in other diatonic degrees. The tonic areas altogether account for 60% of the movement, contrasting with 17% for the dominant and only 2%–4% for each of the peripheral keys.

The Milanese as a Group

Certain characteristics stand out as common to the Milanese group, whether they held regular positions in Milan or travelled across the Alps (Zani, never active at the Milanese court, cannot be regarded as belonging to the main Milanese group). All the Milanese concertos discussed here are in the major mode, an extreme illustration of an increasing preference within the eighteenth-century symphony and concerto. Such avoidance of the minor mode for solo concertos even applies to Giuseppe Sammartini, half of whose output across all genres is in the minor.[25]

The Milanese composers shared the universal trait of opening and closing the ritornello movement with proportionately long sections in the tonic, but they preferred to unfold the central argument as a largely unstable process with modulatory intermediate ritornellos. Zuccari excepted, the second ritornello (R2) generally starts with a short stable area in the dominant and then modulates: this applies in ten of thirteen concertos by Scaccia, eleven of twelve concertos by Giuseppe Sammartini, five of seven by Giovanni Battista Sammartini, and all the Perroni and Brivio concertos analysed here. Zani also favoured this strategy, found in eighteen of his twenty-five concertos in major. By contrast, Vivaldi writes a modulating R2 in only 13% of 232 concertos in major, and Tessarini in

25 Lance, 'The London Sammartini', p. 8.

only one of thirty-five. The entire group adopted the dominant as an axiomatic first move, as does Zani in all but one concerto in major. Yet after the uniformity of the first move, the Milanese repertoire displays a remarkable diversity among the ensuing tonal schemes, most occurring only once or twice in each composer's output. This largely reflects their preference for a succession of two or more peripheral degrees, with each held stable for a short duration or only articulated by a single cadence.

While some movements undoubtedly favour continuity and thematic unity – especially those cello concertos in contrapuntal style apparently destined for Count von Schönborn – in general this repertoire places a high premium on contrasts and unexpected changes of direction. This feature is emphasized not only by harmonic restlessness and instability but also by textural variety. In an unusually high proportion of opening tonic sections, tutti and solo are intermingled, blurring major structural distinctions and emphasizing the lack of correspondence between harmonic and textural functions. It is therefore possible to speak of the Milanese-Viennese group as a more coherent school of concerto composition than any other of this period.

CHAPTER 13

Turin and the French Connection

The concerto must certainly have played a significant role in the musical activities of the Turin court, yet it does not appear to have figured highly in the compositional activity of the violinists working there, to judge from the paucity of surviving sources. Nor can it be said that these few surviving works are of striking individuality or quality, which is perhaps why no Turin concertos reached publication in Amsterdam or elsewhere. The largest single corpus is the group of concertos by G.B. Somis surviving in the Fonds Blancheton, reflecting the close political ties between Turin and Paris described in Chapter 2; others are found in a variety of manuscript collections. The repertoire therefore presents a somewhat disparate picture, without any identifiable focus for the locus of activity; and certainly the idioms and formal structures are too diffuse for us to be able to speak of an integrated Turin school of concerto composition.

Giovanni Battista Somis

Giovanni Battista Somis (*b* Turin, 1686; *d* Turin, 1763), sometimes referred to by his father's nickname 'l'Ardy', was born in Turin into an extensive family of musicians.[1] As early as 1696 he joined the court orchestra as a violinist; and in 1703 the Duke sent him to study with Corelli in Rome, where he also took part in Ottoboni's musical performances. Returning to Turin in 1706, he rejoined the court orchestra, which remained his base for his entire professional career. Although an acknowledged virtuoso, not until 1736 did he become leader of the orchestra, but the following year he was appointed both musical and stage director at the Teatro Regio, a position he held until 1757.

Visiting Italy in 1739–40, Charles de Brosses sought out Somis at the ducal chapel, but finding that 'he does not play every day, and his turn would not come round again for some time', he had to use some persuasion to get him to perform the following day. In the end 'he played a concerto specially for me, and made a blunder': de Brosses thought him a good violinist, but still inferior to Tartini and Veracini.[2] Perhaps Somis's greatest significance was as a noted teacher, counting among his pupils many leading figures in the French violin school (including

---

[1]   The most authoritative biography is Basso, 'Notizie biografiche'. See also Burdette, 'The Violin Sonatas of Giovanni Battista Somis', pp. 1–93; and Ghisi, 'Giovanbattista e Lorenzo Somis'.

[2]   Translated from de Brosses, *Lettres familières*, vol. 2, pp. 579–80.

Canavas, Guignon, Guillemain and Leclair) and two outstanding virtuosi of the later eighteenth century, Giardini and Pugnani. To them he bequeathed a powerful bow-stroke, a rich tone and a grand eloquence that stood in contrast to the more delicate nuances of the Tartini school.

From 1709 onwards Somis was chamber musician to the Prince of Carignano, a member of the Duke's family who moved to Paris in 1718. This connection provided an entrée to musical life in the French capital, and in 1733 Somis performed concertos twice at the Concert Spirituel; he may also have visited Paris on other occasions around this time. The strong French connection is certainly emphasized by the prominent position of Somis's concertos in the Fonds Blancheton, and it is possible that Somis may have advised on the repertoire to be copied.[3]

Six Somis violin concertos are preserved in the Fonds Blancheton: while a further concerto attributed to him is ascribed elsewhere to Vivaldi (RV 302).[4] Four other concertos survive in Dresden and in Manchester (the Ottoboni collection), one of which is also attributed to Scaccia (see Chapter 11). This leaves a total of nine violin concertos whose ascription is not directly in doubt. They make a diverse group, inhibiting any overall summary of Somis's contribution. But it can hardly be argued that Somis brought either a vivid imagination to the genre or a striking individuality in his handling of ritornello form. There is little of the piquant melodic invention that distinguishes his violin sonatas; and the solo writing is all too dependent on routine violinistic figuration. Nevertheless his handling of tonality is distinctive, especially in the remarkable single minor-mode concerto.

For all Somis's early training under Corelli and his allegiance to the sonata, the concertos are unambiguously in the Venetian tradition, with none of the contrapuntal leanings of the Roman school. Indeed Somis prefers a direct, diatonic melodic style and predominantly short phrases, with only limited use of sequential patterns. A trademark is the opening descending arpeggio, sometimes filled in as a major scale (see Catalogue). Five concertos intermingle solos within the opening R1: Som2 in D major even starts with a solo flourish that seems to refer directly to the Vivaldi Gloria, RV 589.

Also straightforward is Somis's approach to ritornello form, with the unaltered motto used extensively to articulate central ritornellos and R4. Somis does, however, show a distinctive awareness of tonal implications in that almost every movement omits secondary-key material from R1 in the recapitulation. Som4 in G major[5] begins with a miniature sonata-form ritornello such as has already been described in connection with G.B. Sammartini (Ex. 13.1a). As Table 13.1 demonstrates, the balance between sharpward and flatward movement is reflected in the tonal plan of the movement as a whole: the recapitulation either omits or transposes dominant-key sections of R1, instead substituting tinges of subdominant harmony (Ex. 13.1b).

---

[3]   Hirshberg, 'The Formation and Destination of the *Fonds Blancheton*'; and Introduction to *Ten Italian Violin Concertos from Fonds Blancheton.*

[4]   Som5 is attributed to Visconti in GB-Ckc, Ms. 240. A further *Concerto a più instrumenti* in F-Pn lies outside this study.

[5]   Ed. Hirshberg, *Ten Italian Violin Concertos*, No. 8.

Ex. 13.1. G.B. Somis, Violin Concerto in G major, Som4

Table 13.1. Opening ritornello and recapitulation of G.B. Somis, Violin Concerto in G major, Som4

R1: Bars	1–2	3–4	5–6	7–10	10–12	13–16	17–18	19–21	22–25
Key	I	→ (V)	I	V	V	V	I	I (IV)	I
Motive	M	a	b	c	d	e	M	f	e

Recap: Bars	81–82	83–84	85–90	90–94	95–98	98–103	103–8	109–11	112–15
Key	I	→ (V)	I (IV)	I	I	I (IV)	I (V)	I (IV)	I
Motive	M	a	solo (new)	solo d'	solo c	solo d"	M a b	f	e

Of the eight major-mode concertos only one clearly articulates a peripheral minor key with a ritornello: remarkably, four prefer the subdominant for R3, a rare option in Vivaldi. This downplaying of the minor mode adds to the air of bright directness, while the balance of dominant and subdominant shows a tonal sensitivity that is rare at this time. A glance at Somis's tonal schemes will clarify this point (Table 13.2). This balance is especially revealing in the unusual Som1

Table 13.2. G.B. Somis's tonal schemes

Circuit		Pendulum	
Tonal scheme	**Number**	**Tonal scheme**	**Number**
Major			
I-V-vi-I	1		
I-V-vi-iii-I	1		
I-V-vi-IV-I	1		
I-V-iii-V-I	1	I-V-iii-I-vi-I	1
		I-V-I-IV-I I-V-I-V-IV-I	2 1
Minor			
		i-III-v-♭VII-ii-IV-i	1

Table 13.3. Timeline of G.B. Somis, Violin Concerto in D major, Som1

Function	R1	R2	S2a	ST	S2b	R3	R4
Bars	1–17	18–32	32–37	37–47	47–57	57–73	73–93
Key	I →	V	V →	I	→	IV →	I
Thematic		most of R1				= R1	= R2 extended

Table 13.4. Timeline of G.B. Somis, Violin Concerto in G minor, Som6

Function	R1	S1	R2	S2	R3	S3	R4
Bars	1–23	24–48	48–71	71–99	99–106	106–124	124–142
Key	i (//III → i)	i // III →	v (// ♭VII → v)	v // ♭VII →	ii // IV	IV →	i
Thematic	M M	a a	M M	a a	M M		= R1 omitting section in III

in D major, which manipulates the normal parameters of ritornello form around a single solo, producing a Schubertian 'subdominant recapitulation' (Table 13.3).

Much more interesting musically, however, and again exceptional in its treatment of ritornello form, is the one minor-mode concerto, Som6 in G minor. This is so different from the other concertos that its authenticity might be called into question. The repeated quavers, sequential patterning and Neapolitan chromatic touches suggest a heavy dependence on Vivaldi's minor-mode idiom. But the tonal scheme is in any case unique (Table 13.4). Already R1 predicts the pattern of rising thirds, articulated by a harmonic hiatus and exact motivic repetition (Ex. 13.2). The rising thirds (i-III-v-♭VII-ii-IV, alternating minor and relative major) create a long, logical chain that eventually leads via the missing E♭ chord (bar 118) to the recapitulation. One important feature of this scheme is the appearance of ii minor and IV major, both extremely rare in the concerto repertoire, and

Ex. 13.2. G.B. Somis, Violin Concerto in G minor, Som6

perhaps a direct result of the one-flat key signature that allows them to be written without accidentals: a similar process to that observed in Locatelli's Op. 3/2.

Lorenzo Somis

(Giovanni) Lorenzo Somis (*b* Turin, 1688; *d* Turin, 1775), though not much younger than his more famous brother, seems to have adopted a more cosmopolitan outlook; and he was also a noted painter, amassing a remarkable art collection of his own. Lorenzo studied with Laurenti in Bologna, and he subsequently worked in Rome and Sicily before eventually settling in Turin. In 1724 he joined the ducal military band; and from 1732 to 1770 he was a violinist in the court orchestra, only leaving Turin to visit Paris in 1753. A close friendship with the Milan musician Ignazio Balbi suggests a possible connection with the Milanese school.[6]

The four surviving violin concertos by Lorenzo Somis represent a curious amalgam of different elements. In two cases the ritornello movement follows a short introduction with precisely notated dotted rhythms, perhaps reflecting the French connections of the Turin court; while a third begins with a full-scale Grave in *da chiesa* manner. To some extent the Allegro idiom is consistent with that of G.B. Somis, in the short diatonic melodies and straightforward approach to ritornello form. Solos include a good deal of frankly routine figuration (see, for example, the second movement of SomL2 in E♭ major).[7] But as the table of tonal schemes suggests (Table 13.5), there is some experimentation and variety. SomL2 unusually prepares for the tonic return with the minor dominant (bars 58–9); while SomL3 recalls his brother's predilection for the subdominant – here introduced by a bold hiatus from vi, a technique encountered nowhere else (Ex. 13.3).

Possible, but by no means decisive, evidence of a Milan connection resides in SomL1 in D major, with its modulating second ritornello (V–I–iii), and in the 'Lombardic' rhythms (reverse dotting) of SomL4.[8] More importantly, both of

6　Everett, *The Manchester Concerto Partbooks*, pp. 381–5.
7　Ed. Geerb (1997).
8　Everett, *The Manchester Concerto Partbooks*, pp. 384–5. Quantz, however, reported that Lombardic rhythms (or Scotch snaps) were invented by Vivaldi around 1722.

Table 13.5. Lorenzo Somis's tonal schemes

Circuit		Pendulum	
Tonal scheme	**Number**	**Tonal scheme**	**Number**
Major			
		I-V-I-vi-I	1
		I-V-I-vi-IV-I	1
		I-V-I-ii-vi-iii-I	1
I-V-vii-vi-v-I	1		

Ex. 13.3. Lorenzo Somis, Violin Concerto in G major, SomL3

these concertos illustrate Lorenzo's partial adumbration of *galant* features, especially in the solos, which now incorporate a small-scale cantabile sensibility as well as typical triplet mannerisms and chromatic inflexions (Ex. 13.4). This more flexible melodic style does not obviate a certain stiffness in the writing, which is particularly evident in those ritornellos where elements of the new idiom are forcedly imposed. In SomL4 the 'Lombardic' rhythms are superimposed on a descending scale (see Catalogue) and then on a routine circle-of-fifths progression, which sounds distinctly uncomfortable under the strain.

Giovanni Pietro Ghignone

The French career of Jean-Pierre Guignon has been described in Chapter 2, but he was born in Turin as Giovanni Pietro Ghignone (*b* Turin, 1702; *d* Versailles, 1774), the son of a Turin merchant and one of the most successful of Somis's students. Two concertos survive in Dresden in Pisendel's hand, possibly dating from the latter's Italian trip in 1716–17, in other words pre-dating Ghignone's move to Paris in 1725. It is certainly possible to identify Turinese characteristics here: Ghi1 begins with the descending scale motive characteristic of G.B. Somis, but here it is in the second violin part, ingeniously counterpointed against another short diatonic motive of the kind associated with the Turin school in general (see Catalogue).[9]

There is little to remark in the ritornello form of these two concertos, with their

---

[9] This concerto is also attributed to Alberti, but on stylistic grounds we have accepted the Ghignone attribution.

Ex. 13.4. Lorenzo Somis, Violin Concerto in D major, SomL1

simple Da Capo at the end and commonly used tonal schemes (I-V-iii-vi-I and I-V-vi-I-iii-I). Very striking, however, is the way the soloist is introduced in the large-scale Ghi2 (Ex. 13.5). The first solo begins as a reworking of the scalic motto, but this immediately develops into a rich-textured fantasy on the tonic chord. The movement is completely becalmed by this unusual gesture, and it is only through a new solo, based on the second bar of the motto, that momentum is renewed. Exactly the same process recurs in the dominant after R2, but with a different and less extended fantasy. This grand conception results in a very substantial movement, although its proportions are kept within bounds by not dwelling on peripheral keys (R3 in iii is kept to a mere three bars).

Considering the reputation of the Somis school of violinists, the concerto repertoire is somewhat disappointing. In this small sample, it is difficult to identify consistent characteristics that would suggest a coherent Turin school. However, isolated works by each of these three composers deserve closer investigation; and once again each develops individual ideas about concerto writing that are not found in any other repertoires considered here.

Ex. 13.5. Ghignone, Violin Concerto in G major, Ghi2

CHAPTER 14

Padua, Tartini and 'la maggior perfezione del buon gusto'

Giuseppe Tartini (*b* Pirano, 1692; *d* Padua, 1770) was born in Pirano in Istria (now part of Slovenia), but he left his native region in 1708 to become a law student at the University of Padua, the city where he was to spend most of his life.[1] A marriage of which his family disapproved led to his abandoning Padua for refuge in Assisi, where he devoted himself to the violin and to composition under the tuition of the organist Bohuslav Černohorský. During the 1710s he made his living as a violinist in northern and central Italy, the experience of hearing Veracini in Venice in 1716 causing him to devote himself still more strenuously to violin practice. Other than this inspiration, and an equally revelatory contact with the patrician Cremonese violinist Gasparo Visconti, there is little to indicate the influences on his violin playing and composition during these formative years; although he must inevitably have been strongly aware of the astounding virtuosity and the latest concertos of Vivaldi and his contemporaries in Venice.

In 1721, thanks to the father of a Venetian pupil, Tartini was appointed *primo violino di concerto* at S Antonio in Padua ('Il Santo'). Apart from a brief intermission in Prague (1723–26), Padua was to be his base for the remainder of his long life, and it was for S Antonio that many of his concertos must have been written, as has been described in Chapter 2. He must also have performed concertos when invited to appear as a celebrity violinist elsewhere in Italy; in 1728, for example, his fee for performing at a major festival of the Chiesa della Steccata in Parma exceeded that of all but one of the singers.[2] Other concertos were presumably intended for his numerous pupils, following the founding of his 'Scuola di Nazioni' in 1727. Clearly, moreover, the concerto was central to Tartini's own artistic career. Even after his own violin playing declined around 1740 as a result of a stroke, it was in the concerto and sonata that he developed his new aesthetic: an almost mystical relationship with his art based on adherence to Nature and vocal expressiveness ('la maggior perfezione del buon gusto').[3]

Tartini was one of the most prolific concerto composers of the period, his

---

[1] The principal biographical source remains Petrobelli, *Giuseppe Tartini*, from which this paragraph is largely drawn. See also Petrobelli, 'Giuseppe Tartini', in *Storia della musica*.
[2] Petrobelli, 'Una presenza di Tartini'.
[3] 'The highest perfection of good taste' (see p. 31).

Ex. 14.1a. Tartini, Violin Concerto in G major, D73 (Op. 2/1)

Ex. 14.1b. Tartini, Violin Concerto in C major, D8

Ex. 14.1c. Tartini, Violin Concerto in C major, D13

surviving repertoire spanning some forty years from around 1720 to 1760.[4] During this time there were obvious changes in melodic idiom and texture, from the elaborate and virtuosic early concertos, very much in Vivaldi's footsteps, through the more elegant *galanterie* of the middle period (marked by efflorescence rather than technical show), to the extreme simplicity and sensitive cantabile of the latest works, supported by the lightest two-violin accompaniment. These three broad layers correspond to the three style periods identified in Minos Dounias's pioneering 1935 monograph: period I (*c*1721–35), period II (*c*1735–50) and period III (*c*1750–70).[5]

Three examples of violin writing, each taken from the closing solo – the traditional place for a climactic heightening of virtuosity – will make the change in attitude abundantly clear (Ex. 14.1). There is, however, a methodological

4   The present study is based on 104 ritornello-form movements from both printed and manuscript sources, the latter mainly from the Padua and Berkeley collections.

5   Dounias, *Die Violinkonzerte Giuseppe Tartinis*. The style periods are indicated in the catalogue, pp. 243–97.

problem in writing about Tartini's stylistic development in this way, since few of the concertos can be reliably dated on documentary grounds; and in any case Tartini is known to have continually revised his concertos over many years. Definitely early are the concertos published as Op. 1 (books 1 and 2) and Op. 2, which appeared between 1728 and 1734;[6] but otherwise chronological attributions are largely dependent on stylistic grounds. Dounias seems to have based his categorizations mainly on melodic idioms and phrasing, his discussion giving only limited consideration to the development of concerto form. We will therefore use his overall perspective to guide our analysis of Tartini's approach to ritornello form, making broad comparisons between fifty 'early' concertos from period I and fifty-four 'late' concertos from periods II and III.

Clearly there is a danger of a tautologous argument here, for Dounias may in reality have been influenced by the very same features that we remark. Used with caution, however, his categorizations provide a useful benchmark. Certainly melodic trends are reflected in Tartini's formal procedures: the early concertos begin with elaborate ritornello movements around complex key schemes, the middle period developed a more compact version of ritornello form, while the latest concertos transformed it into a type of binary design. This final stage will be considered separately at the end of the chapter.

The Opening Ritornello

The motto

Although Tartini's melodic writing may have changed markedly over his career, his motto types can be summarized under a limited number of headings, their usage consistent across early and late groups. Such Vivaldian favourites as hammer-strokes, octave leaps and repeated quavers are infrequent. Instead four types dominate: (i) march (9%), (ii) scalic melody (18%), (iii) broken tonic chord (24%), and (iv) melody circling around a single note, usually the dominant (27%). From the earliest concertos onwards, Tartini shows a strong preference for two- and four-bar units, which may then be repeated either literally or sequentially. Indeed regularity of phrasing and a generally additive approach to melodic construction permeate his writing as a whole (in contrast to almost all the rest of our repertoire), resulting in a somewhat predictable character but also tending to rob the listener of a broader musical perspective.

In the earlier concertos, the typical melodic organization is the extension of a single one-bar motive, which gives the motto its distinctive stamp. Later this technique gives way to longer melodic lines, perhaps the four-bar melody characteristic of the 'classical' period; although, as there, this does not prevent the extraction of a short motive for development during the movement. Some examples will demonstrate the way in which the general categories are transformed

---

6   Op. 1 book 3 contains concertos by Tartini and Visconti, but without specific attributions; some survive in manuscript concordances, but Tartini's authorship remains uncertain (Dounias, *Die Violinkonzerte Giuseppe Tartinis*, pp. 56–9, 295–7). Further on sources and revisions of Tartini's early concertos, see Thomson, 'I primi concerti di Giuseppe Tartini'.

Ex. 14.2a. Tartini, Violin Concerto in D major, D20

Ex. 14.2b. Tartini, Violin Concerto in D major, D33

Ex. 14.2c. Tartini, Violin Concerto in F major, D63

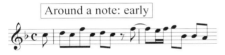

Ex. 14.2d. Tartini, Violin Concerto in F major, D69

between early and late concertos (Ex. 14.2). The last example here illustrates in microcosm the characteristic syncopations, appoggiaturas, and dotted or triplet rhythms of the later idiom.

Construction of R1

As with Vivaldi, a crucial issue in the construction of R1 is the harmonic trajectory, and, in particular, whether a contrasting key is clearly articulated in the middle. The large-scale earlier concertos include a higher proportion of such progressions (81%), even four examples where two separate keys are temporarily established (Table 14.1). In D2 (Op. 2/2) for example, R1 is truly a 'piece within a piece', with strong cadences in both V and vi followed by a reprise (Table 14.2). The corresponding figure in the late concertos, reflecting their more concise and focused approach, is 55%. A particularly common device is to follow the central dominant with a stepwise sequence from ii to I (Ex. 14.3). This is a harmonic progression to which we shall return.

It is never Tartini's practice to follow a full R1 with a tonic solo leading to R1b, yet the soloist contributes strikingly to R1 in a few cases. Thus D58 presents a multisectional tutti-solo complex; while in D89 (Op. 1/1/6) the solo gradually infiltrates the ritornello, eventually expanding into the true solo S1.

Table 14.1. Harmonic structure of R1 in Tartini

Harmonic structure of R1	All	Early	Late
Contains a middle section with chromatic progressions (such as secondary dominants) or diatonic sequential progressions	21%	15%	27%
Entirely in tonic area with diatonic harmony, non-sequential	12%	4%	18%
Contains a middle section in another key, perhaps preceded or followed by sequential progressions	59%	68%	51%
Contains a middle section with two separate keys	4%	9%	0%
Contains a central modulation to another key but immediately returns to the tonic	4%	4%	4%

Table 14.2. Timeline of R1 in Tartini, Violin Concerto in C major, D2 (Op. 2/2)

Bars	1–2	2–4	5–12	13–14	15–20
Key	I	→ V	→ vi	I	(iv, ii) I
Thematic	M	extended	M developed	M	M developed

Ex. 14.3. Tartini, Violin Concerto in E major, D51

The Central Ritornellos and Solos

Thematic structure and R2

Tartini shows a remarkably high consistency in the use of earlier material in the central ritornellos. In 84 out of 104 concertos, R2 is entirely based on material from R1, and of these only six introduce new material into R3. Such consistency is further reflected in the usage of the motto (Table 14.3). In 95% of the repertoire the motto heads the second ritornello, yet it is often absent in the third, resulting in a strong hierarchization in such cases. Furthermore, there is a marked decline in the use of the motto to articulate two central ritornellos (from 58% to 26%), a change partly attributable to the declining presence of R3.

Also highly consistent in Tartini's output is the harmonic treatment of R2. In only eight cases is R2 modulatory, and normally there is an apparently solid block in the secondary key. But this larger stability disguises a much more fluid practice; for Tartini never simply reiterates R1, but consistently takes the opportunity

Table 14.3. Tartini's articulation of intermediate ritornellos

Melodic articulation	All	Early	Late
Both central ritornellos articulated by motto	41%	58%	26%
A single intermediate ritornello articulated by motto	13%	4%	20%
R2 by motto, R3 by another	40%	36%	45%
R2 & R3b by motto, R3a by another	1%	2%	0%
No intermediate ritornello articulated by motto	5%	0%	9%

to vary the material, often with a thoroughgoing recasting of ideas. Thus R2 will frequently revisit much of the material of R1, in order, but melodically varied and written at different pitches. This is particularly evident where R1 contains a central section in another key: Tartini faces the challenge in R2 not merely by following the same modulatory structure but by traversing new keys, resulting in a roving instability before the eventual return to the secondary key. In a few cases the soloist plays a part in this unstable process, so the listener is led to believe that S2 has already begun. In D91 (Op. 1/2/2), for example, it appears that R2 has simply modulated from V to vi, at which point the soloist enters, only for a sequence to pull back to the dominant for a continuing disquisition on earlier material (Ex. 14.4).

Ex. 14.4. Tartini, Violin Concerto in A major, D91 (Op. 1/2/2)

Ex. 14.5. Tartini, Violin Concerto in D major, D20

Thematic relationship between ritornellos and solos

The first main solo almost universally begins with the motto (ninety-seven cases). It may be directly quoted, or it may be ornamented or even transformed altogether in affect, as in D20 (compare Ex. 14.5 with Ex. 14.2a). In thirty concertos, spread across the repertoire, there is an even tighter connection, through S1 incorporating later motives from R1: of these, eight rework the entire ritornello. D83, too long for quotation here but included in the modern collected edition, provides a compelling example. Here S1 presents the first half of R1 (as far as the dominant cadence) with only minor changes, before a solo passage in V intervenes; but then the closing material of R1 returns, now transposed into the dominant. This strongly differentiates and demarcates the dominant area within S1, presaging the 'second subject' of sonata form; and the same cadential phrase recurs at the end of S2 in order to stress vi. Such connections create a strong sense of thematic unity, but this is no mere mechanical repetition, for the reiterations of material are used to articulate stages in the tonal argument.

There is a further consistency about the start of the next solo (S2), which in eighty-seven cases recalls the opening of S1. Indeed in 77% of the repertoire the motto or a close variant introduces each of the first four sections:

R1	S1	R2	S2
M	M	M	M
I	I	V	V

Although Tartini does frequently ornament the motto in the solo, sometimes it is simply presented four times in succession in almost identical form. The pattern is made still more explicit by two devices: (i) the near-universal retention of the same octave for both ritornello and ensuing solo; and (ii) rhythmic separation between sections, the norm between ritornello and solo, and often found *vice versa*. This results in a very clear and almost schematic exposition of the four opening sections. Much less schematic, though, are Tartini's procedures across the rest of the concerto, where strongly varied approaches and subtle formal ambiguities come into play.

Tonal schemes

Tartini's tonal schemes are remarkably consistent in a single aspect: in every case but one, the second ritornello articulates the main secondary key, with the target being either the dominant or else III in minor (Table 14.4). The only exception is the unprecedented D66 in F major, where the dominant is well established in S1,

Table 14.4a. Tartini's tonal schemes in major

Circuit		Pendulum	
Tonal scheme	**Number**	**Tonal scheme**	**Number**
I-V-vi-I	3, **11**	I-V-I-vi-I	**1**
		I-V-I-vi-V-I	**1**
		I-V-vi-I-vi-I	1, **3**
I-V-vi-iii-I	**2**	I-V-I-vi-I-vi-iii-I	1
		I-V-I-vi-I-iii-I	1
		I-V-vi-I-vi-iii-I	1
I-V-vi-ii-I	**1**	I-V-vi-I-ii-I	1
		I-V-I-vi-ii-I	**1**
		I-V-vi-I-ii-I-iii-I	1
		I-V-I-vi-ii-v-vi-iii-I	1
		I-V-I-vi-ii-IV-I	1
		I-V-vi-V-ii-vi-I-iii-I	1
		I-V-vi-V-I-ii-vi-I-iii-I	1
		I-V-vi-I-IV-ii-I	1
I-V-iii-I	1, **7**	I-V-I-iii-I	**1**
I-V-iii-vi-I	2, **5**	I-V-I-iii-vi-I	1
		I-V-iii-I-vi-I	**2**
		I-V-iii-vi-I-iii-I	**1**
		I-V-iii-vi-I-vi-iii-I	1
I-V-iii-ii-I	1		
I-V-iii-V-ii-iii-I	1		
I-V-ii-I	2, **10**		
I-V-ii-vi-I	4, **1**	I-V-ii-I-vi-I	1
		I-V-I-ii-I-vi-I	1
I-V-ii-vi-iii-I	1	I-V-I-ii-vi-iii-I	1
		I-V-ii-I-vi-iii-I	2
		I-V-ii-I-vi-I-iii-I	1
I-V-ii-vi-v-I	1		
		I-V-ii-I-iii-I	**1**
		I-V-ii-v-IV-vi-I-iii-I	1
I-V-ii-IV-I	1		
I-V-ii-IV-vi-I	1		
I-V-ii-IV-v-vi-iii-I	1		
I-V-IV-ii-I	1		
		I-V-^{V}/V-I-V-vi-I-ii-I	1
Total	18, **39**		21, **11**

Late concertos in bold

Table 14.4b. Tartini's tonal schemes in minor

Circuit		Pendulum	
Tonal scheme	**Number**	**Tonal scheme**	**Number**
i-v-III-i	2, **1**	i-v-i-III-♭VII-i-iv-III-i	1
		i-v-i-v-♭VII-i-III-i-iv-i	1
i-III-v-III-i	1	i-III-i-v-i-III-i i-III-v-i-III-v-i-iv-VI-i	1 1
i-III-v-♭VII-i i-III-v-♭VII-III-i i-III-v-♭VII-v-III-i i-III-v-♭VII-iv-I	**1** 1 **1** **1**	i-III-i-v-♭VII-i-iv-i	1
i-III-♭VII-v-i	1	i-III-♭VII-v-♭VII-III-i-III-i	1
Total	**5, 4**		**6, 0**

Late concertos in bold

only to be rejected by a hiatus when the ritornello starts in A minor. Such consistency does not, however, extend to the rest of the ritornello movement. Looking at the early group, the most immediately obvious feature is the wide variety of long and tortuous schemes, many of them unique to Tartini. Rather than visiting each key only once, he tends to return to earlier keys, sometimes within a process of prediction and realization, but often suggesting a rhapsodical approach to ritornello form. Pendulum schemes are in the majority (54%), resulting from either a central debate about secondary and peripheral areas or a later false reprise sidetracked into new departures. D46 (Op. 2/6) provides an example of apparent tonal rambling using the pendulum technique. Here the tonic returns three times in the centre of the movement, including two unmistakable false reprises, both of which strongly imply the recapitulation (Table 14.5). The first of these is particularly deceptive, since it uses the common technique of direct transposition of the motto from peripheral key to tonic; yet the latter is immediately subverted (Ex. 14.6).

By contrast, the later concertos – often shorter and more direct in their musical language – adopt a concentrated approach towards tonality, focusing around a smaller number of options. In 57% there is just a single peripheral key, adding to the two usual options a third that will be considered in a moment. Usually each key is visited only once, in a direct and overarching tonal trajectory that avoids the rhetorical twists and turns of the earlier concertos. Not surprisingly, the proportion of pendulum schemes has declined to 20%.

One striking characteristic of Tartini's major-mode concertos is a propensity for the supertonic. Sometimes this occurs as part of a larger grouping of peripheral keys, but usually it leads directly to the tonic, reflecting a general fondness for sequential patterns falling by a tone. The sequence ii-I is commonly found in binary movements, as a way of returning to the tonic after the central dominant. The same pattern writ large is one of Tartini's favourite tonal schemes in the later

Table 14.5. Timeline of Tartini, Violin Concerto in E major, D46 (Op. 2/6)

Function	R1	S1	R2	S2	R3a	RT
Bars	1–16	17–31	32–45	46–62	63–64	65–66
Key	I (ii, vi)	I → V	V	V → vi → (I) → vi	vi	I
Thematic	M		M		M	M false reprise

R3b/S	ST/S3	R4a	S4	R4b
67–72	73–87	88–92	93–107	108–112
(vi) → ii →	I → iii //	I	I	I
	false reprise	M		

Ex. 14.6. Tartini, Violin Concerto in E major, D46 (Op. 2/6)

concertos; ten of which employ I-V-ii-I, a scheme nowhere to be found in the Vivaldi sample. Numerous others – and this includes many of the early concertos – embed this same succession of keys within more complex schemes.

The role of R3

Table 14.6 demonstrates clearly the hierarchical distinction that Tartini enforces on the peripheral areas. While R2 almost universally begins and ends in the secondary key, such stability does not obtain later in the movement. Already in the early group there is a relatively high figure for the single modulatory R3 (50%): and frequently there are two or more ritornellos in different keys. This tonal instability is further emphasized by short exchanges between tutti and solo not reflected in this table. Such free-flowing diversity is later abandoned in favour of a much reduced role for the tutti in this part of the movement. By far the favoured option in the late concertos is a single modulatory R3, generally short and not headed by the motto.

R3 is lacking altogether in fifteen cases, of which thirteen are in the late group. This does not necessarily mean that there is no peripheral key at all, for it may be clearly articulated within the solo, resulting in the succession S2-S3-S4. But the

Table 14.6. Tonal structure of R3 in Tartini

Tonal structure of R3	All	Early	Late
Entirely in a single key	11%	18%	4%
Modulatory	61%	50%	70%
R3a and R3b each stable in a different peripheral key	4%	8%	0%
R3a stable, R3b modulatory	3%	6%	0%
R3a modulatory, R3b stable	4%	8%	0%
R3a and R3b both modulatory	2%	4%	0%
R3a and R3b both stable, R3c modulatory	1%	2%	0%
No R3	15%	4%	26%

Ex. 14.7. Tartini, Violin Concerto in G major, D83

consequent reduction to three ritornellos certainly weakens the power of the ritornello structure, and suggests a binary division which will be explored below (see Table 14.11).

The recapitulation

Towards the recapitulation

Tartini's propensity for breaks and separations early in the movement is often replicated at the point of recapitulation, which is emphasized by a harmonic hiatus in a surprisingly high forty cases (38%); the percentage for the early group is even higher (48%). The tonic return is thereby strongly highlighted and dramatized. But exactly the opposite effect results from another extremely common technique, one that seems to be unique to Tartini: blurring the approach to the tonic in a deliberately ambiguous way, as exemplified by D83 (Ex. 14.7). Here the modulatory R3 has essentially returned to the tonic, but the final cadence is firmly on the dominant. The soloist presents the motto in a sequential pattern, and there can be no doubt that the recapitulation is initiated here somewhere, but it is

Table 14.7. Point of re-establishment of the tonic in Tartini

Point of re-establishment of the tonic	All	Early	Late
At the beginning of R4, after a modulatory solo	37%	66%	9%
Within a ritornello (R3-R4)	20%	14%	24%
At the beginning of S4, after a modulatory ritornello	18%	10%	26%
Within a solo (S3-S4)	26%	10%	41%

disguised both by the dominant start and by the apparent move towards IV. A similar ambiguity results in other concertos from the substitution of ii at the very moment the tonic is expected, resulting in Tartini's favourite sequential pattern ii–I.

The point of tonic return
The way in which the tonic return is achieved is closely related to its place with the textural structure, and here there is a dramatic change between the early and late groups (Table 14.7). In the early group, the strongest form of articulation predominates, with the recapitulation being initiated by a ritornello: in as many as nineteen of fifty concertos still further emphasis is provided by a harmonic hiatus between S3 and the tutti recapitulation. In the late group, by contrast, this strong emphasis is replaced by a clear preference for solo recapitulation, with as many as 41% taking the weakest option, arriving at the tonic in the middle of an extended solo passage. In part, this obviously reflects the diminishing importance of the third ritornello altogether.

The thematic structure of the recapitulation
The recapitulation provides a further opportunity to vary and rework earlier material, and Tartini is notably inventive in the myriad ways in which he approaches this challenge. Rarely is the recapitulation merely a routine restatement of earlier sections, but instead ritornellos and solos alike explore new combinations and transformations of material from R1 and S1.

To begin with the ritornellos, a complete Da Capo of R1 is extremely rare, found in only three early cases (Table 14.8). A further eight concertos spread a reprise of the complete R1 across two ritornellos (in the case of D89, this incorporates a major expansion of a solo interpolation in R1). But much the strongest preference in the early group is for a compressed or otherwise varied version of the opening ritornello. The simplest and most common approach (fifteen cases) reprises in R4a the first part of R1 and in R4b the closing section, thus omitting or downplaying any unstable central material.

The later group shows a marked change, the preference here being to restrict R4 to the closing section of R1, with no reprise of the opening of the movement at all. The consequence is a significant downgrading of the force of the tonic ritornello: now a short tailpiece, often after a solo cadenza, without the strong impact of the motto. D83 again provides a compelling example. The weight of the recapitulation is here transferred entirely to the soloist, who reprises in S4 both the motto and also secondary material transposed to the tonic: after the pause for a

Table 14.8. Thematic structure of R4a and R4b in Tartini

Thematic structure of R4	Early	Late
Where there is a single R4		
R4 = R1 complete	3	0
R4 = R1 compressed/varied	3	6
R4 = closing section of R1 only, possibly varied	4	27
R4 new	0	1
Total	**10**	**34**
Where there is more than one R4		
R4a-R4b = all of R1, possibly with S4 included	7	1
R4a-R4b = outer elements of R1, possibly varied	26	12
Other	7	7
Total	**40**	**20**

Table 14.9. Thematic structure of S4 in Tartini

Thematic structure of S4	Early	Late
S4 contributes to the reprise of R1	6%	0%
S4 starts as S1, diverges where S1 moves towards secondary key	4%	11%
S4 starts as S1, later transposes some secondary key material	4%	59%
S4 starts with new material, later transposes some secondary key material	2%	4%
S4 uses earlier material in other ways	42%	19%
S4 consists of new material or figuration	30%	7%
No S4	12%	0%

cadenza, a full-blown tutti would be superfluous. Instead R4 rounds off the movement with closing material from R1, characteristically varied to avoid the banality of merely echoing the last phrase of the solo.

This last example has already suggested that the soloist plays a much more significant part in Tartini's recapitulations than in any other repertoire in this study, as is confirmed in Table 14.9. While in the early column the frequencies are comparable to those for Vivaldi (Table 6.11), those in the second column show an extremely dramatic change. Corresponding to the waning tutti role in the recapitulation, the significance of S4 is correspondingly heightened. As many as 74% of the later movements exemplify some form of tonal recapitulation, as against 10% of the early group. In 59% the solo not only stresses the tonic by

Ex. 14.8. Tartini, Violin Concerto in C major, D13

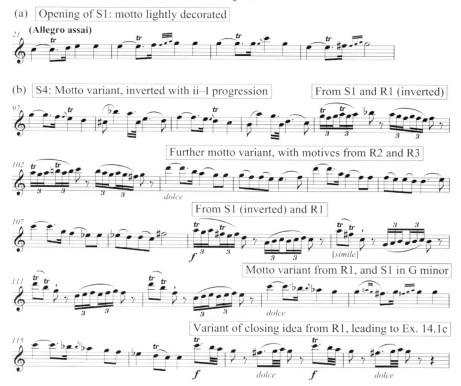

(a) Opening of S1: motto lightly decorated

(b) S4: Motto variant, inverted with ii–I progression   From S1 and R1 (inverted)

Further motto variant, with motives from R2 and R3

From S1 (inverted) and R1

Motto variant from R1, and S1 in G minor

Variant of closing idea from R1, leading to Ex. 14.1c

recalling the opening of S1, usually the motto, but also resolves the secondary material by transposition to the tonic, in the manner of the later 'sonata form' (compare Vivaldi's mere four examples of this strategy).

Yet this is not a purely mechanical procedure, and indeed it is in the recapitulation that Tartini achieves the most imaginative reconstruction of earlier material, often varying and reordering motives from S1 and R1 in diverse combinations. Some suggestion of this has been seen in the relatively straightforward D83, but others present more complex reworkings. In D100, for example, R4a immediately embarks on a modulating development of motives from the motto, ending on the dominant. Rather than simply reprising the motto, the ensuing solo S4 presents a new compressed variant, which leads immediately to two further motives from S1 – now transposed from dominant to tonic, but in reverse order and further manipulated.

More distant in its variants, but no less clearly a recall of earlier material, is the recapitulation in D13, where the material is in a state of continuous evolution. S4 prefers some variants developed in central sections and others in inverted form (Ex. 14.8). Thus the motto is never directly stated in the recapitulation at all; and, since it was not heard in a peripheral key either, it is restricted to its customary four early appearances in tonic and dominant. However it is not entirely lost from view, but rather permeates the later sections in varied allusions.

An Overall View

Tartini's interest in thematic manipulation permeates his entire repertoire. In the early concertos a short motto fragment may be used to bind together the diffuse sections of a long and rhapsodic form. In D55, for example, a simple E minor arpeggio is manipulated not only to provide the basis for the thematic material (sometimes in diminution) but also to underpin a variety of solo material.[7] In the later concertos, melodic ideas contained within the motto are used in much more subtle and allusive ways, as the succeeding solos and ritornellos adapt and transform them into new musical shapes.

Throughout Tartini's output there is a tendency to separate the early sections by clear rests between some or all of the components R1-S1-R2-S2. The early group also includes frequent harmonic hiatuses, not only at the point of recapitulation, but also at such unusual places as the start or end of R2. D3 (Op. 2/5) projects the disjunctures of its opening ritornello across the entire movement, with rhythmic separations between every section as well as numerous hiatuses (Table 14.10). The sense of nervous discontinuity is not dispelled even at the very last opportunity, where the characteristic ii-I sequence is deliberately imposed on the closing section. In later concertos, however, while the early rhythmic separations are generally maintained, there is much more sense of gathering continuity and coherence as the movement proceeds: not only through the progressive thematic working, but also through the deliberate blurring of boundaries such as the ambiguous elision of the point of recapitulation.

Table 14.10. Timeline of Tartini, Violin Concerto in C major, D3 (Op. 2/5)

Function	R1 /	S1 /	R2 /	S2 /	R3a //	ST/RT //	S/R3b /	S/R/S3c //
Bars	1–16	17–28	29–42	43–58	59–62	63–64	65–66	67–79
Key	I	I → V	V	V → vi	vi (^{V}/vi)	I	vi	→ iii
Motto	M	M	M	M	M	M'	M'	

R4a /	S4 //	R4b
80–87	88–100	100–106
I (V)	I	(^{V}/ii) I
M		

Rhythmic separations are indicated by /; hiatus by //

Towards binary form

If there is no R3 and the second solo leads from the motto through peripheral keys to a recapitulation, the movement already begins to demonstrate fundamentally different proportions. This is especially emphasized when the second half of S1 is recapitulated in the tonic, as in D53 (Table 14.11). In such a case, the two long solos (S1 and S2-S3-S4) constitute in themselves a binary movement, framed by

---

[7]   Ed. Bojan (1998).

Table 14.11. Timeline of Tartini, Violin Concerto in E major, D53

Function	R1	S1	R2	S2	S3	S4	R4
Bars	1–13	14–37	38–47	48–53	54–59 60–63	64–75	76–80
Key	I	I → V	V	V →	ii // IV →	I	
Thematic	M	M	M'	M		= 26–37 adapted to remain in I	= 9–13

Table 14.12. Timeline of Tartini, Violin Concerto in B minor, D125

Function	R1	S1	R2	S2	S4	R4
Bars	1–18	‖: 19–33– 45–56	57–64 :‖	65–86–88	89–91–102	103–110
Key	i	i → III→ v	v	III →	i	i
Thematic	M	M M'		M	→ 45–56 transposed to i	

three ritornellos. R3 is prepared but never realized, and the final R4 provides merely a brief closure.

In Tartini's latest concertos (not included in the above analysis), this type of scheme is regularized into an explicit binary structure, by the addition of a central double bar and an indication to repeat all or most of the first half of the movement. The structure may be handled in different ways – the opening ritornello may be included in the repeat or not, the central ritornello may precede or follow the double bar – but never is the peripheral key articulated by a ritornello. The tutti essentially provides a frame for a lightly accompanied binary solo. This is particularly evident where R2 comes at the end of the repeated section, emphasizing its role as a closure rather than a new beginning. D125 provides an extreme example, with the full ritornello heard only at the very beginning, and the motto thereafter reserved for the soloist (Table 14.12).

This new variant of ritornello form is outside the scope of this book, and it clearly allies the concerto not only with the sonata but also with the developing symphony. Yet it did not achieve widespread currency even among his later pupils. The charming *galant* concertos of Angelo Morigi (Op. 3, published in London in 1756) reflect the elegant melodic ease and ornamental decoration of Tartini's middle period, but they retain a strong ritornello form without a central caesura – and even a continuing attachment to R3. The third ritornello was indeed a highly variable element for several more decades. Eventually it was decisively abandoned in favour of a large-scale recapitulation initiated by the tutti (R4a-S4-R4b) as symphonic principles increasingly took hold.[8] By the time of Mozart's piano concertos of the 1780s, the incipient sonata-form elements of Tartini's later conception had become standard practice; but they were allied instead to a four-ritornello frame (R1-R2-R4a-R4b), in which the recapitulation is strongly reasserted by the tutti motto.

---

[8]   See the charts in White, 'First-Movement Form' and *From Vivaldi to Viotti*, pp. 71–5.

CHAPTER 15

The Malleable Model

We started this book from a position of frustration with the idea of a static model for ritornello form. During the course of the book, we have deliberately avoided specifying what such a model might look like, and it is time now to reveal what we have been avoiding. Walter Kolneder, in a widely read text, has summarized Vivaldian ritornello form in a chart which may be translated into our format as follows:[1]

Table 15.1. Walter Kolneder's model for Vivaldi ritornello movements

In major

Function	R1	S1	R2	S2	R3	S3	R4 (Da Capo)
Key	I	→	V	→	vi	→	I

In minor

Function	R1	S1	R2	S2	R3	S3	R4 (Da Capo)
Key	i	→	III	→	v	→	i

To our great surprise, we have not discovered a single first movement that reproduces precisely this succession of events in either the major or minor mode. Kolneder's own Vivaldi example is a minor-mode finale (from RV 393/769), and even this does not correspond exactly.

Now it may be argued that a model is a simplified or 'ideal' synthesis, enshrining certain universal principles that need never come together in a single work (the same could be said of the textbook 'sonata form'). Indeed we must state immediately that we fully concur with the concept of an overall model that guided the process of composition, and that also orientated performers and listeners: our analytic symbols would indicate that this study has been so directed. Yet we challenge the very principle of narrowing down the enormous diversity of options in order to reach a single synthetic and easily memorable model, as well as the methods previously used to achieve one. These attempts have been marred by two severe shortcomings: statistical distortion and conceptual malformation.

---

[1] 'The Solo Concerto', p. 312 (originally in *Die Solokonzertform bei Vivaldi*, p. 38).

Statistical distortion

The Kolneder model given in Table 15.1 inevitably results in an impoverished perspective, since it fails to recognize the diversity of options that are actually used across Vivaldi's repertoire. In fairness, Kolneder does mention some variant patterns, but his basic position is that 'departures from this scheme are comparatively rare'. Our statistical study has, however, demonstrated that the tonal scheme I-V-vi-I emphasized here is found in only 20% of concertos in major, while an even smaller number (12%) combine this tonal scheme with a stable R3. Similarly a mere 10% of concertos in minor use the scheme i-III-v-i.

Still more misleading is the implication that the recapitulation is normally coterminous with a Da Capo of R1: 'Since [the first and last ritornellos] have the function of providing a framework for the whole movement, the ritornello usually appears here complete (the last appearance generally as a *da capo*).'[2] The power of this myth is exemplified by the way it influenced Charles Rosen's discussion of the classical concerto: 'The first ritornello could take on the character of a sonata exposition, or it could keep its older concerto function, in which *the first and last ritornelli were the same – the older form being essentially an ABA form in which the B was much longer and more complex than the outer frame* [our italics].'[3] Yet in reality, in only 21% of the Vivaldi sample is the final ritornello a full Da Capo of R1; and, even more remarkably, there is just a single case where the tonic has not already been firmly established (RV 477).

If the Kolneder model appears to be of only limited application to the Vivaldi repertoire, it has even less relevance for other concerto composers. To take just one instance, the modulatory R2 – which is in any case no stranger in the Vivaldi sample (14%) – is very much the preferred choice for others: Scaccia used this option in nine out of thirteen concertos.

Conceptual malformation

No less problematical than this statistical distortion is a conceptual malformation: the very idea that the ritornellos provide static 'pillars of the formal architecture' around modulatory solos, all within the frame provided by the first and last ritornellos.[4] A set of four pillars, the left and right thicker than the two in the middle, may look fine as a graphic design on paper, but it completely misrepresents the musical process. Listening to a ritornello form movement should be a dynamic experience moving onwards through time towards the recapitulation, which itself usually continues the musical argument still further.

One might claim that such models are unavoidable in any general music history or textbook. Yet this particular artificial model has somehow acquired a status of its own, as the recognized mould from which hundreds of nearly identical concertos supposedly emerged. The conscientious student of the concerto is dangerously led to use the model as a compulsory guide, thereby judging all the many departures either unfavourably as stylistic aberrations or favourably as heroic acts of liberation. Furthermore, we have increasingly come to realize that

---

[2]   Ibid., p. 315.
[3]   *Sonata Forms*, p. 72.
[4]   Bukofzer, *Music in the Baroque Era*, p. 228.

the convenient methodology of comparing each movement to a narrow model unwittingly distorts our conception of the historical process of style change.

Model or Prescription

We are therefore bound to assert that the very clarity and precision of such a model renders it unduly restrictive, and ultimately invalid. The staggering variety of options and strategies implicit in the ritornello concept eludes any clear-cut model, yet this variety was of the essence as far as the concerto composer was concerned. To take but one example, our analysis of the thematic relationship between the first solo and R1 has produced as many as thirteen options, covering almost every possible permutation. It would therefore be quite misleading to select one or two of them as 'the solo model' and consider all others as exceptions.

Any composer approaching the (by then) routine task of inventing a new solo movement in ritornello form must have had in mind not a rigid model, but rather an initial prescription comprising certain universal requirements or 'rules' (in the sense of Leonard Meyer's terminology, discussed in Chapter 1):

(1) an alternation of texturally contrasting ritornellos and solos;
(2) tonal closure, involving departure from and return to the tonic, whether in circuit or in pendulum pattern;
(3) a directional tonal process effected by the hierarchization of key areas;
(4) a unitary form unfolding as a chain of stable and modulatory sections;
(5) a strong thematic identity to each ritornello and solo;
(6) a specialized role for the soloist, through idiomatic virtuosity and cantabile writing, as well as distinct structural functions (such as the modulation to V);
(7) a developing web of relationships between ritornellos and solos, created by recurrence, variation and contrast – with the motto playing a central role;
(8) an expanding range of implications, some realized, others tried and rejected, but always leading to the obligatory recapitulation;
(9) a short time span of about five minutes.

Such a prescription is deliberately vague and open-ended, inherently allowing extreme diversification on the next level down, that of strategies.

A movement written by these rules orientates the listener's perception and understanding, by enabling well-projected events to be easily registered and recalled, and by encouraging anticipation of possible realizations of implications. The listener is challenged to follow the course of a ritornello movement in much the same way as a later sonata-form Allegro. This is therefore not easy listening music that fails to repay close attention: indeed it is hard listening for a modern audience, precisely because the subtleties in the musical argument are not signalled beyond the most obvious textural alternations. The continuous structure with its apparently predictable ritornello pattern can all too readily obscure discontinuities at many different levels.

Here the temporal element is of vital importance, for any ritornello movement involves a quick turnover of tonal and thematic arguments, and at least six separate events (such as R1-S1-R2-S2-R3-R4) occur within a very short time span. For the listener this works both ways: on the one hand it serves to facilitate memory, yet at the same time it demands the most alert and focused attention. Even the apparently simple alternation of solo and tutti creates an intricate web of relationships between the individual and the group. The solo entrance provides an initial commentary on the ritornello – whether by ignoring the motto entirely or by presenting it in some more soloistic guise – and the interaction becomes ever more complex as the listener relates each subsequent ritornello to the former ritornellos, each solo to the former solos, and each solo to the surrounding ritornellos.

On top of this, there is a further layer. Not only is the listener required to follow all the twists and turns of the musical argument, but he is also challenged to consider more fundamental questions about style and genre.

Overlapping Styles

Historians customarily distinguish three broad styles within the early eighteenth-century Italian concerto repertoire:

(1) a contrapuntal style after Corelli, marked by a severe and neutral melodic vocabulary, with interlocking suspensions; a three-voice texture derived from the trio sonata; equality of major and minor modes, and pendulum tonal schemes; thematic and textural uniformity except for incidental concertino contrast;

(2) the Vivaldian concerto style, based on short motives with a sharp rhythmic profile; well-articulated contrasts, strongly characterizing solo and tutti sections; some preference for the major mode and for circuit tonal schemes; predominantly homophonic textures stressing the outer parts;

(3) the early *galant* idiom, predicated on a succession of short-breathed melodies, either in moderate tempo with rococo decoration or in a simple popular vein; predominance of the major mode; emphasis on the upper melodic voice; still mostly irregular phrasing, but sometimes a regular phrase structure with immediate repeats (e.g. a succession of 2+2-bar units, aa-bb-cc etc.).

This familiar picture is usually projected as a broadly chronological development. Yet our analysis of the vast concerto repertoire suggests that these three styles were by no means distinct stages, but instead intermingled to a surprising degree. Many composers were apparently able to adopt one or other at will, or in response to the tastes of a particular patron. Thus the concerto composer does not work 'within a style' but rather controls several styles, alternating between them on different levels so as to create variety within a set of twelve concertos, to contrast movements within a single work, or simply to develop a musical argument across a single ritornello movement. Thus he may interpose trio-sonata suspensions into a Vivaldian Allegro, or dissipate a *stile antico* motto into *galant* homophony, or – in the case of Mossi – superimpose modern violinistic figuration onto an essentially Corellian idiom. This kind of intertextuality raises the possibility that styles themselves can form part of the rhetorical debate. A concerto movement may in fact be 'about' the interaction between strict counterpoint and the virtuosic demands of the soloist, as in Platti's cello concertos; or 'about' the relationship between fugal continuity and the articulatory power of ritornello form, as with the Roman group. Just as there is always a tonal, thematic and textural argument across a movement, so too can there be a stylistic argument.

General, Local, Personal

Having studied hundreds of movements by dozens of Italian composers, we continue to be overwhelmed by the extraordinary diversity of strategies that they devised. Indeed, we have yet to discover two concertos that outline the same trajectory in all tonal, thematic and textural parameters. How then are we to analyze the development of style across all this diversity?

Studies of style history customarily distinguish between 'general practice', local idiom, and personal style. The concept of a statistically defined 'general practice' in connection with sonata form and the symphony has been convincingly challenged by Charles Rosen as 'pure fiction'.[5] It is equally misleading in the case of the early solo concerto. 'General practice' could only ever comprise an artificial synthesis of a large number of variables, obscuring any individual and original traits. While it is true that many concerto composers may indeed converge in certain strategies, any attempt to subsume their oeuvre into a 'general practice' must inevitably result in the statistical distortion already identified, since they will certainly diverge in other strategies. Here we must clearly state that the prescription suggested above does not simply represent 'general practice' by another name, but instead comprises a quite different concept: an overarching guide for concerto composers that at the same time allowed them full rein to develop and establish their own personal styles.

It would likewise be a mistake to exaggerate the importance of local centres. Whereas schools have appropriately been identified in the history of the symphony (as with Mannheim or Milan), it is misleading to attempt to distinguish unified 'concerto schools'. It is true that composers active in close proximity over an extended period were likely to share certain compositional strategies. Yet even in the relatively coherent groups identified in the preceding chapters, each composer, while sharing certain common traits with his colleagues, still explored his own distinctive strategies in other respects. We are therefore inescapably led to the conclusion that the history of the solo concerto was largely generated by individual concerto composers, mostly well-travelled performers with distinct personal temperaments and wide-ranging European experience.

Certainly, individual composers developing their own musical idiolects were not working in isolation. In particular, they all shared the effects of the powerful 'Vivaldian revolution', which abruptly transformed Venetian music during the 1710s and soon penetrated every concerto centre across Italy, as well as further afield. This is not to imply a Vivaldian school, but rather an overarching influence which affected all composers profoundly without obliterating either their local heritage or individual proclivities. Composers of the older generation felt

5   *Sonata Forms*, p. 6.

compelled to integrate at least some aspects of Vivaldi's conception – his innovations in ritornello form, his instrumental writing, his rich expression – into their own practice; younger contemporaries fell completely under his spell.

The immediate impact of Vivaldi's music is all the more impressive, given that he limited his teaching activity to the Pietà. His influence relied on his high reputation as a virtuoso performer and on the rapid international dissemination of his publications, as well as Venice's great prestige as a cultural centre. The deeper reasons for Vivaldi's powerful influence are to be found in Cesare Fertonani's perceptive observation: 'Vivaldi's compositional art is based on a continuous and fruitful dialectic between two contrasting aesthetic premises: simplicity (a category which implies naturalness, spontaneity and clarity) and complexity (which, on the other hand, refers to elaboration, intellectual control and technical mediation).'[6] Each composer following Vivaldi could engage with this dialectic according to his own personal temperament, developing his musical priorities within the flexible context provided by ritornello form.

Central to Vivaldi's achievement in the concerto was his consistently imaginative exploration and expansion of options in every parameter, defying any tendency towards standardization of ritornello form. This proved a blessing for other concerto composers, for it opened the door for them to develop their own ideas, striking off on individual paths that they were to maintain with some consistency. Take, for example, Albinoni's penchant for the pendulum pattern and a final coda, or Montanari's blend of fugal procedures with the new virtuosity; Platti's intricate reworkings in the recapitulation, or Valentini's adoption of elements from binary form; d'Alai's exploration of the properties of $^V/V$ or Brescianello's preference for a central modulatory instability; or Tartini's strategy of following a fourfold motto statement with subtle motivic transformations later. The historian should not be misled by superficial thematic resemblances to Vivaldi's concertos in the works of his contemporaries; for while they always shared certain of his traits, together they vastly expanded the range of options across all the parameters. Indeed one might fairly say that they went out of their way to distinguish themselves from their most famous influence.

The Three-stage Process: Exploration, Selection, Elimination

The emergence of ritornello form initiated an immediate wave of exploration, suggesting a vast laboratory in which composers experimented with the effects of the many options within each parameter and of their innumerable permutations together. The next stage involved the selection of preferred options, at first by personal choice, later as part of a more general consensus. The final stage was the elimination of certain options that were apparently deemed unsatisfactory, or no longer relevant.

The exploratory stage should be viewed in a positive light rather than as a mere prelude to the stages of selection and elimination. Take the crucial aspect of the thematic relationship between R1 and S1, where the two extreme options were

[6]   Translated from *La musica strumentale*, pp. 98–9.

unity (with the motto identically presented) or total contrast. But the question 'does Vivaldi prefer contrast or unity?' is not answerable in this simple form. The early *La stravaganza*, Op. 4, already investigates many possible relationships: S1 starts with different material in seven cases, with the motto in two, with an ornamentation of the motto in two further, and with new material over the motto once. Our analysis of Vivaldi's repertoire as a whole identifies 59% where he selected clear contrast in S1, with the remainder exploiting ten different degrees of thematic integration (see Table 4.7). Tessarini mirrored this range, with a new start to S1 in about half of his concertos, and the rest employing various options in the use of R1 material.

Exploration is still more conspicuous in the dazzling variety of tonal schemes. Vivaldi himself used ninety-eight, and his contemporaries added new options, so that they more than doubled the number of tonal schemes used to well over 200. Each composer developed his own preferences. For example, Zani used VI as a peripheral key in seven of his twelve concertos in minor, a comparatively rare choice in Vivaldi (21%). Similarly, Tartini greatly expanded the number of major-mode schemes including ii, a key which Vivaldi employed only sparingly.

Such exploration not only opens up new possibilities for imaginative compositional strategies, but it also expands the perceptual horizons for the listener, by bringing to his attention the ever-increasing range of options and thereby encouraging comparisons across his own musical experience. Yet at the same time – even within the two parameters just discussed – the contrary process of selection was already under way. This can be easily observed in the matter of the solo opening, where Albinoni and Tartini both strongly favoured the motto, often unadorned and at the same pitch.

A distinction should be made between acts of selection common to most composers and those made by personal decision. Aside from the universal trend towards the major mode, by far the most general act of selection was the establishment of the dominant as the first target in major. Using Meyer's important distinction, we propose that the initial move to the dominant was elevated from the level of 'strategy' to that of a 'rule' lasting throughout the eighteenth century until Beethoven. Yet this was not a decision made by Vivaldi, who called upon every available degree in major, with first targets other than the dominant in a significant minority of 18%. Nor is this an early practice that he eventually abandoned, for the corresponding figure for our late group has increased to 24% – suggesting that Vivaldi either ignored the selection made by his contemporaries or actively resisted it. Likewise, the self-consciously individual Bonporti chose the dominant in only two of the six concertos considered here. Yet in his early concertos, from around 1700, Albinoni had already initiated the selection of the dominant. Tessarini and Locatelli followed suit in all but one idiosyncratic case each; and the dominant as first target in major was simply axiomatic for all the other composers considered here.

Such consistency was by no means the case in the minor mode. Vivaldi used both v and III in nearly equal proportions, and he occasionally promoted iv as a secondary key following the modal tradition. Others followed a similar diversity, oscillating between v and III, or (in Locatelli's case) iv and III. Yet some composers did make a personal selection. D'Alai preserved v as his sole choice, while Tessarini settled exclusively on III – also the trend in Tartini's output, fore-shadowing the universal preference in the later eighteenth century.

If we can, therefore, detect certain selection procedures in the choice of the first target, entire tonal schemes present a much more diverse picture. In general, whether to move from the stage of exploration into that of selection – and, more radically, towards elimination – was a decision taken individually by each composer. With regard to tonal schemes, a comparison of three of the larger repertoires is instructive (see Tables 8.13, 12.1 and 12.6). Tessarini selected I-V-vi-I as his preferred choice in major: including pendulum variants, it is found in as many as 27 out of 35 concertos. Zani, on the other hand, refrained from any selection. His repertoire explored a much greater variety, with 20 tonal schemes in his 25 concertos in major: only four are shared with Tessarini, and I-V-vi-I appears just once. Scaccia's 13 concertos display a similar range, with I-V-vi-I again a rarity. This analysis shows that while Tessarini made his own selection, his two prominent contemporaries persisted in the stage of exploration; and there was no universal trend towards a single preferred tonal scheme. Indeed, it turns out that I-V-vi-I was a surprisingly rare option in the repertoire as a whole.

A Chronological Perspective

The three-stage process therefore moved at a different rate for each of the various parameters, and it would be a fundamental mistake to expect the different elements of style to change in a synchronized way. Three broad chronological patterns can be distinguished across the period of this book.

(1) Selection and elimination during the earliest stages
A fascinating example of early elimination is provided by the various options for the tonal design of R1. A modulatory opening ritornello is intrinsic in the early string concertos of Albinoni, where the ritornello-solo structure is not clearly articulated, and it is also found in concertos in the older manner by Montanari and Mossi. It was also briefly tried in the newer type of solo concerto, as in eight of Torelli's concertos Op. 8 and in four of the early Vivaldi group. Yet this practice was quickly eliminated, appearing in none of Vivaldi's late group and only very exceptionally in concertos by other composers (such as Brescianello's Op. 1/9, where it follows a long solo opening). As R1 settled into a closed, non-modulatory pattern, composers explored instead a variety of internal options, at first expanding the ritornello with long chromatic progressions (as often in Vivaldi) and later including separate sections in other keys. Where, in the concertos of Tessarini and G.B. Sammartini, R1 resembles a short symphony with its own self-contained tonal scheme, it was indeed a 'piece within a piece'.

Still more fundamental is the question of who is to start the concerto. It is, after all, perfectly plausible that the soloist might initiate the drama, whether with an introductory flourish (in the tradition of Valentini's Op. 7/1), or with a strong thematic identity as in Torelli's Op. 8/1. However, this option was largely elimi-nated very early on – just when composers were preferring to open the Da Capo aria with a full-scale ritornello to prepare for the solo entrance. Within the Vivaldi sample the soloist starts proceedings in only fourteen concertos, of which five are in the early group and none in the late. Only very rarely was this option used by others for special effect, playing upon the expectation of a tutti opening, as in the Brescianello concerto just mentioned.

The same tendency towards closure was reflected at the end of the movement in attitudes towards the *attacca* link to the slow movement. This remnant of the *concerto da chiesa*, where contrasting sections flow easily into one another, is found occasionally in early solo concertos (for example, in Torelli), but Vivaldi used it in a mere 3% of the sample. His preference for a self-contained ritornello structure was followed by all his contemporaries, and the *attacca* ending was eliminated altogether.

(2) Constant exploration and expansion of options, only hinting at later selection and elimination
At the other end of the spectrum were parameters where hardly any selection took place within this period. The recapitulation was perhaps the least standardized area of the concerto, offering innumerable options and combinations across every parameter. Among these diverse possibilities was one that came to be selected as the norm later in the century: the final solo that transposed secondary material from S1 into the tonic. This significant gesture of tonal resolution – a distinguishing feature of mature sonata form – is very rare in the present repertoire, appearing in only 3% of the Vivaldi sample and in two concertos by Tessarini. More significant is its appearance in the concertos of Valentini, under the influence of binary form, and again in those of Platti, but it is only in the late Tartini group that it becomes a prominent characteristic (63%). This foreshadows its selection as a hallmark of the high classical concerto, in line with contemporary symphonic practice.

(3) Exploration giving way to selection and elimination during the course of the period
The problem of dating individual concertos makes it particularly difficult to map stylistic changes across the repertoire, even in the case of Vivaldi. Yet an overview of such a large repertoire can point to certain changes of direction. There was, for example, a gradual trend away from techniques that blur the edges between the opening ritornello and solo sections. An early casualty was the device of repeating the tutti motto immediately after the opening ritornello, so that the solo flows almost imperceptibly out of the tutti. Clearly this was felt to diminish the impact of the solo entrance. More long-lasting was the R1a-S1a-R1b complex common in Albinoni's repertoire (where it is associated with the Devise). This did not undermine the solo impact in quite the same way – indeed the Devise had something of the opposite effect, since it served to highlight the very process of the solo entrance. Furthermore the three-section pattern could be used in a rhetorical sense to suggest a tonal debate, such as we have seen in Vivaldi (p. 106). Nevertheless Vivaldi eventually effected a process of selection here too, as this pattern appears in 60% of the early group but in only 11% of the late. A similar trend can be seen in Tessarini's output, where it is found in a significant 29% overall, but in a higher proportion of the early Op. 1.

Younger composers showed a clear preference for a single, continuous S1 leading directly to R2. While this is not to preclude some intermingling of solo passages within R1 (as in Zuccari's substantial tutti-solo complexes), the essential point is that the functions of R1 and S1 are increasingly sharply defined. The ritornello serves to set out the main affect of the movement in a closed section made up of several discrete components; then the soloist is highlighted by a clear and characterful entrance and by being entrusted with the first structural modulation.

If the trend in the first half of the movement was towards sizeable sections with separate functions (R1-S1-R2), in the second half the opposite development may be discerned. The tendency was for ritornellos to become shorter and less weighty as the movement progressed, with the soloist taking a correspondingly more prominent role; and the rapid alternation of textures encouraged a greater interplay and integration between tutti and solo, especially in recapitulation patterns such as S4a-R4a-S4b-R4b. Yet within the peripheral stage of the movement the process of selection was slow and uneven, and many options were essayed. While some composers persisted with full-scale ritornellos in peripheral keys, the Milanese group favoured a series of tutti interjections marking brief staging posts; the later concertos of both Vivaldi and Tartini show a trend towards a shorter, modulatory R3, emphasizing the instability of this part of the movement. At the most extreme, R3 is reduced to a brief reference of one or two bars, leading either dramatically or unobtrusively straight into the recapitulation.

In some concertos by Tartini, R3 simply disappears altogether, so that the soloist outlines a simple binary form across two solo sections (S1 and S2-S3-S4). The debate about the function of R3 continued well into the second half of the century, but it was the latter strategy that eventually prevailed. In Mozart's Piano Concerto, K. 503, for example, only remnants of R3 survive in the modulatory dialogue between piano and orchestra at bars 228–273. By contrast with the Tartini model, however, the recapitulation now takes up a far greater proportion of the movement, beginning with a tutti restatement of the opening section. In this way Mozart builds on the various recapitulatory techniques already developed in the Italian concerto repertoire, achieving a complex reintegration of R1 and S1 to which tutti and soloist equally subscribe.

Many factors contributed to the development of autonomous instrumental music during the eighteenth century, and we would not wish to downplay the significance of the binary dance form or its offsprings, the sonata and symphony. Yet Vivaldi's importance in encouraging Bach as well as other Italian composers to 'think musically' cannot be overstated. In imbuing the instrumental concerto with 'order, connection, and proportion', he created a readily comprehensible yet infinitely flexible way of organizing instrumental structures. Ritornello form provided a means of developing a musical argument through a whole range of rhetorical strategies, opening up opportunities for composers to develop their most imaginative responses along highly diverse and original lines. Vivaldi himself continued to explore the possibilities in unexpected and even bizarre ways. The riches of his later repertoire are as yet unfamiliar to modern performers or audiences, who will find much that is surprising and disturbing when these concertos become more widely known.

Instead of attempting to imitate Vivaldi directly (the conventional misunder-standing), his Italian contemporaries preferred to experiment with their own approaches towards the genre. Almost every composer considered in this book developed a distinctive voice, and there is scarcely a single concerto in the wider repertoire that could be mistaken for one by Vivaldi. The most rewarding concertos discussed here – by Bonporti, Laurenti, Montanari, Platti, Tessarini and Zani, as well as by more familiar names such as Albinoni, Locatelli and Tartini – attain a real presence and individuality; these are composers that deserve wider recognition.

Style history is a multifaceted and elusive concept that defies simple analysis. The early eighteenth-century Italian concerto is not a single river with a number of more or less significant tributaries and backwaters, but a richly varied delta with numerous streams leading off in all kinds of unexpected directions. Some of these streams may have joined to produce trends that were to attain great signifi-cance later in the eighteenth century; others, equally interesting, proved to be more idiosyncratic innovations. Ultimately it is only by studying and listening to the entire range of this extraordinarily rich repertoire that we will come to appre-ciate the originality of the Italian composers' response to the Vivaldian revolution.

Appendix: Catalogue of Repertoire

The catalogue below summarizes the repertoire studied in this book. Concertos are essentially for solo violin unless otherwise indicated. First movements have been studied unless otherwise indicated (I = first movement, II = second movement). In the interests of brevity, concordances are not cited unless they are of particular significance; similarly modern editions are only selectively identified. Publications are identified by *RISM* number, and libraries by *RISM* sigla:

A-Wgm	Vienna, Gesellschaft der Musikfreunde in Wien
A-Wn	Vienna, Österreichische Nationalbibliothek, Musiksammlung
D-B	Berlin, Staatsbibliothek zu Berlin, Preussischer Kulturbesitz
D-Dl	Dresden, Sächsische Landesbibliothek – Staats- und Universitätsbibliothek
D-KA	Karlsruhe, Badische Landesbibliothek
D-SWl	Schwerin, Mecklenburgische Landesbibliothek, Musiksammlung
D-WD	Wiesentheid, Musiksammlung des Grafen von Schönborn-Wiesentheid
F-Pn	Paris, Bibliothèque Nationale
GB-Ckc	Cambridge, King's College, Rowe Music Library
GB-Lbl	London, British Library
GB-Mp	Manchester, Henry Watson Music Library
I-AN	Ancona, Biblioteca Comunale 'L. Benincasa'
I-Gl	Genoa, Conservatorio di Musica Niccolò Paganini (Liceo musicale)
S-L	Lund, Universitetsbiblioteket
S-Skma	Stockholm, Statens Musikbibliotek
S-Uu	Uppsala, Universitetsbiblioteket
US-BEm	Berkeley, University of California, Music Library
US-SFsc	San Francisco State University, Col. Frank V. de Bellis Collection
US-Wc	Washington, Library of Congress

Thematic catalogues relating to manuscript collections include the following:

Berkeley   Duckles and Elmer, *Thematic Catalog of a Manuscript Collection*
              [US-BEm]
Dresden   Pozzi, 'Il concerto strumentale italiano' [D-Dl]
Fonds   de La Laurencie, *Inventaire critique du fonds Blancheton* [F-Pn,
  Blancheton Rés. F 446]
Manchester   Everett, *The Manchester Concerto Partbooks* [GB-Mp, MS 580
              Ct51 and GB-Lbl, R.M. 22.c.28]
Vienna   Haas, *Die Estensischen Musikalien* [A-Wn]
Wiesentheid   Zobeley, *Die Musikalien der Grafen von Schönborn-Wiesentheid*
              [D-WD, microfilm in Deutsches musikgeschichtliches Archiv,
              Kassel]

Anthologies cited are as follows:

Concerts à 5, 6, & 7 instrumens (Amsterdam: Roger, No. 188, 1714)
VI concerts à 5 & 6 instrumens (Amsterdam: J. Roger, No. 417, 1716)
[12] Concerti a cinque (Amsterdam: J. Roger, Nos. 432–3, 1717)
VI concerti à 5 stromenti (Amsterdam: J. Roger, No. 448, *c*1719)
Harmonia Mundi, 2nd collection (London: Walsh, No. 384, 1728)
6 concerti a cinque stromenti (Amsterdam: Witwogel, No. 35, 1735)
VI concerti a cinque stromenti (Amsterdam: Witwogel, No. 48, 1736)
Ten Italian Violin Concertos from Fonds Blancheton, ed. Jehoash Hirshberg,
Recent Researches in the Music of the Classical Era, 19–20 (Madison, WI: A-R
Editions, 1984)

Alberti, Giuseppe Matteo

Thematic catalogue: Talbot, 'A Thematic Catalogue of the Orchestral Works of
Giuseppe Matteo Alberti' [T]

Principal publications:
[10] Concerti per chiesa e per camera, Op. 1 (Bologna, 1713, A665)
XII sinfonie a quattro, Op. 2 (Amsterdam, 1725, A672)

T1 (Op. 2/2, 2vn), T2, T3, T4, T5, T6 (Op. 1/7; ed. Desderi, 1955), T7 (Op. 1/5),
T8, T9, T10, T11 (Op. 1/3; ed. Desderi, 1955), T12 (*Harmonia Mundi*, No. 1),
T14, T15/II, T16 (Op. 1/9), T17 (ed. Hirshberg, *Ten Italian Violin Concertos*,
No. 1), T18, T19, T20 (Op. 1/1), T21 (*VI concerti à 5*, No. 1)

Regarding T13, see Ghignone, Ghi2

Albinoni, Tomaso

Thematic catalogues: in Talbot, *Albinoni: Leben und Werk*; and Rossi, *Tommaso Albinoni: Catalogo tematico*
Catalogue: in Talbot, *Tomaso Albinoni*

Principal publications:
[6] Sinfonie e [6] concerti a cinque, Op. 2 (Venice, 1700, A703; ed. Ammetto and Filocamo, 2003), especially Op. 2/8 and Op. 2/12 [sonatas alternate with concertos, each numbered 1–6; the concertos are here designated Op. 2/2, Op. 2/4 etc.]
[12] Concerti a cinque, Op. 5 (Venice, 1707, A722)
[12] Concerti a cinque, Op. 7 (Amsterdam, 1715, A733) [incl. 4 for ob, 4 for 2ob]
[12] Concerti a cinque, Op. 9 (Amsterdam, 1722, A738) [incl. 4 for ob, 4 for 2ob]
[12] Concerti a cinque, Op. 10 (Amsterdam, 1735–6, A740), especially Nos. 8 and 12

Others: [Talbot numbers] *Co*2 (*Concerti a cinque*, No. 11; ed. Ammetto and Filocamo, 2002), *Co*4 (ed. Ammetto and Filocamo, 2002), *Co*5 (ed. Wanek, 1974)

Modern edition: *Tomaso Giovanni Albinoni: Gesamtausgabe der Instrumentalmusik*, ed. Walter Kolneder (Mainz and Zürich, 1958–)

Bonporti, Francesco Antonio

Thematic catalogue: in Carlini, *Francesco Antonio Bonporti*

Principal publication: *[10] Concerti a quattro*, Op. 11 (Trent, after 1727, B3663; ed. Maxwell Sobel, 1994)

Brescianello, Giuseppe Antonio

Principal publication: *12 concerti et sinphonie*, Op. 1 (Amsterdam, 1738, B4343) [incl. 6 vn concs, numbered 1–6, but alternating with symphonies; here designated Op. 1/1, Op. 1/3 etc.]

Brivio, Giuseppe Ferdinando

D'Alai, Mauro

Principal publication: *Dodici concerti*, Op. 1 (Amsterdam, 1727, AA554a)

See also Zuccari, Zuc6

Ghignone, Giovanni Pietro [Jean-Pierre Guignon]

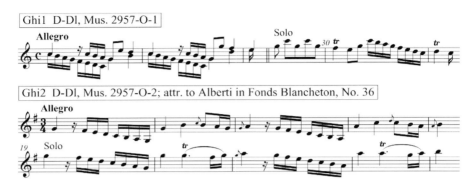

Laurenti, Girolamo Nicolò

Principal publication: *VI concerti*, Op. 1 (Amsterdam, 1727, L1092)

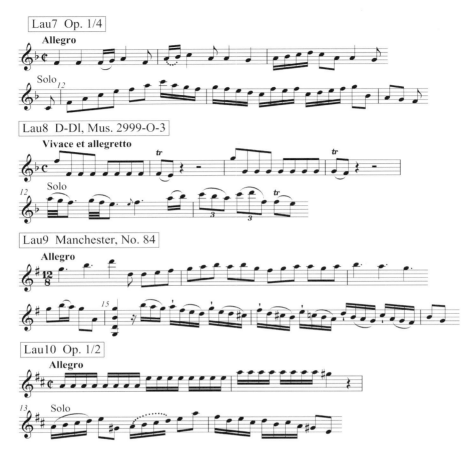

Locatelli, Pietro Antonio

Thematic catalogue: Dunning, ed., *Pietro Antonio Locatelli: Catalogo tematico*

Principal publication: *L'arte del violino: XII concerti*, Op. 3 (Amsterdam, 1733, L2605)
Others: WoO3, WoO4
Some begin with a short introduction

Modern editions: *Pietro Antonio Locatelli: Opera omnia*, 3, ed. Albert Dunning (London: Schott, 2001) and 9, ed. Giacomo Fornari (London: Schott, 1996)

Marcello, Alessandro [*pseud* Eterio Stinfalico]

Thematic catalogue: Selfridge-Field, *The Music of Benedetto and Alessandro Marcello*

Principal publication: *La cetra* (Augsburg, *c*1738, M420) [6 concs for 2ob etc.], (Selfridge-Field) D936–D939, D941, D944
Other: D935 (ob, in *Concerti a cinque*, No. 2; ed. Ruf, 1963)

Marcello, Benedetto

Thematic catalogue: Selfridge-Field, *The Music of Benedetto and Alessandro Marcello*

Principal publication: *[12] Concerti a cinque*, Op. 1 (Venice, 1708, M443)
Since the *violino principale* part is missing, only the following movements have been studied: 2/II (C788) from Bach's transcription (BWV 981), 8/I (C790) from the manuscript compilation C791

Others: C784 (ed. Engländer, 1956), C797 (2vn)

Montanari, Antonio

Principal publication: *VIII concerti*, Op. 1 (Amsterdam, *c*1730, M3306; some II)
Others: D-Dl, Mus. 2767-O-1; S-L, Saml. Engelhart, No. 382

Mossi, Giovanni

Principal publications:
VI concerti a 6 instromenti, Op. 3 (Amsterdam, *c*1720, M3805)
[12] Concerti, Op. 4 (Amsterdam, 1727, M3807)

See Chapter 7 for more details

Perroni [Peroni], Giovanni

Platti, Giovanni Benedetto

Thematic catalogue: Iesuè, *Le Opere di Giovanni Benedetto Platti* [I]

Vn conc: I18 (D-Dl, Mus. 2787-O-1)
Ob conc: I47 (D-WD, Zobeley 644; ed. Winschermann, 1964)
Vc concs (all in D-WD, with Zobeley nos.): I19 (646), I20/II (668), I21/II (669), I22 (650), I23 (651), I24 (652), I25 (653), I26/II (655), I27 (657), I28 (658), I29 (659), I30 (648), I31 (649), I32 (656), I34 (647), I35 (660/645), I36/II (663), I37 (664), I38 (665), I40 (667), I42 (654), I46 (662) [incomplete concertos omitted]

Sammartini, Giuseppe

SamG1 ob: Lbl, R.M. 23.b.8 (12); R.M. 23.b.20

SamG2 ob: D-Dl, Mus. 2763-O-2; vn, S-Skma (J-C D-76)

SamG3 fl: S-Skma

SamG4 fl, II: S-Lu, Saml. Engelhart 114

SamG5 vn [ob?], II: S-Skma (J-C D-80)

SamG6 ob, II: D-Dl, Mus. 2763-O-3; ed. Töttcher (1968)

Sammartini, Giovanni Battista

Thematic catalogue: Jenkins and Churgin, *Thematic Catalogue of the Works of Giovanni Battista Sammartini*
See also Gehann, *Giovanni Battista Sammartini: Die Konzerte*

For works discussed, see the catalogue on p. 267
Modern edition: *Giovanni Battista Sammartini: Four Concertos*, ed. Ada Beate Gehann, Recent Researches in the Music of the Classical Era, Vol. 67 (Middleton, WI: A-R Editions, 2002) [includes J-C 74 and J-C 71 (version A)]

Scaccia, Angelo Maria

Principal publication: *[6] Concerti*, Op. 1 (Amsterdam, *c*1730, S1132)

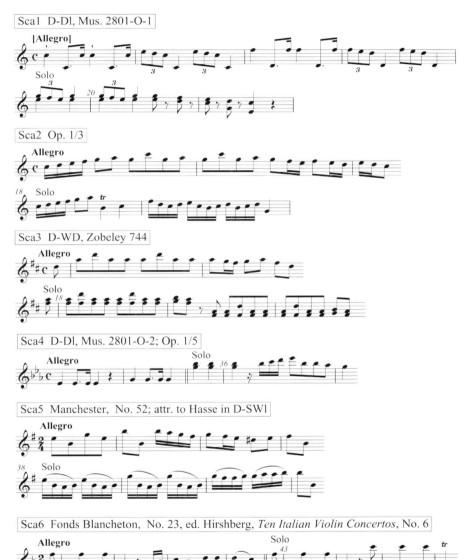

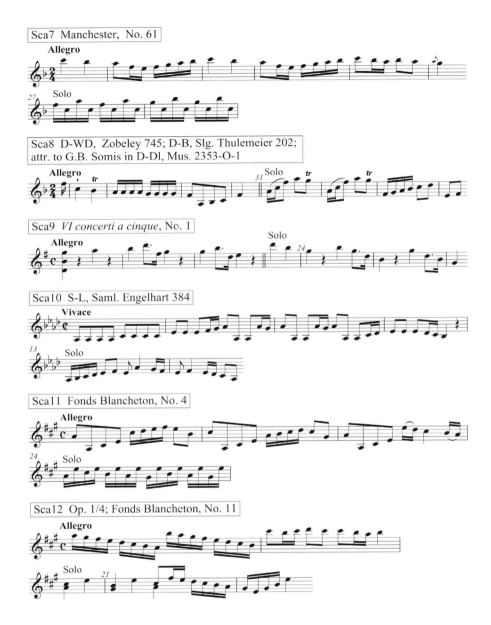

Schiassi, Gaetano Maria

Principal publication: *[12] concerti* (Amsterdam, 1729, S1531)

Somis, Giovanni Battista

See also Scaccia, Sca8

Fonds Blancheton, No. 2, attributed to Somis, is by Vivaldi (RV 302)

Somis, Giovanni Lorenzo

Tartini, Giuseppe

Thematic catalogue: Dounias, *Die Violinkonzerte Giuseppe Tartinis* [D]
See also Duckles and Elmer, *Thematic Catalog of a Manuscript Collection*

Principal publications:
Sei concerti a cinque e sei stromenti, Op. 1/1 (Amsterdam, 1728, T233)
[*Sei concerti a cinque stromenti*, Op. 1/3, by Tartini and Visconti, unattributable (Amsterdam, *c*1728, T236)]
Sei concerti a cinque stromenti, Op. 1/2 (Amsterdam, 1730, T235)
VI concerti a otto stromenti, Op. 2 (Amsterdam, *c*1734, T237)

Modern edition: *Le opere di Giuseppe Tartini*, ed. Eduardo Farina and Claudio Scimone (Milan, 1971–)

Bold type indicates Dounias's period II or III (see Chapter 14)

D1 (*VI concerti a cinque*, No. 5), D2 (Op. 2/2), D3 (Op. 2/5), D4, **D5**, **D7**, **D8**, **D10**, **D13**, **D14c**, D15 (Op. 1/I/4; ed. Abbado, 1971), D16, D17, D18 (Op. 1/II/6), D19, D20, D21 (*Le opere*, 14), D22, **D23a**, **D24** (*Le opere*, 2), **D26**, **D27**, **D28**, **D29**, **D31**, **D32**, **D33**, **D34**, **D35**, **D38**, D43, D44, D46 (Op. 2/6), D47, D48 (ed. Bojan, 2000), **D49**, **D50**, **D51** (ed. Ney, 1973), **D52**, **D53** (ed. Scherchen, n.d.), D55 (Op. 1/I/2, ed. Bojan, 1998), D56 (*Le opere*, 6), D57, D58 (Op. 1/I/5), D59 (Op. 1/II/3), D60 (Op. 1/I/3), D61, D62 (Op. 2/4), D63, **D65**, **D66**, **D68**, **D69**, D71 (Op. 1/II/4), D72, D73 (Op. 2/1), D74, D75, D76, **D77**, **D78** (*Le opere*, 5), **D79**, **D80** (ed. Braun, 1972), **D82** (ed. Bojan, 1999), **D83** (*Le opere*, 11), **D84**, D85 (Op. 1/I/1, ed. Guglielmo, 1973), D86 (ed. Rostal, 1952), **D87**, D88 (Op. 1/II/5), D89 (Op. 1/I/6), D90, D91 (Op. 1/II/2), D92 (ed. Schroeder, *c*1960), D93, D94/II, D95, **D96** (*Le opere*, 3), **D97**, **D99**, **D100**, **D101**, **D102**, **D103**, **D104**, **D105**, **D106**, **D107**, D111 (Op. 1/II/1), D112, **D113**, **D114**, **D115** (*Le opere*, 15), D116, D117/II (*Le opere*, 13), D118, **D119**, **D120**, **D122**, D124 (Op. 2/3); US-BE, **It. 853**, It. 881, It. 941; **Anh. VII**

Tessarini, Carlo

Principal publications:
[12] Concerti a cinque, Op. 1 (Amsterdam, 1724, T580); as *Twelve Violin Concertos Opus 1*, ed. Jehoash Hirshberg and Simon McVeigh, Recent Researches in the Music of the Classical Era, 61 (Middleton, WI: A-R Editions, 2001)
La stravaganza, Op. 4 (Amsterdam, *c*1736/7, T587) [incl. 4 vn concs, 2 concs for 2vn]
[6] Concerti a V, 2 vols. (Paris, *c*1745, T574)
Contrasto armonico, Op. 10 (Paris, *c*1748, T558) [3 concs for 2vn]

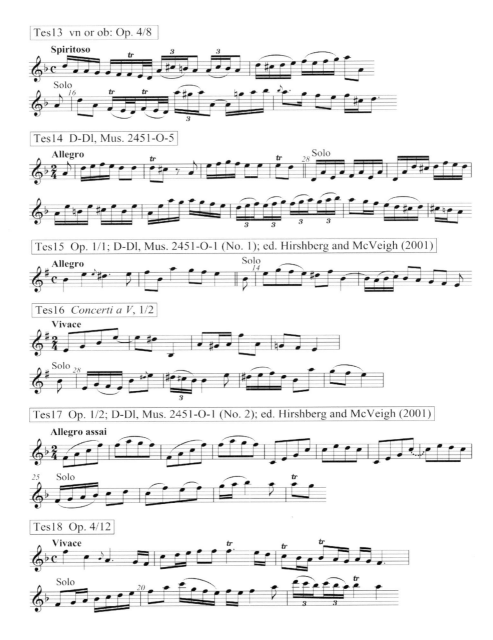

Tes25 2vn: Op. 10/3

Tes26 D-Dl, Mus. 2451-O-2

Tes27 GB-Ckc, Ms. 235

Tes28 GB-Ckc, Ms. 237

Tes29 Op. 1/12; ed. Hirshberg and McVeigh (2001)

Tes30 *Concerti a V*, 2/3

Valentini, Giuseppe

Catalogue: Careri, 'Per un catalogo tematico delle opere di Giuseppe Valentini'
See also Everett, *The Manchester Concerto Partbooks*

Principal publications:
[12] Concerti grossi a quattro e sei strumenti, Op. 7 (Bologna, 1710, V114)
X concerti, Op. 9 (Amsterdam, 1724, V120)

Other:
Two oboe concertos (*Concerti a cinque*, Nos. 3–4)
D-Dl, Mus. 2387-O-1, 2387-O-2, 2387-O-3, 2387-O-5
Manchester, Nos. 25, 26, 28 (ed. Everett. 2001), 30 (= *VI concerts à 5 & 6 instrumens*, No. 1), 31, 51 (ed. Everett, 2000) and 65 (ed. Geerb, 1998)

The concertos of Valentini are variably scored (see Chapters 3 and 7)

Veracini, Francesco Maria

Thematic catalogue: in Hill, *The Life and Works of Francesco Maria Veracini* [Hill]

Concertos: Hill D1, Hill D2 (*VI concerti à 5*, No. 2; ed. Paumgartner, 1960), Hill A1 (*Concerti a cinque*, No. 7), Hill A2, Hill Bb (*VI concerti a cinque*, No. 2)

Vivaldi, Antonio

Thematic catalogues: Ryom, *Répertoire des Oeuvres d'Antonio Vivaldi*; and Ryom, *Verzeichnis der Werke Antonio Vivaldis (RV)*, 2nd edn.

Principal publications:
L'estro armonico, Op. 3 (Amsterdam, 1711, V2201) [4 vn concs, 4 concs for 2vn, 4 concs for 4vn, some with vc]
La stravaganza, Op. 4 (Amsterdam, 1716, V2214) [12 vn concs]
VI concerti a cinque stromenti, Op. 6 (Amsterdam, 1716, V2221)
Concerti a 5 stromenti, Op. 7 (Amsterdam, 1720, V2223) [10 vn concs, 2 ob concs]
Il cimento dell'armonia e dell'inventione, Op. 8 (Amsterdam, 1725, V2225) [10 vn concs, 2 concs for vn or ob]
La cetra, Op. 9 (Amsterdam, 1727, V2229) [11 vn concs, 1 conc for 2vn]
VI concerti, fl, Op. 10 (Amsterdam, 1729, V2230)
Sei concerti, Op. 11 (Amsterdam, 1729, V2231)
Sei concerti, Op. 12 (Amsterdam, 1729, V2232)
Some other works appear in the anthologies listed above
Italic type indicates early works (composed before c1718), **bold** late works (composed after c1722), as discussed on p. 81

Modern editions: *Le opere di Antonio Vivaldi*, ed. G.F. Malipiero and others (Milan: Ricordi, 1947–72)
Nuova edizione critica delle opere di Antonio Vivaldi, various editors (Milan: Ricordi, 1982–)

Some other works appear in the anthologies listed above
Italic type indicates early works (composed before c1718), **bold** late works (composed after c1722), as discussed on p. 81

Modern editions: *Le opere di Antonio Vivaldi*, ed. G.F. Malipiero and others (Milan: Ricordi, 1947–72)
Nuova edizione critica delle opere di Antonio Vivaldi, various editors (Milan: Ricordi, 1982–)

vn concs: RV 170, 171, *172*, **173** (Op. 12/4), *175*, 176, 177, 180 (Op. 8/6), **181a** (Op. 9/1), 182, **183**, 184, *185*/II (Op. 4/7), **186**, 187, *188* (Op. 7/2), **189**, 190, 191, 194, *195*, *196* (Op. 4/10), 197, **198a** (Op. 9/11), 199, 201, **202** (Op. 11/5), *204* (Op. 4/11), 205, 206, **207** (Op. 11/1), *208a* (Op. 7/11), 209, 210 (Op. 8/11), 211, *212a*, **213**, 215, *216* (Op. 6/4), 217, 218, 219, *220*, 221, 222, 224, 225, 226, 227, 228, 229, *230* (Op. 3/9), 231, 232, 233, **234**, 235, 237, **238** (Op. 9/8), *239* (Op. 6/6), 240, 241, 242 (Op. 8/7), 243, **244** (Op. 12/2), 245, 246, 247, **248**, *249* (Op. 4/8), 250, 251, 252, 253 (Op. 8/5), 254, 256, 257, 258, *259* (Op. 6/2), **260**, **261**, 262, **263a** (Op. 9/4), **264**, *265* (Op. 3/12), 266, **267**, 268, 269 (Op. 8/1), **270**, **271**, **273**, *275*, *276*, **277** (Op. 11/2), **278**, *279* (Op. 4/2), *280* (Op. 6/5), 281, **282**, 283, *284* (Op. 4/9), *285a* (Op. 7/5), **286**, 287, **288**, **289**, 293 (Op. 8/3), *294a* (Op. 7/10), 295, 296, 297 (Op. 8/4), *298* (Op. 4/12), *299* (Op. 7/8), **300** (Op. 9/10), *301* (Op. 4/3), 302, 303, 306, **307**, **308** (Op. 11/4), *310* (Op. 3/3), 311, **312**, 313, *314*, 315 (Op. 8/2), *316a* (Op. 4/6), **317** (Op. 12/1), *318* (Op. 6/3), 319, 321, 323, *324* (Op. 6/1), 325, *326* (Op. 7/3), 327, *328*, 329, **330**, 331, 332 (Op. 8/8), 333, **334** (Op. 9/3), *335*, **336** (Op. 11/3), 339, 340, **341**, 342, **343**, 344, **345** (Op. 9/2), 346, *347* (Op. 4/5), **348** (Op. 9/6), **349**, 350, 352, 353, *354* (Op. 7/4), **356** (Op. 3/6), *357* (Op. 4/4), **358** (Op. 9/5), **359** (Op. 9/7), **361** (Op. 12/6), 362 (Op. 8/10), **363**, *364*, **365**, **366**, **367**, 368, **369**, 370, **371**, 372, *374* (Op. 7/6), **375**, 376, 377, **379** (Op. 12/5), **380**, *382*, 383, *383a* (Op. 4/1), 384, **386**, **387**, 388, **389**, **390**, **391** (Op. 9/12), **581**, 582, 583, 761, 762, **763**, 769, 770

va d'a concs: RV 392, 394, 396, 397

vc concs: RV **398**, **399**, 400, 401, *402*, **403**, *404*, *405*, **406**, *407*, 408, 409, **410**, **411**, **412**, **413**, **414**, *416*, **417**, **418**, **419**, *420*, **421**, 422, *423*, **424**

mand conc: RV 425

fl concs: RV **427**, **428** (Op. 10/3), **429**, **431**, **432**, **433** (Op. 10/1), **435** (Op. 10/4), **436**, **437** (Op. 10/6), **438**, **439**/finale (Op. 10/2), **440**

rec concs: RV 441, 442 (basis for Op. 10/5), 443, 444, 445

ob concs: RV 447, 449 (Op. 8/12), 451, 452, 453, 454 (Op. 8/9), 455, 456/II, 461

bn concs: RV 466, 467, 469, 471, 472, **473**, 474, 475, 476, 477, **478**, 479, 480, 481, 483, 484, 485, 486, 487, 488, 489, 490, 491, 492, 493, 494, 495, 496, **497**, 498, 499, **500**, 502, 503, 504

concs for 2vn: RV 505, **506**, 507, 508, 509, *510*, 511, 512, **513**, 514, 515, 516, *517*, *519* (Op. 3/5), 521, *522* (Op. 3/8), 523, 524, 525, 527, 529, **530** (Op. 9/9) other double concertos: RV 531 (2vc), 532 (2mand), **533** (2fl), 534 (2ob), *535* (2ob), 536 (2ob), 537 (2tpt), 538 (2hn), 539 (2hn), **540** (vd'a, lute), 541 (vn, org), 542 (vn, org), 543 (vn, ob unison), 544 (vn, vc), 545 (ob, bn), 546 (vn, vc all'inglese), 547 (vn, vc), 548 (vn, ob), **552** (vn, echo vn), 561 (vn, 2vc), *578*/II (2vn, vc, Op. 3/2), 765 (2vn)

Zani, Andrea

Principal publications:

Sei sinfonie da camera ed altretanti concerti da chiesa, Op. 2 (Casalmaggiore, 1729, Z49; also as Op. 1, Amsterdam, *c*1737, Z50) [incl. 6 vn concs]

Concerti dodeci a quatro, Op. 4 (Vienna, *c*1733, Z51; also as Op. 2, Amsterdam, *c*1741, Z52)

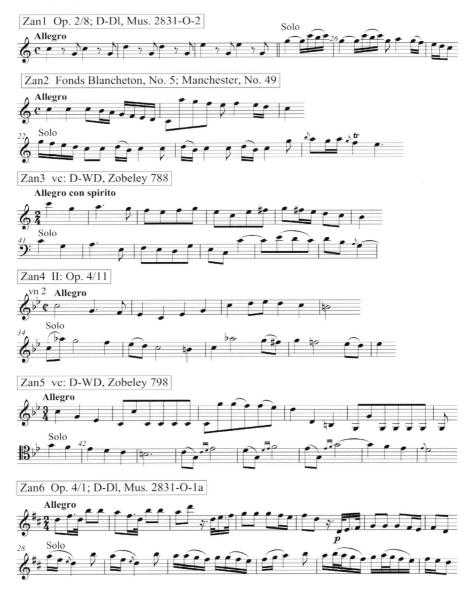

Zan26 Op. 2/6; D-Dl, Mus. 2831-O-8; attr. to Caccia [Scaccia?] in D-Dl, Mus. 2692-O-1

Zan27 vc: D-WD, Zobeley 797

Zan28 Op. 4/2

Zan29 Op. 4/12

Zan30 vc: D-WD, Zobeley 793

Zan31 Op. 2/2; D-Dl, Mus. 2831-O-6; ed. Hirshberg and McVeigh (2001)

Zavateri, Lorenzo Gaetano

Principal publication: *[12] Concerti da chiesa e da camera* (Bologna, 1735; Z105) [incl 6 vn concs]

Zuccari, Carlo

Bibliography

Ahnsehl, Peter, 'Bemerkungen zur Rezeption der Vivaldischen Konzertform durch die mittel- und norddeutschen Komponisten im Umkreis Bachs', in *Vivaldi-Studien: Referate des 3. Dresdner Vivaldi-Kolloquiums*, ed. Wolfgang Reich (Dresden: Sächsische Landesbibliothek, 1981), pp. 59–72

Ahnsehl, Peter, 'Genesis, Wesen, Weiterwirken: Miszellen zur Vivaldischen Ritornellform', *Informazioni e studi vivaldiani*, 6 (1985), pp. 74–87

Allsop, Peter, *Arcangelo Corelli: New Orpheus of our Times* (Oxford: Oxford University Press, 1999)

Atcherson, Walter, 'Key and Mode in Seventeenth-Century Music Theory Books', *Journal of Music Theory*, 17 (1973), pp. 204–32

Avison, Charles, *An Essay on Musical Expression* (London, 1752)

Baldauf-Berdes, Jane L., *Women Musicians of Venice: Musical Foundations, 1525–1855* (Oxford: Clarendon, 1993)

Baldauf-Berdes, Jane L., 'Anna Maria della Pietà: The Woman Musician of Venice Personified', in *Cecilia Reclaimed: Feminist Perspectives on Gender and Music*, ed. Susan C. Cook and Judy S. Tsou (Urbana: University of Illinois Press, 1994), pp. 134–55

Balthazar, Scott L., 'Intellectual History and Concepts of the Concerto: Some Parallels from 1750 to 1850', *Journal of the American Musicological Society*, 36 (1983), pp. 39–72

Barblan, Guglielmo, 'La musica strumentale e cameristica a Milano nel '700', in *Storia di Milano*, 16 (Milan: Fondazione Treccani degli Alfieri per la Storia di Milano, 1962), pp. 619–60

Bartel, Dietrich, *Musica Poetica: Musical-Rhetorical Figures in German Baroque Music* (Lincoln: University of Nebraska Press, 1997)

Basso, Alberto, 'Notizie biografiche sulle famiglie Somis e Somis di Chiavrie', Introduction to G.B. Somis, *Sonate da Camera Op. II*, Monumenti musicali italiani, 2 (Milan, Edizioni Suvini Zerboni, 1976), pp. vii–xxxiii

Bernardi, Alessandra, 'Il mecenatismo musicale a Venezia nel primo Settecento', in Dunning, ed., *Intorno a Locatelli,* vol. 1, pp. 1–128

Bernardini, Alfredo, 'The Oboe in the Venetian Republic, 1692–1797', *Early Music*, 16 (1988), pp. 372–87

Bizzarini, Marco and Giacomo Fornari, *Benedetto Marcello: un musicista tra Venezia e Brescia* (Cremona: Turris, 1990)

Bizzarini, Marco, 'I "buoni fondamenti degli Antichi" e il "gusto moderno": l'eredità di Benedetto Marcello nella formazione culturale e musicale di Pietro Antonio Locatelli', in Dunning, ed., *Intorno a Locatelli,* vol. 1, pp. 129–49

Bombi, Andrea and Maria Nevilla Massaro, *Tartini: il tempo e le opere* (Bologna: Il Mulino, 1994)

Bonta, Stephen, 'The Uses of the *Sonata da Chiesa*', *Journal of the American Musicological Society*, 22 (1969), pp. 54–84

Bouquet-Boyer, Marie-Thérèse, *Musique et musiciens à Turin de 1648 à 1775* (Turin: Accademia delle scienze, 1968)

Brover-Lubovsky, Bella, 'Vivaldi and Contemporary German Music Theory', *Informazioni e studi vivaldiani*, 20 (1999), pp. 59–82

Brover-Lubovsky, Bella, 'Between Modality and Tonality: Vivaldi's Harmony', *Informazioni e studi vivaldiani*, 21 (2000), pp. 111–33

Brover-Lubovsky, Bella, 'Vivaldi's Harmony between Modality and Tonality', Ph.D. diss., Hebrew University, Jerusalem, 2000

Brusa, Marco and Attilio Rossi, 'Sammartini e il suo tempo: fonti manoscritte e stampate della musica a Milano nel Settecento', *Fonti musicali italiane*, 1(1996), Supplemento

Brusniak, Friedhelm, ed., *Italienische Musiker und Musikpflege an deutschen Höfen der Barockzeit* (Cologne: Studio, 1995)

Bukofzer, Manfred, *Music in the Baroque Era* (New York: Norton, 1947)

Burdette, Glenn, 'The Violin Sonatas of Giovanni Battista Somis (1686–1763), including an Edition of Opus 3', Ph.D. diss., University of Cincinnati, 1993

Burney, Charles, *A General History of Music* (1776–89), ed. Frank Mercer, 2 vols. (London: G.T. Foulis, 1935)

Butler, Gregory Gordon, 'J.S. Bach's Reception of Tomaso Albinoni's Mature Concertos', in *Bach Studies*, 2, ed. Daniel R. Melamed (Cambridge: Cambridge University Press, 1995), pp. 20–46

Calmeyer, John Hendrik, 'The Life, Times and Works of Pietro Antonio Locatelli', Ph.D. diss., University of North Carolina, Chapel Hill, 1969

Cantù, Alberto, 'I tre Locatelli e Paganini', *Nuova rivista musicale italiana*, 22 (1988), pp. 221–9

Careri, Enrico, 'Giuseppe Valentini (1681–1753): documenti inediti', *Note d'archivio per la storia musicale*, n.s. 5 (1987), pp. 69–125

Careri, Enrico, *Francesco Geminiani (1687–1762)* (Oxford: Clarendon, 1993)

Careri, Enrico, 'Per un catalogo tematico delle opere di Giuseppe Valentini (1681–1753)', *Studi musicali*, 24 (1995), pp. 63–85

Carlini, Antonio, *Francesco Antonio Bonporti 'Gentilhuomo di Trento': biografia e catalogo tematico dell'opera* (Padua: I Solisti veneti, 2000)

Cattoretti, Anna, ed., *Giovanni Battista Sammartini and his Musical Environment* (Turnhout: Brepols, 2004)

Dangel-Hofmann, Frohmut, ' "Der guthe Houboist von Würtzburg, der platti . . .": Sein kompositorisches Schaffen im Spiegel der Schönbornschen Musikaliensammlung', *Musik in Bayern*, 47 (1993), pp. 11–31

de Brosses, Charles, *Lettres familières sur l'Italie*, ed. Yvonne Bezard, 2 vols. (Paris: Firmin-Didot, 1931)

Degrada, Francesco, ed., *Vivaldi veneziano europeo* (Florence: Olschki, 1980)

Degrassi, Margherita Canale, 'Destinazione e aspetti esecutivi dei Concerti per Violino di Giuseppe Tartini: contributi per un approfondimento', in Dunning, ed., *Intorno a Locatelli*, vol. 1, pp. 151–73

Della Seta, Fabrizio, 'La musica in Arcadia al tempo di Corelli', *Nuovissimi studi corelliani*, ed. Sergio Durante and Pierluigi Petrobelli (Florence: Olschki, 1982), pp. 123–48

Della Seta, Fabrizio, 'I Borghese (1691–1713): La musica di una generazione', *Note d'archivio per la storia musicale*, n.s. 1 (1983), pp. 139–208

Dounias, Minos, *Die Violinkonzerte Giuseppe Tartinis als Ausdruck einer Künstler-persönlichkeit und einer Kulturepoche* (1935, repr. Wolfenbüttel: Möseler, 1966)

Dreyfus, Laurence, 'J.S. Bach's Concerto Ritornellos and the Question of Invention', *The Musical Quarterly*, 71 (1985), pp. 327–58

Dreyfus, Laurence, *Bach and the Patterns of Invention* (Cambridge, MA: Harvard University Press, 1996)

Dubowy, Norbert, 'Anmerkungen zur Form in den frühen Konzerten Antonio Vivaldis', in Fanna and Morelli, eds., *Nuovi studi vivaldiani*, pp. 431–49

Dubowy, Norbert, *Arie und Konzert: zur Entwicklung der Ritornellanlage im 17. und frühen 18. Jahrhundert* (Munich: Fink, 1991)

Dubowy, Norbert, 'Italienische Instrumentalisten in deutschen Hofkapellen', in Strohm, ed., *The Eighteenth-Century Diaspora*, pp. 61–120

Duckles, Vincent and Minnie Elmer, *Thematic Catalog of a Manuscript Collection of Eighteenth-Century Italian Instrumental Music in the University of California, Berkeley, Music Library* (Berkeley: University of California Press, 1963)

Dunning, Albert, 'Some Notes on the Biography of Carlo Tessarini and his Musical Grammar', *Studien zur Musikwissenschaft*, 25 (1962), pp. 115–22

Dunning, Albert, *Pietro Antonio Locatelli: Der Virtuose und seine Welt*, 2 vols. (Buren: Knuf, 1981)

Dunning, Albert, ed., *Intorno a Locatelli: studi in occasione del tricentenario della nascita di Pietro Antonio Locatelli (1695–1764)*, 2 vols. (Lucca: Libreria musicale italiana, 1995)

Dunning, Albert, ed., *Pietro Antonio Locatelli: Catalogo tematico, lettere, documenti & iconografia*, Opera omnia, 10 (London: Schott, 2001)

Dunning, Albert, Introduction to *Pietro Antonio Locatelli: L'arte del violino, XII Concerti per violino solo [Op. 3]*, Opera omnia, 3 (London: Schott, 2002)

Eller, Rudolf, 'Das Formprinzip des Vivaldischen Konzerts. Studien zur Geschichte des Instrumentalkonzerts und zum Stilwandel in der ersten Hälfte des 18. Jahrhunderts', doct. diss., Karl-Marx-Universität, Leipzig, 1957

Eller, Rudolf, 'Geschichtliche Stellung und Wandlung der Vivaldischen Konzertform', *Bericht über den Internationalen Musikwissenschaftlichen Kongress Wien Mozartjahr 1956* (Graz: Böhlau, 1958), pp. 150–5

Eller, Rudolf, 'Die Entstehung der Themenzweiheit in der Frühgeschichte des Instrumentalkonzerts', in *Festschrift Heinrich Besseler zum sechzigsten Geburtstag* (Leipzig: Deutscher Verlag für Musik, 1961), pp. 323–55

Eller, Rudolf, 'Über Character und Geschichte der Dresdner Vivaldi-Manuskripte', *Vivaldiana*, 1 (1969), pp. 57–67

Ellero, Giuseppe, Yolando Scarpa and Carlo Paolucci, *Arte e musica all'Ospedaletto: schede d'archivio sull'attività musicale degli ospedali dei Derelitti e dei Mendicanti di Venezia* (Venice: Stamperia di Venezia, 1978)

Engel, Hans, *Das Instrumentalkonzert* (Leipzig: Breitkopf & Härtel, 1932)

Everett, Paul, 'A Roman Concerto Repertory: Ottoboni's "what not"?', *Proceedings of the Royal Musical Association*, 110 (1983–4), pp. 62–78

Everett, Paul, 'Towards a Chronology of Vivaldi Manuscripts', *Informazioni e studi vivaldiani*, 8 (1987), pp. 90–107

Everett, Paul, 'Towards a Vivaldi Chronology', in Fanna and Morelli, eds., *Nuovi studi vivaldiani*, pp. 729–57

Everett, Paul, *The Manchester Concerto Partbooks*, 2 vols. (New York: Garland, 1989)

Everett, Paul, 'Vivaldi's Paraphrased Oboe Concertos of the 1730s', *Chigiana*, 41 (1989), pp. 197–216

Everett, Paul, 'Vivaldi's Italian Copyists', *Informazioni e studi vivaldiani*, 11 (1990), pp. 27–88

Everett, Paul, 'Vivaldi's Marginal Markings: Clues to Sets of Instrumental Works and their Chronology', in *Musicology in Ireland*, ed. Gerard Gillen and Harry White (Dublin: Irish Academic Press, 1990), pp. 248–63

Everett, Paul, *Vivaldi: 'The Four Seasons' and Other Concertos, Op. 8* (Cambridge: Cambridge University Press, 1996)

Eynard, Marcello, *Il musicista Pietro Antonio Locatelli: un itinerario artistico da Bergamo ad Amsterdam* (Bergamo: Circolo lirico Mayr-Donizetti, 1995)

Fanna, Antonio and Giovanni Morelli, eds., *Nuovi studi vivaldiani: edizione e cronologia critica delle opere*, 2 vols. (Florence: Olschki, 1988)

Fanna, Antonio and Michael Talbot, eds., *Vivaldi vero e falso. Problemi di attribuzione* (Florence: Olschki, 1992)

Fechner, Manfred, 'Bemerkungen zu einigen Dresdner Vivaldi-Manuskripten', in Fanna and Morelli, eds., *Nuovi studi vivaldiani*, pp. 775–84

Fertonani, Cesare, 'Espressione strumentale e poesia nel Settecento italiano: *Il pianto d'Arianna* di Pietro Antonio Locatelli', *Studi musicali*, 22 (1993), pp. 335–63

Fertonani, Cesare, *La musica strumentale di Antonio Vivaldi* (Florence: Olschki, 1998)

Fischer, Wilhelm, 'Zur Entwicklungsgeschichte des Wiener klassischen Stils', *Studien zur Musikwissenschaft*, 3 (1915), pp. 24–84

Fornari, Giacomo, Introduction to *Pietro Antonio Locatelli: Sei concerti a quattro [Op. 7]*, Opera omnia, 7 (London: Schott, 1996)

Fourés, Olivier, and Michael Talbot, 'A New Vivaldi Cantata in Vienna', *Informazioni e studi vivaldiani*, 21 (2000), pp. 99–109

Freeman, Daniel E., 'The Earliest Italian Keyboard Concertos', *The Journal of Musicology*, 4 (1985–6), pp. 121–45

Gambassi, Osvaldo, *La cappella musicale di S Petronio* (Florence: Olschki, 1987)

Gambassi, Osvaldo, *L'Accademia Filarmonica di Bologna. Fondazione, statuti e aggregazioni* (Florence: Olschki, 1992)

Gehann, Ada Beate, *Giovanni Battista Sammartini: Die Konzerte* (Frankfurt am Main: Lang, 1995)

Gehann, Ada Beate, Introduction to *Giovanni Battista Sammartini: Four Concertos*, Recent Researches in the Music of the Classical Era, 67 (Middleton, WI: A-R Editions, 2002)

Gehann, Ada Beate, 'Merkmale der Konzertsatzform in der späten Kompositionsphase G. B. Sammartinis', in Cattoretti, ed., *Giovanni Battista Sammartini and his Musical Environment*

Geyer, Helen and Wolfgang Osthoff, eds., *Musica agli Ospedali/Conservatori veneziani tra il Seicento e Ottocento* (Rome: Edizioni Storia e Letteratura, forthcoming)

Ghisi, Federico, 'Giovanbattista e Lorenzo Somis musicisti piemontesi', *Chigiana*, 20 (1963), pp. 56–65

Giskes, Johan H., 'I dedicatari olandesi delle opere di Pietro Antonio Locatelli', in Dunning, ed., *Intorno a Locatelli*, vol. 1, pp. 275–318

Grattoni, Maurizio, ' "Qui si ferma à piacimento": struttura e funzione della cadenza nei concerti di Vivaldi', in Fanna and Morelli, eds., *Nuovi studi vivaldiani*, pp. 479–92

Haas, Robert, *Die Estensischen Musikalien: thematisches Verzeichnis mit Einleitung* (Regensburg: Bosse, 1927)

Hansell, Sven Hostrup, 'Orchestral Practice at the Court of Cardinal Pietro Ottoboni', *Journal of the American Musicological Society*, 19 (1966), pp. 398–403

Hell, Helmut, 'Ein Doppelkonzert Antonio Vivaldis als Triosonate', *Analecta Musicologica*, 22 (1984), pp. 149–96

Heller, Karl, *Die deutsche Überlieferung der Instrumentalwerke Vivaldis* (Leipzig: Deutscher Verlag für Musik, 1971)

Heller, Karl, 'Vivaldis Ripienkonzerte. Bemerkungen zu einigen ausgewählten Problemen', in *Vivaldi-Studien*, ed. Wolfgang Reich (Dresden: Sächsische Landesbibliothek, 1981), pp. 169–73

Heller, Karl, 'Über die Beziehungen zwischen einigen Concerto- und Sinfonia-Sätzen Vivaldis', *Informazioni e studi vivaldiani*, 4 (1983), pp. 41–60

Heller, Karl, *Antonio Vivaldi: The Red Priest of Venice*, tr. David Marinelli (Portland, OR: Amadeus, 1997)

Hill, John Walter, 'Veracini in Italy', *Music & Letters*, 56 (1975), pp. 257–76

Hill, John Walter, *The Life and Works of Francesco Maria Veracini* (Ann Arbor, MI: UMI, 1979)

Hill, John Walter, 'The Anti-Galant Attitude of F.M. Veracini', in *Studies in Musicology in Honor of Otto E. Albrecht*, ed. John Walter Hill (Kassel: Bärenreiter, 1980), pp. 158–96

Hirshberg, Jehoash, 'The Formation and Destination of the *Fonds Blancheton*', *Current Musicology*, 27 (1979), pp. 36–44

Hirshberg, Jehoash, Introduction to *Ten Italian Violin Concertos from Fonds Blancheton*, Recent Researches in the Music of the Classical Era, 19–20 (Madison, WI: A-R Editions, 1984)

Hirshberg, Jehoash and Simon McVeigh, 'The Making of a Ritornello Movement: Compositional Strategy and Selection in Tessarini's "Opera Prima" ', *Informazioni e studi vivaldiani*, 21 (2000), pp. 35–74

Hirshberg, Jehoash and Simon McVeigh, Introduction to Carlo Tessarini, *Twelve Violin Concertos Opus 1*, Recent Researches in the Music of the Classical Era, 61 (Middleton, WI: A-R Editions, 2001)

Hirshberg, Jehoash and Simon McVeigh, 'In Defence of Positivism Today – or Exploring a Virgin Territory', *Orbis Musicae*, 13 (2003), pp. 91–7

Hirshberg, Jehoash and Simon McVeigh, 'The "Virtuosi Instrumenti" and the Milanese Concerto in the Early Eighteenth Century', in Cattoretti, ed., *Giovanni Battista Sammartini and his Musical Environment*, pp. 203–44

Holman, Peter and Richard Maunder, 'The Accompaniment of Concertos in 18th-Century England', *Early Music*, 28 (2000), pp. 637–50

Hutchings, Arthur, *The Baroque Concerto*, 3rd edn. rev. (London: Faber, 1978)

Iesuè, Alberto, 'Le opere a stampa e manoscrittee di Giovanni Benedetto Platto', *Nuova rivista musicale italiana*, 9 (1975), pp. 541–51

Iesuè, Alberto, *Le Opere di Giovanni Benedetto Platti, 1697–1763: catalogo tematico* (Padua: I Solisti veneti, 1999)

Jenkins, Newell, and Bathia Churgin, *Thematic Catalogue of the Works of Giovanni Battista Sammartini: Orchestral and Vocal Music* (Cambridge, MA: Harvard University Press, 1976)

Kan, Rebecca, 'The Concerto Adagios of Antonio Vivaldi', Ph.D. diss., University of Liverpool, 2003

Kirakowska, Susan, 'Giuseppe Sammartini's Concertos, Opus 8', *The Music Review*, 38 (1977), 258–66

Kirkendale, Ursula, *Antonio Caldara: sein Leben und seine venezianisch-römischen Oratorien* (Graz: Böhlau, 1966)

Kirkendale, Ursula, 'The Ruspoli Documents on Handel', *Journal of the American Musicological Society*, 20 (1967), pp. 222–73

Kolneder, Walter, *Die Solokonzertform bei Vivaldi* (Strasbourg: P. H. Heitz, 1961)

Kolneder, Walter, *Antonio Vivaldi: His Life and Work*, tr. Bill Hopkins (London: Faber, 1970)

Kolneder, Walter, *Melodietypen bei Vivaldi* (Zürich: Amadeus, 1973)

Kolneder, Walter, 'Gibt es einen Vivaldistil?', *Informazioni e studi vivaldiani*, 1 (1980), pp. 9–17

Kolneder, Walter, 'The Solo Concerto', in *Concert Music (1630–1750)*, New Oxford

History of Music, 6, ed. Gerald Abraham (Oxford: Oxford University Press, 1986), pp. 302–76

Kotsoni-Brown, Stavria, 'The Solo Cello Concertos of Antonio Vivaldi', Ph.D. diss., University of Liverpool, 2000

Lance, Evelyn B., 'The London Sammartini', *The Music Review*, 38 (1977), pp. 1–14

Landmann, Ortrun, 'Katalog der Dresdener Vivaldi-Handschriften und -Frühdrucke', *Vivaldi-Studien*, ed. Wolfgang Reich (Dresden: Sächsische Landesbibliothek, 1981), pp. 102–67

Landmann, Ortrun, 'The Dresden Hofkapelle during the Lifetime of Johann Sebastian Bach', *Early Music*, 17 (1989), pp. 17–30

La Laurencie, Lionel de, *Inventaire critique du fonds Blancheton de la Bibliothèque du Conservatoire de Paris*, 2 vols. (Paris: E. Droz, 1930–1)

LaRue, Jan, 'Bifocal Tonality: An Explanation for Ambiguous Baroque Cadences', *Essays on Music in Honor of Archibald Thompson Davison* (Cambridge, MA: Harvard University, 1957), pp. 173–84

LaRue, Jan, 'Significant and Coincidental Resemblance between Classical Themes', *Journal of the American Musicological Society*, 14 (1961), pp. 224–34

LaRue, Jan, *Guidelines for Style Analysis*, 2nd edn. (Michigan: Harmonie Park, 1992)

La Via, Stefano, 'Il Cardinale Ottoboni e la musica: nuovi documenti (1700–1740), nuove letture e ipotesi', in Dunning, ed., *Intorno a Locatelli*, vol. 1, pp. 319–526

Ligi, Bramante, 'La Cappella musicale del Duomo di Urbino', *Note d'archivio per la storia musicale*, 2 (1925), pp. 1–369

Lindgren, Lowell, 'Count Rudolf Franz Erwein von Schönborn (1677–1754) and the Italian Sonatas for Violoncello in his Collection at Wiesentheid', in *Relazioni musicali tra Italia e Germania nell' età barocca*, ed. Alberto Colzani, Norbert Dubowy, Andrea Luppi and Maurizio Padoan (Como: A.M.I.S., 1997), pp. 255–302

Madricardo, Claudio and Franco Rossi, eds., *Benedetto Marcello: la sua opera e il suo tempo* (Florence: Olschki, 1988)

Marissen, Michael, *The Social and Religious Designs of J.S. Bach's Brandenburg Concertos* (Princeton, NJ: Princeton University Press, 1995)

Marx, Hans Joachim, 'Die Musik am Hofe Pietro Kardinal Ottobonis unter Arcangelo Corelli', *Analecta Musicologica*, 5 (1968), pp. 104–77

Marx, Hans Joachim, 'Die "Giustificazioni della Casa Pamphilj" als musikgeschichtliche Quelle', *Studi musicali*, 12 (1983), pp. 121–87

Mattheson, Johann, *Johann Mattheson's 'Der vollkommene Capellmeister'*, tr. Ernest C. Harriss (Ann Arbor, MI: UMI, 1981)

Maunder, Richard, *The Scoring of Baroque Concertos* (Woodbridge: Boydell, 2004)

McClary, Susan, 'The Blasphemy of Talking Politics during Bach Year', in *Music and Society: The Politics of Composition, Performance and Reception*, ed. Richard Leppert and Susan McClary (Cambridge: Cambridge University Press, 1987), pp. 13–62

McVeigh, Simon, *The Violinist in London's Concert Life, 1750–1784: Felice Giardini and his Contemporaries* (New York: Garland, 1989)

McVeigh, Simon, 'Italian Violinists in Eighteenth-century London', in Strohm, ed., *The Eighteenth-Century Diaspora*, pp. 139–76

Meyer, Leonard B., *Explaining Music: Essays and Explorations* (Berkeley: University of California Press, 1973)

Meyer, Leonard B., *Style and Music: Theory, History, and Ideology*, repr. edn. (Chicago: University of Chicago Press, 1996)

MGG = Die Musik in Geschichte und Gegenwart, ed. Friedrich Blume, 17 vols. (Kassel: Bärenreiter, 1949–86)

MGG2 = *Die Musik in Geschichte und Gegenwart*, 2nd edn., ed. Ludwig Finscher, 23 vols. (Kassel: Bärenreiter, 1994–)

Mitchell, James Harris, 'The Works of Guiseppe [*sic*] Antonio Brescianello', Ph.D. diss., University of North Carolina, 1962

Monterosso, Raffaello, *Musicisti cremonesi nella mostra bibliografica della Biblioteca governativa (1949)* (Cremona, 1958)

Monterosso, Raffaello, 'Medaglioni di musicisti lombardi', in *Musicisti lombardi ed emiliani*, ed. Adelmo Damerini and Gino Roncaglia (Siena: Accademia Musicale Chigiana, 1958), pp. 51–60

Monterosso, Rafaello, 'Gasparo Visconti, violinista cremonese del secolo XVIII', *Studien zur Musikwissenschaft*, 25 (1962), pp. 378–88

Morelli, Giovanni, ed., *L'invenzione del gusto: Corelli e Vivaldi: mutazioni culturali, a Roma e Venezia, nel periodo post-barocco* (Milan: Ricordi, 1982)

Narmour, Eugene, *The Analysis and Cognition of Basic Melodic Structures: The Implication-Realization Model* (Chicago: University of Chicago Press, 1990)

NG2 = *The New Grove Dictionary of Music and Musicians*, 2nd edn., ed. Stanley Sadie, 29 vols. (London: Macmillan, 2001)

North, Roger, *Roger North on Music*, ed. John Wilson (London: Novello, 1959)

Passadore, Francesco and Franco Rossi, *San Marco, vitalità di una tradizione: il fondo musicale e la cappella dal Settecento ad oggi*, 4 vols. (Venice: Edizioni Fondazione Levi, 1994–6)

Pelicelli, N., 'Musicisti in Parma', *Note d'archivio per la storia musicale*, 11 (1934), pp. 248–81

Petrobelli, Pierluigi, 'Per l'edizione critica di un concerto tartiniano (D. 21)', *Chigiana*, 19 (1962), pp. 97–128; in Petrobelli, *Tartini: le sue idee*, pp. 109–36

Petrobelli, Pierluigi, 'Una presenza di Tartini a Parma nel 1728', *Aurea Parma*, 50 (1966), pp. 109–24; in Petrobelli, *Tartini: le sue idee*, pp. 65–79

Petrobelli, Pierluigi, 'Tartini, le sue idee e il suo tempo', *Nuova rivista musicale italiana*, 1 (1967), pp. 651–75; in Petrobelli, *Tartini: le sue idee*, pp. 21–49

Petrobelli, Pierluigi, *Giuseppe Tartini: le fonti biografiche* (Venice: Universal Edition, 1968)

Petrobelli, Pierluigi, 'La scuola di Tartini in Germania e la sua influenza', *Analecta Musicologica*, 5 (1968), pp. 1–17

Petrobelli, Pierluigi, 'Tartini e la musica popolare', *Chigiana*, 26–27 (1969–70), pp. 443–50; in Petrobelli, *Tartini: le sue idee*, pp. 101–8

Petrobelli, Pierluigi, 'Tartini e Corelli: preliminari per l'impostazione di un problema', in *Studi corelliani*, ed. Adriano Cavicchi, Oscar Mischiati and Pierluigi Petrobelli (Florence: Olschki, 1972), pp. 99–107

Petrobelli, Pierluigi, 'Giuseppe Tartini', in *Storia della musica al Santo di Padova*, ed. Sergio Durante and Pierluigi Petrobelli (Vicenza: Neri Pozza, 1990), pp. 181–97

Petrobelli, Pierluigi, *Tartini: le sue idee e il suo tempo* (Lucca: Libreria musicale italiana, 1992)

Pincherle, Marc, *Antonio Vivaldi et la musique instrumentale*, 2 vols. (Paris: Floury, 1948)

Piperno, Franco, 'Musica e musicisti per l'Accademia del Disegno di San Luca (1716–1860)', in *La musica a Roma attraverso le fonti d'archivi*, ed. Bianca Maria Antolini, Arnaldo Morelli and Vera Vita Spagnuolo (Lucca: Libreria musicale italiana, 1994), pp. 553–64

Piperno, Franco, ' "Su le sponde del Tebro": eventi, mecenati e istituzioni musicali a Roma negli anni di Locatelli. Saggio di cronologia', in Dunning, ed., *Intorno a Locatelli*, vol. 2, pp. 793–877

Porta, Enzo, 'La tecnica violinistica dell'Arte del Violino di Pietro Antonio Locatelli', in Dunning, ed., *Intorno a Locatelli*, vol. 2, pp. 879–952

Pozzi, Paola, 'Il concerto strumentale italiano alla Corte di Dresda durante la prima metà del Settecento', in Dunning, ed., *Intorno a Locatelli*, vol. 2, pp. 953–1037

Preussner, Eberhard, *Die musikalische Reisen des Herrn von Uffenbach* (Kassel: Bärenreiter, 1949)

Quantz, Johann Joachim, *Versuch einer Anweisung die Flöte traversiere zu spielen* (1752), as *On Playing the Flute*, tr. Edward R. Reilly, 2nd edn. (London: Faber and Faber, 1985)

Ramot, Na'ama, 'The Organization of the First Ritornello in Solo Concertos by Antonio Vivaldi and Carlo Tessarini', MA diss., Hebrew University, Jerusalem, 2000

Rasch, Rudolf, 'I manoscritti musicali nel lascito di Michel-Charles le Cène (1743)', in Dunning, ed., *Intorno a Locatelli*, vol. 2, pp. 1039–70

Rasch, Rudolf, 'La famosa mano di Monsieur Roger: Antonio Vivaldi and his Dutch Publishers', *Informazioni e studi vivaldiani*, 17 (1996), pp. 89–137

Rasch, 'Estienne Roger and John Walsh: Patterns of Competition between Early Eighteenth-Century Dutch and English Music Publishing', in *The North Sea and Culture (1550–1800)*, ed. Juliette Roding and Lex Heerma van Voss (Hilversum: Verloren, 1996), pp. 396–407

Rasch, Rudolf, 'Corelli's Contract: Notes on the Publication History of the *Concerti Grossi . . . Opera Sesta [1714]*', *Tijdschrift van de Koninklijke Vereniging voor Nederlandse Muziekgeschiedenis*, 46 (1996), pp. 83–136

Rasch, Rudolf, 'The Italian Presence in the Musical Life of the Dutch Republic', in Strohm, ed., *The Eighteenth-Century Diaspora*, pp. 177–210

Rasch, Rudolf, 'Il cielo batavo: I compositori italiani e le edizioni olandesi delle loro opere strumentali nel primo Settecento', *Analecta Musicologica*, 32 (2002), pp. 237–66

Ratner, Leonard G., *Classic Music: Expression, Form, and Style* (New York: Schirmer, 1980)

RISM = Répertoire International des Sources Musicales

Roeder, Michael Thomas, *A History of the Concerto* (Portland, OR: Amadeus, 1994)

Rosen, Charles, *Sonata Forms*, rev. edn. (New York: Norton, 1988)

Rossi, Franco, *Tommaso Albinoni: Catalogo tematico delle opere*, 2 vols. (Padua: I Solisti Veneti, 2002)

Rostirolla, Giancarlo, 'L'organizzazione musicale nell'Ospedale veneziano della Pietà al tempo di Vivaldi', *Nuova rivista musicale italiana*, 13 (1979), pp. 168–95

Rostirolla, Giancarlo, 'Maestri di cappella, organisti, cantanti e strumentisti attivi in Roma nella metà del Settecento, *Note d'archivio per la storia musicale*, n.s. 2 (1984), pp. 195–269

Rothstein, William, *Phrase Rhythm in Tonal Music* (New York: Schirmer, 1989)

Ryom, Peter, *Verzeichnis der Werke Antonio Vivaldis (RV): Kleine Ausgabe*, 2nd edn. (Leipzig: Deutscher Verlag, 1974)

Ryom, Peter, *Les manuscrits de Vivaldi* (Copenhagen: Antonio Vivaldi Archives, 1977)

Ryom, Peter, *Répertoire des Oeuvres d'Antonio Vivaldi: Les Compositions Instrumentales* (Copenhagen: Engstrøm & Sødring, 1986)

Schering, Arnold, *Geschichte des Instrumentalkonzerts* (Leipzig: Breitkopf & Härtel, 1905)

Selfridge-Field, Eleanor, 'Vivaldi and Marcello: Clues to Provenance and Chronology', in Fanna and Morelli, eds., *Nuovi studi vivaldiani*, pp. 785–98

Selfridge-Field, Eleanor, *The Music of Benedetto and Alessandro Marcello: A Thematic Catalogue* (Oxford: Clarendon, 1990)

Selfridge-Field, Eleanor, *Venetian Instrumental Music from Gabrieli to Vivaldi*, 3rd edn. (New York: Dover, 1994)

Sgaria, Giovanni, 'Giovanni Mossi, musicista romano del primo Settecento', in Dunning, ed., *Intorno a Locatelli*, vol. 2, pp. 1113–67

Shapiro, Martin L., 'The Treatment of Form in the Violin Concertos of Tomaso Albinoni', Ph.D. diss., University of California at Santa Barbara, 1971

Sheldon, David A., 'The Galant Style Revisited and Re-evaluated', *Acta Musicologica*, 47 (1975), pp. 240–70

Sheldon, David A., 'The Concept *Galant* in the 18th Century', *Journal of Musicological Research*, 9 (1989–90), 89–108

Siegele, Ulrich, 'Proportionierung als kompositorisches Arbeitsinstrument in Konzerten J.S. Bachs', in *Bachs Orchesterwerke*, ed. Martin Geck (Witten: Klangfarben Musikverlag, 1997), pp. 159–71

Simon, Edwin J., 'The Double Exposition in the Classic Concerto', *Journal of the American Musicological Society*, 10 (1957), 111–18

Sofianopulo, Marco, ed., *Giuseppe Tartini nel terzo centenario della nascita* (Trieste: Tipografia Tergeste, 1992)

Solie, John E., 'Form in the Concertos and Sinfonias of Tomaso Albinoni', Ph.D. diss., University of Chicago, 1974

Solie, John E., 'Aria Structure and Ritornello Form in the Music of Albinoni', *The Musical Quarterly*, 63 (1977), 31–47

Stevens, Jane, 'An 18th-Century Description of Concerto First-Movement Form', *Journal of the American Musicological Society*, 24 (1971), pp. 85–95

Stone, Lawrence, 'Prosopography', in *Historical Studies Today*, ed. Felix Gilbert and Stephen R. Graubard (New York: Norton, 1972), pp. 107–40

Strohm, Reinhard, ed., *The Eighteenth-Century Diaspora of Italian Music and Musicians* (Turnhout: Brepols, 2001)

Suess, John G., Introduction, *Giuseppe Torelli: Concerti musicali Opus 6*, Recent Researches in the Music of the Baroque Era, 115 (Middleton, WI: A-R Editions, 2002)

Swack, Jeanne, 'Modular Structure and the Recognition of Ritornello in Bach's Brandenburg Concertos', *Bach Perspectives*, 4 (Lincoln: University of Nebraska Press, 1999), pp. 33–53

Talbot, Michael, 'The Instrumental Music of Tomaso Albinoni, 1671–1741', Ph.D. diss., University of Cambridge, 1969

Talbot, Michael, 'The Concerto Allegro in the Early Eighteenth Century', *Music & Letters*, 52 (1971), pp. 8–18, 159–72

Talbot, Michael, 'Albinoni's Oboe Concertos', *The Consort*, 29 (1973), pp. 14–22; reprinted in Talbot, *Venetian Music*

Talbot, Michael, 'Some Overlooked MSS in Manchester', *Musical Times*, 115 (1974), pp. 942–4

Talbot, Michael, 'A Thematic Catalogue of the Orchestral Works of Giuseppe Matteo Alberti (1685–1751)', *RMA Research Chronicle*, 13 (1976), pp. 1–26

Talbot, Michael, 'Vivaldi's "Manchester" Sonatas', *Proceedings of the Royal Musical Association*, 104 (1977–8), pp. 20–9; reprinted in Talbot, *Venetian Music*

Talbot, Michael, *Albinoni: Leben und Werk* (Adliswil: Kunzelmann, 1980)

Talbot, Michael, 'Charles Jennens and Antonio Vivaldi', in Degrada, ed., *Vivaldi veneziano europeo*, pp. 67–75

Talbot, Michael, 'Vivaldi and a French Ambassador', *Informazioni e studi vivaldiani*, 2 (1981), pp. 31–43

Talbot, Michael, 'A Vivaldi Discovery at the Conservatorio "Benedetto Marcello" ', *Informazioni e studi vivaldiani*, 3 (1982), pp. 3–12

Talbot, Michael, 'A Rival of Corelli: The Violinist-Composer Giuseppe Valentini', in *Nuovissimi studi corelliani*, ed. Sergio Durante and Pierluigi Petrobelli (Florence: Olschki, 1982), pp. 347–65

Talbot, Michael, 'Musical Academies in Eighteenth-Century Venice', *Note d'archivio per la storia musicale*, n.s. 2 (1984), pp. 21–65, reprinted in Talbot, *Venetian Music*

Talbot, Michael, 'Vivaldi in the Sale Catalogue of Nicolaas Selhof', *Informazioni e studi vivaldiani*, 6 (1985), pp. 57–63

Talbot, Michael, 'Vivaldi and the Empire', *Informazioni e studi vivaldiani*, 8 (1987), pp. 31–51; reprinted in Talbot, *Venetian Music*

Talbot, Michael, *Antonio Vivaldi: A Guide to Research* (New York: Garland, 1988)

Talbot, Michael, 'Vivaldi and Rome: Observations and Hypotheses', *Journal of the Royal Musical Association*, 113 (1988), pp. 28–46; reprinted in Talbot, *Venetian Music*

Talbot, Michael, *Tomaso Albinoni: The Venetian Composer and his World* (Oxford: Clarendon, 1990)

Talbot, Michael, ' "Lingua romana in bocca veneziana": Vivaldi, Corelli and the Roman School', in *Studi corelliani IV*, ed. Pierluigi Petrobelli and Gloria Staffieri (Florence: Olschki, 1990), pp. 303–18; reprinted in Talbot, *Venetian Music*

Talbot, Michael, *Vivaldi*, 2nd edn. (London: Dent, 1993)

Talbot, Michael, *Benedetto Vinaccesi: A Musician in Brescia and Venice in the Age of Corelli* (Oxford: Clarendon, 1994)

Talbot, Michael, *The Sacred Vocal Music of Antonio Vivaldi* (Florence: Olschki, 1995)

Talbot, Michael, 'Stylistic Evolution in Corelli's Music', *Studi corelliani V*, ed. Stefano La Via (Florence: Olschki, 1996), pp. 143–58

Talbot, Michael, *Venetian Music in the Age of Vivaldi* (Aldershot: Ashgate, 1999)

Talbot, Michael, *The Finale in Western Instrumental Music* (Oxford: Oxford University Press, 2001)

Talbot, Michael, 'Anna Maria's Partbook', in Geyer and Osthoff, eds., *Musica agli Ospedali*

Tanenbaum, Faun Stacy, 'The Pietà Partbooks and More Vivaldi', *Informazioni e studi vivaldiani*, 8 (1987), pp. 7–12; 'The Pietà Partbooks – Continued', ibid., 9 (1988), pp. 5–13

Thomson, George W., 'I primi concerti di Giuseppe Tartini: fonti, abbozzi e revisioni', in Bombi and Massaro, eds., *Tartini: il tempo e le opere*, pp. 347–62

Torrefranca, Faustino, *Le origini italiane del romanticismo musicale* (Turin: Fratelli Bocca, 1930)

Torrefranca, Fausto, 'Prime ricognizioni dello stile violoncellistica Plattiano', International Musicological Society Fourth Congress Report (Basle: Bärenreiter, c1950), pp. 203–11

Vickers, Brian, 'Figures of Rhetoric/Figures of Music?', *Rhetorica*, 2 (1984), pp. 1–44

Vio, Gastone, 'Precisazioni sui documenti della Pietà in relazione alle "figlie del coro" ', in Degrada, ed., *Vivaldi veneziano europeo*, pp. 101–22

Vio, Gastone, 'Antonio Vivaldi violinista in S Marco?', *Informazioni e studi vivaldiani*, 2 (1981), pp. 51–60

Vitali, Carlo, 'I nove "principi di altezza" corrispondenti di Vivaldi e la dedica enigmatica del Concerto RV 754: Alla ricerca dell'indirizzario perduto', *Informazioni e studi vivaldiani*, 16 (1995), pp. 59–89

White, Chappell, 'First-Movement Form in the Violin Concerto from Vivaldi to Viotti', in *Music East and West: Essays in Honor of Walter Kaufmann*, ed. Thomas Noblitt (New York: Pendragon, 1981), pp. 183–97

White, Chappell, *From Vivaldi to Viotti: A History of the Early Classical Violin Concerto* (Philadelphia: Gordon and Breach, 1992)

White, Mary Gray, 'The Life of Francesco Maria Veracini', *Music & Letters*, 53 (1972), pp. 18–35

White, Micky, 'Biographical Notes on the "Figlie di coro" of the Pietà Contemporary with Vivaldi', *Informazioni e studi vivaldiani*, 21 (2000), pp. 75–97

Whitmore, Philip, 'Towards an Understanding of the Capriccio', *Journal of the Royal Musical Association*, 113 (1988), pp. 47–56

Wolf, Eugene K., Introduction to *Antecedents of the Symphony: The Ripieno Concerto*, The Symphony 1720–1840, ed. Barry S. Brook, Series A, Vol. 1 (New York: Garland, 1983)

Wolff, Christoph, 'Vivaldi's Compositional Art and the Process of "Musical Thinking" ', in Fanna and Morelli, eds., *Nuovi studi vivaldiani*, pp. 1–17

Zobeley, Fritz (with Frohmut Dangel-Hofmann), *Die Musikalien der Grafen von Schönborn-Wiesentheid: thematisch-bibliographischer Katalog*, Part 1, 2 vols. (Tutzing: Schneider, 1967–82)

Zoppelli, Luca, 'Tempeste e stravaganze: fattori estetici e ricettivi in margine alla datazione dei concerti "a programma" ', in Fanna and Morelli, eds., *Nuovi studi vivaldiani*, pp. 801–10

Index

Bold indicates main references to the life and works of each principal composer. Incidental references to Vivaldi are not indexed.